1999 SUPPLEMENT

CASES AND MATERIALS

CONSTITUTIONAL LAW

TENTH EDITION

by

WILLIAM COHEN
C. Wendell and Edith M. Carlsmith
Professor Emeritus, Stanford Law School

JONATHAN D. VARAT
Dean and Professor of Law
University of California, Los Angeles

NEW YORK, NEW YORK
FOUNDATION PRESS
1999

 TEXT IS PRINTED ON 10% POST CONSUMER RECYCLED PAPER

TABLE OF CONTENTS
(**Bold** Indicates Principal Cases)

CHAPTER 11. DEFINING THE SCOPE OF "LIBERTY" AND "PROPERTY" PROTECTED BY THE DUE PROCESS CLAUSE—THE PROCEDURAL DUE PROCESS CASES

Section

1. When Does Due Process Mandate Constitutional Procedures?

   A. What "Property" and "Liberty" is Protected?

*

TABLE OF CASES

Principal cases are in bold type. Non-principal cases are in roman type. References are to Pages.

1999 SUPPLEMENT

CONSTITUTIONAL LAW

*

PART I

The Constitution and the Courts: The Judicial Function in Constitutional Cases

CHAPTER 3

The Jurisdiction of Federal Courts in Constitutional Cases

SECTION 2. Constitutional Litigation Initiated in the Federal Courts

B. Enforcement of Federal Rights in Suits Against State Officers: The Eleventh Amendment

Page 76. Add at end of subsection:

CONGRESSIONAL POWER TO AUTHORIZE SUITS AGAINST STATES IN FEDERAL COURT

Relying on *Seminole Tribe*, the Court held that Congress could not subject States to federal court jurisdiction in damage actions for infringement of

1

trademarks and patents. College Savings Bank v. Florida Prepaid Postsecondary Education Expense Board, 119 S.Ct. ___ (1999); Florida Prepaid Postsecondary Education Expense Board v. College Savings Bank, 119 S.Ct. ___ (1999). In each case, the Court rejected an argument that the abrogation of State sovereign immunity was justified by Section Five of the Fourteenth Amendment.

STATE SOVEREIGN IMMUNITY IN STATE COURT SUITS

In Alden v. Maine, 119 S.Ct. ___ (1999), the Court held that States could assert sovereign immunity when sued in State court, that Congress lacked power to abrogate that immunity, and that States do not waive immunity by permitting suit in similar cases involving state law claims. Affirming a State court decision dismissing an overtime pay claim under the Fair Labor Standards Act, the Court said:

> "the sovereign immunity of the States neither derives from nor is limited by the terms of the Eleventh Amendment. Rather, as the Constitution's structure, and its history, and the authoritative interpretations by this Court make clear, the States' immunity from suit is a fundamental aspect of the sovereignty which the States enjoyed before the ratification of the Constitution, and which they retain today ... except as altered by the plan of the Convention or certain constitutional Amendments."

SECTION 3.   CASES AND CONTROVERSIES

B.   STANDING

3.   TAXPAYER AND CITIZEN STANDING

Page 106. Add at end of subsection:

Raines v. Byrd

521 U.S. 811, 117 S.Ct. 2312, 138 L.Ed.2d 849 (1997).

Chief Justice Rehnquist delivered the opinion of the Court.*

The District Court for the District of Columbia declared the Line Item Veto Act unconstitutional. On this direct appeal, we hold that appellees lack standing to bring this suit, and therefore direct that the judgment of the District Court be vacated and the complaint dismissed.

I

The appellees are six Members of Congress, four of whom served as Senators and two of whom served as Congressmen in the 104th Congress (1995–1996). On March 27, 1996, the Senate passed a bill entitled the Line Item Veto Act by a vote of 69–31. All four appellee Senators voted "nay." ... The next day, the House of Representatives passed the identical bill by a vote of

---

* Justice Ginsburg joins this opinion.

232–177. Both appellee Congressmen voted "nay." ... On April 4, 1996, the President signed the Line Item Veto Act (Act) into law. Pub. L. 104–130, 110 Stat. 1200, codified at 2 U.S.C.A. § 691 et seq. (Supp.1997). The Act went into effect on January 1, 1997.... The next day, appellees filed a complaint in the District Court for the District of Columbia against the two appellants, the Secretary of the Treasury and the Director of the Office of Management and Budget, alleging that the Act was unconstitutional.

The provisions of the Line Item Veto Act do not use the term "veto." Instead, the President is given the authority to "cancel" certain spending and tax benefit measures after he has signed them into law. Specifically, the Act provides:

"[T]he President may, with respect to any bill or joint resolution that has been signed into law pursuant to Article I, section 7, of the Constitution of the United States, cancel in whole-(1) any dollar amount of discretionary budget authority; (2) any item of new direct spending; or (3) any limited tax benefit; if the President—

"(A) determines that such cancellation will—(i) reduce the Federal budget deficit; (ii) not impair any essential Government functions; and (iii) not harm the national interest; and

"(B) notifies the Congress of such cancellation by transmitting a special message ... within five calendar days (excluding Sundays) after the enactment of the law [to which the cancellation applies]." ....

The President's "cancellation" under the Act takes effect when the "special message" notifying Congress of the cancellation is received in the House and Senate. With respect to dollar amounts of "discretionary budget authority," a cancellation means "to rescind." .... With respect to "new direct spending" items or "limited tax benefit[s]," a cancellation means that the relevant legal provision, legal obligation, or budget authority is "prevent[ed] ... from having legal force or effect." ...

The Act establishes expedited procedures in both Houses for the consideration of "disapproval bills," ... bills or joint resolutions which, if enacted into law by the familiar procedures set out in Article I, § 7 of the Constitution, would render the President's cancellation "null and void," .... "Disapproval bills" may only be one sentence long and must read as follows after the enacting clause: "That Congress disapproves of cancellations _____ as transmitted by the President in a special message on _____ regarding _____." .... (The blank spaces correspond to the cancellation reference numbers as set out in the special message, the date of the President's special message, and the public law number to which the special message relates, respectively. ....)

The Act provides that "[a]ny Member of Congress or any individual adversely affected by [this Act] may bring an action, in the United States District Court for the District of Columbia, for declaratory judgment and injunctive relief on the ground that any provision of this part violates the Constitution." ... Appellees brought suit under this provision, claiming that "[t]he Act violates Article I" of the Constitution. Specifically, they alleged that the Act "unconstitutionally expands the President's power," and "violates the requirements of bicameral passage and presentment by granting to the President, acting alone, the authority to 'cancel' and thus repeal provisions of federal law." They alleged that the Act injured them "directly and concretely . . . in their official capacities" in three ways: "The Act . . . (a) alter[s] the legal and practical effect of all votes they may cast on bills containing such separately vetoable items, (b) divest[s] the [appellees] of their constitutional role in the repeal of legislation, and (c) alter[s] the constitutional balance of powers between the Legislative and Executive Branches, both with respect to measures containing separately vetoable items and with respect to other matters coming before Congress."

Appellants moved to dismiss for lack of jurisdiction, claiming . . . that appellees lacked standing to sue and that their claim was not ripe. Both sides also filed motions for summary judgment on the merits. On April 10, 1997, the District Court (i) denied appellants' motion to dismiss, holding that appellees had standing to bring this suit and that their claim was ripe, and (ii) granted appellees' summary judgment motion, holding that the Act is unconstitutional. . . .

. . .

. . . On the merits, the court held that the Act violated the Presentment Clause, Art. I, § 7, cl. 2, and constituted an unconstitutional delegation of legislative power to the President.

The Act provides for a direct, expedited appeal to this Court. . . . On April 18, eight days after the District Court issued its order, appellants filed a jurisdictional statement asking us to note probable jurisdiction. . . . We established an expedited briefing schedule and heard oral argument on May 27. We now hold that appellees have no standing to bring this suit, and therefore direct that the judgment of the District Court be vacated and the complaint dismissed.

II

. . .

We have always insisted on strict compliance with this jurisdictional standing requirement. . . . And our standing inquiry has been especially rigorous when reaching the merits of the dispute would force us to decide whether an action taken by one of the other two branches of the Federal Government was unconstitutional. . . . In the light of this overriding and time-honored concern about keeping the Judiciary's power within its proper constitutional sphere, we must put aside the natural urge to proceed directly to the merits of this important dispute and to "settle" it for the sake of convenience and efficiency. Instead, we must carefully inquire as to whether appellees have met their burden of establishing that their claimed injury is personal, particularized, concrete, and otherwise judicially cognizable.

III

We have never had occasion to rule on the question of legislative standing presented here. In Powell v. McCormack, 395 U.S. 486, 496, 512–514 (1969), we held that a Member of Congress' constitutional challenge to his exclusion from the House of Representatives (and his consequent loss of salary) presented an Article III case or controversy. But *Powell* does not help appellees. First, appellees have not been singled out for specially unfavorable treatment as opposed to other Members of their respective bodies. Their claim is that the Act causes a type of institutional injury (the diminution of legislative power), which necessarily damages all Members of Congress and both Houses of Congress equally.... Second, appellees do not claim that they have been deprived of something to which they personally are entitled—such as their seats as Members of Congress after their constituents had elected them. Rather, appellees' claim of standing is based on a loss of political power, not loss of any private right, which would make the injury more concrete. Unlike the injury claimed by Congressman Adam Clayton Powell, the injury claimed by the Members of Congress here is not claimed in any private capacity but solely because they are Members of Congress. If one of the Members were to retire tomorrow, he would no longer have a claim; the claim would be possessed by his successor instead. The claimed injury thus runs (in a sense) with the Member's seat, a seat which the Member holds (it may quite arguably be said) as trustee for his constituents, not as a prerogative of personal power....

The one case in which we have upheld standing for legislators (albeit state legislators) claiming an institutional injury is Coleman v. Miller, 307 U.S. 433 (1939). Appellees, relying heavily on this case, claim that they, like the state legislators in *Coleman*, "have a plain, direct and adequate interest in maintaining the effectiveness of their votes," ... sufficient to establish standing. In *Coleman*, 20 of Kansas' 40 State Senators voted not to ratify the proposed "Child Labor Amendment" to the Federal Constitution. With the vote deadlocked 20–20, the amendment ordinarily would not have been ratified. However, the State's Lieutenant Governor, the presiding officer of the State Senate, cast a deciding vote in favor of the amendment, and it was deemed ratified (after the State House of Representatives voted to ratify it). The 20 State Senators who had voted against the amendment, joined by a 21st State Senator and three State House Members, filed an action in the Kansas Supreme Court seeking a writ of mandamus that would compel the appropriate state officials to recognize that the legislature had not in fact ratified the amendment. That court held that the members of the legislature had standing to bring their mandamus action, but ruled against them on the merits....

This Court affirmed. By a vote of 5–4, we held that the members of the legislature had standing. In explaining our holding, we repeatedly emphasized that if these legislators (who were suing as a bloc) were correct on the merits, then their votes not to ratify the amendment were deprived of all validity.... It is obvious, then, that our holding in *Coleman* stands (at most) for the proposition that legislators whose votes would have been sufficient to defeat (or enact) a specific legislative act have standing to sue if that legislative action goes into effect (or does not go into effect), on the ground that their votes have been completely nullified.

It should be equally obvious that appellees' claim does not fall within our holding in *Coleman*, as thus understood. They have not alleged that they voted for a specific bill, that there were sufficient votes to pass the bill, and that the bill was nonetheless deemed defeated. In the vote on the Line Item Veto Act, their votes were given full effect. They simply lost that vote. Nor can they allege that the Act will nullify their votes in the future in the same way that the votes of the *Coleman* legislators had been nullified. In the future, a majority of Senators and Congressman can pass or reject appropriations bills; the Act has no effect on this process. In addition, a majority of Senators and Congressman can vote to repeal the Act, or to exempt a given appropriations bill (or a given provision in an appropriations bill) from the Act; again, the Act has no effect on this process. *Coleman* thus provides little meaningful precedent for appellees' argument.

Nevertheless, appellees rely heavily on our statement in *Coleman* that the Kansas senators had "a plain, direct, and adequate interest in maintaining the effectiveness of their votes." Appellees claim that this statement applies to them because their votes on future appropriations bills (assuming a majority of Congress does not decide to exempt those bills from the Act) will be less "effective" than before, and that the "meaning" and "integrity" of their vote has changed. The argument goes as follows. Before the Act, Members of Congress could be sure that when they voted for, and Congress passed, an appropriations bill that included funds for Project X, one of two things would happen: (i) the bill would become law and all of the projects listed in the bill would go into effect, or (ii) the bill would not become law and none of the projects listed in the bill would go into effect. Either way, a vote for the appropriations bill meant a vote for a package of projects that were inextricably linked. After the Act, however, a vote for an appropriations bill that includes Project X means something different. Now, in addition to the two possibilities listed above, there is a third option: the bill will become law and then the President will "cancel" Project X.

Even taking appellees at their word about the change in the "meaning" and "effectiveness" of their vote for appropriations bills which are subject to the Act, we think their argument pulls *Coleman* too far from its moorings. Appellees' use of the word "effectiveness" to link their argument to *Coleman* stretches the word far beyond the sense in which the *Coleman* opinion used it. There is a vast difference between the level of vote nullification at issue in *Coleman* and the abstract dilution of institutional legislative power that is alleged here. To uphold standing here would require a drastic extension of *Coleman*. We are unwilling to take that step.

Not only do appellees lack support from precedent, but historical practice appears to cut against them as well. It is evident from several episodes in our history that in analogous confrontations between one or both Houses of Congress and the Executive Branch, no suit was brought on the basis of claimed injury to official authority or power. The Tenure of Office Act, passed by Congress over the veto of President Andrew Johnson in 1867, was a thorn in the side of succeeding Presidents until it was finally repealed at the behest of President Grover Cleveland in 1887.... It provided that an official whose appointment to an Executive Branch office required confirmation by the Senate could not be removed without the consent of the Senate.... In 1868, Johnson removed his Secretary of War, Edwin M. Stanton. Within a week, the House of Representatives impeached Johnson.... One of the principal charges against him was that his removal of Stanton violated the Tenure of Office Act.... At the conclusion of his trial before the Senate, Johnson was acquitted by one vote.... Surely Johnson had a stronger claim of diminution of his official power as a result of the Tenure of Office Act than do the appellees in the present case. Indeed, if their claim were sustained, it would appear that President Johnson would have had standing to challenge the Tenure of Office

Act before he ever thought about firing a cabinet member, simply on the grounds that it altered the calculus by which he would nominate someone to his cabinet. Yet if the federal courts had entertained an action to adjudicate the constitutionality of the Tenure of Office Act immediately after its passage in 1867, they would have been improperly and unnecessarily plunged into the bitter political battle being waged between the President and Congress.

... A sort of mini-Tenure of Office Act covering only the Post Office Department had been enacted in 1872, ... and it remained on the books after the Tenure of Office Act's repeal in 1887. In the last days of the Woodrow Wilson administration, Albert Burleson, Wilson's Postmaster General, came to believe that Frank Myers, the Postmaster in Portland, Oregon, had committed fraud in the course of his official duties. When Myers refused to resign, Burleson, acting at the direction of the President, removed him. Myers sued in the Court of Claims to recover lost salary. In Myers v. United States, 272 U.S. 52 (1926), more than half a century after Johnson's impeachment, this Court held that Congress could not require senatorial consent to the removal of a Postmaster who had been appointed by the President with the consent of the Senate.... In the course of its opinion, the Court expressed the view that the original Tenure of Office Act was unconstitutional....

If the appellees in the present case have standing, presumably President Wilson ... would ... have had standing, and could have challenged the law preventing the removal of a presidential appointee without the consent of Congress. Similarly, in INS v. Chadha, 462 U.S. 919 (1983), the Attorney General would have had standing to challenge the one-House veto provision because it rendered his authority provisional rather than final. By parity of reasoning, President Gerald Ford could have sued to challenge the appointment provisions of the Federal Election Campaign Act which were struck down in Buckley v. Valeo, 424 U.S. 1 (1976), and a Member of Congress could have challenged the validity of President Coolidge's pocket veto that was sustained in The Pocket Veto Case, 279 U.S. 655 (1929).

There would be nothing irrational about a system which granted standing in these cases; some European constitutional courts operate under one or another variant of such a regime.... But it is obviously not the regime that has obtained under our Constitution to date. Our regime contemplates a more restricted role for Article III courts, well expressed by Justice Powell in his concurring opinion in United States v. Richardson, 418 U.S. 166 (1974): "The irreplaceable value of the power articulated by Mr. Chief Justice Marshall [in Marbury v. Madison, 1 Cranch 137 (1803)] lies in the protection it has afforded the constitutional rights and liberties of individual citizens and minority groups against oppressive or discriminatory government action. It is this role, not some amorphous general supervision of the operations of government, that has maintained public esteem for the federal courts and has permitted the peaceful coexistence of the countermajoritarian implications of judicial review and the democratic principles upon which our Federal Government in the final analysis rests." Id., at 192.

IV

In sum, appellees have alleged no injury to themselves as individuals (contra *Powell*), the institutional injury they allege is wholly abstract and widely dispersed (contra *Coleman*), and their attempt to litigate this dispute at this time and in this form is contrary to historical experience. We attach some importance to the fact that appellees have not been authorized to represent their respective Houses of Congress in this action, and indeed both Houses actively oppose their suit. We also note that our conclusion neither deprives Members of Congress of an adequate remedy (since they may repeal the Act or exempt appropriations bills from its reach), nor forecloses the Act from constitutional challenge (by someone who suffers judicially cognizable injury as a result of the Act). Whether the case would be different if any of these circumstances were different we need not now decide.

We therefore hold that these individual members of Congress do not have a sufficient "personal stake" in this dispute and have not alleged a sufficiently concrete injury to have established Article III standing. The judgment of the District Court is vacated, and the case is remanded with instructions to dismiss the complaint for lack of jurisdiction.

It is so ordered.

Justice Souter, concurring in the judgment, with whom Justice Ginsburg joins, concurring.

Appellees . . . essentially claim that, by granting the President power to repeal statutes, the Act injures them by depriving them of their official role in voting on the provisions that become law. Under our precedents, it is fairly debatable whether this injury is sufficiently "personal" and "concrete" to satisfy the requirements of Article III.

. . . [I]t is at least arguable that the official nature of the harm here does not preclude standing.

Nor is appellees' injury so general that, under our case law, they clearly cannot satisfy the requirement of concreteness. . . .

Because it is fairly debatable whether appellees' injury is sufficiently personal and concrete to give them standing, it behooves us to resolve the question under more general separation-of-powers principles underlying our standing requirements. . . . [R]espect for the separation of powers requires the Judicial Branch to exercise restraint in deciding constitutional issues by resolving those implicating the powers of the three branches of Government as a "last resort," . . . . The counsel of restraint in this case begins with the fact that a dispute involving only officials, and the official interests of those, who serve in the branches of the National Government lies far from the model of the traditional common-law cause of action at the conceptual core of the case-or-controversy requirement. . . . Although the contest here is not formally between the political branches (since Congress passed the bill augmenting Presidential power and the President signed it), it is in substance an inter-branch controversy about calibrating the legislative and executive powers, as well as an intrabranch dispute between segments of Congress itself. Intervention in such a controversy would risk damaging the public confidence that is vital to the functioning of the Judicial Branch. . . .

While it is true that a suit challenging the constitutionality of this Act brought by a party from outside the Federal Government would also involve the Court in resolving the dispute over the allocation of power between the political branches, it would expose the Judicial Branch to a lesser risk. Deciding a suit to vindicate an interest outside the Government raises no specter of judicial readiness to enlist on one side of a political tug-of-war, since "the propriety of such action by a federal court has been recognized since Marbury v. Madison, 1 Cranch 137 (1803)." ... And just as the presence of a party beyond the Government places the Judiciary at some remove from the political forces, the need to await injury to such a plaintiff allows the courts some greater separation in the time between the political resolution and the judicial review. ...

The virtue of waiting for a private suit is only confirmed by the certainty that another suit can come to us. The parties agree, and I see no reason to question, that if the President "cancels" a conventional spending or tax provision pursuant to the Act, the putative beneficiaries of that provision will likely suffer a cognizable injury and thereby have standing under Article III. By depriving beneficiaries of the money to which they would otherwise be entitled, a cancellation would produce an injury that is "actual," "personal and individual," and involve harm to a "legally protected interest," ...; assuming the canceled provision would not apply equally to the entire public, the injury would be "concrete," ... and it would be "fairly trace[able] to the challenged action of the" executive officials involved in the cancellation, ... as well as probably "redress[able] by a favorable decision," .... While the Court has declined to lower standing requirements simply because no one would otherwise be able to litigate a claim, ... the certainty of a plaintiff who obviously would have standing to bring a suit to court after the politics had at least subsided from a full boil is a good reason to resolve doubts about standing against the plaintiff invoking an official interest....

I therefore conclude that appellees' alleged injuries are insufficiently personal and concrete to satisfy Article III standing requirements of personal and concrete harm. Since this would be so in any suit under the conditions here, I accordingly find no cognizable injury to appellees.

Justice Stevens, dissenting.

The Line Item Veto Act purports to establish a procedure for the creation of laws that are truncated versions of bills that have been passed by the Congress and presented to the President for signature. If the procedure were valid, it would deny every Senator and every Representative any opportunity to vote for or against the truncated measure that survives the exercise of the President's cancellation authority. Because the opportunity to cast such votes is a right guaranteed by the text of the Constitution, I think it clear that the persons who are deprived of that right by the Act have standing to challenge its constitutionality. Moreover, because the impairment of that constitutional right has an immediate impact on their official powers, in my judgment they need not wait until after the President has exercised his cancellation authority to bring suit. Finally, the same reason that the respondents have standing provides a sufficient basis for concluding that the statute is unconstitutional.

. . .

... The appellees ... articulated their claim as a combination of the diminished effect of their initial vote and the circumvention of their right to participate in the subsequent repeal. Whether one looks at the claim from this perspective, or as a simple denial of their right to vote on the precise text that will ultimately become law, the basic nature of the injury caused by the Act is the same.

In my judgment, the deprivation of this right—essential to the legislator's office—constitutes a sufficient injury to provide every Member of Congress with standing to challenge the constitutionality of the statute. If the dilution of an individual voter's power to elect representatives provides that voter with standing ... the deprivation of the right possessed by each Senator and Representative to vote for or against the precise text of any bill before it becomes law must also be a sufficient injury to create Article III standing for them. . . .

Moreover, the appellees convincingly explain how the immediate, constant threat of the partial veto power has a palpable effect on their current legislative choices. Because the Act has this immediate and important impact on the powers of Members of Congress, and on the manner in which they undertake their legislative responsibilities, they need not await an exercise of the President's cancellation authority to institute the litigation that the statute itself authorizes. . . .

Given the fact that the authority at stake is granted by the plain and unambiguous text of Article I, it is equally clear to me that the statutory attempt to eliminate it is invalid.

Accordingly, I would affirm the judgment of the District Court.

Justice Breyer, dissenting.

. . .

I concede that there would be no case or controversy here were the dispute before us not truly adversary, or were it not concrete and focused. But the interests that the parties assert are genuine and opposing, and the parties are therefore truly adverse. . . .

Nonetheless, there remains a serious constitutional difficulty due to the fact that this dispute about lawmaking procedures arises between government officials and is brought by legislators. The critical question is whether or not this dispute, for that reason, is so different in form from those "matters that were the traditional concern of the courts at Westminster" that it falls outside the scope of Article III's judicial power. . . . Justice Frankfurter explained this argument in his dissent in *Coleman*, saying that courts traditionally "leave intra-parliamentary controversies to parliaments and outside the scrutiny of law courts. . . ." Justice Frankfurter dissented because, in his view, the "political" nature of the case, which involved legislators, placed the dispute outside the scope of Article III's "case" or "controversy" requirement. Nonetheless, the *Coleman* court rejected his argument.

Although the majority today attempts to distinguish *Coleman*, I do not believe that Justice Frankfurter's argument or variations on its theme can carry the day here. First, as previously mentioned, the jurisdictional statute before us eliminates all but constitutional considerations, and the circumstances mentioned above remove all but the "political" or "intragovernmental" aspect of the constitutional issue.

Second, the Constitution does not draw an absolute line between disputes involving a "personal" harm and those involving an "official" harm.... *Coleman* itself involved injuries in the plaintiff legislators' official capacity. And the majority in this case, suggesting that legislators might have standing to complain of rules that "denied" them "their vote ... in a discriminatory manner," concedes at least the possibility that any constitutional rule distinguishing "official" from "personal" injury is not absolute.

Third, Justice Frankfurter's views were dissenting views, and the dispute before us, when compared to *Coleman*, presents a much stronger claim, not a weaker claim, for constitutional justiciability. The lawmakers in *Coleman* complained of a lawmaking procedure that, at worst, improperly counted Kansas as having ratified one proposed constitutional amendment, which had been ratified by only 5 other States, and rejected by 26, making it unlikely that it would ever become law.... The lawmakers in this case complain of a lawmaking procedure that threatens the validity of many laws (for example, all appropriations laws) that Congress regularly and frequently enacts. The systematic nature of the harm immediately affects the legislators' ability to do their jobs. The harms here are more serious, more pervasive, and more immediate than the harm at issue in *Coleman*....

. . .

In sum, I do not believe that the Court can find this case nonjusticiable without overruling *Coleman*. Since it does not do so, I need not decide whether the systematic nature, seriousness, and immediacy of the harm would make this dispute constitutionally justiciable even in *Coleman*'s absence. Rather, I can and would find this case justiciable on *Coleman*'s authority. I add that because the majority has decided that this dispute is not now justiciable and has expressed no view on the merits of the appeal, I shall not discuss the merits either, but reserve them for future argument.

FEDERAL ELECTION COMMISSION v. AKINS, 524 U.S. 11 (1998). A group of voters brought an administrative complaint before the Commission, alleging that an organization was a "political committee" required by the Federal Election Campaign Act to register and make certain information public. The Commission dismissed the complaint and the voters sought judicial review in the federal courts. The Court held that the voters had standing to challenge the Commission's dismissal of the complaint under the Act, which authorized "any party aggrieved" by an FEC order dismissing a complaint to seek judicial review. Congress had the constitutional power to authorize federal courts to adjudicate the lawsuit. The voters suffered injury in fact from their inability to obtain information that would help them evaluate candidates for public office. That harm was fairly traceable to the Commission's decision, and could be redressed by judicial decision. Justice Breyer's opinion for the Court rejected the argument that there was no standing because the lawsuit involved only a "generalized grievance shared in substantially equal measure by all or a large class of citizens."

"Whether styled as a constitutional or prudential limit on standing, the Court has sometimes determined that where large numbers of Americans suffer alike, the political process, rather than the judicial process, may provide the more appropriate remedy for a widely shared grievance. . . .

"The kind of judicial language . . . invariably appears in cases where the harm at issue is not only widely shared, but is also of an abstract and indefinite nature—for example, harm to the 'common concern for obedience to law.' . . . The abstract nature of the harm—for example, injury to the interest in seeing that the law is obeyed—deprives the case of the concrete specificity that characterized those controversies which were 'the traditional concern of the courts at Westminster,' . . .

"Often the fact that an interest is abstract and the fact that it is widely shared go hand in hand. But their association is not invariable, and where a harm is concrete, though widely shared, the Court has found 'injury in fact.' . . . .Thus the fact that a political forum may be more readily available where an injury is widely shared (while counseling against, say, interpreting a statute as conferring standing) does not, by itself, automatically disqualify an interest for Article III purposes. Such an interest, where sufficiently concrete, may count as an 'injury in fact.' This conclusion seems particularly obvious where (to use a hypothetical example) large numbers of individuals suffer the same common-law injury (say, a widespread mass tort), or where large numbers of voters suffer interference with voting rights conferred by law. . . .We conclude that similarly, the informational injury at issue here, directly related to voting, the most basic of political rights, is sufficiently concrete and specific such that the fact that it is widely shared does not deprive Congress of constitutional power to authorize its vindication in the federal courts."

Justice Scalia, joined by Justices O'Connor and Thomas, dissented. On the constitutional issue, he said, in part:

The Constitution's line of demarcation between the Executive power and the judicial power presupposes a common understanding of the type of interest needed to sustain a 'case or controversy' against the Executive in the courts. A system in which the citizenry at large could sue to compel Executive compliance with the law would be a system in which the courts, rather than of the President, are given the primary responsibility to 'take Care that the Laws be faithfully executed,' " Art. II, § 3. We do not have such a system because the common understanding of the interest necessary to sustain suit has included the requirement, . . . that the complained-of injury be particularized and differentiated, rather than common to all the electorate. When the Executive can be directed by the courts, at the instance of any voter, to remedy a deprivation which affects the entire electorate in precisely the same way—and particularly when that deprivation (here, the unavailability of information) is one inseverable part of a larger enforcement scheme—there has occurred a shift of political responsibility to a branch designed not to protect the public at large but to protect individual rights. 'To permit Congress to convert the undifferentiated public interest in executive officers' compliance with the law into an 'individual right' vindicable in the courts is to permit Congress to transfer from the President to the courts the Chief Executive's most important constitutional duty. . . .' *Lujan,* 504 U.S., at 577. If today's decision is correct, it is within the power of Congress to authorize any interested person to manage (through the courts) the Executive's enforcement of any law that includes a requirement for the filing and public availability of a piece of paper."

Clinton v. City of New York

524 U.S. 417, 118 S.Ct. 2091, 141 L.Ed.2d 393 (1998).

(The report in this case appears infra page 51.)

DEPARTMENT OF COMMERCE v. UNITED STATES HOUSE OF REPRESENTATIVES, 119 S.Ct. 765 (1999). The Census Bureau announced a plan to use statistical sampling in conducting the 2000 Decennial Census. An Act of Congress provides that "[a]ny person aggrieved by the use of any statistical method in violation of the Constitution or any provision of law . . . in connection with the 2000 census or any later decennial census, to determine the population for purposes of the apportionment or redistricting of Members in Congress, may in a civil action obtain declaratory, injunctive, and any other appropriate relief against the use of such method." Suits were brought in federal district courts by the House of Representatives, and by citizens of 13 States, asserting that the Bureau's plan for the 2000 census would violate the Census Act and the Constitution. The Court held that the State residents sufficiently showed that they would suffer injury through loss of State representatives and dilution of voting strength to have Article III standing. The Court did not address the question whether the House of Representatives had standing.

PART II

ALLOCATION OF GOVERNMENTAL POWERS: THE NATION AND THE STATES; THE PRESIDENT, THE CONGRESS, AND THE COURTS

CHAPTER 5

THE SCOPE OF STATE POWER

SECTION 4.   IMPLIED RESTRICTIONS OF THE COMMERCE CLAUSE—PRODUCTION AND TRADE

C.   PRESERVING RESOURCES FOR IN-STATE CONSUMPTION

Page 312.   Add at end of subsection:

Camps Newfound/Owatonna, Inc. v. Town of Harrison
520 U.S. 564, 117 S.Ct. 1590, 137 L.Ed.2d 852 (1997).

Justice Stevens delivered the opinion of the Court.
The question presented is whether an otherwise generally applicable state

property tax violates the Commerce Clause of the United States Constitution, Art. I, § 8, cl. 3, because its exemption for property owned by charitable institutions excludes organizations operated principally for the benefit of non-residents.

ISSUE

I

Petitioner is a Maine nonprofit corporation that operates a summer camp [on 180 lakeshore acres located in the town of Harrison] for the benefit of children of the Christian Science faith.... About 95% of the campers are not residents of Maine....

. . .

The Maine statute at issue, Me.Rev.Stat. Ann., Tit. 36, § 652(1)(A) (Supp. 1996), provides a general exemption from real estate and personal property taxes for "benevolent and charitable institutions incorporated" in the State. With respect to institutions that are "in fact conducted or operated principally for the benefit of persons who are not residents of Maine," however, a charity may only qualify for a more limited tax benefit, and then only if the weekly charge for services provided does not exceed $30 per person. § 652(1)(A)(1). Because most of the campers come from out of State, petitioner could not qualify for a complete exemption. And, since the weekly tuition was roughly $400, petitioner was ineligible for any charitable tax exemption at all.

[Petitioner sued in state court for a refund of real estate and personal property taxes paid from 1989 through 1991, and a continuing exemption from future property taxes. The Superior Court ruled for petitioner, but] the Maine Supreme Judicial Court reversed.... Noting that a Maine statute characterized tax exemptions as "tax expenditures," it viewed the exemption for charitable institutions as the equivalent of a purchase of their services.... Because the exemption statute "treats all Maine charities alike"—given the fact that "all have the opportunity to qualify for an exemption by choosing to dispense the majority of their charity locally"—it "regulates evenhandedly with only inci-dental effects on interstate commerce." ... [A]bsen[t] evidence that petition-er's camp "competes with other summer camps outside of or within Maine," or that the statute "impedes interstate travel" or that it "provides services that are necessary for interstate travel," the Court concluded that petitioner had "not met its heavy burden of persuasion that the statute is unconstitutional."

History

. . .

We ... reverse.

II

. . .

This case involves an issue that we have not previously addressed—the disparate real estate tax treatment of a nonprofit service provider based on the residence of the consumers that it serves. The Town argues that our dormant Commerce Clause jurisprudence is wholly inapplicable to this case, because interstate commerce is not implicated here and Congress has no power to enact a tax on real estate. We first reject these arguments, and then explain why we think our prior cases make it clear that if profit-making enterprises were at issue, Maine could not tax petitioner more heavily than other camp operators simply because its campers come principally from other States. We next address the novel question whether a different rule should apply to a discriminatory tax exemption for charitable and benevolent institutions. Finally, we reject the Town's argument that the exemption should either be viewed as a permissible subsidy or as a purchase of services by the State acting as a "market participant."

III

We are unpersuaded . . . that the dormant Commerce Clause is inapplicable here, either because campers are not "articles of commerce," or more generally because the camp's "product is delivered and 'consumed' entirely within Maine." . . . Even though petitioner's camp does not make a profit, it is unquestionably engaged in commerce, not only as a purchaser, see Katzenbach v. McClung, 379 U.S. 294, 300–301 (1964); United States v. Lopez, 514 U.S. 549, ___–___ (1995), but also as a provider of goods and services. It markets those services, together with an opportunity to enjoy the natural beauty of an inland lake in Maine, to campers who are attracted to its facility from all parts of the Nation. . . . The attendance of these campers necessarily generates the transportation of persons across state lines that has long been recognized as a form of "commerce." Edwards v. California, 314 U.S. 160, 172 (1941); see also Caminetti v. United States, 242 U.S. 470, 491 (1917); Hoke v. United States, 227 U.S. 308, 320 (1913).

Summer camps are comparable to hotels that offer their guests goods and services that are consumed locally. . . . Even when business activities are purely local, if " 'it is interstate commerce that feels the pinch, it does not matter how local the operation which applies the squeeze.' " Heart of Atlanta [Motel, Inc. v. United States, 379 U.S. 241,] at 258 [(1964).]

Although *Heart of Atlanta* involved Congress' affirmative Commerce Clause powers, its reasoning is applicable here. As we stated in Hughes v. Oklahoma, 441 U.S. 322 (1979), "The definition of 'commerce' is the same when relied on to strike down or restrict state legislation as when relied on to support some exertion of federal control or regulation." Id., at 326, n. 2. . . .

. . . The services that petitioner provides to its principally out-of-state campers clearly have a substantial effect on commerce, as do state restrictions on making those services available to nonresidents. Cf. C & A Carbone, Inc. v. Clarkstown, 511 U.S. 383, 391 (1994).

The Town also argues that the dormant Commerce Clause is inapplicable because a real estate tax is at issue. We disagree. A tax on real estate, like any other tax, may impermissibly burden interstate commerce. We may assume as the Town argues (though the question is not before us) that Congress could not impose a national real estate tax. It does not follow that the States may impose real estate taxes in a manner that discriminates against interstate commerce. . . .

To allow a State to avoid the strictures of the dormant Commerce Clause by the simple device of labeling its discriminatory tax a levy on real estate would destroy the barrier against protectionism that the Constitution provides.... [W]ere the Town's theory adopted, a State could create ... a tariff with ease. The State would need only to pass a statute imposing a special real estate tax on property used to store, process, or sell imported goods. By gearing the increased tax to the value of the imported goods at issue, the State could create the functional equivalent of an import tariff....

. . .

IV

[W]ere this statute targeted at profit-making entities, it would violate the dormant Commerce Clause. "State laws discriminating against interstate commerce on their face are 'virtually per se invalid.'" Fulton Corp. v. Faulkner, 516 U.S. 325, ___ (1996).... It is not necessary to look beyond the text of this statute to determine that it discriminates against interstate commerce. The Maine law expressly distinguishes between entities that serve a principally interstate clientele and those that primarily serve an intrastate market, singling out camps that serve mostly in-staters for beneficial tax treatment, and penalizing those camps that do a principally interstate business. As a practical matter, the statute encourages affected entities to limit their out-of-state clientele, and penalizes the principally nonresident customers of businesses catering to a primarily interstate market.

If such a policy were implemented by a statutory prohibition against providing camp services to nonresidents, the statute would almost certainly be invalid. We have "consistently ... held that the Commerce Clause ... precludes a state from mandating that its residents be given a preferred right of access, over out-of-state consumers, to natural resources located within its borders or to the products derived therefrom." New England Power Co. v. New Hampshire, 455 U.S. 331, 338 (1982).... Petitioner's "product" is in part the natural beauty of Maine itself, and in addition the special services that the camp provides. In this way, the Maine statute is like a law that burdens out-of-state access to domestically generated hydroelectric power, *New England Power*, or to local landfills, Philadelphia v. New Jersey, 437 U.S. 617 (1978). In those cases, as in this case, the burden fell on out-of-state access both to a natural resource, and to related services provided by state residents.

Avoiding this sort of "economic Balkanization," Hughes v. Oklahoma, 441 U.S. 322, 325 (1979), and the retaliatory acts of other States that may follow, is one of the central purposes of our negative Commerce Clause jurisprudence.... And, as we noted in Brown–Forman Distillers Corp. v. New York State Liquor Authority, 476 U.S. 573, 580 (1986): "Economic protectionism is not limited to attempts to convey advantages on local merchants; it may include attempts to give local consumers an advantage over consumers in other States."[11] By encouraging economic isolationism, prohibitions on out-of-state access to in-state resources serve the very evil that the dormant Commerce Clause was designed to prevent.

Of course, this case does not involve a total prohibition. Rather, the statute provides a strong incentive for affected entities not to do business with

---

[11] The Town argues that "the Commerce Clause protects out-of-state competitors but does not protect out-of-state consumers." ... [O]ur cases have rejected this view.

nonresidents if they are able to so avoid the discriminatory tax. In this way, the statute is similar to the North Carolina "intangibles tax" that we struck down in Fulton Corp. v. Faulkner, 516 U.S. 325, ___ (1996). That case involved the constitutionality under the Commerce Clause of a State "regime that taxe[d] stock [held by in-State shareholders] only to the degree its issuing corporation participates in interstate commerce." . . . We held the statute facially discriminatory, in part because it tended "to discourage domestic corporations from plying their trades in interstate commerce." . . . Maine's statute has a like effect.

To the extent that affected Maine organizations are not deterred by the statute from doing a principally interstate business, it is clear that discriminatory burdens on interstate commerce imposed by regulation or taxation may also violate the Commerce Clause. We have held that special fees assessed on nonresidents directly by the State when they attempt to use local services impose an impermissible burden on interstate commerce. See, e.g., *Chemical Waste*, 504 U.S., at 342 (discriminatory tax imposed on disposal of out-of-state hazardous waste). That the tax discrimination comes in the form of a deprivation of a generally available tax benefit, rather than a specific penalty on the activity itself, is of no moment... New Energy Co. of Ind. v. Limbach, 486 U.S. 269, 274 (1988).... Given the fact that the burden of Maine's facially discriminatory tax scheme falls by design in a predictably disproportionate way on out-of-staters, the pernicious effect on interstate commerce is the same as in our cases involving taxes targeting out-of-staters alone.

Unlike in *Chemical Waste*, we recognize that here the discriminatory burden is imposed on the out-of-state customer indirectly by means of a tax on the entity transacting business with the non-Maine customer. This distinction makes no analytic difference.... [I]t matters little that it is the camp that is taxed rather than the campers. The record demonstrates that the economic incidence of the tax falls at least in part on the campers, the Town has not contested the point, and the courts below based their decision on this presumption....

With respect to those businesses—like petitioner's—that continue to engage in a primarily interstate trade, the Maine statute therefore functionally serves as an export tariff that targets out-of-state consumers by taxing the businesses that principally serve them. [T]his sort of discrimination is at the very core of activities forbidden by the dormant commerce clause....

. . . In sum, the Maine statute facially discriminates against interstate commerce, and is all but *per se* invalid....

. . . Perhaps realizing the weight of its burden, the Town has made no effort to defend the statute under the *per se* rule, and so we do not address this question.... [16] We have no doubt that if petitioner's camp were a profit-making entity, the discriminatory tax exemption would be impermissible.

---

[16] Justice Scalia submits that we err by . . . declining to address an argument that the Town itself did not think worthy of pressing. But even if there were reason to consider the State's compliance with the *per se* rule, the Town would not prevail. In the single case Justice Scalia points to in which we found the *per se* standard to have been met, Maine v. Taylor, 477 U.S. 131 (1986), the State had no " 'reasonable nondiscriminatory alternatives,' " . . . to the action it had taken....

V

The unresolved question . . . is whether a different rule should apply to tax exemptions for charitable and benevolent institutions. Though we have never had cause to address the issue directly, the applicability of the dormant Commerce Clause to the nonprofit sector of the economy follows from our prior decisions.

Our cases have frequently applied [federal] laws regulating commerce to not-for-profit institutions. . . .

We have already held that the dormant Commerce Clause is applicable to activities undertaken without the intention of earning a profit. In Edwards v. California, 314 U.S. 160 (1941), [invalidating] a California statute prohibiting the transport into that State of indigent persons[,] . . . we noted that "[i]t is immaterial whether or not the transportation is commercial in character." . . .

We see no reason why the nonprofit character of an enterprise should exclude it from the coverage of either the affirmative or the negative aspect of the Commerce Clause. . . . There are a number of lines of commerce in which both for-profit and nonprofit entities participate. Some educational institutions, some hospitals, some child-care facilities, some research organizations, and some museums generate significant earnings; and some are operated by not-for-profit corporations. . . .   *reason 2*

. . . Nothing intrinsic to the nature of nonprofit entities prevents them from engaging in interstate commerce. Summer camps may be operated as for-profit or nonprofit entities; nonprofits may depend—as here—in substantial part on fees charged for their services. . . . Whether operated on a for-profit or nonprofit basis, they purchase goods and services in competitive markets, offer

In contrast, here Maine has ample alternatives short of a facially discriminatory property tax exemption to achieve its apparent goal of subsidizing the attendance of the State's children at summer camp. Maine could, for example, achieve this end by offering direct financial support to parents of resident children. . . . Though we have not had the occasion to address the issue, it might also be permissible for the State to subsidize Maine camps directly to the extent that they serve residents. See West Lynn Creamery, Inc. v. Healy, 512 U.S., at 199, n. 15; New Energy Co. of Ind. v. Limbach, 486 U.S. 269, 278 (1988) (noting that "[d]irect subsidization of domestic industry does not ordinarily run afoul" of the Commerce Clause); Hughes v. Alexandria Scrap Corp., 426 U.S. 794, 816 (1976) (Stevens, J., concurring).

While the Town does argue its case under the less exacting analysis set forth in, e.g., Pike v. Bruce Church, Inc., 397 U.S. 137, 142 (1970), "this lesser scrutiny is only available 'where other [nondiscriminatory] legislative objectives are credibly advanced *and* there is *no* patent discrimination against in-

terstate trade.'" *Chemical Waste*, 504 U.S., at 343, n. 5 (quoting Philadelphia v. New Jersey, 437 U.S. 617, 624 (1978) (emphasis added)). Because the Maine statute is facially discriminatory, the more deferential standard is inapplicable. Contrary to Justice Scalia's suggestion, this case is quite unlike General Motors Corp. v. Tracy, 519 U.S. 278 (1997). There, the Court premised its holding that the statute at issue was not facially discriminatory on the view that sellers of "bundled" and "unbundled" natural gas were principally competing in different markets. See id., at ——, —— ("dormant Commerce Clause protects markets and participants in markets, not taxpayers as such"). While it may be true that "[d]isparate treatment constitutes discrimination only if the objects of the disparate treatment are . . . similarly situated," there is no question that the statute at issue here is facially discriminatory because it disparately treats identically situated Maine nonprofit camps depending upon whether they favor in-state, as opposed to out-of-state, campers.

their facilities to a variety of patrons, and derive revenues from a variety of sources, some of which are local and some out of State.

For purposes of Commerce Clause analysis, any categorical distinction between the activities of profit-making enterprises and not-for-profit entities is therefore wholly illusory. Entities in both categories are major participants in interstate markets. And, although the summer camp involved in this case may have a relatively insignificant impact on the commerce of the entire Nation, the interstate commercial activities of nonprofit entities as a class are unquestionably significant.[18] See Wickard v. Filburn, 317 U.S. 111, 127–128 (1942); *Lopez*, 514 U.S., at ___, ___–___.

From the State's standpoint it may well be reasonable to use tax exemptions as a means of encouraging nonprofit institutions to favor local citizens, notwithstanding any possible adverse impact on the larger markets in which those institutions participate. Indeed, if we view the issue solely from the State's perspective, it is equally reasonable to use discriminatory tax exemptions as a means of encouraging the growth of local trade. But as our cases clearly hold, such exemptions are impermissible.... Protectionism, whether targeted at for-profit entities or serving, as here, to encourage nonprofits to keep their efforts close to home, is forbidden under the dormant Commerce Clause. If there is need for a special exception for nonprofits, Congress not only has the power to create it, but also is in a far better position than we to determine its dimensions.

Rule 2

VI

Rather than urging us to create a categorical exception for nonprofit entities, the Town argues that Maine's exemption statute should be viewed as an expenditure of government money designed to lessen its social service burden and to foster the societal benefits provided by charitable organizations. So characterized, the Town submits that its tax exemption scheme is either a legitimate discriminatory subsidy of only those charities that choose to focus their activities on local concerns, or alternatively a governmental "purchase" of charitable services falling within the narrow exception to the dormant Com-

---

[18] We are informed by *amici* that "the nonprofit sector spends over $389 billion each year in operating expenses—approximately seven percent of the gross national product." Brief for American Council on Education et al. as *Amici Curiae* 19. In recent years, nonprofits have employed approximately seven percent of the Nation's paid workers, roughly 9.3 million people in 1990....

Justice Scalia wrongly suggests that Maine's law offers only a "narrow tax exemption," which he implies has no substantial effect on interstate commerce and serves only "to relieve the State of its burden of caring for its residents." This characterization is quite misleading. The statute expressly exempts from tax property used by such important nonprofit service industries as nursing homes and child care centers. See Me.Rev. Stat. Ann., Tit. 36, § 652(1)(A)(1) (Supp. 1996).... Nationally, nonprofit nursing homes had estimated revenues of $18 billion in 1994 [and] compete[d] with a sizeable for-profit nursing home sector, which had revenues of approximately $40 billion in 1994.... Similarly, the $5 billion nonprofit market in child day care services competes with an $11 billion for-profit industry....

Nonprofit hospitals and health maintenance organizations also receive an exemption from Maine's property tax. See Me.Rev. Stat. Ann., Tit. 36, § 652(1)(A), (K) (Supp. 1996).... Nonprofit hospitals had national revenues of roughly $305 billion in 1994, considerably more than the $34 billion in revenues collected by hospitals operated on a for-profit basis.

. . .

merce Clause for States in their role as "market participants," see, e.g., Hughes v. Alexandria Scrap Corp., 426 U.S. 794 (1976); Reeves, Inc. v. Stake, 447 U.S. 429 (1980). We find these arguments unpersuasive. Although tax exemptions and subsidies serve similar ends, they differ in important and relevant respects, and our cases have recognized these distinctions. As for the "market participant" argument, we have already rejected the Town's position in a prior case, and in any event respondents' open-ended exemption for charitable and benevolent institutions is not analogous to the industry-specific state actions that we reviewed in *Alexandria Scrap* and *Reeves*.

. . . We have "never squarely confronted the constitutionality of subsidies," and we need not . . . today. Assuming, *arguendo*, that . . . a direct subsidy benefitting only those nonprofits serving principally Maine residents would be permissible, our cases do not sanction a tax exemption serving similar ends.[22]

In Walz v. Tax Comm'n of City of New York, 397 U.S. 664 (1970), notwithstanding our assumption that a direct subsidy of religious activity would be invalid, we held that New York's tax exemption for church property did not violate the Establishment Clause of the First Amendment. That holding rested, in part, on the premise that there is a constitutionally significant difference between subsidies and tax exemptions. We have expressly recognized that this distinction is also applicable to claims that certain state action designed to give residents an advantage in the market place is prohibited by the Commerce Clause.

In New Energy Co. of Ind. v. Limbach, 486 U.S. 269 (1988), we . . . noted: "The Commerce Clause does not prohibit all state action designed to give its residents an advantage in the marketplace, but only action of that description *in connection with the State's regulation of interstate commerce*. Direct subsidization of domestic industry does not ordinarily run afoul of that prohibition; discriminatory taxation . . . does." *Ibid.* (emphasis in original). . . .

. . . .

[Nor can] Maine's tax exemption statute . . . be characterized as a proprietary activity falling within the market-participant exception. . . . A tax exemption is not the sort of direct state involvement in the market that falls within the market-participation doctrine.

Even if we were prepared to expand the exception . . ., the Maine tax statute at issue here would be a poor candidate. Like the tax exemption upheld in *Walz*—which applied to libraries, art galleries, and hospitals as well as churches—the exemption that has been denied to petitioner is available to a broad category of charitable and benevolent institutions. For that reason, nothing short of a dramatic expansion of the "market participant" exception would support its application to this case. *Alexandria Scrap* involved Maryland's entry into the market for automobile hulks, a discrete activity focused on a single industry. Similarly, South Dakota's participation in the market for

---

[22] [U]nder Maine law an exemption is categorized as a "tax expenditure." Me.Rev. Stat. Ann., Tit. 36, § 196 (1990). The Town's effort to argue that this state statutory categorization allows it to elide the Federal constitutional distinction between tax exemptions and subsidies is unavailing. We recognized long ago that a tax exemption can be viewed as a form of government spending. . . . The distinction we have drawn for dormant Commerce Clause purposes does not turn on this point.

cement was—in part because of its narrow scope—readily conceived as a proprietary action of the State. In contrast, Maine's tax exemption—which sweeps to cover broad swathes of the nonprofit sector—must be viewed as action taken in the State's sovereign capacity rather than a proprietary decision to make an entry into all of the markets in which the exempted charities function.... The Town's version of the "market participant" exception would swallow the rule against discriminatory tax schemes. [T]he notion that whenever a State provides a discriminatory tax abatement it is "purchasing" some service in its proprietary capacity is not readily confined to the charitable context. A special tax concession for liquors indigenous to Hawaii, for example, might be conceived as a "purchase" of the jobs produced by local industry, or an investment in the unique local cultural value provided by these beverages. Cf. Bacchus, 468 U.S., at 270–271. Discriminatory schemes favoring local farmers might be seen as the "purchase" of agricultural services in order to ensure that the State's citizens will have a steady local supply of the product....

VII

... The history of our Commerce Clause jurisprudence has shown that even the smallest scale discrimination can interfere with the project of our federal Union. [T]o countenance discrimination of the sort that Maine's statute represents would invite significant inroads on our "national solidarity" ....

The judgment of the Maine Supreme Judicial Court is reversed.

Justice Scalia, with whom The Chief Justice, Justice Thomas and Justice Ginsburg join, dissenting.

The Court's negative-commerce-clause jurisprudence has drifted far from its moorings. Originally designed to create a national market for commercial activity, it is today invoked to prevent a State from giving a tax break to charities that benefit the State's inhabitants. In my view, Maine's tax exemption, which excuses from taxation only that property used to relieve the State of its burden of caring for its residents, survives even our most demanding commerce-clause scrutiny.

I

. . .

While the "virtually per se rule of invalidity" entails application of the "strictest scrutiny," Hughes v. Oklahoma, 441 U.S. 322, 337 (1979), it does not necessarily result in the invalidation of facially discriminatory State legislation, see, e.g., Maine v. Taylor, 477 U.S. 131 (1986) (upholding absolute ban on the importation of baitfish into Maine), for "what may appear to be a 'discriminatory' provision in the constitutionally prohibited sense—that is, a protectionist enactment—may on closer analysis not be so," New Energy Co. of Ind. v. Limbach, 486 U.S. 269, 278 (1988). Thus, even a statute that erects an absolute barrier to the movement of goods across state lines will be upheld if "the discrimination is demonstrably justified by a valid factor unrelated to economic protectionism," id., at 274, or to put a finer point on it, if the State law "advances a legitimate local purpose that cannot be adequately served by reasonable nondiscriminatory alternatives," id., at 278.

[W]e have also preserved from judicial invalidation laws that confer advantages upon the State's residents but do so without *regulating* interstate commerce. We have therefore excepted the State from scrutiny when it participates in markets rather than regulates them—by selling cement, for example, see Reeves, Inc. v. Stake, 447 U.S. 429 (1980), or purchasing auto hulks, see Hughes v. Alexandria Scrap Corp., 426 U.S. 794 (1976), or hiring contractors, see White v. Massachusetts Council of Construction Employers, 460 U.S. 204 (1983). Likewise, we have said that direct subsidies to domestic industry do not run afoul of the Commerce Clause. See *New Energy Co.*, 486 U.S., at 278. In sum, we have declared that "[t]he Commerce Clause does not prohibit all state action designed to give its residents an advantage in the marketplace, but only action of that description *in connection with the State's regulation of interstate commerce.*" . . .

II

. . . A review of Maine law demonstrates that the provision at issue here is a narrow tax exemption, designed merely to compensate or subsidize those organizations that contribute to the public fisc by dispensing public benefits the State might otherwise provide.

[T]he exemption . . . does not extend to all non-profit[s—]only to those . . . "organized and conducted *exclusively* for benevolent and charitable purposes," § 652(1)(C)(1) (emphasis added), and only to those parcels of real property and items of personal property that are used "solely," § 652(1)(A), "to further the organization's charitable purposes," . . . .

. . .

. . . [A]t issue . . . is not whether a summer camp can properly be regarded as relieving the State of social costs, but rather whether, *assuming it can*, a distinction between charities serving mainly residents and charities operated principally for the benefit of nonresidents is constitutional.[1]

III

. . . The Court readily concludes that . . . the statute "facially discriminates" against interstate commerce. That seems to me not necessarily true. Disparate treatment constitutes discrimination only if the objects of the dispa-

---

[1] . . . [T]he point of our emphasizing . . . the narrowness of the challenged limitation . . . is (1) that Maine's limitation focuses upon a particular state interest that is deserving of exemption from negative-commerce-clause invalidation, and (2) that acknowledging the principle of such an exemption . . . will not place the "national market" in any peril. [T]he Court . . . misdescrib[es] the exemption we defend as "a categorical exemption of nonprofit activities from dormant Commerce Clause scrutiny."

The Court . . . attempt[s] to contest on the merits the narrowness of the exemption, suggesting a massive effect upon interstate commerce by reciting the multi-billion-dollar annual revenues of nonprofit nursing homes, child care centers, hospitals and health maintenance organizations. But . . . most of the services provided by those institutions are provided locally, to local beneficiaries. (In that regard the summer camp that is the subject of the present suit is most atypical.) The record does not show the number of nonprofit nursing homes, child care centers, hospitals and HMOs in Maine that have been denied the charitable exemption because their property is not used "principally for the benefit of persons who are Maine residents"; but it would be a good bet that the number is zero.

rate treatment are, for the relevant purposes, similarly situated. See General Motors Corp. v. Tracy, 117 S.Ct., at 823–824. And for purposes of entitlement to a tax subsidy from the State, it is certainly reasonable to think that property gratuitously devoted to relieving the State of some of its welfare burden is not similarly situated to property used "principally for the benefit of persons who are not residents of [the State]," § 652(1)(A). As we have seen, the theory underlying the exemption is that it is a *quid pro quo* for uncompensated expenditures that lessen the State's burden of providing assistance to its residents.

The Court seeks to establish "facial discrimination" by showing that the effect of treating disparate property disparately is to produce higher costs for those users of the property who come from out of State. But that could be regarded as an *indirect* effect upon interstate commerce produced by a tax scheme that is *not* facially discriminatory, which means that the proper mode of analysis would be the more lenient "balancing" standard....

Even if, however, the Maine statute displays "facial discrimination" against interstate commerce, that is not the end of the analysis. The most remarkable thing about today's judgment is that it is rendered without inquiry into whether the purposes of the tax exemption *justify* its favoritism.... The Town has asserted that the State's interest in encouraging private entities to shoulder part of its social-welfare burden validates this provision under the negative Commerce Clause. Whether it does so because the presence of that interest causes the resident-benefiting charities not to be "similarly situated" to the non-resident-benefiting charities, and hence *negates* "facial discrimination," or rather because the presence of that interest *justifies* "facial discrimination," is ... of no consequence [and] probably unanswerable. To strike down this statute because the Town's lawyers put the argument in one form rather than the other is truly senseless.

[T]his is one of those cases in which the "virtually *per se* rule of invalidity" does not apply. Facially discriminatory or not, the exemption is no more an artifice of economic protectionism than any state law which dispenses public assistance only to the State's residents.[3] Our cases have always recognized the legitimacy of limiting state provided welfare benefits to bona fide residents....

[3] [T]he Court does briefly address whether the statute fails the "virtually *per se* rule of invalidity." It concludes that it does fail because "Maine has ample alternatives short of a facially discriminatory property tax exemption," such as offering direct cash subsidies to parents of resident children or to camps that serve residents. These are *no-regulatory* alternatives (and hence immune from negative-commerce-clause attack), but they are not *nondiscriminatory* alternatives, which is what the exception to the "virtually *per se* rule of invalidity" requires.... Surely, for example, our decision in *Maine v. Taylor*, which upheld Maine's regulatory ban on the importation of baitfish, would not have come out the other way if it had been shown that a state *subsidy* of sales of in-state baitfish could have achieved the same goal—by making the out-of-state fish noncompetitive and thereby excluding them from the market even more effectively than a difficult-to-police ban on importation. Where regulatory discrimination against out-of-state interests is appropriate, the negative Commerce Clause is not designed to push a State into nonregulatory discrimination instead. It permits State regulatory action disfavoring out-of-staters where disfavoring them is indispensable to the achievement of an important and nonprotectionist State objective. As applied to the present case: it is obviously impossible for a State to distribute social welfare benefits only to its residents without discriminating against nonresidents.

States have restricted public assistance to their own bona fide residents since colonial times, . . . and such self-interested behavior . . . is inherent in the very structure of our federal system. . . .

. . . [T]he Court today relies not on any discrimination against out-of-state nonprofits, but on the supposed discrimination against nonresident would-be *recipients* of charity (the nonprofits' "customers"); surely those individuals are similarly discriminated against in the direct distribution of state benefits. The problem . . . [includes] municipal employment[,] free public schooling, . . . libraries, orphanages, homeless shelters and refuges for battered women. One could hardly explain the constitutionality of a State's limiting its provision of these to its own residents on the theory that the State is a "market participant." These are traditional governmental functions, far removed from commercial activity and utterly unconnected to any genuine private market.

If, however, a State that provides social services directly *may* limit its largesse to its own residents, I see no reason why a State that chooses to provide some of its social services indirectly—by compensating or subsidizing private charitable providers—cannot be similarly restrictive. . . .

Finally, even if Maine's property tax exemption for local charities constituted facial discrimination against out-of-state commerce, and even if its policy justification (unrelated to economic protectionism) were insufficient to survive our "virtually *per se* rule of invalidity," there would remain the question whether we should not recognize an additional exception to the negative Commerce Clause, as we have in *Tracy*. As that case explains, just as a public health justification unrelated to economic protectionism may justify an overt discrimination against goods moving in interstate commerce, "so may health and safety considerations be weighed in the process of deciding the threshold question whether the conditions entailing application of the dormant Commerce Clause are present." ___ U.S., at ___ . . . .* As we explicitly acknowledge

---

* [In *Tracy,* the Court rejected the claim of General Motors ("GM"), which bought nearly all the natural gas for its Ohio plants from deregulated out-of-state marketers, that a longstanding Ohio sales and use tax exemption for natural gas sales to in-state consumers by regulated natural gas utilities (or "LCDs"—local distribution companies), impermissibly discriminated against interstate commerce by denying the exemption to deregulated gas sellers, such as producers and independent marketers. Perceiving the LCDs' gas, bundled with regulatory "services and protections," to be a different product than the deregulated "marketer's unbundled gas," the Court said that "in the absence of actual or prospective competition between the supposedly favored and disfavored entities in a single market there can be no local preference, whether by express discrimination against interstate commerce or undue burden upon it, to which the dormant Commerce Clause may apply. The dormant Commerce Clause protects markets and participants in markets, not taxpayers as such."

For the captive market of small, typically residential consumers that regulated natural monopolies historically have served, "competition would not be served by eliminating any tax differential as between sellers, and the dormant Commerce Clause has no job to do." For the noncaptive market of large, typically industrial consumers who could, post-deregulation, buy natural gas from either LCDs or independent marketers, the Court felt it had to decide whether "to accord controlling significance to the noncaptive market in which they compete, or to the noncompetitive, captive market in which the local utilities alone operate." The Court opted for the latter, primarily to protect deliveries to the captive consumers—a concern implicating "health and safety considerations [that may be] weighed in the process of deciding the threshold question whether the conditions entailing application of the dormant Commerce Clause are present"—and secondarily because the Court doubted its capacity to predict the effects of judicial intervention "on the utilities' capacity to serve this captive market" and

in *Tracy*—which effectively creates what might be called a "public utilities" exception to the negative Commerce Clause—the "subsidy" and "market participant" exceptions do not exhaust the realm of state actions that we should abstain from scrutinizing under the Commerce Clause. In my view, the provision by a State of free public schooling, public assistance, and other forms of social welfare to only (or principally) its own residents—whether it be accomplished directly or by providing tax exemptions, cash or other property to private organizations that perform the work for the State—implicates none of the concerns underlying our negative-commerce-clause jurisprudence....

.   .   .

Justice Thomas, with whom Justice Scalia joins, and with whom Chief Justice Rehnquist joins as to Part I, dissenting.

The tax at issue here is a tax on real estate, the quintessential asset that does not move in interstate commerce.... By invalidating Maine's tax assessment on the real property of charitable organizations primarily serving non-Maine residents, because of the tax's alleged *indirect* effect on interstate commerce, the majority has essentially created a "dormant" Necessary and Proper Clause to supplement the "dormant" Commerce Clause. This move works a significant, unwarranted, and ... improvident expansion in our "dormant," or "negative," Commerce Clause jurisprudence....

I write separately, ... because I believe that the improper expansion undertaken today is possible only because our negative Commerce Clause jurisprudence, developed primarily to invalidate discriminatory state taxation of interstate commerce, was already both overbroad and unnecessary. It was overbroad because, unmoored from any constitutional text, it brought within the supervisory authority of the federal courts state action far afield from the discriminatory taxes it was primarily designed to check. It was unnecessary because the Constitution would seem to provide an express check on the States' power to levy certain discriminatory taxes on the commerce of other States—not in the judicially created negative Commerce Clause, but in the Article I, § 10 Import–Export Clause, our decision in Woodruff v. Parham, 8 Wall. 123 (1869), notwithstanding. That ... today's decision finds some support in the morass of our negative Commerce Clause caselaw only serves to highlight the need to abandon that failed jurisprudence and to consider restoring the original Import–Export Clause check on discriminatory state taxation to what appears to be its proper role....

I

The negative Commerce Clause has no basis in the text of the Constitution, makes little sense, and has proved virtually unworkable in application....

[T]he Court has historically offered two different theories in support of its negative Commerce Clause jurisprudence. The first theory posited was that the Commerce Clause itself constituted an exclusive grant of power to Congress. See, e.g., Passenger Cases, 7 How. 283, 393–400 (1849). The "exclusivity" rationale was likely wrong from the outset, however. See, e.g., The Federalist

because "Congress has both the resources and the power to strike the balance between the needs of the competitive and captive markets."—Ed.]

No. 32, p. 154 (M. Beloff ed. 1987) (A.Hamilton) ("[N]otwithstanding the affirmative grants of general authorities, there has been the most pointed care in those cases where it was deemed improper that the like authorities should reside in the states, to insert negative clauses prohibiting the exercise of them by the states"). It was seriously questioned even in early cases. See License Cases, 5 How. 504, 583, 615, 618, 624 (1847) (Four, and arguably five, of the seven participating Justices contending that the Commerce Clause was not exclusive). And, in any event, the Court has long since "repudiated" the notion that the Commerce Clause operates as an exclusive grant of power to Congress, and thereby forecloses state action respecting interstate commerce....

... And, as this Court's definition of the scope of congressional authority under the positive Commerce Clause has expanded, the exclusivity rationale has moved from untenable to absurd.

The second theory ... is that Congress, by its silence, pre-empts state legislation.... [W]e presumed that congressional "inaction" was "equivalent to a declaration that inter-State commerce shall be free and untrammelled." Welton v. Missouri, 91 U.S. 275, 282 (1876). To the extent that the "preemption-by-silence" rationale ever made sense, it too has long since been rejected by this Court in virtually every analogous area of the law.

. . .

[E]ven where Congress has legislated in an area subject to its authority, our pre-emption jurisprudence explicitly rejects the notion that mere congressional silence on a particular issue may be read as preempting state law....

To be sure, we have overcome our reluctance to preempt state law in two types of situations: (1) where a state law directly conflicts with a federal law; and (2) where Congress, through extensive legislation, can be said to have pre-empted the field. See Gade v. National Solid Wastes Management Assn., 505 U.S. 88, 98 (1992). But those two forms of pre-emption provide little aid to defenders of the negative Commerce Clause. Conflict pre-emption only applies when there is a direct clash between an Act of Congress and a state statute, but the very premise of the negative Commerce Clause is the absence of congressional action.

Field pre-emption likewise is of little use in areas where Congress has failed to enter the field.... Furthermore, field pre-emption is itself suspect, at least as applied in the absence of a congressional command that a particular field be pre-empted. Perhaps recognizing this problem, our recent cases have frequently rejected field pre-emption in the absence of statutory language expressly requiring it. See, e.g., O'Melveny & Myers v. FDIC, 512 U.S. 79, 85 (1994).... Even when an express pre-emption provision has been enacted by Congress, we have narrowly defined the area to be pre-empted....

In the analogous context of statutory construction, we have similarly refused to rely on congressional *inaction* to alter the proper construction of a pre-existing statute.... And, even more troubling, the "preemption-by-silence" rationale virtually amounts to legislation by default, in apparent violation of the constitutional requirements of bi-cameralism and presentment. Cf. INS v. Chadha, 462 U.S. 919, 951–959 (1983). Thus, even were we wrongly to assume that congressional silence evidenced a desire to pre-empt some undefined category of state laws, and an intent to delegate such policy-laden categorization to the courts, treating unenacted congressional intent as if it were law would be constitutionally dubious.

In sum, neither of the Court's proffered theoretical justifications—exclusivity or preemption-by-silence—currently supports our negative Commerce Clause jurisprudence, if either ever did. . . .

Moreover, our negative Commerce Clause jurisprudence has taken us well beyond the invalidation of obviously discriminatory taxes on interstate commerce. We have used the Clause to make policy-laden judgments that we are ill-equipped and arguably unauthorized to make. . . . In so doing, we have developed multifactor tests in order to assess the perceived "effect" any particular state tax or regulation has on interstate commerce. . . . And in an unabashedly legislative manner, we have balanced that "effect" against the perceived interests of the taxing or regulating State, as the very description of our "general rule" [in *Pike v. Bruce Church*] indicates. . . .

Any test that requires us to assess (1) whether a particular statute serves a "legitimate" local public interest; (2) whether the effects of the statute on interstate commerce are merely "incidental" or "clearly excessive in relation to the putative benefits"; (3) the "nature" of the local interest; and (4) whether there are alternative means of furthering the local interest that have a "lesser impact" on interstate commerce, and even then makes the question "one of degree," surely invites us, if not compels us, to function more as legislators than as judges. . . .

. . .

[N]one of this policy-laden decisionmaking is proper. Rather, the Court should confine itself to interpreting the text of the Constitution, which itself seems to prohibit in plain terms certain of the more egregious state taxes on interstate commerce . . . and leaves to Congress the policy choices necessary for any further regulation of interstate commerce.

II

Article I, § 10, cl. 2 of the Constitution provides that "[n]o State shall, without the Consent of the Congress, lay any Imposts or Duties on Imports or Exports. . . ." To the 20–century reader, the Clause appears only to prohibit States from levying certain kinds of taxes on goods imported from or exported to *foreign* nations. But a strong argument can be made that for the Constitution's Framers and ratifiers—representatives of States which still viewed themselves as semi-independent sovereigns—the terms "imports" and "exports" encompassed not just trade with foreign nations, but trade with *other States* as well.

[After referring to historical materials to bolster this suggestion, Justice Thomas continued.]

Our Civil War era decision in Woodruff v. Parham, 8 Wall. 123 (1869), . . . held that the Import–Export Clause applied only to foreign trade. None of the parties to these proceedings have challenged that holding, but given that the common 18th-century understanding of the words used in the Clause extended to interstate as well as foreign trade, it is worth assessing the *Woodruff* Court's reasoning with an eye toward reconsidering that decision in an appropriate case.

[An extended analysis of *Woodruff* and its relation to other precedents led Justice Thomas to conclude:]

In sum, it would seem that *Woodruff* was, in all likelihood, wrongly decided. Of course, much of what the Import–Export Clause appears to have been designed to protect against has since been addressed under the negative Commerce Clause. As the majority recognizes, discriminatory State taxation of interstate commerce is one of the core pieces of our negative Commerce Clause jurisprudence. Were it simply a matter of invalidating state laws under one clause of the Constitution rather than another, I might be inclined to leave well enough alone. Indeed, our rule that state taxes that discriminate against interstate commerce are virtually *per se* invalid under the negative Commerce Clause may well approximate the apparent prohibition of the Import–Export Clause itself. But ... without the proper textual roots, our negative Commerce Clause has gone far afield of its core—and we have yet to articulate either a coherent rationale for permitting the courts effectively to legislate in this field, or a workable test for assessing which state laws pass negative Commerce Clause muster. Precedent as unworkable as our negative Commerce Clause jurisprudence has become is simply not entitled to the weight of *stare decisis*.... And it is quite possible that, were we to revisit *Woodruff*, we might find that the Constitution already affords us a textual mechanism with which to address the more egregious of State actions discriminating against interstate commerce.

III

... [T]he Import–Export Clause only prohibits States from levying "duties" and "imposts." ...

The Maine property tax ... is almost certainly not an impost, for, as 18th-century usage of the word indicates, an impost was a tax levied on *goods* at the time of *importation*.... Because the tax ... is levied on real property—property that cannot possibly have been "imported"—the tax would not seem to fit within any of the commonly accepted definitions of "impost."

. . .

[Also,] real property ... taxes were classified as "direct" taxes at the time of the Framing, and were not within the class of "indirect" taxes encompassed by the common understanding of the word "duties." The amount of the Maine tax is tied to the value of the real property on which it is imposed, not to any particular goods, and not even to the number of campers served. It does not appear, therefore, to be a "duty" on "imports" in any sense of the words. Even when coupled with the tax exemption for certain Maine charities (which is, in truth, no different than a subsidy paid out of the State's general revenues), Maine's property tax would not seem to be a "Duty or Impost on Imports or Exports" within the meaning of the Import–Export Clause. Thus, were we to overrule *Woodruff* and apply the Import–Export Clause to this case, I would in all likelihood sustain this tax under that Clause as well.

SOUTH CENTRAL BELL TELEPHONE CO. v. ALABAMA, 119 S.Ct. 1180 (1999). The Court unanimously invalidated as unjustifiably discriminatory against interstate commerce an Alabama franchise tax that gave "domestic corporations the ability to reduce their franchise tax liability simply by reducing the par value of their stock, while den[ying] foreign corporations that same ability." Any claim that "the foreign franchise tax is a 'complementary' or 'compensatory' tax that offsets the tax burden that the domestic shares tax imposes upon domestic corporations" failed, because the State could not "prove[] that the special burden that the franchise tax imposes upon foreign corporations is 'roughly ... approximate' to the special burden on domestic corporations, and that the taxes are similar enough 'in substance' to serve as 'mutually exclusive' proxies for one another."

Justice Breyer's opinion for the Court refused to "entertain [the State's] invitation to reconsider our longstanding negative Commerce Clause doctrine, ... because the State did not make clear it intended to make this argument until it filed its brief on the merits." In a separate concurring opinion, Justice O'Connor noted further "that the State does nothing that would persuade me to reconsider or abandon our well-established body of negative Commerce Clause jurisprudence."

D.   PRESERVING STATE–OWNED RESOURCES FOR IN–STATE USE

Page 322. Add at end of subsection:

Camps Newfound/Owatonna, Inc. v. Town of Harrison

520 U.S. 564, 117 S.Ct. 1590, 137 L.Ed.2d 852 (1997).

[The report in this case appears *supra,* page 14.]

CHAPTER 6

INTERGOVERNMENTAL RELATIONSHIPS WITHIN THE FEDERAL SYSTEM

SECTION 2. STATE REGULATORY IMMUNITY

Page 406. Add at end of chapter:

Printz v. United States

521 U.S. 898, 117 S.Ct. 2365, 138 L.Ed.2d 914 (1997).

Justice Scalia delivered the opinion of the Court.

The question presented in these cases is whether certain interim provisions of the Brady Handgun Violence Prevention Act, Pub.L. 103–159, 107 Stat. 1536, commanding state and local law enforcement officers to conduct background checks on prospective handgun purchasers and to perform certain related tasks, violate the Constitution. *issue*

I

The Gun Control Act of 1968 (GCA), 18 U.S.C. § 921 et seq., establishes a detailed federal scheme governing the distribution of firearms....

In 1993, Congress amended the GCA by enacting the Brady Act. The Act requires the Attorney General to establish a national instant background check system by November 30, 1998, Pub.L. 103–159, as amended, Pub.L. 103–322, 103 Stat.2074, note following 18 U.S.C. § 922, and immediately puts in place certain interim provisions until that system becomes operative. Under the interim provisions, a firearms dealer who proposes to transfer a handgun must first: (1) receive from the transferee a statement (the Brady Form), § 922(s)(1)(A)(i)(I), containing the name, address and date of birth of the proposed transferee along with a sworn statement that the transferee is not among any of the classes of prohibited purchasers, § 922(s)(3); (2) verify the identity of the transferee by examining an identification document, § 922(s)(1)(A)(i)(II); and (3) provide the "chief law enforcement officer" (CLEO) of the transferee's residence with notice of the contents (and a copy) of the Brady Form, §§ 922(s)(1)(A)(i)(III) and (IV). With some exceptions, the dealer must then wait five business days before consummating the sale, unless the CLEO earlier notifies the dealer that he has no reason to believe the transfer would be illegal. § 922(s)(1)(A)(ii). *facts of the act*

31

The Brady Act creates two significant alternatives to the foregoing scheme. A dealer may sell a handgun immediately if the purchaser possesses a state handgun permit issued after a background check, § 922(s)(1)(C), or if state law provides for an instant background check, § 922(s)(1)(D). In States that have not rendered one of these alternatives applicable to all gun purchasers, CLEOs are required to perform certain duties. When a CLEO receives the required notice of a proposed transfer from the firearms dealer, the CLEO must "make a reasonable effort to ascertain within 5 business days whether receipt or possession would be in violation of the law, including research in whatever State and local recordkeeping systems are available and in a national system designated by the Attorney General." § 922(s)(2). The Act does not require the CLEO to take any particular action if he determines that a pending transaction would be unlawful; he may notify the firearms dealer to that effect, but is not required to do so. If, however, the CLEO notifies a gun dealer that a prospective purchaser is ineligible to receive a handgun, he must, upon request, provide the would-be purchaser with a written statement of the reasons for that determination. § 922(s)(6)(C). Moreover, if the CLEO does not discover any basis for objecting to the sale, he must destroy any records in his possession relating to the transfer, including his copy of the Brady Form. § 922(s)(6)(B)(i). Under a separate provision of the GCA, any person who "knowingly violates [the section of the GCA amended by the Brady Act] shall be fined under this title, imprisoned for no more than 1 year, or both." § 924(a)(5).

[T]he CLEOs for Ravalli County, Montana, and Graham County, Arizona . . . filed separate actions challenging the constitutionality of the Brady Act's interim provisions. In each case, the District Court held that the provision requiring CLEOs to perform background checks was unconstitutional, but concluded that that provision was severable from the remainder of the Act, effectively leaving a voluntary background-check system in place. . . . A divided panel of the Court of Appeals for the Ninth Circuit reversed, finding none of the Brady Act's interim provisions to be unconstitutional. . . .

II

[T]he Brady Act purports to direct state law enforcement officers to participate, albeit only temporarily, in the administration of a federally enacted regulatory scheme. Regulated firearms dealers are required to forward Brady Forms not to a federal officer or employee, but to the CLEOs, whose obligation to accept those forms is implicit in the duty imposed upon them to make "reasonable efforts" within five days to determine whether the sales reflected in the forms are lawful. While the CLEOs are subjected to no federal requirement that they prevent the sales determined to be unlawful (it is perhaps assumed that their state-law duties will require prevention or apprehension), they are empowered to grant, in effect, waivers of the federally prescribed 5-day waiting period for handgun purchases by notifying the gun dealers that they have no reason to believe the transactions would be illegal.

The petitioners here object to being pressed into federal service, and contend that congressional action compelling state officers to execute federal laws is unconstitutional. Because there is no constitutional text speaking to this precise question, the answer to the CLEOs' challenge must be sought in historical understanding and practice, in the structure of the Constitution, and in the jurisprudence of this Court. . . .

Petitioners contend that compelled enlistment of state executive officers for the administration of federal programs is, until very recent years at least, unprecedented. The Government contends, to the contrary, that "the earliest Congresses enacted statutes that required the participation of state officials in the implementation of federal laws," Brief for United States 28. The Government's contention demands our careful consideration, since early congressional enactments "provid[e] 'contemporaneous and weighty evidence' of the Constitution's meaning," Bowsher v. Synar, 478 U.S. 714, 723–724, 106 S.Ct. 3181, 92 L.Ed.2d 583 (1986) (quoting Marsh v. Chambers, 463 U.S. 783, 790, 103 S.Ct. 3330, 77 L.Ed.2d 1019 (1983)). Indeed, such "contemporaneous legislative exposition of the Constitution . . ., acquiesced in for a long term of years, fixes the construction to be given its provisions." Myers v. United States, 272 U.S. 52, 175, 47 S.Ct. 21, 71 L.Ed. 160 (1926) (citing numerous cases). Conversely if, as petitioners contend, earlier Congresses avoided use of this highly attractive power, we would have reason to believe that the power was thought not to exist.

The Government observes that statutes enacted by the first Congresses required state courts to [perform a variety of enforcement functions.] . . .

These early laws establish, at most, that the Constitution was originally understood to permit imposition of an obligation on state *judges* to enforce federal prescriptions, insofar as those prescriptions related to matters appropriate for the judicial power. That assumption was perhaps implicit in one of the provisions of the Constitution, and was explicit in another. In accord with the so-called Madisonian Compromise, Article III, § 1, established only a Supreme Court, and made the creation of lower federal courts optional with the Congress—even though it was obvious that the Supreme Court alone could not hear all federal cases throughout the United States. . . . And the Supremacy Clause, Art. VI, cl. 2, announced that "the Laws of the United States . . . shall be the supreme Law of the Land; and the Judges in every State shall be bound thereby." It is understandable why courts should have been viewed distinctively in this regard; unlike legislatures and executives, they applied the law of other sovereigns all the time. . . . The Constitution itself, in the Full Faith and Credit Clause, Art. IV, § 1, generally required such enforcement with respect to obligations arising in other States. . . .

For these reasons, we do not think the early statutes imposing obligations on state courts imply a power of Congress to impress the state executive into its service. Indeed, it can be argued that the numerousness of these statutes, contrasted with the utter lack of statutes imposing obligations on the States' executive (notwithstanding the attractiveness of that course to Congress), suggests an assumed absence of such power.[2] The only early federal law the Government has brought to our attention that imposed duties on state executive officers is the Extradition Act of 1793, which required the "executive authority" of a State to cause the arrest and delivery of a fugitive from justice upon the request of the executive authority of the State from which the fugitive

---

2 . . . None of the early statutes directed to state judges or court clerks required the performance of functions more appropriately characterized as executive than judicial. . . .

had fled.... That was in direct implementation, however, of the Extradition Clause of the Constitution itself, see Art. IV, § 2.

Not only do the enactments of the early Congresses ... contain no evidence of an assumption that the Federal Government may command the States' executive power in the absence of a particularized constitutional authorization, they contain some indication of precisely the opposite assumption. On September 23, 1789—the day before its proposal of the Bill of Rights ...—the First Congress enacted a law aimed at obtaining state assistance of the most rudimentary and necessary sort for the enforcement of the new Government's laws: the holding of federal prisoners in state jails at federal expense. Significantly, the law issued not a command to the States' executive, but a recommendation to their legislatures. Congress "recommended to the legislatures of the several States to pass laws, making it expressly the duty of the keepers of their gaols, to receive and safe keep therein all prisoners committed under the authority of the United States," and offered to pay 50 cents per month for each prisoner.... Moreover, when Georgia refused to comply with the request, ... Congress's only reaction was a law authorizing the marshal in any State that failed to comply ... to rent a temporary jail until provision for a permanent one could be made....

[T]he Government also ... points to portions of The Federalist which reply to criticisms that Congress's power to tax will produce two sets of revenue officers. "Publius" responded that Congress will probably "make use of the State officers and State regulations, for collecting" federal taxes, The Federalist No. 36, p. 221 (C. Rossiter ed. 1961) (A.Hamilton) (hereinafter The Federalist), and predicted that "the eventual collection [of internal revenue] under the immediate authority of the Union, will generally be made by the officers, and according to the rules, appointed by the several States," id., No. 45, at 292 (J. Madison). The Government also invokes the Federalist's more general observations that the Constitution would "enable the [national] government to employ the ordinary magistracy of each [State] in the execution of its laws," id., No. 27, at 176 (A.Hamilton), and that it was "extremely probable that in other instances, particularly in the organization of the judicial power, the officers of the States will be clothed in the correspondent authority of the Union," id., No. 45, at 292 (J. Madison). But none of these statements necessarily implies—what is the critical point here—that Congress could impose these responsibilities *without the consent of the States*. They appear to rest on the natural assumption that the States would consent to allowing their officials to assist the Federal Government, ... an assumption proved correct by the extensive mutual assistance the States and Federal Government voluntarily provided one another in the early days of the Republic, ... including voluntary *federal implementation of state law* ....

Another passage of The Federalist reads as follows:

"It merits particular attention ..., that the laws of the Confederacy as to the *enumerated* and *legitimate* objects of its jurisdiction will become the SUPREME LAW of the land; to the observance of which all officers, legislative, executive, and judicial in each State will be bound by the sanctity of an oath. Thus, the legislatures, courts, and magistrates, of the respective members will be incorporated into the operations of the national government *as far as its just and constitutional authority extends*; and will be rendered auxiliary to the enforcement of its laws." The Federalist No. 27, at 177 (A.Hamilton) (emphasis in original).

. . . Justice Souter finds "[t]he natural reading" of the phrases "will be incorporated into the operations of the national government" and "will be rendered auxiliary to the enforcement of its laws" to be that the National Government will have "authority . . ., when exercising an otherwise legitimate power (the commerce power, say), to require state 'auxiliaries' to take appropriate action." There are several obstacles to such an interpretation. First, . . . if the passage means that state officers must take an active role in the implementation of federal law, it means that they must do so without the necessity for a congressional directive that they implement it. But no one has ever thought, and no one asserts in the present litigation, that that is the law. [S]econd[,] Justice Souter's reading is that it makes state *legislatures* subject to federal direction. (The passage in question, after all, does not include legislatures merely incidentally, as by referring to "all state officers"; it refers to legislatures *specifically* and *first of all*.) We have held, however, that state legislatures are *not* subject to federal direction. New York v. United States, 505 U.S. 144 (1992).

These problems are avoided . . . if the calculatedly vague consequences the passage recites—"incorporated into the operations of the national government" and "rendered auxiliary to the enforcement of its laws"—are taken to refer to nothing more (or less) than the duty owed to the National Government, on the part of *all* state officials, to enact, enforce, and interpret state law in such fashion as not to obstruct the operation of federal law, and the attendant reality that all state actions constituting such obstruction, even legislative acts, are *ipso facto* invalid. . . . It also reconciles the passage with Hamilton's statement in Federalist No. 36, at 222, that the Federal Government would in some circumstances do well "to employ the state officers as much as possible, and to attach them to the Union by an accumulation of their emoluments"— which surely suggests inducing state officers to come aboard by paying them, rather than merely commandeering their official services.

. . .

To complete the historical record, we must note that there is not only an absence of executive-commandeering statutes in the early Congresses, but there is an absence of them in our later history as well, at least until very recent years. . . .

. . .

The Government points to a number of federal statutes enacted within the past few decades that require the participation of state or local officials in implementing federal regulatory schemes. . . . Even assuming they represent assertion of the very same congressional power challenged here, they are of such recent vintage that they are no more probative than the statute before us of a constitutional tradition that lends meaning to the text. Their persuasive force is far outweighed by almost two centuries of apparent congressional avoidance of the practice. . . .

III

The constitutional practice we have examined above tends to negate the existence of the congressional power asserted here, but is not conclusive. We turn next to consideration of the structure of the Constitution. . . .

A

It is incontestible that the Constitution established a system of "dual sovereignty." Gregory v. Ashcroft, 501 U.S. 452 (1991); Tafflin v. Levitt, 493 U.S. 455, 458 (1990). Although the States surrendered many of their powers to the new Federal Government, they retained "a residuary and inviolable sovereignty," The Federalist No. 39, at 245 (J. Madison). This is reflected throughout the Constitution's text, Lane County v. Oregon, 7 Wall. 71, 76 (1869); Texas v. White, 7 Wall. 700, 725 (1869), including (to mention only a few examples) the prohibition on any involuntary reduction or combination of a State's territory, Art. IV, § 3; the Judicial Power Clause, Art. III, § 2, and the Privileges and Immunities Clause, Art. IV, § 2, which speak of the "Citizens" of the States; the amendment provision, Article V, which requires the votes of three-fourths of the States to amend the Constitution; and the Guarantee Clause, Art. IV, § 4, which "presupposes the continued existence of the states and . . . those means and instrumentalities which are the creation of their sovereign and reserved rights," Helvering v. Gerhardt, 304 U.S. 405, 414–415 (1938). Residual state sovereignty was also implicit, of course, in the Constitution's conferral upon Congress of not all governmental powers, but only discrete, enumerated ones, Art. I, § 8, which implication was rendered express by the Tenth Amendment's assertion that "[t]he powers not delegated to the United States by the Constitution, nor prohibited by it to the States, are reserved to the States respectively, or to the people."

The Framers' experience under the Articles of Confederation had persuaded them that using the States as the instruments of federal governance was both ineffectual and provocative of federal-state conflict. See The Federalist No. 15. Preservation of the States as independent political entities being the price of union, and "[t]he practicality of making laws, with coercive sanctions, for the States as political bodies" having been, in Madison's words, "exploded on all hands," 2 Records of the Federal Convention of 1787, p. 9 (M. Farrand ed.1911), the Framers rejected the concept of a central government that would act upon and through the States, and instead designed a system in which the state and federal governments would exercise concurrent authority over the people—who were, in Hamilton's words, "the only proper objects of government," The Federalist No. 15, at 109. We have set forth the historical record in more detail elsewhere, see New York v. United States, 505 U.S., at 161–166, and need not repeat it here. It suffices to repeat the conclusion: "The Framers explicitly chose a Constitution that confers upon Congress the power to regulate individuals, not States." . . . The Constitution thus contemplates that a State's government will represent and remain accountable to its own citizens. . . .

This separation of the two spheres is one of the Constitution's structural protections of liberty. . . . The power of the Federal Government would be augmented immeasurably if it were able to impress into its service—and at no cost to itself—the police officers of the 50 States.

B

We have thus far discussed the effect that federal control of state officers would have upon the first element of the "double security" alluded to by Madison: the division of power between State and Federal Governments. It would also have an effect upon the second element: the separation and equilibration of powers between the three branches of the Federal Government itself. The Constitution does not leave to speculation who is to administer the laws enacted by Congress; the President, it says, "shall take Care that the Laws be faithfully executed," Art. II, § 3, personally and through officers whom he appoints (save for such inferior officers as Congress may authorize to be appointed by the "Courts of Law" or by "the Heads of Departments" who are themselves presidential appointees), Art. II, § 2. The Brady Act effectively transfers this responsibility to thousands of CLEOs in the 50 States, who are left to implement the program without meaningful Presidential control (if indeed meaningful Presidential control is possible without the power to appoint and remove). The insistence of the Framers upon unity in the Federal Executive—to insure both vigor and accountability—is well known. See The Federalist No. 70 (A.Hamilton).... That unity would be shattered, and the power of the President would be subject to reduction, if Congress could act as effectively without the President as with him, by simply requiring state officers to execute its laws.[12]

C

The dissent ... reasons that the power to regulate the sale of handguns under the Commerce Clause, coupled with the power to "make all Laws which shall be necessary and proper for carrying into Execution the foregoing Powers," Art. I, § 8, conclusively establishes the Brady Act's constitutional validity, because the Tenth Amendment imposes no limitations on the exercise of *delegated* powers but merely prohibits the exercise of powers "*not* delegated to the United States." What destroys the dissent's Necessary and Proper Clause argument, however, is not the Tenth Amendment but the Necessary and Proper Clause itself. When a "La[w] ... for carrying into Execution" the Commerce Clause violates the principle of state sovereignty reflected in the various constitutional provisions we mentioned earlier, it is not a "La[w] ... *proper* for carrying into Execution the Commerce Clause," and is thus, in the words of The Federalist, "merely [an] ac[t] of usurpation" which "deserve[s] to be treated as such." The Federalist No. 33, at 204 (A.Hamilton)....

dissent's argument

majority's answer

. . .

IV

Finally, and most conclusively in the present litigation, we turn to the prior jurisprudence of this Court. Federal commandeering of state governments

---

[12] There is not, as the dissent believes, "tension" between the proposition that impressing state police officers into federal service will massively augment *federal* power, and the proposition that it will also sap the power of the Federal *Presidency*. It is quite possible to have a more powerful Federal Government that is, by reason of the destruction of its Executive unity, a less efficient one. The dissent is correct that control by the unitary Federal Executive is also sacrificed when States voluntarily administer federal programs, but the condition of voluntary state participation significantly reduces the ability of Congress to use this device as a means of reducing the power of the Presidency.

is such a novel phenomenon that this Court's first experience with it did not occur until the 1970's, when the Environmental Protection Agency promulgated regulations requiring States to prescribe auto emissions testing, monitoring and retrofit programs, and to designate preferential bus and carpool lanes. The Courts of Appeals for the Fourth and Ninth Circuits invalidated the regulations on statutory grounds in order to avoid what they perceived to be grave constitutional issues, see Maryland v. EPA, 530 F.2d 215, 226 (C.A.4 1975); Brown v. EPA, 521 F.2d 827, 838–842 (C.A.9 1975); and the District of Columbia Circuit invalidated the regulations on both constitutional and statutory grounds, see District of Columbia v. Train, 521 F.2d 971, 994 (C.A.D.C. 1975). After we granted certiorari to review the statutory and constitutional validity of the regulations, the Government declined even to defend them, and instead rescinded some and conceded the invalidity of those that remained, leading us to vacate the opinions below and remand for consideration of mootness. EPA v. Brown, 431 U.S. 99 (1977).

[L]ater opinions of ours have made clear that the Federal Government may not compel the States to implement, by legislation or executive action, federal regulatory programs. In Hodel v. Virginia Surface Mining & Reclamation Assn., Inc., 452 U.S. 264 (1981), and FERC v. Mississippi, 456 U.S. 742 (1982), we sustained statutes against constitutional challenge only after assuring ourselves that they did not require the States to enforce federal law. In *Hodel* we ... concluded that the Surface Mining Control and Reclamation Act ... merely made compliance with federal standards a precondition to continued state regulation in an otherwise pre-empted field.... In *FERC*, we construed the most troubling provisions of the Public Utility Regulatory Policies Act of 1978, to contain only the "command" that state agencies "consider" federal standards, and again only as a precondition to continued state regulation of an otherwise pre-empted field.... We warned that "this Court never has sanctioned explicitly a federal command to the States to promulgate and enforce laws and regulations,".....

When we were at last confronted squarely with a federal statute that unambiguously required the States to enact or administer a federal regulatory program ... in New York v. United States, 505 U.S. 144 (1992), ... [we held:] "The Federal Government," ... "may not compel the States to enact or administer a federal regulatory program." Id., at 188.

The Government contends that *New York* is distinguishable on the following ground: unlike the "take title" provisions invalidated there, the background-check provision of the Brady Act does not require state legislative or executive officials to make policy, but instead issues a final directive to state CLEOs. It is permissible, the Government asserts, for Congress to command state or local officials to assist in the implementation of federal law so long as "Congress itself devises a clear legislative solution that regulates private conduct" and requires state or local officers to provide only "limited, non-policymaking help in enforcing that law." "[T]he constitutional line is crossed only when Congress compels the States to make law in their sovereign capacities." Brief for United States 16.

The Government's distinction between "making" law and merely "enforcing" it, between "policymaking" and mere "implementation," is ... reminiscent of, the line that separates proper congressional conferral of Executive power from unconstitutional delegation of legislative authority for federal separation-of-powers purposes. See A.L.A. Schechter Poultry Corp. v. United States, 295 U.S. 495, 530 (1935); Panama Refining Co. v. Ryan, 293 U.S. 388, 428–429 (1935). This Court has not been notably successful in describing the latter line.... We are doubtful that the new line the Government proposes would be any more distinct. Executive action that has utterly no policymaking component is rare, particularly at an executive level as high as a jurisdiction's chief law-enforcement officer. Is it really true that there is no policymaking involved in deciding, for example, what "reasonable efforts" shall be expended to conduct a background check? It may well satisfy the Act for a CLEO to direct that (a) no background checks will be conducted that divert personnel time from pending felony investigations, and (b) no background check will be permitted to consume more than one-half hour of an officer's time. But nothing in the Act *requires* a CLEO to be so parsimonious; diverting at least *some* felony-investigation time, and permitting at least *some* background checks beyond one-half hour would certainly not be *un*reasonable. Is this decision whether to devote maximum "reasonable efforts" or minimum "reasonable efforts" not preeminently a matter of policy? It is quite impossible, in short, to draw the Government's proposed line at "no policymaking," and we would have to fall back upon a line of "not too much policymaking." How much is too much is not likely to be answered precisely; and an imprecise barrier against federal intrusion upon state authority is not likely to be an effective one.

Even assuming, moreover, that the Brady Act leaves no "policymaking" discretion with the States, we fail to see how that improves rather than worsens the intrusion upon state sovereignty. Preservation of the States as independent and autonomous political entities is arguably less undermined by requiring them to make policy in certain fields than ... by "reduc[ing] [them] to puppets of a ventriloquist Congress," Brown v. EPA, 521 F.2d, at 839. It is an essential attribute of the States' retained sovereignty that they remain independent and autonomous within their proper sphere of authority. See Texas v. White, 7 Wall., at 725, 19 L.Ed. 227. It is no more compatible with this independence and autonomy that their officers be "dragooned" ... into administering federal law, than it would be compatible with the independence and autonomy of the United States that its officers be impressed into service for the execution of state laws.

. . .

The Government also maintains that requiring state officers to perform discrete, ministerial tasks specified by Congress does not violate the principle of *New York* because it does not diminish the accountability of state or federal officials. This argument fails even on its own terms. By forcing state governments to absorb the financial burden of implementing a federal regulatory program, Members of Congress can take credit for "solving" problems without having to ask their constituents to pay for the solutions with higher federal taxes. And even when the States are not forced to absorb the costs of implementing a federal program, they are still put in the position of taking the blame for its burdensomeness and for its defects.... Under the present law, for example, it will be the CLEO and not some federal official who stands between the gun purchaser and immediate possession of his gun. And it will likely be the CLEO, not some federal official, who will be blamed for any error (even one in the designated federal database) that causes a purchaser to be mistakenly rejected.

The dissent ... advances ... [the] even more implausible theory [that t]he Brady Act ... is different from the "take title" provisions invalidated in *New York* because the former is addressed to individuals—namely CLEOs—while the latter were directed to the State itself. That ... cannot be a constitutionally significant [difference]. While the Brady Act is directed to "individuals," it is directed to them in their official capacities as state officers; it controls their actions, not as private citizens, but as the agents of the State.... To say that the Federal Government cannot control the State, but can control all of its officers, is to say nothing of significance....

Finally, the Government puts forward a cluster of arguments that can be grouped under the heading: "The Brady Act serves very important purposes, is most efficiently administered by CLEOs during the interim period, and places a minimal and only temporary burden upon state officers." ... Assuming *all* ... were true, [it] might be relevant if we were evaluating whether the incidental application to the States of a federal law of general applicability excessively interfered with the functioning of state governments. See, e.g., Fry v. United States, 421 U.S. 542, 548 (1975); National League of Cities v. Usery, 426 U.S. 833, 853 (1976) (overruled by Garcia v. San Antonio Metropolitan Transit Authority, 469 U.S. 528 (1985)).... But where, as here, it is the whole *object* of the law to direct the functioning of the state executive, and hence to compromise the structural framework of dual sovereignty, such a "balancing" analysis is inappropriate. It is the very *principle* of separate state sovereignty that such a law offends, and no comparative assessment of the various interests can overcome that fundamental defect....

We ... conclude categorically, as we concluded categorically in *New York*: "The Federal Government may not compel the States to enact or administer a federal regulatory program." The mandatory obligation imposed on CLEOs to perform background checks on prospective handgun purchasers plainly runs afoul of that rule.

. . .

We held in *New York* that Congress cannot compel the States to enact or enforce a federal regulatory program. Today we hold that Congress cannot circumvent that prohibition by conscripting the State's officers directly. The Federal Government may neither issue directives requiring the States to address particular problems, nor command the States' officers, or those of their political subdivisions, to administer or enforce a federal regulatory program. It matters not whether policymaking is involved, and no case-by-case weighing of the burdens or benefits is necessary; such commands are fundamentally incompatible with our constitutional system of dual sovereignty....

Justice O'Connor, concurring.

Our precedent and our Nation's historical practices support the Court's holding today....

[T]he Court appropriately refrains from deciding whether other purely ministerial reporting requirements imposed by Congress on state and local authorities pursuant to its Commerce Clause powers are similarly invalid. See, e.g., 42 U.S.C. § 5779(a) (requiring state and local law enforcement agencies to report cases of missing children to the Department of Justice). The provisions invalidated here, however, which directly compel state officials to administer a federal regulatory program, utterly fail to adhere to the design and structure of our constitutional scheme.

Justice Thomas, concurring.

. . .

In my "revisionist" view, the Federal Government's authority under the Commerce Clause does not extend to the regulation of wholly *intra*state, point-of-sale transactions. See United States v. Lopez, 514 U.S. 549, 584 (1995) (concurring opinion). Absent the underlying authority to regulate the intrastate transfer of firearms, Congress surely lacks the corollary power to impress state law enforcement officers into administering and enforcing such regulations. . . .

Even if we construe Congress' authority to regulate interstate commerce to encompass those intrastate transactions that "substantially affect" interstate commerce, I question whether Congress can regulate the particular transactions at issue here. . . . If . . . the Second Amendment is read to confer a *personal* right to "keep and bear arms," a colorable argument exists that the Federal Government's regulatory scheme, at least as it pertains to the purely intrastate sale or possession of firearms, runs afoul of that Amendment's protections. As the parties did not raise this argument, however, we need not consider it here. . . . In the meantime, I join the Court's opinion striking down the challenged provisions of the Brady Act as inconsistent with the Tenth Amendment.

Justice Stevens, with whom Justice Souter, Justice Ginsburg, and Justice Breyer join, dissenting.

When Congress exercises the powers delegated to it by the Constitution, it may impose affirmative obligations on executive and judicial officers of state and local governments as well as ordinary citizens. This conclusion is firmly supported by the text of the Constitution, the early history of the Nation, decisions of this Court, and a correct understanding of the basic structure of the Federal Government.

These cases do not implicate the more difficult questions associated with congressional coercion of state legislatures addressed in New York v. United States, 505 U.S. 144 (1992). . . . The question is whether Congress, acting on behalf of the people of the entire Nation, may require local law enforcement officers to perform certain duties during the interim needed for the development of a federal gun control program. It is remarkably similar to the question, heavily debated by the Framers of the Constitution, whether the Congress could require state agents to collect federal taxes. Or the question whether Congress could impress state judges into federal service to entertain and decide cases that they would prefer to ignore.

. . . Matters such as the enlistment of air raid wardens, the administration of a military draft, the mass inoculation of children to forestall an epidemic, or perhaps the threat of an international terrorist, may require a national response before federal personnel can be made available to respond. If the Constitution empowers Congress and the President to make an appropriate response, is there anything in the Tenth Amendment, "in historical understanding and practice, in the structure of the Constitution, [or] in the jurisprudence of this Court" that forbids the enlistment of state officers to make that response effective? More narrowly, what basis is there in any of those sources for concluding that it is the Members of this Court, rather than the elected representatives of the people, who should determine whether the Constitution contains the unwritten rule that the Court announces today?

. . .

The Brady Act was passed in response to what Congress described as an "epidemic of gun violence." H. R. Rep. No. 103–344, p. 8 (1993). . . . [It] has met with remarkable success. Between 1994 and 1996, approximately 6,600 firearm sales each month to potentially dangerous persons were prevented by Brady Act checks; over 70% of the rejected purchasers were convicted or indicted felons. See U.S. Dept. of Justice, Bureau of Justice Statistics Bulletin, A National Estimate: Presale Firearm Checks 1 (Feb.1997). . . . [T]he congressional decision surely warrants more respect than it is accorded in today's unprecedented decision.

I

The text of the Constitution provides a sufficient basis for a correct disposition of this case . . .

Congress['s] power to regulate commerce among the States . . . adequately supports the regulation of commerce in handguns effected by the Brady Act. Moreover, the additional grant of authority . . . "[t]o make all Laws which shall be necessary and proper for carrying into Execution the foregoing Powers" is surely adequate to support the temporary enlistment of local police officers in the process of identifying persons who should not be entrusted with the possession of handguns. . . .

Unlike the First Amendment, which prohibits the enactment of a category of laws that would otherwise be authorized by Article I, the Tenth Amendment imposes no restriction on the exercise of delegated powers. . . . Thus, the Amendment provides no support for a rule that immunizes local officials from obligations that might be imposed on ordinary citizens.[2] Indeed, it would be more reasonable to infer that federal law may impose greater duties on state officials than on private citizens because another provision of the Constitution requires that "all executive and judicial Officers, both of the United States and of the several States, shall be bound by Oath or Affirmation, to support this Constitution." U.S. Const., Art. VI, cl. 3.

It is appropriate for state officials to make an oath or affirmation to support the Federal Constitution because, as explained in The Federalist, they

---

[2] . . . The majority's . . . claim that, while the Brady Act may be legislation "necessary" to Congress' execution of its undisputed Commerce Clause authority to regulate firearms sales, it is nevertheless not "proper" because it violates state sovereignty, is wholly circular. . . . Moreover, this reading of the term "proper" gives it a meaning directly contradicted by Chief Justice Marshall in McCulloch v. Maryland, 4 Wheat. 316 (1819). As the Chief Justice explained, the Necessary and Proper Clause by "[i]ts terms purport[s] to enlarge, not to diminish the powers vested in the government. It purports to be an additional power, not a restriction on those already granted." . . .

"have an essential agency in giving effect to the federal Constitution." The Federalist No. 44, p. 312 (E. Bourne ed. 1947) (J. Madison). There can be no conflict between their duties to the State and those owed to the Federal Government because Article VI unambiguously provides that federal law "shall be the supreme Law of the Land," binding in every State. U.S. Const., Art. VI, cl. 2. Thus, not only the Constitution, but every law enacted by Congress as well, establishes policy for the States just as firmly as do laws enacted by state legislatures.

. . .

There is not a clause, sentence, or paragraph in the entire text of the Constitution of the United States that supports the proposition that a local police officer can ignore a command contained in a statute enacted by Congress pursuant to an express delegation of power enumerated in Article I.

II

Under the Articles of Confederation the National Government had the power to issue commands to the several sovereign states, but it had no authority to govern individuals directly. Thus, it raised an army and financed its operations by issuing requisitions to the constituent members of the Confederacy, rather than by creating federal agencies to draft soldiers or to impose taxes.

That method of governing proved to be unacceptable, not because it demeaned the sovereign character of the several States, but rather because it was cumbersome and inefficient. Indeed, a confederation that allows each of its members to determine the ways and means of complying with an overriding requisition is obviously more deferential to state sovereignty concerns than a national government that uses its own agents to impose its will directly on the citizenry. The basic change in the character of the government that the Framers conceived was designed to enhance the power of the national government, not to provide some new, unmentioned immunity for state officers. . . .

Indeed, the historical materials strongly suggest that the Founders intended to enhance the capacity of the federal government by empowering it—as a part of the new authority to make demands directly on individual citizens—to act through local officials. Hamilton made clear that the new Constitution, "by extending the authority of the federal head to the individual citizens of the several States, will enable the government to employ the ordinary magistracy of each, in the execution of its laws." The Federalist No. 27, at 180. Hamilton's meaning was unambiguous; the federal government was to have the power to demand that local officials implement national policy programs. . . .

More specifically, during the debates concerning the ratification of the Constitution, it was assumed that state agents would act as tax collectors for the federal government. . . .

. . .

[E]specially clear i[s] Hamilton's statement that "the legislatures, courts, and magistrates, of the respective members, will be incorporated into the operations of the national government *as far as its just and constitutional authority extends; and will be rendered auxiliary to the enforcement of its laws.*"

Ibid. It is hard to imagine a more unequivocal statement that state judicial and executive branch officials may be required to implement federal law where the National Government acts within the scope of its affirmative powers.

The Court makes two unpersuasive attempts to discount the force of this statement. First, according to the majority, because Hamilton mentioned the Supremacy Clause without specifically referring to any "congressional directive," the statement does not mean what it plainly says. But the mere fact that the Supremacy Clause is the source of the obligation of state officials to implement congressional directives does not remotely suggest that they might be " 'incorporat[ed] into the operations of the national government' " before their obligations have been defined by Congress.... Second, the majority suggests that interpreting this passage to mean what it says would conflict with our decision in New York v. United States. But since the *New York* opinion did not mention Federalist No. 27, it does not affect either the relevance or the weight of the historical evidence provided by No. 27 insofar as it relates to state courts and magistrates.

Bereft of support in the history of the founding, the Court rests its conclusion on the claim that there is little evidence the National Government actually exercised such a power in the early years of the Republic.... [W]e have never suggested that the failure of the early Congresses to address the scope of federal power in a particular area or to exercise a particular authority was an argument against its existence....

More importantly, the fact that Congress did elect to rely on state judges and the clerks of state courts to perform a variety of executive functions is surely evidence of a contemporary understanding that their status as state officials did not immunize them from federal service....

[After disputing the majority's characterization of these functions as adjudicative, rather than executive, Justice Stevens continued:]

The Court assumes that the imposition of such essentially executive duties on state judges and their clerks sheds no light on the question whether executive officials might have an immunity from federal obligations. Even assuming that the enlistment of state judges in their judicial role for federal purposes is irrelevant to the question whether executive officials may be asked to perform the same function—a claim disputed below—the majority's analysis is badly mistaken.

... The majority's insistence that ... evidence of federal enlistment of state officials to serve executive functions is irrelevant simply because the assistance of "judges" was at issue rests on empty formalistic reasoning of the highest order.

The Court's evaluation of the historical evidence, furthermore, fails to acknowledge the important difference between policy decisions that may have been influenced by respect for state sovereignty concerns, and decisions that are compelled by the Constitution.[12] Thus, for example, the decision by Con-

[12] Indeed, an entirely appropriate concern for the prerogatives of state government readily explains Congress' sparing use of this otherwise "highly attractive" power. Congress' discretion, contrary to the majority's suggestion, indicates not that the power does not exist, but rather that the interests of the States are more than sufficiently protected by

gress to give President Wilson the authority to utilize the services of state officers in implementing the World War I draft, see Act of May 18, 1917, ch. 15, § 6, 40 Stat. 80–81, surely indicates that the national legislature saw no constitutional impediment to the enlistment of state assistance during a federal emergency. The fact that the President was able to implement the program by respectfully "request[ing]" state action, rather than bluntly commanding it, is evidence that he was an effective statesman, but surely does not indicate that he doubted either his or Congress' power to use mandatory language if necessary. . . .

. . . [T]he majority's opinion consists almost entirely of arguments *against* the substantial evidence weighing in opposition to its view; the Court's ruling is strikingly lacking in affirmative support. Absent even a modicum of textual foundation for its judicially crafted constitutional rule, there should be a presumption that if the Framers had actually intended such a rule, at least one of them would have mentioned it.

III

The Court's "structural" arguments are not sufficient to rebut that presumption. . . .

. . . Given the fact that the Members of Congress are elected by the people of the several States, with each State receiving an equivalent number of Senators in order to ensure that even the smallest States have a powerful voice in the legislature, it is quite unrealistic to assume that they will ignore the sovereignty concerns of their constituents. It is far more reasonable to presume that their decisions to impose modest burdens on state officials from time to time reflect a considered judgment that the people in each of the States will benefit therefrom.

Indeed, the presumption of validity that supports all congressional enactments has added force with respect to policy judgments concerning the impact of a federal statute upon the respective States. . . .

. . . The majority expresses special concern that were its rule not adopted the Federal Government would be able to avail itself of the services of state government officials "at no cost to itself." . . . But this specific problem of federal actions that have the effect of imposing so-called "unfunded mandates" on the States has been identified and meaningfully addressed by Congress in recent legislation.[18] See Unfunded Mandates Reform Act of 1995, Pub.L. 104–4, 109 Stat. 48.

their participation in the National Government.

[18] The majority also makes the more general claim that requiring state officials to carry out federal policy causes states to "tak[e] the blame" for failed programs. . . . This concern is vastly overstated.

Unlike state legislators, local government executive officials routinely take action in response to a variety of sources of authority: local ordinance, state law, and federal law. It doubtless may therefore require some so-

phistication to discern under which authority an executive official is acting, just as it may not always be immediately obvious what legal source of authority underlies a judicial decision. In both cases, affected citizens must look past the official before them to find the true cause of their grievance. . . . But the majority's rule neither creates nor alters this basic truth.

The problem is of little real consequence in any event, because to the extent that a particular action proves politically unpopular,

... Whatever the ultimate impact of the new legislation, its passage demonstrates that unelected judges are better off leaving the protection of federalism to the political process in all but the most extraordinary circumstances.

Perversely, the majority's rule seems more likely to damage than to preserve the safeguards against tyranny provided by the existence of vital state governments. By limiting the ability of the Federal Government to enlist state officials in the implementation of its programs, the Court creates incentives for the National Government to aggrandize itself. In the name of State's rights, the majority would have the Federal Government create vast national bureaucracies to implement its policies. This is exactly the sort of thing that the early Federalists promised would not occur, in part as a result of the National Government's ability to rely on the magistracy of the states. See, e.g., The Federalist No. 36, at 234–235 (Hamilton); id., No. 45, at 318 (Madison).

[T]he Court suggests that the unity in the Executive Branch of the Federal Government "would be shattered, and the power of the President would be subject to reduction, if Congress could ... require ... state officers to execute its laws." Putting to one side the obvious tension between the majority's claim that impressing state police officers will unduly tip the balance of power in favor of the federal sovereign and this suggestion that it will emasculate the Presidency, the Court's reasoning contradicts New York v. United States.

That decision squarely approved of cooperative federalism programs, designed at the national level but implemented principally by state governments.... Congress may require the States to implement its programs as a condition of federal spending, in order to avoid the threat of unilateral federal action in the area, or as a part of a program that affects States and private parties alike. The majority's suggestion in response to this dissent that Congress' ability to create such programs is limited, n. 12, is belied by the importance and sweep of the federal statutes that meet this description....

Nor is there force to the assumption undergirding the Court's entire opinion that if this trivial burden on state sovereignty is permissible, the entire structure of federalism will soon collapse.... [T]his case, unlike any precedent in which the Court has held that Congress exceeded its powers, merely involves the imposition of modest duties on individual officers....

Far more important than the concerns that the Court musters in support of its new rule is the fact that the Framers entrusted Congress with the task of creating a working structure of intergovernmental relationships around the framework that the Constitution authorized.... As a general matter, Congress has followed the sound policy of authorizing federal agencies and federal agents to administer federal programs. That general practice, however, does not

we may be confident that elected officials charged with implementing it will be quite clear to their constituents where the source of the misfortune lies. These cases demonstrate the point. Sheriffs Printz and Mack have made public statements, including their decisions to serve as plaintiffs in these actions, denouncing the Brady Act.... Moreover, we can be sure that CLEOs will inform disgruntled constituents who have been denied permission to purchase a handgun about the origins of the Brady Act requirements. The Court's suggestion that voters will be confused over who is to "blame" for the statute reflects a gross lack of confidence in the electorate that is at war with the basic assumptions underlying any democratic government.

negate the existence of power to rely on state officials in occasional situations in which such reliance is in the national interest. . . .

IV

Finally, the Court advises us that the "prior jurisprudence of this Court" is the most conclusive support for its position. That "prior jurisprudence" is New York v. United States. . . .

. . .

The majority relies upon dictum in *New York* to the effect that "[t]he Federal Government may not compel the States to enact *or administer* a federal regulatory program." . . . To the extent that it has any substance at all, *New York*'s administration language may have referred to the possibility that the State might have been able to take title to and devise an elaborate scheme for the management of the radioactive waste through purely executive policy-making. But despite the majority's effort to suggest that similar activities are required by the Brady Act, it is hard to characterize the minimal requirement that CLEOs perform background checks as one involving the exercise of substantial policymaking discretion on that essentially legislative scale.

. . .

Importantly, the majority either misconstrues or ignores . . . cases that are more directly on point. In *FERC*, we upheld a federal statute requiring state utilities commissions, *inter alia*, to take the affirmative step of considering federal energy standards in a manner complying with federally specified notice and comment procedures, and to report back to Congress periodically. The state commissions could avoid this obligation only by ceasing regulation in the field, a "choice" that we recognized was realistically foreclosed, since Congress had put forward no alternative regulatory scheme to govern this very important area. . . . The burden on state officials that we approved in FERC was far more extensive than the minimal, temporary imposition posed by the Brady Act.

. . .

[T]he majority provides an incomplete explanation of our decision in Testa v. Katt, 330 U.S. 386 (1947), and demeans its importance. In that case the Court unanimously held that state courts of appropriate jurisdiction must occupy themselves adjudicating claims brought by private litigants under the federal Emergency Price Control Act of 1942, regardless of how otherwise crowded their dockets might be with state law matters. That is a much greater imposition on state sovereignty than the Court's characterization of the case as merely holding that "state courts cannot refuse to apply federal law." That characterization describes only the narrower duty to apply federal law in cases that the state courts have consented to entertain.

The language drawn from the Supremacy Clause upon which the majority relies ("the Judges in every State shall be bound [by federal law], any Thing in the Constitution or Laws of any state to the Contrary notwithstanding"), expressly embraces that narrower conflict of laws principle. Art. VI, cl. 2. But the Supremacy Clause means far more. As *Testa* held, because the "Laws of the United States . . . [are] the supreme Law of the Land," state courts of appropriate jurisdiction must hear federal claims whenever a federal statute . . . requires them to do so. . . .

. . . Th[e] language command[ing] state judges to "apply federal law" in cases that they entertain . . . is not the source of their duty to accept jurisdiction of federal claims that they would prefer to ignore. Our opinions in *Testa* . . . rested generally on the language of the Supremacy Clause, without any specific focus on the reference to judges.

. . .

Even if . . . the reference to judges in the Supremacy Clause, rather than the central message of the entire Clause, [had] dictated the result in *Testa*, the Court's . . . argument that the Framers therefore did not intend to permit the enlistment of other state officials is implausible. . . . The notion that the Framers would have had no reluctance to "press state judges into federal service" against their will but would have regarded the imposition of a similar—indeed, far lesser—burden on town constables as an intolerable affront to principles of state sovereignty, can only be considered perverse. If such a distinction had been contemplated by the learned and articulate men who fashioned the basic structure of our government, surely some of them would have said so.

* * *

The provision of the Brady Act that crosses the Court's newly defined constitutional threshold is more comparable to a statute requiring local police officers to report the identity of missing children to the Crime Control Center of the Department of Justice than to an offensive federal command to a sovereign state. If Congress believes that such a statute will benefit the people of the Nation, and serve the interests of cooperative federalism better than an enlarged federal bureaucracy, we should respect both its policy judgment and its appraisal of its constitutional power.

Accordingly, I respectfully dissent.

Justice Souter, dissenting.

I join Justice Stevens's dissenting opinion, but subject to the following qualifications. . . . I do not find anything dispositive in the paucity of early examples of federal employment of state officers for executive purposes. . . .

[I]t is The Federalist that finally determines my position. . . .

Hamilton in No. 27 . . . addresses the combined effect of the proposed Supremacy Clause, U.S. Const., Art. VI, cl. 2, and state officers's oath requirement, U.S. Const., Art. VI, cl. 3, and he states that "the Legislatures, Courts and Magistrates of the respective members will be incorporated into the operations of the national government, *as far as its just and constitutional authority extends*; and will be rendered auxiliary to the enforcement of its laws." . . . The natural reading of this language is not merely that the officers of the various branches of state governments may be employed in the performance of national functions; Hamilton says that the state governmental machinery "will be incorporated" into the Nation's operation, and because the "auxiliary" status of the state officials will occur because they are "bound by the sanctity of an oath," . . . I take him to mean that their auxiliary functions will be the products of their obligations thus undertaken to support federal law, not of their own, or the States', unfettered choices.[1]

. . .

... I cannot persuade myself that the statements from No. 27 speak of anything less than the authority of the National Government, when exercising an otherwise legitimate power (the commerce power, say), to require state "auxiliaries" to take appropriate action. To be sure, it does not follow that any conceivable requirement may be imposed on any state official. I continue to agree, for example, that Congress may not require a state legislature to enact a regulatory scheme and that New York v. United States, 505 U.S. 144 (1992) was rightly decided (even though I now believe its dicta went too far toward immunizing state administration as well as state enactment of such a scheme from congressional mandate); after all, the essence of legislative power, within the limits of legislative jurisdiction, is a discretion not subject to command. But insofar as national law would require nothing from a state officer inconsistent with the power proper to his branch of tripartite state government (say, by obligating a state judge to exercise law enforcement powers), I suppose that the reach of federal law as Hamilton described it would not be exceeded....

... I do not read any of The Federalist material as requiring the conclusion that Congress could require administrative support without an obligation to pay fair value for it ... If, therefore, my views were prevailing in these cases, I would remand for development and consideration of petitioners' points, that they have no budget provision for work required under the Act and are liable for unauthorized expenditures....

Justice Breyer, with whom Justice Stevens joins, dissenting.

... The federal systems of Switzerland, Germany, and the European Union ... provide that constituent states, not federal bureaucracies, will themselves implement many of the laws, rules, regulations, or decrees enacted by the central "federal" body.... They do so in part because they believe that such a system interferes less, not more, with the independent authority of the "state," member nation, or other subsidiary government, and helps to safeguard individual liberty as well....

Of course, we are interpreting our own Constitution, not those of other nations, and there may be relevant political and structural differences between their systems and our own.... But their experience may nonetheless cast an empirical light on the consequences of different solutions to a common legal problem—in this case the problem of reconciling central authority with the need to preserve the liberty-enhancing autonomy of a smaller constituent governmental entity.... And that experience here offers empirical confirmation of the implied answer to a question Justice Stevens asks: Why, or how,

---

[1] ...

The Court reads Hamilton's description of state officers' role in carrying out federal law as nothing more than a way of describing the duty of state officials "not to obstruct the operation of federal law," with the consequence that any obstruction is invalid. But I doubt that Hamilton's English was quite as bad as all that. Someone whose virtue consists of not obstructing administration of the law is not described as "incorporated into the operations" of a government or as an "auxiliary" to its law enforcement. One simply cannot escape from Hamilton by reducing his prose to inapposite figures of speech.

would what the majority sees as a constitutional alternative—the creation of a new federal gun-law bureaucracy, or the expansion of an existing federal bureaucracy—better promote either state sovereignty or individual liberty?

As comparative experience suggests, there is no need to interpret the Constitution as containing an absolute principle—forbidding the assignment of virtually any federal duty to any state official. Nor is there a need to read the Brady Act as permitting the Federal Government to overwhelm a state civil service. The statute uses the words "reasonable effort," 18 U.S.C. § 922(s)(2)— words that easily can encompass the considerations of, say, time or cost, necessary to avoid any such result.

... [T]hat direct federal assignment of duties to state officers is not common ... likely reflects, not a widely shared belief that any such assignment is incompatible with basic principles of federalism, but rather a widely shared practice of assigning such duties in other ways.... [T]here is neither need nor reason to find in the Constitution an absolute principle, the inflexibility of which poses a surprising and technical obstacle to the enactment of a law that Congress believed necessary to solve an important national problem.

. . .

CHAPTER 7

SEPARATION OF POWERS

SECTION 1. THE PRESIDENT'S POWER TO DETERMINE NATIONAL POLICY

Page 422. Add at end of section:

D. THE LEGISLATIVE VETO

Clinton v. City of New York

524 U.S. 417, 118 S.Ct. 2091, 141 L.Ed.2d 393 (1998).

Justice Stevens delivered the opinion of the Court.

The Line Item Veto Act (Act), 110 Stat. 1200, 2 U. S. C. § 691 et seq. (1994 ed., Supp. II), was enacted in April 1996 and became effective on January 1, 1997. The following day, six Members of Congress who had voted against the Act brought suit in the District Court for the District of Columbia challenging its constitutionality. ... We determined, however, that the Members of Congress did not have standing to sue because they had not "alleged a sufficiently concrete injury to have established Article III standing," Raines v. Byrd, 521 U.S. 811, ___ (1997)....

Less than two months after our decision in that case, the President exercised his authority to cancel one provision in the Balanced Budget Act of 1997, ... and two provisions in the Taxpayer Relief Act of 1997 ... Appellees, claiming that they had been injured by two of those cancellations, filed these cases in the District Court. That Court again held the statute invalid, ... and we again expedited our review.... We now hold that these appellees have standing to challenge the constitutionality of the Act and, reaching the merits, we agree that the cancellation procedures set forth in the Act violate the Presentment Clause, Art. I, § 7, cl. 2, of the Constitution.

I

We begin by reviewing the canceled items that are at issue in these cases.

Title XIX of the Social Security Act, ... authorizes the Federal Government to transfer huge sums of money to the States to help finance medical care for the indigent. ...In 1991, Congress directed that those federal subsidies be reduced by the amount of certain taxes levied by the States on health care providers. In 1994, the Department of Health and Human Services (HHS) notified the State of New York that 15 of its taxes were covered by the 1991 Act, and that as of June 30, 1994, the statute therefore required New York to return $955 million to the United States. The notice advised the State that it could apply for a waiver on certain statutory grounds. New York did request a waiver for those tax programs, as well as for a number of others, but HHS has not formally acted on any of those waiver requests. New York has estimated that the amount at issue for the period from October 1992 through March 1997 is as high as $2.6 billion.

Because HHS had not taken any action on the waiver requests, New York turned to Congress for relief. . . . Section 4722(c) of the Balanced Budget Act of 1997 identifies the disputed taxes and provides that they "are deemed to be permissible health care related taxes and in compliance with the requirements" of the relevant provisions of the 1991 statute.

On August 11, 1997, the President sent identical notices to the Senate and to the House of Representatives canceling "one item of new direct spending," specifying § 4722(c) as that item . . .

A person who realizes a profit from the sale of securities is generally subject to a capital gains tax. Under existing law, however, an ordinary business corporation can acquire a corporation, including a food processing or refining company, in a merger or stock-for-stock transaction in which no gain is recognized to the seller . . .; the seller's tax payment, therefore, is deferred. If, however, the purchaser is a farmers' cooperative, the parties cannot structure such a transaction because the stock of the cooperative may be held only by its members, . . .; thus, a seller dealing with a farmers' cooperative cannot obtain the benefits of tax deferral.

In § 968 of the Taxpayer Relief Act of 1997, Congress amended § 1042 of the Internal Revenue Code to permit owners of certain food refiners and processors to defer the recognition of gain if they sell their stock to eligible farmers' cooperatives. The purpose of the amendment, as repeatedly explained by its sponsors, was "to facilitate the transfer of refiners and processors to farmers' cooperatives." The amendment to § 1042 was one of the 79 "limited tax benefits" authorized by the Taxpayer Relief Act of 1997 and specifically identified in Title XVII of that Act as "subject to [the] line item veto."

On the same date that he canceled the "item of new direct spending" involving New York's health care programs, the President also canceled this limited tax benefit. . . .

II

Appellees filed two separate actions against the President and other federal officials challenging these two cancellations. The plaintiffs in the first case are the City of New York, two hospital associations, one hospital, and two unions representing health care employees. The plaintiffs in the second are a farmers' cooperative consisting of about 30 potato growers in Idaho and an individual farmer who is a member and officer of the cooperative. The District Court consolidated the two cases and determined that at least one of the plaintiffs in each had standing under Article III of the Constitution.

. . .

On the merits, the District Court held that the cancellations did not conform to the constitutionally mandated procedures for the enactment or repeal of laws . . .

III

As in the prior challenge to the Line Item Veto Act, we initially confront jurisdictional questions. The appellees invoked the jurisdiction of the District Court under the section of the Act entitled "Expedited Review." That section, 2 U. S. C. § 692(a)(1), expressly authorizes "[a]ny Member of Congress or any individual adversely affected" by the Act to bring an action for declaratory judgment or injunctive relief on the ground that any provision of the Act is unconstitutional. [T]he Government . . . argues that, with the exception of Mike Cranney, the appellees are not "individuals" within the meaning of § 692(a)(1). . . . [T]he argument poses a jurisdictional question (although not one of constitutional magnitude), it is not waived by the failure to raise it in the District Court. . . . [I]n the context of the entire section Congress undoubtedly intended the word 'individual' to be construed as synonymous with the word "person."

. . .

We are also unpersuaded by the Government's argument that appellees' challenge to the constitutionality of the Act is nonjusticiable. . . . Our disposition of the first challenge to the constitutionality of this Act demonstrates our recognition of the importance of respecting the constitutional limits on our jurisdiction, even when Congress has manifested an interest in obtaining our views as promptly as possible. But these cases differ from *Raines*, not only because the President's exercise of his cancellation authority has removed any concern about the ripeness of the dispute, but more importantly because the parties have alleged a "personal stake" in having an actual injury redressed rather than an "institutional injury" that is "abstract and widely dispersed." . . .

In both the New York and the Snake River cases, the Government argues that the appellees are not actually injured because the claims are too speculative and, in any event, the claims are advanced by the wrong parties. We find no merit in the suggestion that New York's injury is merely speculative because HHS has not yet acted on the State's waiver requests. The State now has a multibillion dollar contingent liability that had been eliminated by § 4722(c) of the Balanced Budget Act of 1997. The District Court correctly concluded that the State, and the appellees, "suffered an immediate, concrete injury the moment that the President used the Line Item Veto to cancel section 4722(c) and deprived them of the benefits of that law." . . .

We also reject the Government's argument that New York's claim is advanced by the wrong parties because the claim belongs to the State of New York, and not appellees. Under New York statutes that are already in place, it is clear that both the City of New York and the appellee health care providers will be assessed by the State for substantial portions of any recoupment payments that the State may have to make to the Federal Government. To the extent of such assessments, they have the same potential liability as the State does.

The Snake River farmers' cooperative also suffered an immediate injury when the President canceled the limited tax benefit that Congress had enacted to facilitate the acquisition of processing plants. Three critical facts identify the specificity and the importance of that injury. First, Congress enacted § 968 for the specific purpose of providing a benefit to a defined category of potential purchasers of a defined category of assets. The members of that statutorily defined class received the equivalent of a statutory "bargaining chip" to use in carrying out the congressional plan to facilitate their purchase of such assets. Second, the President selected § 968 as one of only two tax benefits in the Taxpayer Relief Act of 1997 that should be canceled. The cancellation rested on his determination that the use of those bargaining chips would have a significant impact on the Federal budget deficit. Third, the Snake River cooperative was organized for the very purpose of acquiring processing facilities, it had concrete plans to utilize the benefits of § 968, and it was engaged in ongoing negotiations with the owner of a processing plant who had expressed an interest in structuring a tax-deferred sale when the President canceled § 968. Moreover, it is actively searching for other processing facilities for possible future purchase if the President's cancellation is reversed; and there are ample processing facilities in the State that Snake River may be able to purchase. By depriving them of their statutory bargaining chip, the cancellation inflicted a sufficient likelihood of economic injury to establish standing . . .

. . .

As with the New York case, the Government argues that the wrong parties are before the Court—that because the sellers of the processing facilities would have received the tax benefits, only they have standing to challenge the cancellation of § 968. This argument not only ignores the fact that the cooperatives were the intended beneficiaries of § 968, but also overlooks the self-evident proposition that more than one party may have standing to challenge a particular action or inaction. Once it is determined that a particular plaintiff is harmed by the defendant, and that the harm will likely be redressed by a favorable decision, that plaintiff has standing—regardless of whether there are others who would also have standing to sue. Thus, we are satisfied that both of these actions are Article III 'Cases' that we have a duty to decide.

IV

The Line Item Veto Act gives the President the power to "cancel in whole" three types of provisions that have been signed into law: "(1) any dollar amount of discretionary budget authority; (2) any item of new direct spending; or (3) any limited tax benefit." . . . It is undisputed that the New York case involves an "item of new direct spending" and that the Snake River case involves a "limited tax benefit" as those terms are defined in the Act. It is also undisputed that each of those provisions had been signed into law pursuant to Article I, § 7, of the Constitution before it was canceled.

The Act requires the President to adhere to precise procedures whenever he exercises his cancellation authority. In identifying items for cancellation he must consider the legislative history, the purposes, and other relevant information about the items. . . . He must determine, with respect to each cancellation, that it will "(i) reduce the Federal budget deficit; (ii) not impair any essential Government functions; and (iii) not harm the national interest." . . . Moreover, he must transmit a special message to Congress notifying it of each cancellation within five calendar days (excluding Sundays) after the enactment of the canceled provision. . . . It is undisputed that the President meticulously followed these procedures in these cases.

A cancellation takes effect upon receipt by Congress of the special message from the President. . . . If, however, a "disapproval bill" pertaining to a special message is enacted into law, the cancellations set forth in that message become "null and void." . . . The Act sets forth a detailed expedited procedure for the consideration of a "disapproval bill," . . . but no such bill was passed for either of the cancellations involved in these cases. A majority vote of both Houses is sufficient to enact a disapproval bill. The Act does not grant the President the authority to cancel a disapproval bill, . . . but he does, of course, retain his constitutional authority to veto such a bill.

The effect of a cancellation is plainly stated in § 691e, which defines the principal terms used in the Act. With respect to both an item of new direct spending and a limited tax benefit, the cancellation prevents the item "from having legal force or effect." . . . Thus, under the plain text of the statute, the two actions of the President that are challenged in these cases prevented one section of the Balanced Budget Act of 1997 and one section of the Taxpayer Relief Act of 1997 "from having legal force or effect." The remaining provisions of those statutes, with the exception of the second canceled item in the latter, continue to have the same force and effect as they had when signed into law.

In both legal and practical effect, the President has amended two Acts of Congress by repealing a portion of each. . . . There is no provision in the Constitution that authorizes the President to enact, to amend, or to repeal statutes. . . .

There are important differences between the President's "return" of a bill pursuant to Article I, § 7, and the exercise of the President's cancellation authority pursuant to the Line Item Veto Act. The constitutional return takes place before the bill becomes law; the statutory cancellation occurs after the bill becomes law. The constitutional return is of the entire bill; the statutory cancellation is of only a part. Although the Constitution expressly authorizes the President to play a role in the process of enacting statutes, it is silent on the subject of unilateral Presidential action that either repeals or amends parts of duly enacted statutes.

There are powerful reasons for construing constitutional silence on this profoundly important issue as equivalent to an express prohibition. The procedures governing the enactment of statutes set forth in the text of Article I were the product of the great debates and compromises that produced the Constitution itself. . . . . Our first President understood the text of the Presentment Clause as requiring that he either "approve all the parts of a Bill, or reject it in toto." What has emerged in these cases from the President's exercise of his statutory cancellation powers, however, are truncated versions of two bills that passed both Houses of Congress. They are not the product of the "finely wrought" procedure that the Framers designed.

At oral argument, the Government suggested that the cancellations at issue in these cases do not effect a "repeal" of the canceled items because under the special "lockbox" provisions of the Act, a canceled item "retain[s] real, legal budgetary effect" insofar as it prevents Congress and the President from spending the savings that result from the cancellation. The text of the Act expressly provides, however, that a cancellation prevents a direct spending or tax benefit provision "from having legal force or effect." That a canceled item may have "real, legal budgetary effect" as a result of the lockbox procedure does not change the fact that by canceling the items at issue in these cases, the President made them entirely inoperative as to appellees. Section 968 of the Taxpayer Relief Act no longer provides a tax benefit, and § 4722(c) of the Balanced Budget Act of 1997 no longer relieves New York of its contingent liability. Such significant changes do not lose their character simply because the canceled provisions may have some continuing financial effect on the Government. The cancellation of one section of a statute may be the functional equivalent of a partial repeal even if a portion of the section is not canceled.

V

The Government advances two related arguments to support its position that despite the unambiguous provisions of the Act, cancellations do not amend or repeal properly enacted statutes in violation of the Presentment Clause. First, relying primarily on Field v. Clark, 143 U. S. 649 (1892), the Government contends that the cancellations were merely exercises of discretionary authority granted to the President by the Balanced Budget Act and the Taxpayer Relief Act read in light of the previously enacted Line Item Veto Act. Second, the Government submits that the substance of the authority to cancel tax and spending items "is, in practical effect, no more and no less than the power to 'decline to spend' specified sums of money, or to 'decline to implement' specified tax measures."

In Field v. Clark, the Court upheld the constitutionality of the Tariff Act of 1890. Act of Oct. 1, 1890, 26 Stat. 567. That statute contained a "free list" of almost 300 specific articles that were exempted from import duties "unless otherwise specially provided for in this act." ... Section 3 was a special provision that directed the President to suspend that exemption for sugar, molasses, coffee, tea, and hides "whenever, and so often" as he should be satisfied that any country producing and exporting those products imposed duties on the agricultural products of the United States that he deemed to be "reciprocally unequal and unreasonable...." ... The section then specified the duties to be imposed on those products during any such suspension. The Court provided this explanation for its conclusion that § 3 had not delegated legislative power to the President:

> "Nothing involving the expediency or the just operation of such legislation was left to the determination of the President... .[W]hen he ascertained the fact that duties and exactions, reciprocally unequal and unreasonable, were imposed upon the agricultural or other products of the United States by a country producing and exporting sugar, molasses, coffee, tea or hides, it became his duty to issue a proclamation declaring the suspension, as to that country, which Congress had determined should occur. He had no discretion in the premises except in respect to the duration of the suspension so ordered. But that related only to the enforcement of the policy established by Congress. As the suspension was absolutely required when the President ascertained the existence of a

particular fact, it cannot be said that in ascertaining that fact and in issuing his proclamation, in obedience to the legislative will, he exercised the function of making laws. . . .It was a part of the law itself as it left the hands of Congress that the provisions, full and complete in themselves, permitting the free introduction of sugars, molasses, coffee, tea and hides, from particular countries, should be suspended, in a given contingency, and that in case of such suspensions certain duties should be imposed."

This passage identifies three critical differences between the power to suspend the exemption from import duties and the power to cancel portions of a duly enacted statute. First, the exercise of the suspension power was contingent upon a condition that did not exist when the Tariff Act was passed: the imposition of "reciprocally unequal and unreasonable" import duties by other countries. In contrast, the exercise of the cancellation power within five days after the enactment of the Balanced Budget and Tax Reform Acts necessarily was based on the same conditions that Congress evaluated when it passed those statutes. Second, under the Tariff Act, when the President determined that the contingency had arisen, he had a duty to suspend; in contrast, while it is true that the President was required by the Act to make three determinations before he canceled a provision, . . ., those determinations did not qualify his discretion to cancel or not to cancel. Finally, whenever the President suspended an exemption under the Tariff Act, he was executing the policy that Congress had embodied in the statute. In contrast, whenever the President cancels an item of new direct spending or a limited tax benefit he is rejecting the policy judgment made by Congress and relying on his own policy judgment. Thus, the conclusion in Field v. Clark that the suspensions mandated by the Tariff Act were not exercises of legislative power does not undermine our opinion that cancellations pursuant to the Line Item Veto Act are the functional equivalent of partial repeals of Acts of Congress that fail to satisfy Article I, § 7.

The Government's reliance upon other tariff and import statutes, discussed in *Field*, that contain provisions similar to the one challenged in *Field* is unavailing for the same reasons. Some of those statutes authorized the President to "suspen[d] and discontinu[e]" statutory duties upon his determination that discriminatory duties imposed by other nations had been abolished. . . .A slightly different statute . . . provided that certain statutory provisions imposing duties on foreign ships "shall be repealed" upon the same no-discrimination determination by the President. . . .

The cited statutes all relate to foreign trade, and this Court has recognized that in the foreign affairs arena, the President has "a degree of discretion and freedom from statutory restriction which would not be admissible were domestic affairs alone involved." United States v. Curtiss–Wright Export Corp., 299 U. S. 304, 320 (1936). . . .More important, when enacting the statutes discussed in *Field*, Congress itself made the decision to suspend or repeal the particular provisions at issue upon the occurrence of particular events subsequent to enactment, and it left only the determination of whether such events occurred up to the President. The Line Item Veto Act authorizes the President himself to effect the repeal of laws, for his own policy reasons, without observing the procedures set out in Article I, § 7. The fact that Congress intended such a result is of no moment. Although Congress presumably anticipated that the

President might cancel some of the items in the Balanced Budget Act and in the Taxpayer Relief Act, Congress cannot alter the procedures set out in Article I, § 7, without amending the Constitution.

Neither are we persuaded by the Government's contention that the President's authority to cancel new direct spending and tax benefit items is no greater than his traditional authority to decline to spend appropriated funds. The Government has reviewed in some detail the series of statutes in which Congress has given the Executive broad discretion over the expenditure of appropriated funds. For example, the First Congress appropriated "sum[s] not exceeding" specified amounts to be spent on various Government operations. ...In those statutes, as in later years, the President was given wide discretion with respect to both the amounts to be spent and how the money would be allocated among different functions. It is argued that the Line Item Veto Act merely confers comparable discretionary authority over the expenditure of appropriated funds. The critical difference between this statute and all of its predecessors, however, is that unlike any of them, this Act gives the President the unilateral power to change the text of duly enacted statutes. None of the Act's predecessors could even arguably have been construed to authorize such a change.

VI

. . .

... [O]ur decision rests on the narrow ground that the procedures authorized by the Line Item Veto Act are not authorized by the Constitution. The Balanced Budget Act of 1997 is a 500–page document that became "Public Law 105–33" after three procedural steps were taken: (1) a bill containing its exact text was approved by a majority of the Members of the House of Representatives; (2) the Senate approved precisely the same text; and (3) that text was signed into law by the President. The Constitution explicitly requires that each of those three steps be taken before a bill may "become a law." Art. I, § 7. If one paragraph of that text had been omitted at any one of those three stages, Public Law 105–33 would not have been validly enacted. If the Line Item Veto Act were valid, it would authorize the President to create a different law—one whose text was not voted on by either House of Congress or presented to the President for signature. Something that might be known as "Public Law 105–33 as modified by the President" may or may not be desirable, but it is surely not a document that may "become a law" pursuant to the procedures designed by the Framers of Article I, § 7, of the Constitution.

If there is to be a new procedure in which the President will play a different role in determining the final text of what may "become a law," such change must come not by legislation but through the amendment procedures set forth in Article V of the Constitution. . . .

The judgment of the District Court is affirmed.

It is so ordered.

Justice Kennedy, concurring.

. . .

I write to respond to my colleague Justice Breyer, who observes that the statute does not threaten the liberties of individual citizens, a point on which I disagree. The argument is related to his earlier suggestion that our role is lessened here because the two political branches are adjusting their own powers between themselves .. To say the political branches have a somewhat free hand to reallocate their own authority would seem to require acceptance of two premises: first, that the public good demands it, and second, that liberty is not at risk. The former premise is inadmissible. The Constitution's structure requires a stability which transcends the convenience of the moment. ...The latter premise, too, is flawed. Liberty is always at stake when one or more of the branches seek to transgress the separation of powers.

Separation of powers was designed to implement a fundamental insight: concentration of power in the hands of a single branch is a threat to liberty. . . . .

In recent years, perhaps, we have come to think of liberty as defined by that word in the Fifth and Fourteenth Amendments and as illuminated by the other provisions of the Bill of Rights. The conception of liberty embraced by the Framers was not so confined. They used the principles of separation of powers and federalism to secure liberty in the fundamental political sense of the term, quite in addition to the idea of freedom from intrusive governmental acts. The idea and the promise were that when the people delegate some degree of control to a remote central authority, one branch of government ought not possess the power to shape their destiny without a sufficient check from the other two. In this vision, liberty demands limits on the ability of any one branch to influence basic political decisions. . . .

. . .

The principal object of the statute, it is true, was not to enhance the President's power to reward one group and punish another, to help one set of taxpayers and hurt another, to favor one State and ignore another. Yet these are its undeniable effects. The law establishes a new mechanism which gives the President the sole ability to hurt a group that is a visible target, in order to disfavor the group or to extract further concessions from Congress. The law is the functional equivalent of a line item veto and enhances the President's powers beyond what the Framers would have endorsed.

. . .

... With these observations, I join the opinion of the Court.

Justice Breyer, with whom Justice O'Connor and Justice Scalia join as to Part III, dissenting.

I

I agree with the Court that the parties have standing, but I do not agree with its ultimate conclusion. In my view the Line Item Veto Act does not violate any specific textual constitutional command, nor does it violate any implicit Separation of Powers principle. Consequently, I believe that the Act is constitutional.

II

I approach the constitutional question before us with three general considerations in mind. First, the Act represents a legislative effort to provide the President with the power to give effect to some, but not to all, of the expenditure and revenue-diminishing provisions contained in a single massive appropriations bill. And this objective is constitutionally proper.

When our Nation was founded, Congress could easily have provided the President with this kind of power. . . . At that time, a Congress, wishing to give a President the power to select among appropriations, could simply have embodied each appropriation in a separate bill, each bill subject to a separate Presidential veto.

Today, however, . . . Congress cannot divide such a bill into thousands, or tens of thousands, of separate appropriations bills, each one of which the President would have to sign, or to veto, separately. Thus, the question is whether the Constitution permits Congress to choose a particular novel means to achieve this same, constitutionally legitimate, end.

Second, the case in part requires us to focus upon the Constitution's generally phrased structural provisions, provisions that delegate all "legislative" power to Congress and vest all "executive" power in the President. The Court, when applying these provisions, has interpreted them generously in terms of the institutional arrangements that they permit. . . .

Indeed, Chief Justice Marshall, in a well-known passage, explained,

"To have prescribed the means by which government should, in all future time, execute its powers, would have been to change, entirely, the character of the instrument, and give it the properties of a legal code. It would have been an unwise attempt to provide, by immutable rules, for exigencies which, if foreseen at all, must have been seen dimly, and which can be best provided for as they occur." McCulloch v. Maryland, 4 Wheat. 316, 415 (1819).

This passage . . . calls attention to the genius of the Framers' pragmatic vision, which . . . find[s] constitutional room for necessary institutional innovation.

Third, we need not here referee a dispute among the other two branches. . . .

These three background circumstances mean that, when one measures the literal words of the Act against the Constitution's literal commands, the fact that the Act may closely resemble a different, literally unconstitutional, arrangement is beside the point. . . .

. . .

III

The Court believes that the Act violates the literal text of the Constitution. A simple syllogism captures its basic reasoning:

Major Premise: The Constitution sets forth an exclusive method for enacting, repealing, or amending laws.

Minor Premise: The Act authorizes the President to "repea[l] or amen[d]" laws in a different way, namely by announcing a cancellation of a portion of a previously enacted law.

Conclusion: The Act is inconsistent with the Constitution.

I find this syllogism unconvincing, however, because its Minor Premise is faulty. When the President "canceled" the two appropriation measures now before us, he did not repeal any law nor did he amend any law. He simply followed the law, leaving the statutes, as they are literally written, intact.

. . .

. . . Literally speaking, the President has not "repealed" or "amended" anything. He has simply executed a power conferred upon him by Congress, which power is contained in laws that were enacted in compliance with the exclusive method set forth in the Constitution. See Field v. Clark, . . .

Nor can one dismiss this literal compliance as some kind of formal quibble, as if it were somehow "obvious" that what the President has done "amounts to," "comes close to," or is "analogous to" the repeal or amendment of a previously enacted law. That is because the power the Act grants the President (to render designated appropriations items without "legal force or effect") also "amounts to," "comes close to," or is "analogous to" a different legal animal, the delegation of a power to choose one legal path as opposed to another . . .

. . .

[T]he Act contains a "lockbox" feature, which gives legal significance to the enactment of a particular appropriations item even if, and even after, the President has rendered it without "force or effect." . . . In essence, the "lockbox" feature: (1) points to a Gramm–Rudman–Hollings Act requirement that, when Congress enacts a "budget-busting" appropriation bill, automatically reduces authorized spending for a host of federal programs in a pro rata way; (2) notes that cancellation of an item (say, a $2 billion item) would, absent the lockbox provision, neutralize (by up to $2 billion) the potential "budget busting" effects of other bills (and therefore potentially the President could cancel items in order to "save" the other programs from the mandatory cuts, resulting no net deficit reduction); and (3) says that this "neutralization" will not occur (i.e., the pro rata reductions will take place just as if the $2 billion item had not been canceled), so that the canceled items truly provide additional budget savings over and above the Gramm–Rudman–Hollings regime. . . . [D]espite the Act's use of the word "cancel," the Act does not delegate to the President the power truly to cancel a line item expenditure (returning the legal status quo to one in which the item had never been enacted). Rather, it delegates to the President the power to decide how to spend the money to which the line item refers—either for the specific purpose mentioned in the item, or for general deficit reduction via the "lockbox" feature.

. . .

IV

Because I disagree with the Court's holding of literal violation, I must consider whether the Act nonetheless violates Separation of Powers principles—principles that arise out of the Constitution's vesting of the "executive

Power" in "a President," U. S. Const., Art. II, § 1, and "[a]ll legislative Powers" in "a Congress," Art. I, § 1. There are three relevant Separation of Powers questions here: (1) Has Congress given the President the wrong kind of power, i.e., "non-Executive" power? (2) Has Congress given the President the power to "encroach" upon Congress' own constitutionally reserved territory? (3) Has Congress given the President too much power, violating the doctrine of "nondelegation?" ... [W]ith respect to this Act, the answer to all these questions is "no."

A

Viewed conceptually, the power the Act conveys is the right kind of power. It is "executive." As explained above, an exercise of that power "executes" the Act. Conceptually speaking, it closely resembles the kind of delegated authority—to spend or not to spend appropriations, to change or not to change tariff rates—that Congress has frequently granted the President, any differences being differences in degree, not kind.

The fact that one could also characterize this kind of power as "legislative," say, if Congress itself (by amending the appropriations bill) prevented a provision from taking effect, is beside the point. This Court has frequently found that the exercise of a particular power, such as the power to make rules of broad applicability, ... can fall within the constitutional purview of more than one branch of Government. ...

The Court has upheld congressional delegation of rulemaking power and adjudicatory power to federal agencies, ... and prosecutor-appointment power to judges ... It is far easier conceptually to reconcile the power at issue here with the relevant constitutional description ("executive") than in many of these cases. ....

If there is a Separation of Powers violation, then, it must rest, not upon purely conceptual grounds, but upon some important conflict between the Act and a significant Separation of Powers objective.

B

The Act does not undermine what this Court has often described as the principal function of the Separation of Powers, which is to maintain the tripartite structure of the Federal Government—and thereby protect individual liberty ...

... [O]ne cannot say that the Act "encroaches" upon Congress' power, when Congress retained the power to insert, by simple majority, into any future appropriations bill, into any section of any such bill, or into any phrase of any section, a provision that says the Act will not apply. ... Thus this Act is not the sort of delegation "without ... sufficient check" that concerns Justice Kennedy ...

Nor can one say that the Act's basic substantive objective is constitutionally improper, for the earliest Congresses could have, and often did, confer on the President this sort of discretionary authority over spending, ... Where the burden of overcoming legislative inertia lies is within the power of Congress to determine by rule. Where is the encroachment?

Nor can one say the Act's grant of power "aggrandizes" the Presidential office. The grant is limited to the context of the budget. It is limited to the power to spend, or not to spend, particular appropriated items, and the power to permit, or not to permit, specific limited exemptions from generally applicable tax law from taking effect. ...The delegation of those powers to the President may strengthen the Presidency, but any such change in Executive Branch authority seems minute when compared with the changes worked by delegations of other kinds of authority that the Court in the past has upheld. ...

C

The "nondelegation" doctrine represents an added constitutional check upon Congress' authority to delegate power to the Executive Branch. ...[I]n Chief Justice Taft's ... words, the Constitution permits only those delegations where Congress "shall lay down by legislative act an intelligible principle to which the person or body authorized to [act] is directed to conform." ...

The Act before us seeks to create such a principle in three ways. The first is procedural. The Act tells the President that, in "identifying dollar amounts [or] ... items ... for cancellation" (which I take to refer to his selection of the amounts or items he will "prevent from having legal force or effect"), he is to "consider," among other things,

> "the legislative history, construction, and purposes of the law which contains [those amounts or items, and] ... any specific sources of information referenced in such law or ... the best available information...." ...

The second is purposive. The clear purpose behind the Act, confirmed by its legislative history, is to promote "greater fiscal accountability" and to "eliminate wasteful federal spending and ... special tax breaks." ...

The third is substantive. The President must determine that, to "prevent" the item or amount "from having legal force or effect" will "reduce the Federal budget deficit; ... not impair any essential Government functions; and ... not harm the national interest." ...

The resulting standards are broad. But this Court has upheld standards that are equally broad, or broader. ...

. . .

... I believe that the power the Act grants the President to prevent spending items from taking effect does not violate the "nondelegation" doctrine.

. . .

... [T]he "limited tax benefit" provisions do not differ enough from the "spending" provisions to warrant a different "nondelegation" result.

V

In sum, I recognize that the Act before us is novel. In a sense, it skirts a constitutional edge. But that edge has to do with means, not ends. The means chosen do not amount literally to the enactment, repeal, or amendment of a law. Nor, for that matter, do they amount literally to the "line item veto" that the Act's title announces. Those means do not violate any basic Separation of Powers principle. They do not improperly shift the constitutionally foreseen balance of power from Congress to the President. Nor, since they comply with Separation of Powers principles, do they threaten the liberties of individual citizens. They represent an experiment that may, or may not, help representative government work better. The Constitution, in my view, authorizes Congress and the President to try novel methods in this way. Consequently, with respect, I dissent.

Justice Scalia, with whom Justice O'Connor joins, and with whom Justice Breyer joins as to Part III, concurring in part and dissenting in part.

Today the Court acknowledges the " 'overriding and time-honored concern about keeping the Judiciary's power within its proper constitutional sphere,' " ... It proceeds, however, to ignore the prescribed statutory limits of our jurisdiction by permitting the expedited-review provisions of the Line Item Veto Act to be invoked by persons who are not "individual[s]," ... and to ignore the constitutional limits of our jurisdiction by permitting one party to challenge the Government's denial to another party of favorable tax treatment from which the first party might, but just as likely might not, gain a concrete benefit. In my view, the Snake River appellees lack standing to challenge the President's cancellation of the "limited tax benefit," and the constitutionality of that action should not be addressed. I think the New York appellees have standing to challenge the President's cancellation of an "item of new direct spending"; I believe we have statutory authority (other than the expedited-review provision) to address that challenge; but unlike the Court I find the President's cancellation of spending items to be entirely in accord with the Constitution.

I

The Court's unrestrained zeal to reach the merits of this case is evident in its disregard of the statute's expedited-review provision, which extends that special procedure to "[a]ny Member of Congress or any individual adversely affected by [the Act]," ... With the exception of Mike Cranney, a natural person, the appellees—corporations, cooperatives, and governmental entities—are not "individuals" under any accepted usage of that term. ...

. . .

II

Not only must we be satisfied that we have statutory jurisdiction to hear this case; we must be satisfied that we have jurisdiction under Article III. ...

In the first action before us, ... [t]he Snake River appellees have standing, in the Court's view, because § 968 gave them "the equivalent of a statutory 'bargaining chip,' " and "[b]y depriving them of their statutory bargaining chip, the cancellation inflicted a sufficient likelihood of economic injury to establish standing under our precedents." It is unclear whether the Court means that deprivation of a "bargaining chip" itself suffices for standing, or that such deprivation suffices in the present case because it creates a likelihood of economic injury. The former is wrong as a matter of law, and the latter is wrong as a matter of fact, on the facts alleged.

... Snake River does not challenge the Line Item Veto Act on equal-protection grounds, ... And I know of no case outside the equal-protection field in which the mere detriment to one's "bargaining position," as opposed to a demonstrated loss of some bargain, has been held to confer standing. ...

But even if harm to one's bargaining position were a legally cognizable injury, Snake River has not alleged, as it must, facts sufficient to demonstrate that it personally has suffered that injury. ...Snake River has presented no evidence to show that it was engaged in bargaining, and that that bargaining was impaired by the President's cancellation of § 968. The Court says that Snake River "was engaged in ongoing negotiations with the owner of a processing plant who had expressed an interest in structuring a tax-deferred sale when the President canceled § 968." There is, however, no evidence of "negotiations," only of two "discussions." ...

Nor has Snake River demonstrated, as the Court finds, that "the cancellation inflicted a sufficient likelihood of economic injury to establish standing under our precedents." Presumably the economic injury the Court has in mind is Snake River's loss of a bargain purchase of a processing plant. But there is no evidence, and indeed not even an allegation, that before the President's action such a purchase was likely. ...

. . .

... While Snake River in the present case may indeed have enough of a "stake" to assure adverseness, the matter it brings before us is inappropriate for our resolution because its allegations do not establish an injury in fact, attributable to the Presidential action it challenges, and remediable by this Court's invalidation of that Presidential action.

Because, in my view, Snake River has no standing to bring this suit, we have no jurisdiction to resolve its challenge to the President's authority to cancel a "limited tax benefit."

III

I agree with the Court that the New York appellees have standing to challenge the President's cancellation of § 4722(c) of the Balanced Budget Act of 1997 as an "item of new direct spending." The tax liability they will incur under New York law is a concrete and particularized injury, fairly traceable to the President's action, and avoided if that action is undone. Unlike the Court, however, I do not believe that Executive cancellation of this item of direct spending violates the Presentment Clause.

... [T]he Court's problem with the Act is not that it authorizes the President to veto parts of a bill and sign others into law, but rather that it authorizes him to "cancel"—prevent from "having legal force or effect"—certain parts of duly enacted statutes.

Article I, § 7 of the Constitution obviously prevents the President from canceling a law that Congress has not authorized him to cancel. ...It was certainly arguable, as an original matter, that Art. I, § 7 also prevents the President from canceling a law which itself authorizes the President to cancel it. But as the Court acknowledges, that argument has long since been made and rejected. ...

As much as the Court goes on about Art. I, § 7, therefore, that provision does not demand the result the Court reaches. It no more categorically prohibits the Executive reduction of congressional dispositions in the course of implementing statutes that authorize such reduction, than it categorically prohibits the Executive augmentation of congressional dispositions in the course of implementing statutes that authorize such augmentation—generally known as substantive rulemaking. There are, to be sure, limits upon the former just as there are limits upon the latter.... Those limits are established, however, not by some categorical prohibition of Art. I, § 7, which our cases conclusively disprove, but by what has come to be known as the doctrine of unconstitutional delegation of legislative authority ...

It is this doctrine, and not the Presentment Clause, ... that is the issue presented by the statute before us here. That is why the Court is correct to distinguish prior authorizations of Executive cancellation ... on the ground that they were contingent upon an Executive finding of fact, and on the ground that they related to the field of foreign affairs ... These distinctions have nothing to do with whether the details of Art. I, § 7 have been complied with, but everything to do with whether the authorizations went too far by transferring to the Executive a degree of political, law-making power that our traditions demand be retained by the Legislative Branch.

    . . .

... [T]here is not a dime's worth of difference between Congress's authorizing the President to cancel a spending item, and Congress's authorizing money to be spent on a particular item at the President's discretion. And the latter has been done since the Founding of the Nation. ...

    . . .

The short of the matter is this: Had the Line Item Veto Act authorized the President to "decline to spend" any item of spending contained in the Balanced Budget Act of 1997, there is not the slightest doubt that authorization would have been constitutional. What the Line Item Veto Act does instead—authorizing the President to "cancel" an item of spending—is technically different. But the technical difference does not relate to the technicalities of the Presentment Clause, which have been fully complied with; and the doctrine of unconstitutional delegation, which is at issue here, is preeminently not a doctrine of technicalities. The title of the Line Item Veto Act, which was perhaps designed to simplify for public comprehension, or perhaps merely to comply with the terms of a campaign pledge, has succeeded in faking out the Supreme Court. The President's action it authorizes in fact is not a line-item veto and thus does not offend Art. I, § 7; and insofar as the substance of that action is concerned, it is no different from what Congress has permitted the President to do since the formation of the Union.

    . . .

SECTION 3.   PRESIDENTIAL AND CONGRESSIONAL IMMUNITIES

Page 454. Add after Nixon v. Fitzgerald:

Clinton v. Jones

520 U.S. 681, 117 S.Ct. 1636, 137 L.Ed.2d 945 (1997).

Justice Stevens delivered the opinion of the Court.

This case raises a constitutional and a prudential question concerning the Office of the President of the United States. Respondent, a private citizen, seeks to recover damages from the current occupant of that office based on actions allegedly taken before his term began. The President submits that in all but the most exceptional cases the Constitution requires federal courts to defer such litigation until his term ends and that, in any event, respect for the office warrants such a stay. Despite the force of the arguments supporting the President's submissions, we conclude that they must be rejected.

I

Petitioner, William Jefferson Clinton, was elected to the Presidency in 1992, and re-elected in 1996. His term of office expires on January 20, 2001. In 1991 he was the Governor of the State of Arkansas. Respondent, Paula Corbin Jones, is a resident of California. In 1991 she lived in Arkansas, and was an employee of the Arkansas Industrial Development Commission.

On May 6, 1994, she commenced this action in the United States District Court for the Eastern District of Arkansas by filing a complaint naming petitioner and Danny Ferguson, a former Arkansas State Police officer, as defendants. The complaint alleges two federal claims, and two state law claims over which the federal court has jurisdiction because of the diverse citizenship of the parties....

Th[e] allegations [in the complaint] principally describe events that are said to have occurred on the afternoon of May 8, 1991, during an official conference held at the Excelsior Hotel in Little Rock, Arkansas. The Governor delivered a speech at the conference; respondent—working as a state employee-staffed the registration desk. She alleges that Ferguson persuaded her to leave her desk and to visit the Governor in a business suite at the hotel, where he made "abhorrent" sexual advances that she vehemently rejected. She further claims that her superiors at work subsequently dealt with her in a hostile and rude manner, and changed her duties to punish her for rejecting those advances. Finally, she alleges that after petitioner was elected President, Ferguson defamed her by making a statement to a reporter that implied she had accepted petitioner's alleged overtures, and that various persons authorized to speak for the President publicly branded her a liar by denying that the incident had occurred.

... Her complaint contains four counts. The first charges that petitioner, acting under color of state law, deprived her of rights protected by the Constitution, in violation of ... 42 U.S.C. § 1983. The second charges that petitioner and Ferguson engaged in a conspiracy to violate her federal rights, also actionable under federal law. See ... 42 U.S.C. § 1985. The third is a state common-law claim for intentional infliction of emotional distress, grounded primarily on the incident at the hotel. The fourth count, also based on state law, is for defamation, embracing both the comments allegedly made to the press by Ferguson and the statements of petitioner's agents.... With the exception of the last charge, which arguably may involve conduct within the outer perimeter of the President's official responsibilities, ... the alleged misconduct of petitioner was unrelated to any of his official duties as President of the United States and, indeed, occurred before he was elected to that office.

II

In response to the complaint, petitioner promptly advised the District Court that he intended to file a motion to dismiss on grounds of Presidential immunity, and requested the court to defer all other pleadings and motions until after the immunity issue was resolved. . . .

The District Judge denied the motion to dismiss on immunity grounds and ruled that discovery in the case could go forward, but ordered any trial stayed until the end of petitioner's Presidency. . . .

Both parties appealed. A divided panel of the Court of Appeals affirmed the denial of the motion to dismiss, but because it regarded the order postponing the trial until the President leaves office as the "functional equivalent" of a grant of temporary immunity, it reversed that order. . . .

. . .

III

. . .

. . . The representations made on behalf of the Executive Branch as to the potential impact of the precedent established by the Court of Appeals merit our respectful and deliberate consideration.

. . . [There are] two important constitutional issues not encompassed within the questions presented by the petition for certiorari that we need not address today.

First, because the claim of immunity is asserted in a federal court and relies heavily on the doctrine of separation of powers . . ., it is not necessary to consider or decide whether a comparable claim might succeed in a state tribunal. If this case were being heard in a state forum, instead of advancing a separation of powers argument, petitioner would presumably rely on federalism and comity concerns,[13] as well as the interest in protecting federal officials from possible local prejudice that underlies the authority to remove certain cases brought against federal officers from a state to a federal court . . .

Second, our decision rejecting the immunity claim and allowing the case to proceed does not require us to confront the question whether a court may compel the attendance of the President at any specific time or place. We assume that the testimony of the President, both for discovery and for use at trial, may be taken at the White House at a time that will accommodate his busy schedule, and that, if a trial is held, there would be no necessity for the President to attend in person, though he could elect to do so.[14]

[13] Because the Supremacy Clause makes federal law "the supreme Law of the Land," Art. VI, cl. 2, any direct control by a state court over the President, who has principal responsibility to ensure that those laws are "faithfully executed," Art. II, § 3, may implicate concerns that are quite different from the interbranch separation of powers questions addressed here. . . .

[14] Although Presidents have responded to written interrogatories, given depositions, and provided videotaped trial testimony, no sitting President has ever testified, or been ordered to testify, in open court.

IV

Petitioner's principal submission—that "in all but the most exceptional cases," the Constitution affords the President temporary immunity from civil damages litigation arising out of events that occurred before he took office— cannot be sustained on the basis of precedent.

Only three sitting Presidents have been defendants in civil litigation involving their actions prior to taking office. Complaints against Theodore Roosevelt and Harry Truman had been dismissed before they took office; the dismissals were affirmed after their respective inaugurations. Two companion cases arising out of an automobile accident were filed against John F. Kennedy in 1960 during the Presidential campaign. After taking office, he unsuccessfully argued that his status as Commander in Chief gave him a right to a stay under the Soldiers' and Sailors' Civil Relief Act of 1940.... The motion for a stay was denied by the District Court, and the matter was settled out of court. Thus, none of those cases sheds any light on the constitutional issue before us.

The principal rationale for affording certain public servants immunity from suits for money damages arising out of their official acts is inapplicable to unofficial conduct.... That rationale provided the principal basis for our holding that a former President of the United States was "entitled to absolute immunity from damages liability predicated on his official acts," *Fitzgerald*, 457 U. S., at 749.... Our central concern was to avoid rendering the President "unduly cautious in the discharge of his official duties." ...

This reasoning provides no support for an immunity for *unofficial* conduct. As we explained in *Fitzgerald*, "the sphere of protected action must be related closely to the immunity's justifying purposes." ... Because of the President's broad responsibilities, we recognized in that case an immunity from damages claims arising out of official acts extending to the "outer perimeter of his authority." ... But we have never suggested that the President, or any other official, has an immunity that extends beyond the scope of any action taken in an official capacity....

Moreover, when defining the scope of an immunity for acts clearly taken *within* an official capacity, we have applied a functional approach. "Frequently our decisions have held that an official's absolute immunity should extend only to acts in performance of particular functions of his office." ... As our opinions have made clear, immunities are grounded in "the nature of the function performed, not the identity of the actor who performed it." ...

Petitioner's effort to construct an immunity from suit for unofficial acts grounded purely in the identity of his office is unsupported by precedent.

V

We are also unpersuaded by the evidence from the historical record to which petitioner has called our attention. He points to a comment by Thomas Jefferson protesting the subpoena *duces tecum* Chief Justice Marshall directed to him in the Burr trial, a statement in the diaries kept by Senator William Maclay of the first Senate debates, in which then Vice–President John Adams and Senator Oliver Ellsworth are recorded as having said that "the President personally [is] not ... subject to any process whatever," lest it be "put ... in the power of a common Justice to exercise any Authority over him and Stop the

Whole Machine of Government," and to a quotation from Justice Story's Commentaries on the Constitution. None of these sources sheds much light on the question at hand.

Respondent, in turn, has called our attention to conflicting historical evidence. Speaking in favor of the Constitution's adoption at the Pennsylvania Convention, James Wilson—who had participated in the Philadelphia Convention at which the document was drafted—explained that, although the President "is placed [on] high," "not a single privilege is annexed to his character; far from being above the laws, he is amenable to them in his private character as a citizen, and in his public character by impeachment." This description is consistent with both the doctrine of presidential immunity as set forth in *Fitzgerald*, and rejection of the immunity claim in this case. With respect to acts taken in his "public character"—that is official acts—the President may be disciplined principally by impeachment, not by private lawsuits for damages. But he is otherwise subject to the laws for his purely private acts.

In the end, as applied to the particular question before us, we reach the same conclusion about these historical materials that Justice Jackson described when confronted with an issue concerning the dimensions of the President's power. "Just what our forefathers did envision, or would have envisioned had they foreseen modern conditions, must be divined from materials almost as enigmatic as the dreams Joseph was called upon to interpret for Pharoah. A century and a half of partisan debate and scholarly speculation yields no net result but only supplies more or less apt quotations from respected sources on each side.... They largely cancel each other." Youngstown Sheet & Tube Co. v. Sawyer, 343 U.S. 579, 634–635 (1952) (concurring opinion).

VI

Petitioner's strongest argument supporting his immunity claim is based on the text and structure of the Constitution. He does not contend that the occupant of the Office of the President is "above the law," in the sense that his conduct is entirely immune from judicial scrutiny. The President argues merely for a postponement of the judicial proceedings that will determine whether he violated any law. His argument is grounded in the character of the office that was created by Article II of the Constitution, and relies on separation of powers principles that have structured our constitutional arrangement since the founding.

As a starting premise, petitioner contends that he occupies a unique office with powers and responsibilities so vast and important that the public interest demands that he devote his undivided time and attention to his public duties. He submits that—given the nature of the office—the doctrine of separation of powers places limits on the authority of the Federal Judiciary to interfere with the Executive Branch that would be transgressed by allowing this action to proceed.

We have no dispute with the initial premise of the argument. Former presidents, from George Washington to George Bush, have consistently endorsed petitioner's characterization of the office.... As Justice Jackson has pointed out, the Presidency concentrates executive authority "in a single head in whose choice the whole Nation has a part, making him the focus of public hopes and expectations. In drama, magnitude and finality his decisions so far overshadow any others that almost alone he fills the public eye and ear." *Youngstown Sheet & Tube Co. v. Sawyer,* 343 U. S., at 653 (Jackson, J., concurring). We have, in short, long recognized the "unique position in the constitutional scheme" that this office occupies. *Fitzgerald,* 457 U. S., at 749. Thus, while we suspect that even in our modern era there remains some truth to Chief Justice Marshall's suggestion that the duties of the Presidency are not entirely "unremitting," *United States v. Burr,* 25 F. Cas. 30, 34 (C.C.Va.1807), we accept the initial premise of the Executive's argument.

It does not follow, however, that separation of powers principles would be violated by allowing this action to proceed. The doctrine of separation of powers is concerned with the allocation of official power among the three co-equal branches of our Government. . . .

Of course the lines between the powers of the three branches are not always neatly defined. . . . But in this case there is no suggestion that the Federal Judiciary is being asked to perform any function that might in some way be described as "executive." Respondent is merely asking the courts to exercise their core Article III jurisdiction to decide cases and controversies. Whatever the outcome of this case, there is no possibility that the decision will curtail the scope of the official powers of the Executive Branch. The litigation of questions that relate entirely to the unofficial conduct of the individual who happens to be the President poses no perceptible risk of misallocation of either judicial power or executive power.

Rather than arguing that the decision of the case will produce either an aggrandizement of judicial power or a narrowing of executive power, petitioner contends that—as a by—product of an otherwise traditional exercise of judicial power—burdens will be placed on the President that will hamper the performance of his official duties. . . . [P]etitioner contends that this particular case— as well as the potential additional litigation that an affirmance of the Court of Appeals judgment might spawn—may impose an unacceptable burden on the President's time and energy, and thereby impair the effective performance of his office.

Petitioner's predictive judgment finds little support in either history or the relatively narrow compass of the issues raised in this particular case. As we have already noted, in the more than 200–year history of the Republic, only three sitting Presidents have been subjected to suits for their private actions. If the past is any indicator, it seems unlikely that a deluge of such litigation will ever engulf the Presidency. As for the case at hand, if properly managed by the District Court, it appears to us highly unlikely to occupy any substantial amount of petitioner's time.

Of greater significance, petitioner errs by presuming that interactions between the Judicial Branch and the Executive, even quite burdensome interactions, necessarily rise to the level of constitutionally forbidden impairment of the Executive's ability to perform its constitutionally mandated functions. . . . The fact that a federal court's exercise of its traditional Article III jurisdiction may significantly burden the time and attention of the Chief Executive is not sufficient to establish a violation of the Constitution. Two long-settled propositions, first announced by Chief Justice Marshall, support that conclusion.

First, we have long held that when the President takes official action, the Court has the authority to determine whether he has acted within the law. Perhaps the most dramatic example of such a case is our holding that President Truman exceeded his constitutional authority when he issued an order directing the Secretary of Commerce to take possession of and operate most of the Nation's steel mills in order to avert a national catastrophe. Youngstown Sheet & Tube Co. v. Sawyer, 343 U.S. 579 (1952). Despite the serious impact of that decision on the ability of the Executive Branch to accomplish its assigned mission, and the substantial time that the President must necessarily have devoted to the matter as a result of judicial involvement, we exercised our Article III jurisdiction to decide whether his official conduct conformed to the law. Our holding was an application of the principle established in Marbury v. Madison, 1 Cranch 137 (1803), that "[i]t is emphatically the province and duty of the judicial department to say what the law is." . . .

Second, it is also settled that the President is subject to judicial process in appropriate circumstances. Although Thomas Jefferson apparently thought otherwise, Chief Justice Marshall, when presiding in the treason trial of Aaron Burr, ruled that a subpoena *duces tecum* could be directed to the President. United States v. Burr, 25 F. Cas. 30 (No. 14,692D) (CC Va. 1807). We unequivocally and emphatically endorsed Marshall's position when we held that President Nixon was obligated to comply with a subpoena commanding him to produce certain tape recordings of his conversations with his aides. United States v. Nixon, 418 U.S. 683 (1974). . . .

Sitting Presidents have responded to court orders to provide testimony and other information with sufficient frequency that such interactions between the Judicial and Executive Branches can scarcely be thought a novelty. President Monroe responded to written interrogatories, ... President Nixon—as noted above—produced tapes in response to a subpoena *duces tecum*, see United States v. Nixon, President Ford complied with an order to give a deposition in a criminal trial, United States v. Fromme, 405 F. Supp. 578 (E.D.Cal.1975), and President Clinton has twice given videotaped testimony in criminal proceedings, see United States v. McDougal, 934 F. Supp. 296 (E.D.Ark.1996); United States v. Branscum, No., LRP–CR–96–49 (ED Ark., June 7, 1996). Moreover, sitting Presidents have also voluntarily complied with judicial requests for testimony. President Grant gave a lengthy deposition in a criminal case under such circumstances, . . . and President Carter similarly gave videotaped testimony for use at a criminal trial. . . .

In sum, "[i]t is settled law that the separation-of-powers doctrine does not bar every exercise of jurisdiction over the President of the United States." *Fitzgerald*, 457 U. S., at 753–754. If the Judiciary may severely burden the Executive Branch by reviewing the legality of the President's official conduct, and if it may direct appropriate process to the President himself, it must follow that the federal courts have power to determine the legality of his unofficial conduct. The burden on the President's time and energy that is a mere by-product of such review surely cannot be considered as onerous as the direct burden imposed by judicial review and the occasional invalidation of his official actions. We therefore hold that the doctrine of separation of powers does not require federal courts to stay all private actions against the President until he leaves office.

The reasons for rejecting such a categorical rule apply as well to a rule that would require a stay "in all but the most exceptional cases." Indeed, if the Framers of the Constitution had thought it necessary to protect the President from the burdens of private litigation, we think it far more likely that they would have adopted a categorical rule than a rule that required the President to litigate the question whether a specific case belonged in the "exceptional case" subcategory. In all events, the question whether a specific case should receive exceptional treatment is more appropriately the subject of the exercise of judicial discretion than an interpretation of the Constitution. Accordingly, we turn to the question whether the District Court's decision to stay the trial until after petitioner leaves office was an abuse of discretion.

VII

The Court of Appeals described the District Court's discretionary decision to stay the trial as the "functional equivalent" of a grant of temporary immunity.... Although we ultimately conclude that the stay should not have been granted, we think the issue is more difficult than the opinion of the Court of Appeals suggests.

Strictly speaking the stay was not the functional equivalent of the constitutional immunity that petitioner claimed, because the District Court ordered discovery to proceed. Moreover, a stay of either the trial or discovery might be justified by considerations that do not require the recognition of any constitutional immunity. The District Court has broad discretion to stay proceedings as an incident to its power to control its own docket.... Although we have rejected the argument that the potential burdens on the President violate separation of powers principles, those burdens are appropriate matters for the District Court to evaluate in its management of the case. The high respect that is owed to the office of the Chief Executive, though not justifying a rule of categorical immunity, is a matter that should inform the conduct of the entire proceeding, including the timing and scope of discovery.

Nevertheless, we are persuaded that it was an abuse of discretion for the District Court to defer the trial until after the President leaves office. Such a lengthy and categorical stay takes no account whatever of the respondent's interest in bringing the case to trial. The complaint was filed within the statutory limitations period-albeit near the end of that period-and delaying trial would increase the danger of prejudice resulting from the loss of evidence, including the inability of witnesses to recall specific facts, or the possible death of a party.

The decision to postpone the trial was, furthermore, premature. The proponent of a stay bears the burden of establishing its need.... In this case, at the stage at which the District Court made its ruling, there was no way to assess whether a stay of trial after the completion of discovery would be warranted. Other than the fact that a trial may consume some of the President's time and attention, there is nothing in the record to enable a judge to assess the potential harm that may ensue from scheduling the trial promptly after discovery is concluded. We think the District Court may have given undue weight to the concern that a trial might generate unrelated civil actions that could conceivably hamper the President in conducting the duties of his office. If and when that should occur, the court's discretion would permit it to manage those actions in such fashion (including deferral of trial) that interference with the President's duties would not occur. But no such impingement upon the President's conduct of his office was shown here.

VIII

We add a final comment on two matters that are discussed at length in the briefs: the risk that our decision will generate a large volume of politically motivated harassing and frivolous litigation, and the danger that national security concerns might prevent the President from explaining a legitimate need for a continuance.

We are not persuaded that either of these risks is serious. Most frivolous and vexatious litigation is terminated at the pleading stage or on summary judgment, with little if any personal involvement by the defendant.... Moreover, the availability of sanctions provides a significant deterrent to litigation directed at the President in his unofficial capacity for purposes of political gain or harassment. History indicates that the likelihood that a significant number of such cases will be filed is remote. Although scheduling problems may arise, there is no reason to assume that the District Courts will be either unable to accommodate the President's needs or unfaithful to the tradition—especially in matters involving national security—of giving "the utmost deference to Presidential responsibilities." ...

If Congress deems it appropriate to afford the President stronger protection, it may respond with appropriate legislation.... If the Constitution embodied the rule that the President advocates, Congress, of course, could not repeal it. But our holding today raises no barrier to a statutory response to these concerns.

The Federal District Court has jurisdiction to decide this case. Like every other citizen who properly invokes that jurisdiction, respondent has a right to an orderly disposition of her claims. Accordingly, the judgment of the Court of Appeals is affirmed.

It is so ordered.

Justice Breyer, concurring in the judgment.

I agree with the majority that the Constitution does not automatically grant the President an immunity from civil lawsuits based upon his private conduct....

In my view, however, once the President sets forth and explains a conflict between judicial proceeding and public duties, the matter changes. At that point, the Constitution permits a judge to schedule a trial in an ordinary civil damages action (where postponement normally is possible without overwhelming damage to a plaintiff) only within the constraints of a constitutional principle—a principle that forbids a federal judge in such a case to interfere with the President's discharge of his public duties. I have no doubt that the Constitution contains such a principle applicable to civil suits, based upon Article II's vesting of the entire "executive Power" in a single individual, implemented through the Constitution's structural separation of powers, and revealed both by history and case precedent.

I recognize that this case does not require us now to apply the principle specifically, thereby delineating its contours; nor need we now decide whether lower courts are to apply it directly or categorically through the use of presumptions or rules of administration. Yet I fear that to disregard it now may appear to deny it. I also fear that the majority's description of the relevant precedents de-emphasizes the extent to which they support a principle of the President's independent authority to control his own time and energy.... Further, if the majority is wrong in predicting the future infrequency of private civil litigation against sitting Presidents, acknowledgement and future delineation of the constitutional principle will prove a practically necessary institutional safeguard....

. . .

I agree with the majority that [historical] precedents reject any absolute Presidential immunity from all court process. But they do not cast doubt upon Justice Story's basic conclusion that "in civil cases," a sitting President "possess[es] an official inviolability" as necessary to permit him to "perform" the duties of his office without "obstruction or impediment."

. . .

Case law, particularly, Nixon v. Fitzgerald, strongly supports the principle that judges hearing a private civil damages action against a sitting President may not issue orders that could significantly distract a President from his official duties.

. . .

... Its key paragraph, explaining why the President enjoys an absolute immunity rather than a qualified immunity, contains seven sentences, four of which focus primarily upon time and energy *distraction* and three of which focus primarily upon official decision *distortion*.

. . .

... [A] lawsuit that significantly distracts an official from his public duties can distort the content of a public decision just as can a threat of potential future liability. If the latter concern can justify an "absolute" immunity in the case of a President no longer in office, where distraction is no longer a consideration, so can the former justify, not immunity, but a postponement, in the case of a sitting President.

. . .

... [T]his Court has now made clear that such lawsuits may proceed against a sitting President. The consequence, as the Court warned in *Fitzgerald*, is that a sitting President, given "the visibility of his office," could well become "an easily identifiable target for suits for civil damages," .... The threat of sanctions could well discourage much unneeded litigation, but some lawsuits (including highly intricate and complicated ones) could resist ready evaluation and disposition; and individual district court procedural rulings could pose a significant threat to the President's official functions.

I concede the possibility that district courts, supervised by the Courts of Appeals and perhaps this Court, might prove able to manage private civil damage actions against sitting Presidents without significantly interfering with the discharge of Presidential duties—at least if they manage those actions with the constitutional problem in mind. Nonetheless, predicting the future is difficult, and I am skeptical. Should the majority's optimism turn out to be misplaced, then, in my view, courts will have to develop administrative rules applicable to such cases (including postponement rules of the sort at issue in this case) in order to implement the basic constitutional directive. A Constitution that separates powers in order to prevent one branch of Government from significantly threatening the workings of another could not grant a single judge more than a very limited power to second guess a President's reasonable determination (announced in open court) of his scheduling needs, nor could it permit the issuance of a trial scheduling order that would significantly interfere with the President's discharge of his duties—in a private civil damage action the trial of which might be postponed without the plaintiff suffering enormous harm.... I agree with the majority's determination that a constitutional defense must await a more specific showing of need; I do not agree with what I believe to be an understatement of the "danger." And I believe that ordinary case-management principles are unlikely to prove sufficient to deal with private civil lawsuits for damages unless supplemented with a constitutionally based requirement that district courts schedule proceedings so as to avoid significant interference with the President's ongoing discharge of his official responsibilities.

. . .

PART III

Government and the Individual: The Protection of Liberty and Property Under the Due Process and Equal Protection Clauses

CHAPTER 8

The Bill of Rights, The Civil War Amendments and Their Inter–Relationship

SECTION 2.   The Initial Interpretation of the Civil War Amendments

Page 478. Add at end of Note, "The Privileges and Immunities Clause of the Fourteenth Amendment:"

The Court's opinion in Saenz v. Roe, 119 S.Ct. 1518 (1999), reported fully infra at page 137, again highlighted the question whether, after the Slaughter-house Cases, the Fourteenth Amendment Privileges and Immunities Clause does any independent constitutional work. Justice Stevens' majority opinion, holding unconstitutional a California law limiting welfare benefits for families residing in the State less than a year to the amounts they would have received in their States of previous residence, found "the right of the newly arrived citizen to the same privileges and immunities enjoyed by other citizens of the same State . . . protected not only by the new arrival's status as a state citizen, but also by her status as a citizen of the United States. . . . Despite fundamentally differing views concerning the coverage of the Privileges or Immunities Clause of the Fourteenth Amendment, most notably expressed in the majority and dissenting opinions in the Slaughter–House Cases, 16 Wall. 36 (1872), it has always been common ground that this Clause protects [that right]." Later in the opinion, Justice Stevens wrote that "the protection afforded to the citizen by the Citizenship Clause of that Amendment is a limitation on the powers of the National Government as well as the States[,]" and at the end of the opinion he wrote: "Citizens of the United States, whether rich or poor, have the right to choose to be citizens 'of the State wherein they reside.' U.S. Const., Amdt. 14, § 1. The States, however, do not have any right to select their citizens." Does Justice Stevens' reasoning and conclusion depend on the Privileges and Immunities Clause itself?

In dissent, Chief Justice Rehnquist, joined by Justice Thomas, objected to the Court's "breath[ing] new life into the previously dormant Privileges or Immunities Clause of the Fourteenth Amendment . . . ." In another dissent, Justice Thomas, joined by the Chief Justice, expressed the view that "the majority attributes a meaning to the Privileges or Immunities Clause that likely was unintended when the Fourteenth Amendment was enacted and ratified." Is Justice Stevens' opinion really a departure from the Court's interpretation of the Fourteenth Amendment Privileges and Immunities Clause in the Slaughterhouse Cases?

CHAPTER 9

THE DUE PROCESS, CONTRACT, AND JUST COMPENSATION CLAUSES AND THE REVIEW OF THE REASONABLENESS OF LEGISLATION

SECTION 1. ECONOMIC REGULATORY LEGISLATION

C. THE JUST COMPENSATION CLAUSE OF THE FIFTH AMENDMENT—WHAT DOES IT ADD TO DUE PROCESS?

Page 541. Replace "(subsections 1. and 2.)" in the second sentence of the Introduction with "subsections 1., 2., and 3.)" and "subsection 3." in the third sentence with "subsection 4."

Page 555. Add at the end of the first paragraph of footnote 1:

A 5–4 majority of the Court again applied this common law rule that "interest follows principal" in Phillips v. Washington Legal Foundation, 524 U.S. 156 (1998), where federal tax and banking regulations seemed effectively to preclude earning of interest on client funds held by lawyers in trust accounts as part of normal legal practice, if the interest from deposits of these funds that, individually, were nominal in amount or would be held in the trust account for short time periods, were to be paid to the client, but these regulations permitted interest to be earned if it was to be paid to nonprofit charitable organizations. The Court ruled that the interest earned on client funds held in Interest on Lawyers Trust Account (IOLTA) programs–adopted in 48 States in response to the federal scheme for the purpose of funding nonprofit legal services organizations serving the poor–remained the "property" of the clients, despite not having "economically realizable value to its owner," since "possession, control, and disposition are nonetheless valuable rights that inhere in the property." The Court remanded the case, however, expressing "no view" concerning whether the State had "taken" the interest generated by the IOLTA program or what amount of " 'just compensation', if any" was due. In one dissent, Justice Souter (for 4 Justices) found the majority's conclusion an "abstract proposition" and urged a remand without deciding whether the IOLTA interest was client "property," because the "taking" and "just compensation" questions were "serious ones" in light of the "most salient fact" that with or without IOLTA the client "would have no net interest." Justice Breyer's dissent (for the same 4 Justices) contended that without the IOLTA program no interest could have been earned on these client funds and thus "the most that Texas law could have taken from the client is ... a right to prevent the principal from being put to productive use by others." He thought that the "interest follows principal" rule followed in *Webb's Fabulous Pharmacies* did not and should not apply where the client's principal would earn nothing absent government intervention, and thus that the interest earned on IOLTA accounts was not the client's "property" within the meaning of the Takings Clause.

Page 567. Add after Dolan v. City of Tigard:

CITY OF MONTEREY v. DEL MONTE DUNES, 119 S.Ct. 1624 (1999). In a suit challenging as a regulatory taking the city's repeated denials of permission to develop an ocean-front parcel (where the city had imposed on the developer increasingly restrictive conditions with each new application), a portion of Justice Kennedy's opinion that spoke for all nine Justices contained the following passage:

> "Although in a general sense concerns for proportionality animate the Takings Clause, ... we have not extended the rough-proportionality test of *Dolan* beyond the special context of exactions—land-use decisions conditioning approval of development on the dedication of property to public use.... The rule applied in *Dolan* considers whether dedications demanded as conditions of development are proportional to the development's anticipated impacts. It was not designed to address, and is not readily applicable to, the much different questions arising where, as here, the landowner's challenge is based not on excessive exactions but on denial of development. We believe, accordingly, that the rough-proportionality test of *Dolan* is inapposite to a case such as this one."

Page 568. Add a new subsection 3. and change existing subsection 3. to 4., as follows:

3. ECONOMIC REGULATION IMPOSING RETROACTIVE LIABILITY–TAKINGS OR DUE PROCESS?

Eastern Enterprises v. Apfel

524 U.S. 498, 118 S.Ct. 2131, 141 L.Ed.2d 451 (1998).

Justice O'Connor announced the judgment of the Court and delivered an opinion, in which The Chief Justice, Justice Scalia, and Justice Thomas join.

In this case, the Court considers a challenge under the Due Process and Takings Clauses of the Constitution to the Coal Industry Retiree Health Benefit Act of 1992 (Coal Act), 26 U. S. C. §§ 9701–9722 (1994 ed. and Supp. II), which establishes a mechanism for funding health care benefits for retirees from the coal industry and their dependents. We conclude that the Coal Act, as applied to petitioner Eastern Enterprises, effects an unconstitutional taking.

I

For a good part of this century, employers in the coal industry have been involved in negotiations with the United Mine Workers of America (UMWA or Union) regarding the provision of employee benefits to coal miners. [A pattern developed, beginning with the National Bituminous Coal Wage Agreement of 1947 (1947 NBCWA), which established the 'United Mine Workers of America Welfare and Retirement Fund' (1947 W & R Fund), and the 1950 NBCWA and its 1950 W & R Fund, of using coal production royalties to fund, among other things, the medical expenses of miners and their dependents, but without guaranteeing benefit entitlements. Instead, fund trustees were authorized to determine benefit types and levels within budgetary constraints. Annual reports of the 1950 W & R Fund reiterated that benefits were subject to change and "although persons involved in the coal industry may have made occasional statements intimating that the 1950 W & R Fund promised lifetime health benefits, . . . it is clear that the 1950 W & R Fund did not, by its terms, guarantee lifetime health benefits for retirees and their dependents." In fact, "[b]etween 1950 and 1974, the trustees often exercised their prerogative to alter the level of benefits according to the Fund's budget."]

. . . [T]he Employee Retirement Income Security Act of 1974 (ERISA), 29 U. S. C. § 1001 et seq., introduced specific funding and vesting requirements for pension plans. To comply with ERISA, the UMWA and the BCOA [Bituminous Coal Operators' Association] entered into a new agreement, the 1974 NBCWA, which created four trusts . . . to replace the 1950 W & R Fund[, two of which, the 1950 Benefit Plan and the 1974 Benefit Plan,] provided nonpension benefits, including medical benefits. Miners who retired before January 1, 1976, and their dependents were covered by the 1950 Benefit Plan, while active miners and those who retired after 1975 were covered by the 1974 Benefit Plan.

The 1974 NBCWA thus was the first agreement between the UMWA and the BCOA to expressly reference health benefits for retirees[, including] a Health Services card for retired miners until their death, and to their widows until their death or remarriage. . . . Despite the expanded benefits, the 1974 NBCWA did not alter the employers' obligation to contribute only a fixed amount of royalties, nor did it extend employers' liability beyond the life of the agreement. . . .

[The broadened coverage under the 1974 NBCWA dramatically increased the number of eligible benefit recipients, and combined with a decline in the amount of coal produced, the retirement of a generation of miners, and rapid escalation of health care costs, financial problems for the 1950 and 1974 Benefit Plans soon developed. In response, the 1978 NBCWA assigned responsibility to signatory employers for the health care of their own active and retired employees.] To ensure the Plans' solvency, [under] the 1978 NBCWA . . . the coal operators' liability to the Benefit Plans shifted from a defined contribution obligation, under which employers were responsible only for a predetermined amount of royalties, to a form of defined benefit obligation, under which employers were to fund specific benefits.

Despite the 1978 changes, the Benefit Plans continued to suffer financially as costs increased and employers who had signed the 1978 NBCWA withdrew from the agreement, either to continue in business with nonunion employees or to exit the coal business altogether. As more and more coal operators abandoned the Benefit Plans, the remaining signatories were forced to absorb the increasing cost of covering retirees left behind by exiting employers. . . .

[An Advisory Commission on UMWA Retiree Health Benefits, the Coal Commission, proposed alternative funding plans to Congress, which eventually passed the Coal Act. The Act] merged the 1950 and 1974 Benefit Plans into a . . . Combined Fund [that] provides 'substantially the same' health benefits to retirees and their dependents that they were receiving under the 1950 and 1974 Benefit Plans. See §§ 9703(b)(1), (f). It is financed by annual premiums assessed against 'signatory coal operators,' i.e., coal operators that signed any

NBCWA or any other agreement requiring contributions to the 1950 or 1974 Benefit Plans. See §§ 9701(b)(1), (3); § 9701(c)(1). Any signatory operator who 'conducts or derives revenue from any business activity, whether or not in the coal industry,' may be liable for those premiums. § 9706(a); § 9701(c)(7). . . .

The Commissioner of Social Security (Commissioner) calculates the premiums due from any signatory operator based on [a formula that assigns retirees to signatory operators which "remain in business" and which, if there is no signatory to the 1978 or a later agreement who most recently employed the retiree for at least two years or at all, "employed the coal industry retiree in the coal industry for a longer period of time than any other signatory operator prior to the effective date of the 1978 coal wage agreement." § 9706(a). Eastern, which operated coal mines from1929 until 1965 and then transferred its coal-related operations to a subsidiary, EACC, which assumed all its liabilities, continues to operate other businesses and, "although . . . no longer involved in the coal industry, . . . is 'in business' within the meaning of the Coal Act." By virtue of its stock interest in EACC through another subsidiary, CPC, Eastern did receive dividends of over $100 million until 1987, when it sold its interest in CPC to Peabody Holding Co. pursuant to an agreement that transferred responsibility for payments to relevant benefit plans to Peabody, CPC and EACC. Pursuant to the terms of the 1992 Coal Act,] the Commissioner assigned to Eastern the obligation for Combined Fund premiums respecting over 1,000 retired miners who had worked for the company before 1966, based on Eastern's status as the pre–1978 signatory operator for whom the miners had worked for the longest period of time. See 26 U. S. C. § 9706(a). Eastern's premium for a 12–month period exceeded $5 million. . . .

Eastern [sued] the Commissioner, as well as the Combined Fund and its trustees, . . . assert[ing] that the Coal Act, either on its face or as applied, violates substantive due process and constitutes a taking of its property in violation of the Fifth Amendment. [Eastern sought declaratory and injunctive relief against enforcement of the Coal Act, not compensation. The lower federal courts rejected Eastern's claims.]

. . .

IV

A

. . .

This case does not present the "classi[c] taking" in which the government directly appropriates private property for its own use. See United States v. Security Industrial Bank, 459 U.S. 70, 78 (1982). Although takings problems are more commonly presented when "the interference with property can be characterized as a physical invasion by government, than when interference arises from some public program adjusting the benefits and burdens of economic life to promote the common good," Penn Central Transp. Co. v. New York City, 438 U. S. 104, 124 (1978) (citation omitted), economic regulation such as the Coal Act may nonetheless effect a taking, see Security Industrial Bank, supra, at 78. See also Calder v. Bull, 3 Dall. 386, 388 (1798) (Chase, J.) ("It is against all reason and justice" to presume that the legislature has been entrusted with the power to enact "a law that takes property from A. and gives it to B"). By operation of the Act, Eastern is "permanently deprived of those assets necessary to satisfy its statutory obligation, not to the Government, but to [the Combined Benefit Fund]," Connolly, supra, at 222, and "a strong public desire to improve the public condition is not enough to warrant achieving the desire by a shorter cut than the constitutional way of paying for the change," Pennsylvania Coal Co. v. Mahon, 260 U. S. 393, 416 (1922).

Of course, a party challenging governmental action as an unconstitutional taking bears a substantial burden.... [E]valuating a regulation's constitutionality involves an examination of the "justice and fairness" of the governmental action[; t]hat inquiry, by its nature, does not lend itself to any set formula, ... and the determination whether "justice and fairness" require that "economic injuries caused by public action [must] be compensated by the government, rather than remain disproportionately concentrated on a few persons," is essentially ad hoc and fact intensive, Kaiser Aetna v. United States, 444 U. S. 164, 175 (1979).... [S]everal factors, however, ... have particular significance: "the economic impact of the regulation, its interference with reasonable investment backed expectations, and the character of the governmental action." ...

B

Our analysis in this case is informed by previous decisions considering the constitutionality of somewhat similar legislative schemes....

[After reviewing Usery v. Turner Elkhorn Mining Co., 428 U. S. 1 (1976), Pension Benefit Guaranty Corporation v. R. A. Gray & Co., 467 U. S. 717 (1984), Connolly v. Pension Benefit Guaranty Corporation, 475 U. S. 211 (1986), and Concrete Pipe & Products of Cal., Inc. v. Construction Laborers Pension Trust for Southern Cal., 508 U. S. 602 (1993), Justice O'Connor continued:] Our opinions in *Turner Elkhorn*, *Connolly*, and *Concrete Pipe*, make clear that Congress has considerable leeway to fashion economic legislation, including the power to affect contractual commitments between private parties. Congress also may impose retroactive liability to some degree, particularly where it is "confined to short and limited periods required by the practicalities of producing national legislation." *Gray*, 467 U. S., at 731.... Our decisions, however, have left open the possibility that legislation might be unconstitutional if it imposes severe retroactive liability on a limited class of parties that could not have anticipated the liability, and the extent of that liability is substantially disproportionate to the parties' experience.

C

We believe that the Coal Act's allocation scheme, as applied to Eastern, presents such a case. We reach that conclusion by applying the three factors that traditionally have informed our regulatory takings analysis....

As to the first factor ..., economic impact, there is no doubt that the Coal Act has forced a considerable financial burden upon Eastern. The parties estimate that Eastern's cumulative payments under the Act will be on the order of $50 to $100 million.... Eastern's liability is thus substantial, and the company is clearly deprived of the amounts it must pay the Combined Fund....

That liability is not, of course, a permanent physical occupation of Eastern's property of the kind that we have viewed as a *per se* taking. See Loretto v. Teleprompter Manhattan CATV Corp., 458 U. S. 419, 441 (1982). But our decisions ... suggest that an employer's statutory liability for multiemployer plan benefits should reflect some "proportion[ality] to its experience with the plan." Concrete Pipe, supra, at 645 ...; see also Connolly, supra, at 225.... In *Concrete Pipe* and *Connolly*, the employers had "voluntarily negotiated and maintained a pension plan which was determined to be within the strictures of ERISA," and consequently, the statutory liability was linked to the employers' conduct.

Here, however, while Eastern contributed to the 1947 and 1950 W & R Funds, it ceased its coal mining operations in 1965 and neither participated in negotiations nor agreed to make contributions in connection with the Benefit Plans under the 1974, 1978, or subsequent NBCWA's. It is the latter agreements that first suggest an industry commitment to the funding of lifetime health benefits for both retirees and their family members. Although EACC continued mining coal until 1987 as a subsidiary of Eastern, Eastern's liability under the Act bears no relationship to its ownership of EACC; the Act assigns Eastern responsibility for benefits relating to miners that Eastern itself, not EACC, employed, while EACC would be assigned the responsibility for any miners that it had employed. See 26 U.S.C. §§ 9706(a). Thus, the Act does not purport, as Justice Breyer suggests, to assign liability to Eastern based on the " 'last man out' problem" that developed after benefits were significantly expanded in 1974. During the years in which Eastern employed miners, retirement and health benefits were far less extensive than under the 1974 NBCWA, were unvested, and were fully subject to alteration or termination. Before 1974, as Justice Breyer notes, Eastern could not have contemplated liability for the provision of lifetime benefits to the widows of deceased miners, a beneficiary class that is likely to be substantial.... The company's obligations under the Act depend solely on its roster of employees some 30 to 50 years before the statute's enactment, without any regard to responsibilities that Eastern accepted under any benefit plan the company itself adopted.

. . .

For similar reasons, the Coal Act substantially interferes with Eastern's reasonable investment-backed expectations. The Act's beneficiary allocation scheme reaches back 30 to 50 years to impose liability against Eastern based on the company's activities between 1946 and 1965. Thus, even though the Act mandates only the payment of future health benefits, it nonetheless "attaches new legal consequences to [an employment relationship] completed before its enactment." Landgraf v. USI Film Products, 511 U. S. 244, 270 (1994).

Retroactivity is generally disfavored in the law, Bowen v. Georgetown Univ. Hospital, 488 U. S. 204, 208 (1988), in accordance with "fundamental notions of justice" that have been recognized throughout history, Kaiser Aluminum & Chemical Corp. v. Bonjorno, 494 U. S. 827, 855 (1990) (Scalia, J., concurring)....

Our Constitution expresses concern with retroactive laws through several of its provisions, including the Ex Post Facto and Takings Clauses....

[T]he Coal Act operates retroactively, divesting Eastern of property long after the company believed its liabilities under the 1950 W & R Fund to have been settled. And the extent of Eastern's retroactive liability is substantial and particularly far reaching.... The distance into the past that the Act reaches back to impose a liability on Eastern and the magnitude of that liability raise substantial questions of fairness....

Respondents and their amici curiae assert that the extent of retroactive liability is justified because there was an implicit, industrywide agreement during the time that Eastern was involved in the coal industry to fund lifetime health benefits for qualifying miners and their dependents. That contention, however, is not supported by the pre–1974 NBCWA's.... Moreover, even though retirees received medical benefits before 1974, and perhaps developed a corresponding expectation that those benefits would continue, the Coal Act imposes liability respecting a much broader range of beneficiaries. In any event, the question is not whether miners had an expectation of lifetime benefits, but whether Eastern should bear the cost of those benefits as to miners it employed before 1966.

Eastern only participated in the 1947 and 1950 W & R Funds, which operated on a pay-as-you-go basis, and under which the degree of benefits and the classes of beneficiaries were subject to the trustees' discretion. Not until 1974, when ERISA forced revisions to the 1950 W & R Fund, could lifetime medical benefits under the multiemployer agreement have been viewed as promised. Eastern was no longer in the industry when the ... 1978 and subsequent NBCWA's shifted the 1950 and 1974 Benefit Plans from a defined contribution framework to a guarantee of defined benefits, at least for the life of the agreements.... Thus, unlike the pension withdrawal liability upheld in *Concrete Pipe* and *Connolly*, the Coal Act's scheme for allocation of Combined Fund premiums is not calibrated either to Eastern's past actions or to any agreement—implicit or otherwise—by the company. Nor would the pattern of the Federal Government's involvement in the coal industry have given Eastern "sufficient notice" that lifetime health benefits might be guaranteed to retirees several decades later. See Connolly, supra, at 227.

... Eastern might be responsible for employment-related health problems of all former employees whether or not the cost was foreseen at the time of employment, ... but there is no such connection here.... [T]he Constitution does not permit a solution to the problem of funding miners' benefits that imposes such a disproportionate and severely retroactive burden upon Eastern.

Finally, the nature of the governmental action in this case is quite unusual. That Congress sought a legislative remedy for what it perceived to be a grave problem in the funding of retired coal miners' health benefits is understandable; complex problems of that sort typically call for a legislative solution. When, however, that solution singles out certain employers to bear a burden that is substantial in amount, based on the employers' conduct far in the past, and unrelated to any commitment that the employers made or to any injury they caused, the governmental action implicates fundamental principles of fairness underlying the Takings Clause. Eastern cannot be forced to bear the expense of lifetime health benefits for miners based on its activities decades before those benefits were promised. Accordingly, in the specific circumstances of this case, we conclude that the Coal Act's application to Eastern effects an unconstitutional taking.

D

Eastern also claims that the manner in which the Coal Act imposes liability upon it violates substantive due process. To succeed, Eastern would be required to establish that its liability under the Act is "arbitrary and irrational." Turner Elkhorn, supra, at 15. Our analysis of legislation under the Takings and Due Process Clauses is correlated to some extent, see Connolly, supra, at 223, and there is a question whether the Coal Act violates due process in light of the Act's severely retroactive impact. At the same time, this Court has expressed concerns about using the Due Process Clause to invalidate economic legislation. See Ferguson v. Skrupa, 372 U. S. 726, 731 (1963) ...; see also Williamson v. Lee Optical of Okla., Inc., 348 U. S. 483, 488 (1955).... Because we have determined that the ... Coal Act's allocation scheme violates the Takings Clause as applied to Eastern, we need not address Eastern's due process claim....

V

... [W]e conclude that the Coal Act's allocation of liability to Eastern violates the Takings Clause, and that 26 U. S. C. § 9706(a)(3) should be enjoined as applied to Eastern. The judgment ... is reversed....

. . .

Justice Thomas, concurring.

Justice O'Connor's opinion correctly concludes that the Coal Act's imposition of retroactive liability on petitioner violates the Takings Clause. I write separately to emphasize that the Ex Post Facto Clause of the Constitution, Art. I., § 9, cl. 3, even more clearly reflects the principle that "[r]etrospective laws are, indeed, generally unjust." 2 J. Story, Commentaries on the Constitution § 1398, p. 272 (5th ed. 1981). Since Calder v. Bull, 3 Dall. 386 (1798), however, this Court has considered the Ex Post Facto Clause to apply only in the criminal context. I have never been convinced of the soundness of this limitation, which in *Calder* was principally justified because a contrary interpretation would render the Takings Clause unnecessary. See id., at 394 (opinion of Chase, J.). In an appropriate case, therefore, I would be willing to reconsider *Calder* and its progeny to determine whether a retroactive civil law that passes muster under our current Takings Clause jurisprudence is nonetheless unconstitutional under the Ex Post Facto Clause....

Justice Kennedy, concurring in the judgment and dissenting in part.

The plurality's careful assessment of the history and purpose of the statute in question demonstrates the necessity to hold it arbitrary and beyond the legitimate authority of the Government to enact. In my view, which is in full accord with many of the plurality's conclusions, the relevant portions of the ... Coal Act ... must be invalidated as contrary to essential due process principles, without regard to the Takings Clause of the Fifth Amendment. I concur in the judgment holding the Coal Act unconstitutional but disagree with the plurality's Takings Clause analysis, which, it is submitted, is incorrect and quite unnecessary for decision of the case. I must record my respectful dissent on this issue.

I

. . .

Our cases do not support the plurality's conclusion that the Coal Act takes property. The Coal Act imposes a staggering financial burden on the petitioner, Eastern Enterprises, but it regulates the former mine owner without regard to property. It does not operate upon or alter an identified property interest, and it is not applicable to or measured by a property interest.... The law simply imposes an obligation to perform an act, the payment of benefits. The statute is indifferent as to how the regulated entity elects to comply or the property it uses to do so. To the extent it affects property interests, it does so in a manner similar to many laws; but until today, none were thought to constitute takings. To call this sort of governmental action a taking as a matter of constitutional interpretation is both imprecise and . . . unwise.

. . .

Until today, . . . one constant limitation has been that in all of the cases where the regulatory taking analysis has been employed, a specific property right or interest has been at stake.... The regulations . . . were challenged as being so excessive as to destroy, or take, a specific property interest....

The difficulties in determining whether there is a taking or a regulation even where a property right or interest is identified ought to counsel against extending the regulatory takings doctrine to cases lacking this specificity.... The plurality opinion would throw one of the most difficult and litigated areas of the law into confusion, subjecting States and municipalities to the potential of new and unforeseen claims in vast amounts....

True, the burden imposed by the Coal Act may be just as great if the Government had appropriated one of Eastern's plants, but the mechanism by which the Government injures Eastern is so unlike the act of taking specific property that it is incongruous to call the Coal Act a taking, even as that concept has been expanded by the regulatory takings principle. In the terminology of our regulatory takings analysis, the character of the governmental action renders the Coal Act not a taking of property....

[W]e have been careful not to lose sight of the importance of identifying the property allegedly taken, lest all governmental action be subjected to examination under the constitutional prohibition against taking without just compensation, with the attendant potential for money damages. We have asked how the challenged governmental action is implemented with particular emphasis on the extent to which a specific property right is affected.... The Coal Act neither targets a specific property interest nor depends upon any particular property for the operation of its statutory mechanisms. The liability imposed on Eastern no doubt will reduce its net worth and its total value, but this can be said of any law which has an adverse economic effect.

. . .

If the plurality is adopting its novel and expansive concept of a taking in order to avoid making a normative judgment about the Coal Act, it fails in the attempt; for it must make the normative judgment in all events.... The imprecision of our regulatory takings doctrine does open the door to normative considerations about the wisdom of government decisions.... This sort of analysis is in uneasy tension with our basic understanding of the Takings Clause, which has not been understood to be a substantive or absolute limit on the Government's power to act. The Clause operates as a conditional limitation, permitting the Government to do what it wants so long as it pays the charge [and] presupposes what the Government intends to do is otherwise constitutional.... Given that the constitutionality of the Coal Act appears to turn on the legitimacy of Congress' judgment rather than on the availability of compensation, the more appropriate constitutional analysis arises under general due process principles rather than under the Takings Clause.

. . .

II

When the constitutionality of the Coal Act is tested under the Due Process Clause, it must be invalidated....

Although ... hesitant to subject economic legislation to due process scrutiny as a general matter, the Court has given careful consideration to due process challenges to legislation with retroactive effects .....

The Court's due process jurisprudence reflects this distrust....

These cases reflect our recognition that retroactive lawmaking is a particular concern for the courts because of the legislative "tempt[ation] to use retroactive legislation as a means of retribution against unpopular groups or individuals." Landgraf v. USI Film Products, 511 U. S. 244, 266 (1994).... If retroactive laws change the legal consequences of transactions long closed, the change can destroy the reasonable certainty and security which are the very objects of property ownership. As a consequence, due process protection for property must be understood to incorporate our settled tradition against retroactive laws of great severity. Groups targeted by retroactive laws, were they to be denied all protection, would have a justified fear that a government once formed to protect expectations now can destroy them. Both stability of investment and confidence in the constitutional system, then, are secured by due process restrictions against severe retroactive legislation.

The case before us represents one of the rare instances where the Legislature has exceeded the limits imposed by due process. The plurality opinion demonstrates in convincing fashion that the remedy created by the Coal Act bears no legitimate relation to the interest which the Government asserts in support of the statute. [I]n creating liability for events which occurred 35 years ago the Coal Act has a retroactive effect of unprecedented scope.

. . .

Justice Stevens, with whom Justice Souter, Justice Ginsburg, and Justice Breyer join, dissenting.

... [D]uring the 1950's and 1960's ... there was an implicit understanding on both sides of the bargaining table that the operators would provide the miners with lifetime health benefits. ...

My understanding of this critical fact is shared by [a consensus of Court of Appeals judges who have appraised the issue;] the same understanding ... motivated the members of the Coal Commission to conclude that the operators who had employed the "orphaned miners" should share responsibility for their health benefits [and] led legislators in both political parties to conclude that the Coal Act of 1992 represented a fair solution to a difficult problem.

Given the critical importance of the reasonable expectations of both the miners and the operators during the period before their implicit agreement was made explicit in 1974, I am unable to agree with the plurality's conclusion that the retroactive application of the 1992 Act is an unconstitutional "taking" of Eastern's property. Rather, it seems to me that the plurality and Justice Kennedy have substituted their judgment about what is fair for the better informed judgment of the Members of the Coal Commission and Congress.

Accordingly, ... whether ... analyzed under the Takings Clause or the Due Process Clause, Eastern has not carried its burden of overcoming the presumption of constitutionality accorded to an act of Congress, by demonstrating that the provision is unsupported by the reasonable expectations of the parties in interest.

Justice Breyer, with whom Justice Stevens, Justice Souter, and Justice Ginsburg join, dissenting.

We must decide whether it is fundamentally unfair for Congress to require Eastern Enterprises to pay the health care costs of retired miners who worked for Eastern before 1965, when Eastern stopped mining coal. For many years Eastern benefited from the labor of those miners. Eastern helped to create conditions that led the miners to expect continued health care benefits for themselves and their families after they retired. And Eastern, until 1987, continued to draw sizable profits from the coal industry though a wholly owned subsidiary. For these reasons, I believe that Congress did not act unreasonably or otherwise unjustly in imposing these health care costs upon Eastern. Consequently, in my view, the statute before us is constitutional.

I

As a preliminary matter, I agree with Justice Kennedy that the ... Takings Clause does not apply. ... [A]t the heart of the Clause lies a concern, not with preventing arbitrary or unfair government action, but with providing compensation for legitimate government action that takes "private property" to serve the "public" good.

The "private property" upon which the Clause traditionally has focused is a specific interest in physical or intellectual property. ... This case involves, not an interest in physical or intellectual property, but an ordinary liability to pay money, and not to the Government, but to third parties.

. . .

... [A]pplication of the Takings Clause here bristles with conceptual difficulties. If the Clause applies when the government simply orders A to pay

B, why does it not apply when the government simply orders A to pay the government, i.e., when it assesses a tax? . . . Would that Clause apply to some or to all statutes and rules that "routinely creat[e] burdens for some that directly benefit others"? Connolly, supra, at 223. Regardless, could a court apply the same kind of Takings Clause analysis when violation means the law's invalidation, rather than simply the payment of "compensation?" . . . .

We need not face these difficulties, however, for there is no need to torture the Takings Clause to fit this case. The question involved—the potential unfairness of retroactive liability—finds a natural home in the Due Process Clause, a Fifth Amendment neighbor. . . . It safeguards citizens from arbitrary or irrational legislation. And the Due Process Clause can offer protection against legislation that is unfairly retroactive at least as readily as the Takings Clause might, for . . . a law that is fundamentally unfair because of its retroactivity is a law which is basically arbitrary. . . .

Nor does application of the Due Process Clause automatically trigger the Takings Clause, just because the word "property" appears in both. That word appears in the midst of different phrases with somewhat different objectives, thereby permitting differences in the way in which the term is interpreted. . . .

Insofar as the plurality avoids reliance upon the Due Process Clause for fear of resurrecting Lochner v. New York, 198 U. S. 45 (1905), and related doctrines of "substantive due process," that fear is misplaced. . . . As the plurality points out, an unfair retroactive assessment of liability upsets settled expectations, and it thereby undermines a basic objective of law itself. . . .

To find that the Due Process Clause protects against this kind of fundamental unfairness—that it protects against an unfair allocation of public burdens through this kind of specially arbitrary retroactive means—is to read the Clause in light of a basic purpose: the fair application of law, which purpose hearkens back to the Magna Carta. It is not to resurrect long-discredited substantive notions of "freedom of contract." See, e.g., Ferguson v. Skrupa, 372 U. S. 726, 729–732 (1963).

Thus, like the plurality I would inquire if the law before us is fundamentally unfair or unjust. But I would ask this question because like Justice Kennedy, I believe that, if so, the Coal Act would "deprive" Eastern of "property, without due process of law." . . .

II

The substantive question before us is whether or not it is fundamentally unfair to require Eastern to make future payments for health care costs of retired miners and their families, on the basis of Eastern's past association with these miners. Congress might have assessed all those who now use coal, or the taxpayer, in order to pay for those retired coal miners' health benefits. But Congress, instead, imposed this liability on Eastern. . . . The "fairness" question is, why Eastern?

The answer cannot lie in a contractual promise to pay, for Eastern made no such contractual promise. Nor did Eastern participate in any benefit plan that made such a contractual promise, prior to its departure from the coal industry in 1965. . . .

[Yet] I believe several features of this case demonstrate that the relationship between Eastern and the payments demanded by the Act is special enough to pass the Constitution's fundamental fairness test. . . .

For one thing, the liability that the statute imposes upon Eastern extends only to miners whom Eastern itself employed. . . . They are miners whose labor benefited Eastern when they were younger and healthier. . . .

. . . [T]he special tie between a firm and its former employee . . . helps to explain the special retroactive liability. . . .

More importantly, the record demonstrates that Eastern, before 1965, contributed to the making of an important 'promise' to the miners. That 'promise,' even if not contractually enforceable, led the miners to 'develo[p]' a reasonable 'expectation' that they would continue to receive '[retiree] medical benefits.' The relevant history . . . shows that industry action (including action by Eastern), combined with Federal Government action and the miners' own forbearance, produced circumstances that made it natural for the miners to believe that either industry or government (or both) would make every effort to see that they received health benefits after they retired—regardless of what terms were explicitly included in previously signed bargaining agreements.

. . . .

. . . [I]n labor relations, as in human relations, one can create promises and understandings which, even in the absence of a legally enforceable contract, others reasonably expect will be honored. Indeed, in labor relations such industry-wide understandings may spell the difference between labor war and labor peace, for the parties may look to a strike, not to a court, for enforcement. It is that kind of important, mutual understanding that is at issue here. For the record shows that pre–1965 statements and other conduct led management to understand, and labor legitimately to expect, that health care benefits for retirees and their dependents would continue to be provided.

Finally, Eastern continued to obtain profits from the coal mining industry long after 1965. . . .

Taken together, these circumstances explain why it is not fundamentally unfair for Congress to impose upon Eastern liability for the future health care costs of miners whom it long ago employed—rather than imposing that liability, for example, upon the present industry, coal consumers, or taxpayers. Each diminishes the reasonableness of Eastern's expectation that, by leaving the industry, it could fall within the Constitution's protection against unfairly retroactive liability.

These circumstances . . . mean that Eastern knew of the potential funding problems that arise in any multiemployer benefit plan . . . before it left the industry. Eastern knew or should have known that, in light of the structure of the benefit plan and the frequency with which coal operators went out of business, a "last man out" problem could exacerbate the health plan's funding difficulties. . . . Eastern also knew or should have known that because of prior federal involvement, future federal intervention to solve any such problem was a serious possibility. . . . And, most importantly, Eastern played a significant role in creating the miners' expectations that led to this legislation. Add to these circumstances the two others I have mentioned—that Eastern had benefited from the labor of the miners for whose future health care it must provide, and that Eastern remained in the industry, drawing from it substantial profits (though doing business through a subsidiary, which usually, but not always, insulates an owner from liability).

. . . .

. . . The law imposes upon Eastern the burden of showing that the statute, because of its retroactive effect, is fundamentally unfair or unjust. The circumstances I have mentioned convince me that Eastern cannot show a sufficiently reasonable expectation that it would remain free of future health care cost liability for the workers whom it employed. Eastern has therefore failed to show that the law unfairly upset its legitimately settled expectations. . . .

SECTION 2.   PROTECTION OF PERSONAL LIBERTIES

C.   PERSONAL AUTONOMY

Page 644. Add after Planned Parenthood of Southeastern Pennsylvania v. Casey:

VOINOVICH v. WOMEN'S MEDICAL PROFESSIONAL CORP., 505 U.S. 833, 118 S.Ct. 1347, 140 L.Ed.2d 496 (1998). A federal Court of Appeals held an Ohio law prohibiting postviability abortions unconstitutional, in part because its exception for abortions "necessary to prevent the death of the pregnant woman or a serious risk of the substantial and irreversible impairment of a major bodily function of the pregnant woman" did not provide an exception for abortions based upon the pregnant woman's "mental health." Dissenting from the majority's denial of review of this case, Justice Thomas, joined by the Chief Justice and Justice Scalia, noted that the "vast majority of the 38 States that have enacted postviability abortion restrictions have not specified whether such abortions must be permitted on mental health grounds[,]" and he claimed that no Court ruling "supports the proposition that, after viability, a mental health exception is required as a matter of federal constitutional law."

Page 655.   Replace Cruzan v. Director, Missouri Department of Health with the following:

Washington v. Glucksberg

521 U.S. 702, 117 S.Ct. 2258, 138 L.Ed.2d 772 (1997).

Chief Justice Rehnquist delivered the opinion of the Court.

The question presented in this case is whether Washington's prohibition against "caus[ing]" or "aid[ing]" a suicide offends the Fourteenth Amendment to the United States Constitution. We hold that it does not.

It has always been a crime to assist a suicide in the State of Washington. . . . Today, Washington law provides: "A person is guilty of promoting a suicide attempt when he knowingly causes or aids another person to attempt suicide." Wash. Rev. Code 9A.36.060(1) (1994). "Promoting a suicide attempt" is a felony, punishable by up to five years' imprisonment and up to a $10,000 fine. §§ 9A.36.060(2) and 9A.20.021(1)(c). At the same time, Washington's Natural Death Act, enacted in 1979, states that the "withholding or withdrawal of life-sustaining treatment" at a patient's direction "shall not, for any purpose, constitute a suicide." Wash. Rev. Code § 70.122.070(1). . . .

. . . Respondents . . . are physicians who practice in Washington[,] occasionally treat terminally ill, suffering patients, and declare that they would assist these patients in ending their lives if not for Washington's assisted-suicide ban. In January 1994, respondents, along with three gravely ill, pseudonymous plaintiffs who have since died and Compassion in Dying, a nonprofit organization that counsels people considering physician-assisted suicide, sued in the United States District Court, seeking a declaration that Wash Rev. Code 9A.36.060(1) (1994) is, on its face, unconstitutional. . . .

The plaintiffs asserted "the existence of a liberty interest protected by the Fourteenth Amendment which extends to a personal choice by a mentally competent, terminally ill adult to commit physician-assisted suicide." . . . Relying primarily on Planned Parenthood v. Casey, 505 U.S. 833 (1992), and Cruzan v. Director, Missouri Dept. of Health, 497 U.S. 261 (1990), the District Court agreed . . . and concluded that Washington's assisted-suicide ban is unconstitutional because it "places an undue burden on the exercise of [that] constitutionally protected liberty interest." . . .

. . . The Ninth Circuit . . . en banc . . . affirmed . . . [,] conclud[ing] that "the Constitution encompasses a due process liberty interest in controlling the time and manner of one's death—that there is, in short, a constitutionally-recognized 'right to die.' " . . . After "[w]eighing and then balancing" this interest against Washington's various interests, the court held that the State's assisted-suicide ban was unconstitutional "as applied to terminally ill competent adults who wish to hasten their deaths with medication prescribed by their physicians."[6] We . . . reverse.

I

We begin, as we do in all due-process cases, by examining our Nation's history, legal traditions, and practices. See, e.g., Casey, 505 U. S., at 849–850; Cruzan, 497 U. S., at 269–279; Moore v. East Cleveland, 431 U.S. 494, 503 (1977) (plurality opinion) (noting importance of "careful 'respect for the teachings of history' "). In almost every State—indeed, in almost every western democracy—it is a crime to assist a suicide. The States' assisted-suicide bans are not innovations. Rather, they are longstanding expressions of the States' commitment to the protection and preservation of all human life. . . . Indeed, opposition to and condemnation of suicide—and, therefore, of assisting suicide—are consistent and enduring themes of our philosophical, legal, and cultural heritages. See generally . . . New York State Task Force on Life and the Law, When Death is Sought: Assisted Suicide and Euthanasia in the Medical Context 77–82 (May 1994) (hereinafter New York Task Force).

[6] It is . . . the court's holding that Washington's physician-assisted suicide statute is unconstitutional as applied to the "class of terminally ill, mentally competent patients" that is before us today.

More specifically, for over 700 years, the Anglo–American common-law tradition has punished or otherwise disapproved of both suicide and assisting suicide.... [As of] the 13th century, ... "[t]he principle that suicide of a sane person, for whatever reason, was a punishable felony was ... introduced into English common law." ... Blackstone emphasized that "the law has ... ranked [suicide] among the highest crimes," ... although, anticipating later developments, he conceded that the harsh and shameful punishments imposed for suicide "borde[r] a little upon severity." ...

For the most part, the early American colonies adopted the common-law approach....

Over time, however, the American colonies abolished the[] harsh common-law penalties [of criminal property forfeiture]....

[H]owever, ... the movement away from the common law's harsh sanctions did not represent an acceptance of suicide; rather, ... this change reflected the growing consensus that it was unfair to punish the suicide's family for his wrongdoing.... Nonetheless, ... courts continued to condemn it as a grave public wrong....

That suicide remained a grievous, though nonfelonious, wrong is confirmed by the fact that colonial and early state legislatures and courts did not retreat from prohibiting assisting suicide.... And the prohibitions against assisting suicide never contained exceptions for those who were near death....

The earliest American statute explicitly to outlaw assisting suicide was enacted in New York in 1828, ... and many of the new States and Territories followed New York's example.... By the time the Fourteenth Amendment was ratified, it was a crime in most States to assist a suicide.... In this century, the Model Penal Code also prohibited "aiding" suicide, prompting many States to enact or revise their assisted-suicide bans. The Code's drafters observed that "the interests in the sanctity of life that are represented by the criminal homicide laws are threatened by one who expresses a willingness to participate in taking the life of another, even though the act may be accomplished with the consent, or at the request, of the suicide victim." American Law Institute, Model Penal Code § 210.5, Comment 5, p. 100 (Official Draft and Revised Comments 1980).

Though deeply rooted, the States' assisted-suicide bans have in recent years been reexamined and, generally, reaffirmed. Because of advances in medicine and technology, Americans today are increasingly likely to die in institutions, from chronic illnesses.... Public concern and democratic action are therefore sharply focused on how best to protect dignity and independence at the end of life, with the result that there have been many significant changes in state laws and in the attitudes these laws reflect. Many States, for example, now permit "living wills," surrogate health-care decisionmaking, and the withdrawal or refusal of life-sustaining medical treatment.... At the same time, however, voters and legislators continue for the most part to reaffirm their States' prohibitions on assisting suicide.

The Washington statute at issue in this case ... was enacted in 1975 as part of a revision of that State's criminal code. Four years later, Washington passed its Natural Death Act, which specifically stated that the "withholding or withdrawal of life-sustaining treatment ... shall not, for any purpose, constitute a suicide" and that "[n]othing in this chapter shall be construed to condone, authorize, or approve mercy killing...." ... In 1991, Washington voters rejected a ballot initiative which, had it passed, would have permitted a form of physician-assisted suicide. Washington then added a provision to the Natural Death Act expressly excluding physician-assisted suicide....

California voters rejected an assisted-suicide initiative similar to Washington's in 1993. On the other hand, in 1994, voters in Oregon enacted, also through ballot initiative, that State's "Death With Dignity Act," which legalized physician-assisted suicide for competent, terminally ill adults. Since the Oregon vote, many proposals to legalize assisted-suicide have been and continue to be introduced in the States' legislatures, but none has been enacted. And just last year, Iowa and Rhode Island joined the overwhelming majority of States explicitly prohibiting assisted suicide.... Also, on April 30, 1997, President Clinton signed the Federal Assisted Suicide Funding Restriction Act of 1997, which prohibits the use of federal funds in support of physician-assisted suicide.... [16]

Thus, the States are currently engaged in serious, thoughtful examinations of physician-assisted suicide and other similar issues. For example, New York State's Task Force on Life and the Law—an ongoing, blue-ribbon commission composed of doctors, ethicists, lawyers, religious leaders, and interested laymen—was convened in 1984 and commissioned with "a broad mandate to recommend public policy on issues raised by medical advances." ... After studying physician-assisted suicide, however, the Task Force unanimously concluded that "[l]egalizing assisted suicide and euthanasia would pose profound risks to many individuals who are ill and vulnerable.... [T]he potential dangers of this dramatic change in public policy would outweigh any benefit that might be achieved." ...

Attitudes toward suicide itself have changed since Bracton, but our laws have consistently condemned, and continue to prohibit, assisting suicide. Despite changes in medical technology and notwithstanding an increased emphasis on the importance of end-of-life decisionmaking, we have not retreated from this prohibition. Against this backdrop of history, tradition, and practice, we now turn to respondents' constitutional claim.

II

The Due Process Clause guarantees more than fair process, and the "liberty" it protects includes more than the absence of physical restraint.... The Clause also provides heightened protection against government interference with certain fundamental rights and liberty interests.... We have also assumed, and strongly suggested, that the Due Process Clause protects the traditional right to refuse unwanted lifesaving medical treatment. *Cruzan*, 497 U. S., at 278–279.

But we "ha[ve] always been reluctant to expand the concept of substantive due process because guideposts for responsible decisionmaking in this unchartered area are scarce and open-ended." ... By extending constitutional protection to an asserted right or liberty interest, we, to a great extent, place the matter outside the arena of public debate and legislative action. We must

[16] Other countries are embroiled in simi-   lar debates....

therefore "exercise the utmost care whenever we are asked to break new ground in this field," ... lest the liberty protected by the Due Process Clause be subtly transformed into the policy preferences of the members of this Court, *Moore*, 431 U. S., at 502 (plurality opinion).

Our established method of substantive-due-process analysis has two primary features: First, we have regularly observed that the Due Process Clause specially protects those fundamental rights and liberties which are, objectively, "deeply rooted in this Nation's history and tradition," id., at 503 (plurality opinion); Snyder v. Massachusetts, 291 U.S. 97, 105 (1934) ("so rooted in the traditions and conscience of our people as to be ranked as fundamental"), and "implicit in the concept of ordered liberty," such that "neither liberty nor justice would exist if they were sacrificed," Palko v. Connecticut, 302 U.S. 319, 325, 326 (1937). Second, we have required in substantive-due-process cases a "careful description" of the asserted fundamental liberty interest.... Our Nation's history, legal traditions, and practices thus provide the crucial "guideposts for responsible decisionmaking," that direct and restrain our exposition of the Due Process Clause....

Justice Souter, relying on Justice Harlan's dissenting opinion in *Poe v. Ullman*, would largely abandon this restrained methodology, and instead ask "whether [Washington's] statute sets up one of those 'arbitrary impositions' or 'purposeless restraints' at odds with the Due Process Clause of the Fourteenth Amendment" (quoting Poe, 367 U.S. 497, 543 (1961) (Harlan, J., dissenting)). In our view, however, the development of this Court's substantive-due-process jurisprudence ... has been a process whereby the outlines of the "liberty" specially protected by the Fourteenth Amendment—never fully clarified, to be sure, and perhaps not capable of being fully clarified—have at least been carefully refined by concrete examples involving fundamental rights found to be deeply rooted in our legal tradition. This approach tends to rein in the subjective elements that are necessarily present in due-process judicial review. In addition, by establishing a threshold requirement—that a challenged state action implicate a fundamental right—before requiring more than a reasonable relation to a legitimate state interest to justify the action, it avoids the need for complex balancing of competing interests in every case.

... [W]e have a tradition of carefully formulating the interest at stake in substantive-due-process cases. For example, although *Cruzan* is often described as a "right to die" case, ... we were, in fact, more precise: we assumed that the Constitution granted competent persons a "constitutionally protected right to refuse lifesaving hydration and nutrition." ... The Washington statute at issue in this case prohibits "aid[ing] another person to attempt suicide," ... and, thus, the question before us is whether the "liberty" specially protected by the Due Process Clause includes a right to commit suicide which itself includes a right to assistance in doing so.

We now inquire whether this asserted right has any place in our Nation's traditions. Here ... we are confronted with a consistent and almost universal tradition that has long rejected the asserted right, and continues explicitly to reject it today, even for terminally ill, mentally competent adults. To hold for respondents, we would have to reverse centuries of legal doctrine and practice, and strike down the considered policy choice of almost every State....

Respondents contend, however, that the liberty interest they assert *is* consistent with this Court's substantive-due-process line of cases, if not with this Nation's history and practice. Pointing to *Casey* and *Cruzan*, respondents read our jurisprudence in this area as reflecting a general tradition of "self-sovereignty," ... and as teaching that the "liberty" protected by the Due Process Clause includes "basic and intimate exercises of personal autonomy,".... According to respondents, our liberty jurisprudence, and the broad, individualistic principles it reflects, protects the "liberty of competent, terminally ill adults to make end-of-life decisions free of undue government interference." ... The question presented in this case, however, is whether the protections of the Due Process Clause include a right to commit suicide with another's assistance. With this "careful description" of respondents' claim in mind, we turn to *Casey* and *Cruzan*.

In *Cruzan*, we considered whether Nancy Beth Cruzan, who had been severely injured in an automobile accident and was in a persistive vegetative state, "ha[d] a right under the United States Constitution which would require the hospital to withdraw life-sustaining treatment" at her parents' request.... We began with the observation that "[a]t common law, even the touching of one person by another without consent and without legal justification was a battery." ... We then discussed the related rule that "informed consent is generally required for medical treatment." ... After reviewing a long line of relevant state cases, we concluded that "the common-law doctrine of informed consent is viewed as generally encompassing the right of a competent individual to refuse medical treatment." ... Next, we reviewed our own cases on the subject, and stated that "[t]he principle that a competent person has a constitutionally protected liberty interest in refusing unwanted medical treatment may be inferred from our prior decisions." ... Therefore, "for purposes of [that] case, we assume[d] that the United States Constitution would grant a competent person a constitutionally protected right to refuse lifesaving hydration and nutrition." ... We concluded that, notwithstanding this right, the Constitution permitted Missouri to require clear and convincing evidence of an incompetent patient's wishes concerning the withdrawal of life-sustaining treatment....

Respondents contend that in *Cruzan* we "acknowledged that competent, dying persons have the right to direct the removal of life-sustaining medical treatment and thus hasten death," ... and that "the constitutional principle behind recognizing the patient's liberty to direct the withdrawal of artificial life support applies at least as strongly to the choice to hasten impending death by consuming lethal medication,".... Similarly, the Court of Appeals concluded that "*Cruzan*, by recognizing a liberty interest that includes the refusal of artificial provision of life-sustaining food and water, necessarily recognize[d] a liberty interest in hastening one's own death." ...

The right assumed in *Cruzan*, however, was not simply deduced from abstract concepts of personal autonomy. Given the common-law rule that forced medication was a battery, and the long legal tradition protecting the decision to refuse unwanted medical treatment, our assumption was entirely consistent with this Nation's history and constitutional traditions. The decision to commit suicide with the assistance of another may be just as personal and profound as the decision to refuse unwanted medical treatment, but it has never enjoyed similar legal protection. Indeed, the two acts are widely and reasonably regarded as quite distinct. See Vacco v. Quill, post, [117 S.Ct. 2293].[a] In *Cruzan* itself,

[a] In *Quill*, decided with *Glucksberg*, the Court reversed a decision of the Second Circuit Court of Appeals holding that New York's prohibition on assisted suicide violated the Equal Protection Clause insofar as it prevented prescribing lethal medication for mentally competent, terminally ill patients, because New York law allowed such patients to refuse life-sustaining medical treatment, and the distinction was "not rationally related to any legitimate state interest." Chief Justice Rehnquist's majority opinion concluded that "the distinction between assisting suicide and withdrawing life-sustaining treatment, a distinction widely recognized and endorsed in the medical profession and in our legal traditions, is both important and logical; it is certainly rational." The Chief Justice continued:

> "The distinction comports with fundamental legal principles of causation and intent. First, when a patient refuses life-sustaining medical treatment, he dies from an underlying fatal disease or pathology; but if a patient ingests lethal medication prescribed by a physician, he is killed by that medication. . . .

> "Furthermore, a physician who withdraws, or honors a patient's refusal to begin, life-sustaining medical treatment purposefully intends, or may so intend, only to respect his patient's wishes and 'to cease doing useless and futile or degrading things to the patient when [the patient] no longer stands to benefit from them.' . . . The same is true when a doctor provides aggressive palliative care; in some cases, painkilling drugs may hasten a patient's death, but the physician's purpose and intent is, or may be, only to ease his patient's pain. A doctor who assists a suicide, however, 'must, necessarily and indubitably, intend primarily that the patient be made dead.' . . . Similarly, a patient who commits suicide with a doctor's aid necessarily has the specific intent to end his or her own life, while a patient who refuses or discontinues treatment might not. . . .

> "The law has long used actors' intent or purpose to distinguish between two acts that may have the same result. . . . Put differently, the law distinguishes actions taken 'because of' a given end from actions taken 'in spite of' their unintended but foreseen consequences. . . .

> "Given these general principles, it is not surprising that many courts, including New York courts, have carefully distinguished refusing life-sustaining treatment from suicide. . . .

> "Similarly, the overwhelming majority of state legislatures have drawn a clear line between assisting suicide and withdrawing or permitting the refusal of unwanted lifesaving medical treatment by prohibiting the former and permitting the latter. . . .

> " . . .

> "This Court has also recognized, at least implicitly, the distinction between letting a patient die and making that patient die. In [*Cruzan*], . . . our assumption of a right to refuse treatment was grounded not, as the Court of Appeals supposed, on the proposition that patients have a general and abstract 'right to hasten death,' but on well established, traditional rights to bodily integrity and freedom from unwanted touching. . . . *Cruzan* therefore provides no support for the notion that refusing life-sustaining medical treatment is 'nothing more nor less than suicide.'

> " . . . Logic and contemporary practice support New York's judgment that the two acts are different, and New York may therefore, consistent with the Constitution, treat them differently. . . .

> "New York's reasons for recognizing and acting on this distinction . . . are discussed in greater detail in our opinion in *Glucksberg* [and] easily satisfy the constitutional requirement that a legislative classification bear a rational relation to some legitimate end."

Each of the concurring opinions in *Glucksberg* also applied to this case, except that Justice Souter here said this:

> "Even though I do not conclude that assisted suicide is a fundamental right entitled to recognition at this time, I accord the claims raised by the patients and physicians in this case and Washington v. Glucksberg a high degree of importance, requiring a commensurate justification. See Washington v. Glucksberg (Souter, J., concurring in judgment). The reasons that lead me to conclude in *Glucksberg* that the prohibition on assisted suicide is not arbitrary under the

we recognized that most States outlawed assisted suicide—and even more do today—and we certainly gave no intimation that the right to refuse unwanted medical treatment could be somehow transmuted into a right to assistance in committing suicide. . . .

Respondents also rely on *Casey*. . . .

The Court of Appeals, like the District Court, found *Casey* " 'highly instructive' " and " 'almost prescriptive' " for determining " 'what liberty interest may inhere in a terminally ill person's choice to commit suicide' ":

"Like the decision of whether or not to have an abortion, the decision how and when to die is one of 'the most intimate and personal choices a person may make in a lifetime,' a choice 'central to personal dignity and autonomy.' " . . .

Similarly, respondents emphasize the statement in *Casey* that:

"At the heart of liberty is the right to define one's own concept of existence, of meaning, of the universe, and of the mystery of human life. Beliefs about these matters could not define the attributes of personhood were they formed under compulsion of the State." . . .

By choosing this language, the Court's opinion in *Casey* described, in a general way and in light of our prior cases, those personal activities and decisions that this Court has identified as so deeply rooted in our history and traditions, or so fundamental to our concept of constitutionally ordered liberty, that they are protected by the Fourteenth Amendment. . . . That many of the rights and liberties protected by the Due Process Clause sound in personal autonomy does not warrant the sweeping conclusion that any and all important, intimate, and personal decisions are so protected, . . . and *Casey* did not suggest otherwise.

The history of the law's treatment of assisted suicide in this country has been and continues to be one of the rejection of nearly all efforts to permit it. That being the case, our decisions lead us to conclude that the asserted "right" to assistance in committing suicide is not a fundamental liberty interest protected by the Due Process Clause. The Constitution also requires, however, that Washington's assisted-suicide ban be rationally related to legitimate government interests. . . . This requirement is unquestionably met here. . . .

First, Washington has an "unqualified interest in the preservation of human life." Cruzan, 497 U. S., at 282. The State's prohibition on assisted suicide, like all homicide laws, both reflects and advances its commitment to this interest. . . .

. . . The Court of Appeals . . . held that the "weight" of this interest depends on the "medical condition and the wishes of the person whose life is at stake." . . . Washington, however, . . . insists that all persons' lives, from beginning to end, regardless of physical or mental condition, are under the full protection of the law. . . . As we have previously affirmed, the States "may properly decline to make judgments about the 'quality' of life that a particular

due process standard also support the distinction between assistance to suicide, which is banned, and practices such as termination of artificial life support and death-hastening pain medication, which are permitted. I accordingly concur in the judgment of the Court."

individual may enjoy," Cruzan, 497 U. S., at 282. This remains true, as *Cruzan* makes clear, even for those who are near death.

Relatedly, all admit that suicide is a serious public-health problem, especially among persons in otherwise vulnerable groups. . . .

Those who attempt suicide—terminally ill or not—often suffer from depression or other mental disorders. . . . Research indicates, however, that many people who request physician-assisted suicide withdraw that request if their depression and pain are treated. H. Hendin, Seduced by Death: Doctors, Patients and the Dutch Cure 24–25 (1997) (suicidal, terminally ill patients "usually respond well to treatment for depressive illness and pain medication and are then grateful to be alive"); New York Task Force 177–178. The New York Task Force, however, expressed its concern that, because depression is difficult to diagnose, physicians and medical professionals often fail to respond adequately to seriously ill patients' needs. Id., at 175. Thus, legal physician-assisted suicide could make it more difficult for the State to protect depressed or mentally ill persons, or those who are suffering from untreated pain, from suicidal impulses.

The State also has an interest in protecting the integrity and ethics of the medical profession. . . . [T]he American Medical Association, like many other medical and physicians' groups, has concluded that "[p]hysician-assisted suicide is fundamentally incompatible with the physician's role as healer." . . . And physician-assisted suicide could, it is argued, undermine the trust that is essential to the doctor-patient relationship by blurring the time-honored line between healing and harming. . . .

Next, the State has an interest in protecting vulnerable groups—including the poor, the elderly, and disabled persons—from abuse, neglect, and mistakes. . . . We have recognized . . . the real risk of subtle coercion and undue influence in end-of-life situations. *Cruzan*, 497 U. S., at 281. . . . If physician-assisted suicide were permitted, many might resort to it to spare their families the substantial financial burden of end-of-life health-care costs.

The State's interest here goes beyond protecting the vulnerable from coercion; it extends to protecting disabled and terminally ill people from prejudice, negative and inaccurate stereotypes, and "societal indifference." . . . The State's assisted-suicide ban reflects and reinforces its policy that the lives of terminally ill, disabled, and elderly people must be no less valued than the lives of the young and healthy, and that a seriously disabled person's suicidal impulses should be interpreted and treated the same way as anyone else's. . . .

Finally, the State may fear that permitting assisted suicide will start it down the path to voluntary and perhaps even involuntary euthanasia. The Court of Appeals struck down Washington's assisted-suicide ban only "as applied to competent, terminally ill adults who wish to hasten their deaths by obtaining medication prescribed by their doctors." . . . Washington insists, however, that the impact of the court's decision will not and cannot be so limited. . . . The Court of Appeals' decision, and its expansive reasoning, provide ample support for the State's concerns. The court noted, for example, that the "decision of a duly appointed surrogate decision maker is for all legal purposes the decision of the patient himself," . . .; that "in some instances, the patient may be unable to self-administer the drugs and . . . administration by the physician ... may be the only way the patient may be able to receive them," ...; and that not only physicians, but also family members and loved ones, will inevitably participate in assisting suicide.... Thus, it turns out that what is couched as a limited right to "physician-assisted suicide" is likely, in effect, a much broader license, which could prove extremely difficult to police and contain. Washington's ban on assisting suicide prevents such erosion.

This concern is further supported by evidence about the practice of euthanasia in the Netherlands ... suggest[ing] that, despite the existence of various reporting procedures, euthanasia in the Netherlands has not been limited to competent, terminally ill adults who are enduring physical suffering, and that regulation of the practice may not have prevented abuses in cases involving vulnerable persons, including severely disabled neonates and elderly persons suffering from dementia.... Washington, like most other States, reasonably ensures against this risk by banning, rather than regulating, assisting suicide....

We need not weigh exactingly the relative strengths of these various interests. They are unquestionably important and legitimate, and Washington's ban on assisted suicide is at least reasonably related to their promotion and protection. We therefore hold that Wash. Rev. Code § 9A.36.060(1) (1994) does not violate the Fourteenth Amendment, either on its face or "as applied to competent, terminally ill adults who wish to hasten their deaths by obtaining medication prescribed by their doctors." ...[24]

* * *

Throughout the Nation, Americans are engaged in an earnest and profound debate about the morality, legality, and practicality of physician-assisted suicide. Our holding permits this debate to continue, as it should in a democratic society....

Justice O'Connor, concurring.*

. . .

... I join the Court's opinions because I agree that there is no generalized right to "commit suicide." But respondents urge us to address the narrower question whether a mentally competent person who is experiencing great suffering has a constitutionally cognizable interest in controlling the circumstances of his or her imminent death. I see no need to reach that question in the context of the facial challenges to the New York and Washington laws at issue here.... The parties and *amici* agree that in these States a patient who is

---

[24] ... We emphasize that we today reject the Court of Appeals' specific holding that the statute is unconstitutional "as applied" to a particular class. See n. 6, supra. Justice Stevens agrees with this holding, but would not "foreclose the possibility that an individual plaintiff seeking to hasten her death, or a doctor whose assistance was sought, could prevail in a more particularized challenge." Our opinion does not absolutely foreclose such a claim. However, given our holding that the Due Process Clause of the Fourteenth Amendment does not provide heightened protection to the asserted liberty interest in ending one's life with a physician's assistance, such a claim would have to be quite different from the ones advanced by respondents here.

* Justice Ginsburg concurs in the Court's judgments substantially for the reasons stated in this opinion. Justice Breyer joins this opinion except insofar as it joins the opinions of the Court.

suffering from a terminal illness and who is experiencing great pain has no legal barriers to obtaining medication, from qualified physicians, to alleviate that suffering, even to the point of causing unconsciousness and hastening death. . . . In this light, even assuming that we would recognize such an interest, I agree that the State's interests in protecting those who are not truly competent or facing imminent death, or those whose decisions to hasten death would not truly be voluntary, are sufficiently weighty to justify a prohibition against physician-assisted suicide.

Every one of us at some point may be affected by our own or a family member's terminal illness. There is no reason to think the democratic process will not strike the proper balance between the interests of terminally ill, mentally competent individuals who would seek to end their suffering and the State's interests in protecting those who might seek to end life mistakenly or under pressure. . . .

In sum, there is no need to address the question whether suffering patients have a constitutionally cognizable interest in obtaining relief from the suffering that they may experience in the last days of their lives. There is no dispute that dying patients in Washington and New York can obtain palliative care, even when doing so would hasten their deaths. The difficulty in defining terminal illness and the risk that a dying patient's request for assistance in ending his or her life might not be truly voluntary justifies the prohibitions on assisted suicide we uphold here.

Justice Stevens, concurring in the judgments.

. . .

Today, the Court decides that Washington's statute prohibiting assisted suicide is not invalid "on its face," that is to say, in all or most cases in which it might be applied. That holding, however, does not foreclose the possibility that some applications of the statute might well be invalid.

. . .

History and tradition provide ample support for refusing to recognize an open-ended constitutional right to commit suicide. Much more than the State's paternalistic interest in protecting the individual from the irrevocable consequences of an ill-advised decision motivated by temporary concerns is at stake. . . . The State has an interest in preserving and fostering the benefits that every human being may provide to the community—a community that thrives on the exchange of ideas, expressions of affection, shared memories and humorous incidents as well as on the material contributions that its members create and support. The value to others of a person's life is far too precious to allow the individual to claim a constitutional entitlement to complete autonomy in making a decision to end that life. Thus, I fully agree with the Court that the "liberty" protected by the Due Process Clause does not include a categorical "right to commit suicide which itself includes a right to assistance in doing so."

But just as our conclusion that capital punishment is not always unconstitutional did not preclude later decisions holding that it is sometimes impermissibly cruel, so is it equally clear that a decision upholding a general statutory prohibition of assisted suicide does not mean that every possible application of the statute would be valid. . . .

II

In Cruzan v. Director, Mo. Dept. of Health, 497 U.S. 261 (1990), the Court assumed that the interest in liberty protected by the Fourteenth Amendment encompassed the right of a terminally ill patient to direct the withdrawal of life-sustaining treatment.... We have recognized, however, that this common-law right to refuse treatment is neither absolute nor always sufficiently weighty to overcome valid countervailing state interests.... In most cases, the individual's constitutionally protected interest in his or her own physical autonomy, including the right to refuse unwanted medical treatment, will give way to the State's interest in preserving human life.

Cruzan, however, was not the normal case.... When this Court reviewed the case and upheld Missouri's requirement that there be clear and convincing evidence establishing Nancy Cruzan's intent to have life-sustaining nourishment withdrawn, it made two important assumptions: (1) that there was a "liberty interest" in refusing unwanted treatment protected by the Due Process Clause; and (2) that this liberty interest did not "end the inquiry" because it might be outweighed by relevant state interests.... I agree with both of those assumptions, but I insist that the source of Nancy Cruzan's right to refuse treatment was not just a common-law rule. Rather, this right is an aspect of a far broader and more basic concept of freedom that is even older than the common law. This freedom embraces, not merely a person's right to refuse a particular kind of unwanted treatment, but also her interest in dignity, and in determining the character of the memories that will survive long after her death....

. . .

The *Cruzan* case demonstrated that some state intrusions on the right to decide how death will be encountered are also intolerable. The now-deceased plaintiffs in this action may in fact have had a liberty interest even stronger than Nancy Cruzan's because, not only were they terminally ill, they were suffering constant and severe pain. Avoiding intolerable pain and the indignity of living one's final days incapacitated and in agony is certainly "[a]t the heart of [the] liberty ... to define one's own concept of existence, of meaning, of the universe, and of the mystery of human life." Casey, 505 U. S., at 851.

... *Cruzan* [gave] recognition, not just to vague, unbridled notions of autonomy, but to the more specific interest in making decisions about how to confront an imminent death. Although there is no absolute right to physician-assisted suicide, *Cruzan* makes it clear that some individuals who no longer have the option of deciding whether to live or to die because they are already on the threshold of death have a constitutionally protected interest that may outweigh the State's interest in preserving life at all costs. The liberty interest at stake in a case like this differs from, and is stronger than, both the common-law right to refuse medical treatment and the unbridled interest in deciding whether to live or die. It is an interest in deciding how, rather than whether, a critical threshold shall be crossed.

III

The state interests supporting a general rule banning the practice of physician-assisted suicide do not have the same force in all cases. First and foremost of these interests is the " 'unqualified interest in the preservation of human life,' ".... Properly viewed, however, this interest is not a collective interest that should always outweigh the interests of a person who because of pain, incapacity, or sedation finds her life intolerable, but rather, an aspect of individual freedom.

... Although as a general matter the State's interest in the contributions each person may make to society outweighs the person's interest in ending her life, this interest does not have the same force for a terminally ill patient faced not with the choice of whether to live, only of how to die. Allowing the individual, rather than the State, to make judgments " 'about the "quality" of life that a particular individual may enjoy,' " does not mean that the lives of terminally-ill, disabled people have less value than the lives of those who are healthy. Rather, it gives proper recognition to the individual's interest in choosing a final chapter that accords with her life story, rather than one that demeans her values and poisons memories of her....

... I agree that the State has a compelling interest in preventing persons from committing suicide because of depression, or coercion by third parties. But the State's legitimate interest in preventing abuse does not apply to an individual who is not victimized by abuse, who is not suffering from depression, and who makes a rational and voluntary decision to seek assistance in dying.... [P]rofessionals expert in working with dying patients can help patients cope with depression and pain, and help patients assess their options....

Relatedly, the State and *amici* express the concern that patients whose physical pain is inadequately treated will be more likely to request assisted suicide. Encouraging the development and ensuring the availability of adequate pain treatment is of utmost importance; palliative care, however, cannot alleviate all pain and suffering.... An individual adequately informed of the care alternatives thus might make a rational choice for assisted suicide. For such an individual, the State's interest in preventing potential abuse and mistake is only minimally implicated.

The final major interest asserted by the State is its interest in preserving the traditional integrity of the medical profession.... But for some patients, it would be a physician's refusal to dispense medication to ease their suffering and make their death tolerable and dignified that would be inconsistent with the healing role.... Furthermore, because physicians are already involved in making decisions that hasten the death of terminally ill patients—through termination of life support, withholding of medical treatment, and terminal sedation—there is in fact significant tension between the traditional view of the physician's role and the actual practice in a growing number of cases.[12]

... Although, as the Court concludes today, the[] potential harms are sufficient to support the State's general public policy against assisted suicide, they will not always outweigh the individual liberty interest of a particular patient.... I do not ... foreclose the possibility that an individual plaintiff seeking to hasten her death, or a doctor whose assistance was sought, could prevail in a more particularized challenge....

---

[12] [T]here is evidence that a significant number of physicians support the practice of hastening death in particular situations....

IV

In New York, a doctor must respect a competent person's decision to refuse or to discontinue medical treatment even though death will thereby ensue, but the same doctor would be guilty of a felony if she provided her patient assistance in committing suicide. Today we hold that the Equal Protection Clause is not violated by the resulting disparate treatment of two classes of terminally ill people who may have the same interest in hastening death. I agree that the distinction between permitting death to ensue from an underlying fatal disease and causing it to occur by the administration of medication or other means provides a constitutionally sufficient basis for the State's classification. Unlike the Court, however, I am not persuaded that in all cases there will in fact be a significant difference between the intent of the physicians, the patients or the families in the two situations.

There may be little distinction between the intent of a terminally-ill patient who decides to remove her life-support and one who seeks the assistance of a doctor in ending her life; in both situations, the patient is seeking to hasten a certain, impending death. The doctor's intent might also be the same in prescribing lethal medication as it is in terminating life support. A doctor who fails to administer medical treatment to one who is dying from a disease could be doing so with an intent to harm or kill that patient. Conversely, a doctor who prescribes lethal medication does not necessarily intend the patient's death—rather that doctor may seek simply to ease the patient's suffering and to comply with her wishes. The illusory character of any differences in intent or causation is confirmed by the fact that the American Medical Association unequivocally endorses the practice of terminal sedation—the administration of sufficient dosages of pain-killing medication to terminally ill patients to protect them from excruciating pain even when it is clear that the time of death will be advanced. The purpose of terminal sedation is to ease the suffering of the patient and comply with her wishes, and the actual cause of death is the administration of heavy doses of lethal sedatives. This same intent and causation may exist when a doctor complies with a patient's request for lethal medication to hasten her death.

Thus, although the differences the majority notes in causation and intent between terminating life-support and assisting in suicide support the Court's rejection of the respondents' facial challenge, these distinctions may be inapplicable to particular terminally ill patients and their doctors. Our holding today in Vacco v. Quill that the Equal Protection Clause is not violated by New York's classification, just like our holding in Washington v. Glucksberg that the Washington statute is not invalid on its face, does not foreclose the possibility that some applications of the New York statute may impose an intolerable intrusion on the patient's freedom.

... In my judgment, ... it is clear that the so-called "unqualified interest in the preservation of human life," ... is not itself sufficient to outweigh the interest in liberty that may justify the only possible means of preserving a dying patient's dignity and alleviating her intolerable suffering.

Justice Souter, concurring in the judgment.

... The question is whether the statute sets up one of those "arbitrary impositions" or "purposeless restraints" at odds with the Due Process Clause of the Fourteenth Amendment. Poe v. Ullman, 367 U.S. 497, 543 (1961) (Harlan, J., dissenting)....

. . .

... Justice Harlan's *Poe* dissent ... is important for three things that point to our responsibilities today. The first is Justice Harlan's respect for the tradition of substantive due process review itself, and his acknowledgement of the Judiciary's obligation to carry it on.... The text of the Due Process Clause ... imposes nothing less than an obligation to give substantive content to the words "liberty" and "due process of law."

... The second of the dissent's lessons is a reminder that the business of such review is not the identification of extratextual absolutes but scrutiny of a legislative resolution (perhaps unconscious) of clashing principles, each quite possibly worthy in and of itself, but each to be weighed within the history of our values as a people. It is a comparison of the relative strengths of opposing claims that informs the judicial task, not a deduction from some first premise. Thus informed, judicial review still has no warrant to substitute one reasonable resolution of the contending positions for another, but authority to supplant the balance already struck between the contenders only when it falls outside the realm of the reasonable.... [T]he dissent's third [point] takes the form of an object lesson in the explicit attention to detail that is no less essential to the intellectual discipline of substantive due process review than an understanding of the basic need to account for the two sides in the controversy and to respect legislation within the zone of reasonableness.

III

My understanding of unenumerated rights in the wake of the *Poe* dissent and subsequent cases avoids the absolutist failing of many older cases without embracing the opposite pole of equating reasonableness with past practice described at a very specific level. See Planned Parenthood of Southeastern Pa. v. Casey, 505 U.S. 833, 847–849 (1992). That understanding begins with a concept of "ordered liberty," Poe, 367 U. S., at 549 (Harlan, J.); see also Griswold, 381 U. S., at 500, comprising a continuum of rights to be free from "arbitrary impositions and purposeless restraints," Poe, 367 U. S., at 543 (Harlan, J., dissenting).

> "Due Process has not been reduced to any formula; its content cannot be determined by reference to any code. The best that can be said is that through the course of this Court's decisions it has represented the balance which our Nation, built upon postulates of respect for the liberty of the individual, has struck between that liberty and the demands of organized society. If the supplying of content to this Constitutional concept has of necessity been a rational process, it certainly has not been one where judges have felt free to roam where unguided speculation might take them. The balance of which I speak is the balance struck by this country, having regard to what history teaches are the traditions from which it developed as well as the traditions from which it broke. That tradition is a living thing. A decision of this Court which radically departs from it could not long survive, while a decision which builds on what has survived is likely to

be sound. No formula could serve as a substitute, in this area, for judgment and restraint." Id., at 542. . . .

. . .

This approach calls for a court to assess the relative "weights" or dignities of the contending interests, and to this extent the judicial method is familiar to the common law. Common law method is subject, however, to two important constraints in the hands of a court engaged in substantive due process review. First, such a court is bound to confine the values that it recognizes to those truly deserving constitutional stature, either to those expressed in constitutional text, or those exemplified by "the traditions from which [the Nation] developed," or revealed by contrast with "the traditions from which it broke."

. . .

[S]econd[,] . . . [i]t is no justification for judicial intervention merely to identify a reasonable resolution of contending values that differs from the terms of the legislation under review. It is only when the legislation's justifying principle, critically valued, is so far from being commensurate with the individual interest as to be arbitrarily or pointlessly applied that the statute must give way. Only if this standard points against the statute can the individual claimant be said to have a constitutional right. . . . [10]

The *Poe* dissent . . . reminds us that the process of substantive review by reasoned judgment . . . is one of close criticism going to the details of the opposing interests and to their relationships with the historically recognized principles that lend them weight or value.

. . . Exact analysis and characterization of any due process claim is critical to the method and to the result.

. . .

. . . [The *Poe* dissent] points to the importance of evaluating the claims of the parties now before us with comparable detail. For here we are faced with an individual claim not to a right on the part of just anyone to help anyone else commit suicide under any circumstances, but to the right of a narrow class to help others also in a narrow class under a set of limited circumstances. And the claimants are met with the State's assertion, among others, that rights of such narrow scope cannot be recognized without jeopardy to individuals whom the State may concededly protect through its regulations.

IV

A

Respondents claim that a patient facing imminent death, who anticipates physical suffering and indignity, and is capable of responsible and voluntary choice, should have a right to a physician's assistance in providing counsel and drugs to be administered by the patient to end life promptly. . . . They seek the option to obtain the services of a physician to give them the benefit of advice

---

[10] Our cases have used various terms to refer to fundamental liberty interests. . . . Precision in terminology, however, favors reserving the label "right" for instances in which the individual's liberty interest actually trumps the government's countervailing interests; only then does the individual have anything legally enforceable as against the state's attempt at regulation.

and medical help, which is said to enjoy a tradition so strong and so devoid of specifically countervailing state concern that denial of a physician's help in these circumstances is arbitrary when physicians are generally free to advise and aid those who exercise other rights to bodily autonomy.

. . .

This liberty interest in bodily integrity was phrased in a general way by then-Judge Cardozo when he said, "[e]very human being of adult years and sound mind has a right to determine what shall be done with his own body" in relation to his medical needs. Schloendorff v. Society of New York Hospital, 211 N.Y. 125, 129, 105 N.E. 92, 93 (1914).... Constitutional recognition of the right to bodily integrity underlies the assumed right, good against the State, to require physicians to terminate artificial life support, *Cruzan*, ... and the affirmative right to obtain medical intervention to cause abortion, see *Casey*, supra, at 857, 896; cf. Roe v. Wade, 410 U. S., at 153.

It is, indeed, in the abortion cases that the most telling recognitions of the importance of bodily integrity and the concomitant tradition of medical assistance have occurred. In Roe v. Wade, ... we stressed the importance of the relationship between patient and physician....

The analogies between the abortion cases and this one are several. Even though the State has a legitimate interest in discouraging abortion, ... the Court recognized a woman's right to a physician's counsel and care. Like the decision to commit suicide, the decision to abort potential life can be made irresponsibly and under the influence of others, and yet the Court has held in the abortion cases that physicians are fit assistants. Without physician assistance in abortion, the woman's right would have too often amounted to nothing more than a right to self-mutilation, and without a physician to assist in the suicide of the dying, the patient's right will often be confined to crude methods of causing death, most shocking and painful to the decedent's survivors.

There is, finally, one more reason for claiming that a physician's assistance here would fall within the accepted tradition of medical care in our society, and the abortion cases are only the most obvious illustration of the further point.... [T]he good physician is not just a mechanic of the human body whose services have no bearing on a person's moral choices, but one who does more than treat symptoms, one who ministers to the patient. This idea of the physician as serving the whole person is a source of the high value traditionally placed on the medical relationship. Its value is surely as apparent here as in the abortion cases, for just as the decision about abortion is not directed to correcting some pathology, so the decision in which a dying patient seeks help is not so limited. The patients here sought not only an end to pain (which they might have had, although perhaps at the price of stupor) but an end to their short remaining lives with a dignity that they believed would be denied them by powerful pain medication, as well as by their consciousness of dependency and helplessness as they approached death. In that period when the end is imminent, they said, the decision to end life is closest to decisions that are generally accepted as proper instances of exercising autonomy over one's own body, instances recognized under the Constitution and the State's own law, instances in which the help of physicians is accepted as falling within the traditional norm.

. . .

The argument supporting respondents' position thus progresses through three steps of increasing forcefulness. First, it emphasizes the decriminalization of suicide ... [as one of] society's occasional choices to reject traditions of the legal past. See Poe v. Ullman, 367 U. S., at 542 (Harlan, J., dissenting). [S]econd[,] the State's own act of decriminalization gives a freedom of choice much like the individual's option in recognized instances of bodily autonomy. One of these, abortion, is a legal right to choose in spite of the interest a State may legitimately invoke in discouraging the practice, just as suicide is now subject to choice, despite a state interest in discouraging it. [T]hird[,] ... [r]espondents base their claim on the traditional right to medical care and counsel, subject to the limiting conditions of informed, responsible choice when death is imminent, conditions that support a strong analogy to rights of care in other situations in which medical counsel and assistance have been available as a matter of course. There can be no stronger claim to a physician's assistance than at the time when death is imminent, a moral judgment implied by the State's own recognition of the legitimacy of medical procedures necessarily hastening the moment of impending death.

In my judgment, the importance of the individual interest here, as within that class of "certain interests" demanding careful scrutiny of the State's contrary claim, see *Poe*, supra, at 543, cannot be gainsaid. Whether that interest might in some circumstances, or at some time, be seen as "fundamental" to the degree entitled to prevail is not, however, a conclusion that I need draw here, for I am satisfied that the State's interests described in the following section are sufficiently serious to defeat the present claim that its law is arbitrary or purposeless.

B

The State has put forward several interests to justify the Washington law as applied to physicians treating terminally ill patients, even those competent to make responsible choices: protecting life generally, ... discouraging suicide even if knowing and voluntary, ... and protecting terminally ill patients from involuntary suicide and euthanasia, both voluntary and nonvoluntary....

[T]he third is dispositive for me. That third justification is different from the first two, for it addresses specific features of respondents' claim, and it opposes that claim not with a moral judgment contrary to respondents', but with a recognized state interest in the protection of nonresponsible individuals and those who do not stand in relation either to death or to their physicians as do the patients whom respondents describe.... [M]istaken decisions may result from inadequate palliative care or a terminal prognosis that turns out to be error; coercion and abuse may stem from the large medical bills that family members cannot bear or unreimbursed hospitals decline to shoulder. Voluntary and involuntary euthanasia may result once doctors are authorized to prescribe lethal medication in the first instance, for they might find it pointless to distinguish between patients who administer their own fatal drugs and those who wish not to, and their compassion for those who suffer may obscure the distinction between those who ask for death and those who may be unable to request it. The argument is that a progression would occur, obscuring the line between the ill and the dying, and between the responsible and the unduly influenced, until ultimately doctors and perhaps others would abuse a limited freedom to aid suicides by yielding to the impulse to end another's suffering under conditions going beyond the narrow limits the respondents propose. The State thus argues, essentially, that respondents' claim is not as narrow as it sounds, simply because no recognition of the interest they assert could be limited to vindicating those interests and affecting no others. . . .

. . .

The State . . . argue[s] that . . . the lines proposed here (particularly the requirement of a knowing and voluntary decision by the patient) would be more difficult to draw than the lines that have limited other recently recognized due process rights. . . . [T]he knowing and responsible mind is harder to assess. Second, this difficulty could become the greater by combining with another fact within the realm of plausibility, that physicians simply would not be assiduous to preserve the line. They have compassion, and those who would be willing to assist in suicide at all might be the most susceptible to the wishes of a patient, whether the patient were technically quite responsible or not. Physicians, and their hospitals, have their own financial incentives, too, in this new age of managed care. Whether acting from compassion or under some other influence, a physician who would provide a drug for a patient to administer might well go the further step of administering the drug himself; so, the barrier between assisted suicide and euthanasia could become porous, and the line between voluntary and involuntary euthanasia as well. The case for the slippery slope is fairly made out here, not because recognizing one due process right would leave a court with no principled basis to avoid recognizing another, but because there is a plausible case that the right claimed would not be readily containable by reference to facts about the mind that are matters of difficult judgment, or by gatekeepers who are subject to temptation, noble or not.

Respondents propose . . . the answer of state regulation with teeth. . . .

But at least at this moment there are reasons for caution in predicting the effectiveness of the teeth proposed. Respondents' proposals . . . sound much like the guidelines now in place in the Netherlands, the only place where experience with physician-assisted suicide and euthanasia has yielded empirical evidence about how such regulations might affect actual practice. . . . Some commentators marshall evidence that the Dutch guidelines have in practice failed to protect patients from involuntary euthanasia and have been violated with impunity. . . . This evidence is contested. . . . The day may come when we can say with some assurance which side is right, but for now it is the substantiality of the factual disagreement, and the alternatives for resolving it, that matter. They are, for me, dispositive of the due process claim at this time.

. . .

Legislatures . . . have superior opportunities to obtain the facts necessary for a judgment about the present controversy. . . .

. . .

... The experimentation that should be out of the question in constitutional adjudication displacing legislative judgments is entirely proper, as well as highly desirable, when the legislative power addresses an emerging issue like assisted suicide. The Court should accordingly stay its hand to allow reasonable legislative consideration. While I do not decide for all time that respondents' claim should not be recognized, I acknowledge the legislative institutional competence as the better one to deal with that claim at this time.

Justice Ginsburg, concurring in the judgments.

I concur in the Court's judgments in these cases substantially for the reasons stated by Justice O'Connor in her concurring opinion.

Justice Breyer, concurring in the judgments.

I believe that Justice O'Connor's views, which I share, have greater legal significance than the Court's opinion suggests. I join her separate opinion, except insofar as it joins the majority....

I agree with the Court in Vacco v. Quill that the articulated state interests justify the distinction drawn between physician assisted suicide and withdrawal of life-support. I also agree with the Court that the critical question in both of the cases before us is whether "the 'liberty' specially protected by the Due Process Clause includes a right" of the sort that the respondents assert.... I do not agree, however, with the Court's formulation of that claimed "liberty" interest. The Court describes it as a "right to commit suicide with another's assistance." But I would not reject the respondents' claim without considering a different formulation, for which our legal tradition may provide greater support. That formulation would use words roughly like a "right to die with dignity." But irrespective of the exact words used, at its core would lie personal control over the manner of death, professional medical assistance, and the avoidance of unnecessary and severe physical suffering—combined.

As Justice Souter points out, Justice Harlan's dissenting opinion in Poe v. Ullman, 367 U.S. 497 (1961), offers some support for such a claim. In that opinion, Justice Harlan referred to the "liberty" that the Fourteenth Amendment protects as including "a freedom from all substantial arbitrary impositions and purposeless restraints" and also as recognizing that "certain interests require particularly careful scrutiny of the state needs asserted to justify their abridgment." ... The "certain interests" to which Justice Harlan referred may well be similar (perhaps identical) to the rights, liberties, or interests that the Court today, as in the past, regards as "fundamental." ...

... [R]espondents ... argue that one can find a "right to die with dignity" by examining the protection the law has provided for related, but not identical, interests relating to personal dignity, medical treatment, and freedom from state-inflicted pain....

I do not believe, however, that this Court need or now should decide whether or a not such a right is "fundamental." That is because, in my view, the avoidance of severe physical pain (connected with death) would have to comprise an essential part of any successful claim and because, as Justice O'Connor points out, the laws before us do not force a dying person to undergo that kind of pain. Rather, the laws of New York and of Washington do not prohibit doctors from providing patients with drugs sufficient to control pain despite the risk that those drugs themselves will kill.... And under these circumstances the laws of New York and Washington would overcome any remaining significant interests and would be justified, regardless.

. . .

Were the legal circumstances different—for example, were state law to prevent the provision of palliative care, including the administration of drugs as needed to avoid pain at the end of life—then the law's impact upon serious and otherwise unavoidable physical pain (accompanying death) would be more directly at issue. And as Justice O'Connor suggests, the Court might have to revisit its conclusions in these cases.

COUNTY OF SACRAMENTO v. LEWIS, 523 U.S. 833 (1998). The Court held that a police officer involved in a high-speed car chase aimed at apprehending a criminal suspect does not violate substantive due process by causing a death through deliberate or reckless indifference to life, for "in such circumstances only a purpose to cause harm unrelated to the legitimate object of arrest will satisfy the element of arbitrary conduct shocking to the conscience, necessary for a due process violation." Noting that with respect to the core due process concept of "protection against arbitrary action" the "criteria to identify what is fatally arbitrary" differ as between legislative and executive action, Justice Souter's majority opinion identified "the cognizable level of executive abuse of power as that which shocks the conscience." Deliberate indifference might shock the conscience in a custodial prison situation where "forethought about an inmate's welfare is not only feasible but obligatory under a regime that incapacitates a prisoner to exercise ordinary responsibility for his own welfare[,]" but "a much higher standard of fault than deliberate indifference has to be shown for officer liability in a prison riot" and similar considerations of lack of time for "unhurried judgments" or "repeated reflection" led the Court to conclude that "when unforeseen circumstances demand an officer's instant judgment, even precipitate recklessness fails to inch close enough to harmful purpose to spark the [requisite] shock. . . ."

Justice Scalia, joined by Justice Thomas, complained in an opinion concurring in the judgment that the majority had now embraced an inappropriate "highly subjective substantive-due-process methodolog[y]" in direct contradiction of its rejection of both Justice Souter's concurrence, and the "shocks the conscience" test, in Washington v. Glucksberg, *supra*. Justice Scalia found the application of that test "only to executive action ... original with today's opinion[,]" and while happy to limit its use, he found it a "puzzlement why substantive due process protects some liberties against executive officers but not against legislatures." He urged that adherence to *Glucksberg* required asking, not "whether the police conduct here at issue shocks my unelected conscience"—an inquiry that would allow "not judicial review but judicial governance"—but "whether our Nation has traditionally protected the right" asserted. The absence of "textual or historical support" for an alleged due process right to be free from deliberate or reckless indifference to life in this sort of high-speed car chase should have been the basis of the Court's decision, he concluded.

For the majority, Justice Souter responded in a footnote that Justice Scalia had misperceived a conflict with *Glucksberg*, because there "the differences of opinion turned on the issues of how much history indicating recognition of the asserted right, viewed at what level of specificity, is necessary to support the finding of a substantive due process right entitled to prevail over state legislation." By contrast, "a case challenging executive action on substantive due process grounds ... presents an issue antecedent to any question about the need for historical examples of enforcing a liberty interest of the sort claimed. For executive action challenges raise a particular need to preserve the constitutional proportions of constitutional claims, lest the Constitution be demoted to ... a font of tort law. Thus, in a due process challenge to executive action, the threshold question is whether the behavior of the governmental officer is so egregious, so outrageous, that it may fairly be said to shock the contemporary conscience. That judgment may be informed by a history of liberty protection, but it necessarily reflects an understanding of traditional executive behavior, of contemporary practice, and of the standards of blame generally applied to them. Only if the necessary condition of egregious behavior were satisfied would there be a possibility of recognizing a substantive due process right to be free of such executive action, and only then might there be a debate about the sufficiency of historical examples of enforcement of the right claimed, or its recognition in other ways. ...In sum, the difference of opinion in *Glucksberg* was about the need for historical examples of recognition of the claimed liberty protection at some appropriate level of specificity. In an executive action case, no such issue can arise if the conduct does not reach the degree of the egregious."

Justice Kennedy, joined by Justice O'Connor—comprising two of the six Justices joining the majority opinion—filed a concurring opinion to explain "the objective character of our substantive due process analysis." Opining that the "shocks the conscience" test "has the unfortunate connotation of a standard laden with subjective assessments [and thus] must be viewed with considerable skepticism[,]" he nonetheless maintained that it "can be used to mark the beginning point in asking whether or not the objective character of certain conduct is consistent with our traditions, precedents, and historical understanding of the Constitution and its meaning":

"That said, it must be added that history and tradition are the starting point, but not in all cases the ending point of the substantive due process inquiry. There is room as well for an objective assessment of the necessities of law enforcement, in which the police must be given substantial latitude and discretion, acknowledging, of course, the primacy of the interest in life which the State, by the Fourteenth Amendment, is bound to respect. I agree with the Court's assessment of the State's interests in this regard...."

"Though I share Justice Scalia's concerns about using the phrase 'shocks the conscience' in a manner suggesting that it is a self-defining test, the reasons the Court gives in support of its judgment go far toward establishing that objective considerations, including history and precedent, are the controlling principle, regardless of whether the State's action is legislative or executive in character. To decide this case, ... [i]t suffices to conclude that neither our legal traditions nor the present needs of law enforcement justify finding a due process violation when unintended injuries occur after the police pursue a suspect who disobeys their lawful order to stop."

CHAPTER 10

THE EQUAL PROTECTION CLAUSE AND THE REVIEW OF THE REASONABLENESS OF LEGISLATION

SECTION 2. SOCIAL AND ECONOMIC REGULATORY LEGISLATION

Page 688. Add after Heller v. Doe:

CENTRAL STATE UNIVERSITY v. AMERICAN ASSOCIATION OF UNIVERSITY PROFESSORS, 119 S.Ct. 1162 (1999). An Ohio statute aimed at increasing the time that public university professors spent teaching required development of an instructional workload policy that would be exempt from collective bargaining. In a suit brought by the professors' collective bargaining agent, a majority of the Ohio Supreme Court held that the statute denied the professors equal protection of the laws, because no evidence in the record linked collective bargaining to a decline in teaching and the State had failed to demonstrate "any rational basis for singling out university faculty members as the only public employees ... precluded from bargaining over their workload." The Supreme Court summarily reversed per curiam, finding

> "that the Ohio Supreme Court's holding cannot be reconciled with the requirements of the Equal Protection Clause.... One of the statute's objectives was to increase the time spent by faculty in the classroom; the imposition of a faculty workload policy not subject to collective bargaining was an entirely rational step to accomplish this objective. The legislature could quite reasonably have concluded that the policy animating the law would have been undercut and likely varied if it were subject to collective bargaining.

> "The fact that the record before the Ohio courts did not show that collective bargaining in the past had lead to the decline in classroom time for faculty does not detract from the rationality of the legislative decision.... The legislature wanted a uniform workload policy to be in place by a certain date. It could properly conclude that collective bargaining about that policy in the future would interfere with the attainment of this end. Under our precedent, this is sufficient to sustain the exclusion of university professors from the otherwise general collective-bargaining scheme for public employees."

Justice Ginsburg's concurring opinion, joined by Justice Breyer, noted both "that a summary disposition is not a fit occasion for elaborate discussion of our rational basis standards of review" and that "the Ohio Supreme Court is of course at liberty to resolve the matter under the Ohio Constitution."

In dissent, Justice Stevens indicated that he believed the Court should have denied review, because the case had "little, if any, national significance" and because "[s]even of the eleven Ohio judges who reviewed the case concluded that the Ohio statute violated the Ohio Constitution." He objected as well to summary decision and in any event purported to

"identify a serious flaw in the Court's mechanistic analysis. The Court assumes that the question improperly answered by the Ohio Supreme Court is whether collective bargaining may interfere with the attainment of a uniform workload policy. But that is not the issue, because this case involves the Equal Protection Clause, and not the principles of substantive due process.

"The question posed by this case is whether there is a rational basis for discriminating against faculty members by depriving them of bargaining assistance that is available to all other public employees in the State of Ohio. Even the Court's speculation about the possible adverse consequences of collective bargaining about faculty workload does not explain why collective bargaining about the workloads of all other public employees might not give rise to the same adverse consequences arising from lack of state-wide uniformity. Indeed, I would suppose that the interest in protecting the academic freedom of university faculty members might provide a rational basis for giving them more bargaining assistance than other public employees. In any event, no one has explained why there is a rational basis for concluding that they should receive less."

SECTION 3. Suspect Classifications

C. Classifications Based on Gender

Page 784. Add after United States v. Virginia:

Miller v. Albright

523 U.S. 420, 118 S.Ct. 1428, 140 L.Ed.2d 575 (1998).

Justice Stevens announced the judgment of the Court and delivered an opinion, in which The Chief Justice joined.

There are "two sources of citizenship, and two only: birth and naturalization." United States v. Wong Kim Ark, 169 U.S. 649, 702 (1898). Within the former category, the Fourteenth Amendment of the Constitution guarantees that every person "born in the United States, and subject to the jurisdiction thereof, becomes at once a citizen of the United States, and needs no naturalization." 169 U.S., at 702. Persons not born in the United States acquire citizenship by birth only as provided by Acts of Congress. Id., at 703.

The petitioner in this case challenges the constitutionality of the statutory provisions governing the acquisition of citizenship at birth by children born out of wedlock and outside of the United States. The specific challenge is to the distinction drawn by § 309 of the Immigration and Nationality Act (INA), 66 Stat. 238, as amended, 8 U.S.C. § 1409, between the child of an alien father and a citizen mother, on the one hand, and the child of an alien mother and a citizen father, on the other. Subject to residence requirements for the citizen parent, the citizenship of the former is established at birth; the citizenship of the latter is not established unless and until either the father or his child takes certain affirmative steps to create or confirm their relationship. Petitioner contends that the statutory requirement that those steps be taken while the child is a minor violates the Fifth Amendment because the statute contains no limitation on the time within which the child of a citizen mother may prove that she became a citizen at birth.

We find no merit in the challenge because the statute does not impose any limitation on the time within which the members of either class of children may prove that they qualify for citizenship. It does establish different qualifications for citizenship for the two classes of children, but we are persuaded that the qualifications for the members of each of those classes, so far as they are implicated by the facts of this case, are well supported by valid governmental interests. We therefore conclude that the statutory distinction is neither arbitrary nor invidious.

I

[Petitioner, Lorelyn Penero Miller, was born out of wedlock in the Phillipines in 1970 to Luz Penero, a Filipino national.] At least until after her 21st birthday, she never lived in the United States. . . .

Petitioner's father, Charlie Miller, is an American citizen residing in Texas. He apparently served in the United States Air Force and was stationed in the Philippines at the time of petitioner's conception. . . . He never married petitioner's mother, and there is no evidence that he was in the Philippines at the time of petitioner's birth or that he ever returned there after completing his tour of duty. In 1992, Miller filed a[n unopposed] petition in a Texas court to establish his relationship with petitioner. The . . . court entered a "Voluntary Paternity Decree" finding him "to be the biological and legal father of Lorelyn Penero Miller." The decree provided that "[t]he parent-child relationship is created between the father and the child as if the child were born to the father and mother during marriage." . . .

[Petitioner's subsequent application] for registration as a United States citizen with the State Department . . . was . . . denied on the ground that the Texas decree did not satisfy "the requirements of Section 309(a)(4) INA, which requires that a child born out of wedlock be legitimated before age eighteen in order to acquire U.S. citizenship under Section 301(g) INA (formerly Section 301(a)(7) INA)."

II

[P]etitioner and her father [sued] the Secretary of State in [Federal] District Court [in Texas], seeking a judgment declaring [her to be] a citizen of the United States [with] the right to possess an American passport. They alleged that the INA's different treatment of citizen mothers and citizen fathers violated Mr. Miller's "right to equal protection under the laws by utilizing the suspect classification of gender without justification." [T]he District Court concluded that Mr. Miller did not have standing[,] dismissed him as a party[, and] transferred the case to the District Court for the District of Columbia, the site of the Secretary's residence. [T]hat court [denied relief on the view] that federal courts do not have the power to "grant citizenship." ...

The Court of Appeals ... affirmed, but on ... the merits....

. . .

III

... [S]tatutory distinctions between "illegitimate" and "legitimate" children ... are not encompassed in the question presented in this case and ... we therefore do not consider [them].

... § 1409(a), as amended in 1986, imposes four requirements concerning unmarried citizen fathers that must be satisfied to confer citizenship "as of the date of birth" on a person born out of wedlock to an alien mother in another country. Citizenship for such persons is established if:

"(1) a blood relationship between the person and the father is established by clear and convincing evidence,

"(2) the father had the nationality of the United States at the time of the person's birth,

"(3) the father (unless deceased) has agreed in writing to provide financial support for the person until the person reaches the age of 18 years, and

"(4) while the person is under the age of 18 years—

"(A) the person is legitimated under the law of the person's residence or domicile,

"(B) the father acknowledges paternity of the person in writing under oath, or

"(C) the paternity of the person is established by adjudication of a competent court." 8 U.S.C. § 1409(a).

Only the second of these four requirements is expressly included in § 1409(c), the provision applicable to unwed citizen mothers.... Petitioner ... argues that there is no rational basis for imposing the other three requirements on children of citizen fathers but not citizen mothers. The first requirement is not at issue here, however, because the Government does not question Mr. Miller's blood relationship with petitioner.

Moreover, even though the parties have disputed the validity of the third condition—and even though that condition is repeatedly targeted in Justice Breyer's dissent—we need not resolve that debate because it is unclear whether the requirement even applies in petitioner's case; it was added in 1986, after her birth, and she falls within a special interim provision that allows her to elect application of the pre-amendment § 1409(a), which required only legitimation before age 21. ...And even if the condition did apply to her claim of citizenship, the State Department's refusal to register petitioner as a citizen was expressly based on § 1409(a)(4). Indeed, since that subsection is written in the disjunctive, it is only necessary to uphold the least onerous of the three alternative methods of compliance to sustain the Government's position. Thus, the only issue presented by the facts of this case is whether the requirement in § 1409(a)(4)—that children born out of wedlock to citizen fathers, but not citizen mothers, obtain formal proof of paternity by age 18, either through legitimation, written acknowledgment by the father under oath, or adjudication by a competent court—violates the Fifth Amendment.

It is of significance that ... petitioner ... is not challenging the denial of an application for special status. She is contesting the Government's refusal to register and treat her as a citizen. If she were to prevail, the judgment in her favor would confirm her pre-existing citizenship rather than grant her rights that she does not now possess. We therefore agree with the Court of Appeals that she has standing to invoke the jurisdiction of the federal courts.... Moreover, because her claim relies heavily on the proposition that her citizen father should have the same right to transmit citizenship as would a citizen mother, we shall evaluate the alleged discrimination against him as well as its impact on her. See, e.g., Craig v. Boren, 429 U.S. 190, 193–197 (1976).

IV

Under the terms of the INA, the joint conduct of a citizen and an alien that results in conception is not sufficient to produce an American citizen, regardless of whether the citizen parent is the male or the female partner. If the two parties engage in a second joint act—if they agree to marry one another—citizenship will follow. The provision at issue in this case, however, deals only with cases in which no relevant joint conduct occurs after conception; it determines the ability of each of those parties, acting separately, to confer citizenship on a child born outside of the United States.

If the citizen is the unmarried female, she must first choose to carry the pregnancy to term and reject the alternative of abortion—an alternative that is available by law to many, and in reality to most, women around the world. She must then actually give birth to the child. Section 1409(c) rewards that choice and that labor by conferring citizenship on her child.

If the citizen is the unmarried male, he need not participate in the decision to give birth rather than to choose an abortion; he need not be present at the birth; and for at least 17 years thereafter he need not provide any parental support, either moral or financial, to either the mother or the child, in order to preserve his right to confer citizenship on the child pursuant to § 1409(a). In order retroactively to transmit his citizenship to the child as of the date of the child's birth, all that § 1409(a)(4) requires is that he be willing and able to acknowledge his paternity in writing under oath while the child is still a minor. 8 U.S.C. § 1409(a)(4)(B). In fact, § 1409(a)(4) requires even less of the unmarried father—that provision is alternatively satisfied if, before the child turns 18, its paternity "is established by adjudication of a competent court." § 1409(a)(4)(C). It would appear that the child could obtain such an adjudication absent any affirmative act by the father, and perhaps even over his express objection.

There is thus a vast difference between the burdens imposed on the respective parents of potential citizens born out of wedlock in a foreign land. It seems obvious that the burdens imposed on the female citizen are more severe than those imposed on the male citizen by § 1409(a)(4), the only provision at issue in this case. It is nevertheless argued that the male citizen and his offspring are the victims of irrational discrimination because § 1409(a)(4) is the product of " 'overbroad stereotypes about the relative abilities of men and women.' " We find the argument singularly unpersuasive.[11]

Insofar as the argument rests on the fact that the male citizen parent will "forever forfeit the right to transmit citizenship" if he does not come forward while the child is a minor, whereas there is no limit on the time within which the citizen mother may prove her blood relationship, the argument overlooks the difference between a substantive condition and a procedural limitation. The substantive conduct of the unmarried citizen mother that qualifies her child for citizenship is completed at the moment of birth; the relevant conduct of the unmarried citizen father or his child may occur at any time within 18 years thereafter. There is, however, no procedural hurdle that limits the time or the method by which either parent (or the child) may provide the State Department with evidence that the necessary steps were taken to transmit citizenship to the child.

The substantive requirement embodied in § 1409(a)(4) serves, at least in part, to ensure that a person born out of wedlock who claims citizenship by birth actually shares a blood relationship with an American citizen. . . .

There is no doubt that ensuring reliable proof of a biological relationship between the potential citizen and its citizen parent is an important governmental objective. See Trimble v. Gordon, 430 U.S. 762 (1977); Fiallo, 430 U.S., at 799, n. 8. Nor can it be denied that the male and female parents are differently situated in this respect. The blood relationship to the birth mother is immediately obvious and is typically established by hospital records and birth certificates; the relationship to the unmarried father may often be undisclosed and unrecorded in any contemporary public record. Thus, the requirement that the father make a timely written acknowledgment under oath, or that the child obtain a court adjudication of paternity, produces the rough equivalent of the documentation that is already available to evidence the blood relationship between the mother and the child. If the statute had required the citizen parent, whether male or female, to obtain appropriate formal documentation within 30 days after birth, it would have been "gender-neutral" on its face, even though in practical operation it would disfavor unmarried males because in virtually every case such a requirement would be superfluous for the mother. Surely the fact that the statute allows 18 years in which to provide evidence that is comparable to what the mother provides immediately after birth cannot be viewed as discriminating against the father or his child.

Nevertheless, petitioner reiterates the suggestion that it is irrational to require a formal act such as a written acknowledgment or a court adjudication because the advent of reliable genetic testing fully addresses the problem of proving paternity, and subsection (a)(1) already requires proof of paternity by clear and convincing evidence. . . . We respectfully disagree. Nothing in subsec-

---

[11] . . . Deference to the political branches dictates "a narrow standard of review of decisions made by the Congress or the President in the area of immigration and naturalization." Mathews v. Diaz, 426 U.S. 67, 82 (1976). Even if, as petitioner and her amici argue, the heightened scrutiny that normally governs gender discrimination claims applied in this context, see United States v. Virginia, 518 U.S. 515, ___–___(1996), we are persuaded that the requirement imposed by § 1409(a)(4) on children of unmarried male, but not female, citizens is substantially related to important governmental objectives.

tion (a)(1) requires the citizen father or his child to obtain a genetic paternity test. It is difficult, moreover, to understand why signing a paternity acknowledgment under oath prior to the child's 18th birthday is more burdensome than obtaining a genetic test, which is relatively expensive, normally requires physical intrusion for both the putative father and child, and often is not available in foreign countries. Congress could fairly conclude that despite recent scientific advances, it still remains preferable to require some formal legal act to establish paternity, coupled with a clear-and-convincing evidence standard to deter fraud. The time limitation, in turn, provides assurance that the formal act is based upon reliable evidence, and also deters fraud.[15] Congress is of course free to revise its collective judgment and permit genetic proof of paternity rather than requiring some formal legal act by the father or a court, but the Constitution does not now require any such change.

Section 1409 also serves two other important purposes that are unrelated to the determination of paternity: the interest in encouraging the development of a healthy relationship between the citizen parent and the child while the child is a minor; and the related interest in fostering ties between the foreign-born child and the United States. When a child is born out of wedlock outside of the United States, the citizen mother, unlike the citizen father, certainly knows of her child's existence and typically will have custody of the child immediately after the birth. Such a child thus has the opportunity to develop ties with its citizen mother at an early age, and may even grow up in the United States if the mother returns. By contrast, due to the normal interval of nine months between conception and birth, the unmarried father may not even know that his child exists, and the child may not know the father's identity. Section 1409(a)(4) requires a relatively easy, formal step by either the citizen father or his child that shows beyond doubt that at least one of the two knows of their blood relationship, thus assuring at least the opportunity for them to develop a personal relationship.

The facts of this very case provide a ready example of the concern. Mr. Miller and petitioner both failed to take any steps to establish a legal relationship with each other before petitioner's 21st birthday, and there is no indication in the record that they had any contact whatsoever before she applied for a United States passport. Given the size of the American military establishment that has been stationed in various parts of the world for the past half century, it is reasonable to assume that this case is not unusual. In 1970, when petitioner was born, about 683,000 service personnel were stationed in the Far East, 24,000 of whom were in the Philippines ... Of all Americans in the military at that time, only one percent were female. These figures, coupled with the interval between conception and birth and the fact that military personnel regularly return to the United States when a tour of duty ends, suggest that Congress had legitimate concerns about a class of children born abroad out of wedlock to alien mothers and to American servicemen who would not necessarily know about, or be known by, their children. It was surely reasonable when the INA was enacted in 1952, and remains equally reasonable today, for Congress to condition the award of citizenship to such children on an act that demonstrates, at a minimum, the possibility that those who become citizens

---

[15] Once a child reaches the legal age of majority, a male citizen could make a fraudulent claim of paternity on the person's behalf without any risk of liability for child support.

will develop ties with this country—a requirement that performs a meaningful purpose for citizen fathers but normally would be superfluous for citizen mothers.

It is of course possible that any child born in a foreign country may ultimately fail to establish ties with its citizen parent and with this country, even though the child's citizen parent has engaged in the conduct that qualifies the child for citizenship.... [T]hat the interest in fostering ties with this country may not be fully achieved for either class of children does not qualify the legitimacy or the importance of that interest. If, as Congress reasonably may have assumed, the formal requirements in § 1409(a)(4) tend to make it just as likely that fathers will have the opportunity to develop a meaningful relationship with their children as does the fact that the mother knows of her baby's existence and often has custody at birth, the statute's effect will reduce, rather than aggravate, the disparity between the two classes of children.

We are convinced not only that strong governmental interests justify the additional requirement imposed on children of citizen fathers, but also that the particular means used in § 1409(a)(4) are well tailored to serve those interests. It is perfectly appropriate to require some formal act, not just any evidence that the father or his child know of the other's existence. Such a formal act, whether legitimation, written acknowledgment by the father, or a court adjudication, lessens the risk of fraudulent claims made years after the relevant conduct was required. As for the requirement that the formal act take place while the child is a minor, Congress obviously has a powerful interest in fostering ties with the child's citizen parent and the United States during his or her formative years. If there is no reliable, contemporaneous proof that the child and the citizen father had the opportunity to form familial bonds before the child turned 18, Congress reasonably may demand that the child show sufficient ties to this country on its own rather than through its citizen parent in order to be a citizen.

. . .

V

The words "stereotype," "stereotyping," and "stereotypical" are used repeatedly in petitioner's and her amici's briefs....

The gender equality principle that was implicated in those cases is only indirectly involved in this case for two reasons. First, the conclusion that petitioner is not a citizen rests on several coinciding factors, not just the gender of her citizen parent. On the facts of this case, even if petitioner's mother had been a citizen and her father had been the alien, petitioner would not qualify for citizenship because her mother has never been to the United States. Alternatively, if her citizen parent had been a female member of the Air Force and, like Mr. Miller, had returned to the States at the end of her tour of duty, § 1409 quite probably would have been irrelevant and petitioner would have become a citizen at birth by force of the Constitution itself. Second, it is not merely the sex of the citizen parent that determines whether the child is a citizen under the terms of the statute; rather, it is an event creating a legal relationship between parent and child—the birth itself for citizen mothers, but post-birth conduct for citizen fathers and their offspring. Nevertheless, we may assume that if the classification in § 1409 were merely the product of an outmoded stereotype, it would be invalid.

The "gender stereotypes" on which § 1409 is supposedly premised are (1) "that the American father is never anything more than the proverbial breadwinner who remains aloof from day-to-day child rearing duties," and (2) "that a mother will be closer to her child born out of wedlock than a father will be to his." Even disregarding the statute's separate, non-stereotypical purpose of ensuring reliable proof of a blood relationship, neither of those propositions fairly reflects the justifications for the classification actually at issue.

Section 1409(a)(4) is not concerned with either the average father or even the average father of a child born out of wedlock. It is concerned with a father (a) whose child was born in a foreign country, and (b) who is unwilling or unable to acknowledge his paternity, and whose child is unable or unwilling to obtain a court paternity adjudication. A congressional assumption that such a father and his child are especially unlikely to develop a relationship, and thus to foster the child's ties with this country, has a solid basis even if we assume that all fathers who have made some effort to become acquainted with their children are as good, if not better, parents than members of the opposite sex.

Nor does the statute assume that all mothers of illegitimate children will necessarily have a closer relationship with their children than will fathers. It does assume that all of them will be present at the event that transmits their citizenship to the child, that hospital records and birth certificates will normally make a further acknowledgment and formal proof of parentage unnecessary, and that their initial custody will at least give them the opportunity to develop a caring relationship with the child. Section 1409(a)(4)—the only provision that we need consider—is therefore supported by the undisputed assumption that fathers are less likely than mothers to have the opportunity to develop relationships, not simply, as Justice Breyer contends, that they are less likely to take advantage of that opportunity when it exists. These assumptions are firmly grounded and adequately explain why Congress found it unnecessary to impose requirements on the mother that were entirely appropriate for the father.

None of the premises on which the statutory classification is grounded can be fairly characterized as an accidental byproduct of a traditional way of thinking about the members of either sex. The biological differences between single men and single women provide a relevant basis for differing rules governing their ability to confer citizenship on children born in foreign lands. Indeed, it is the suggestion that simply because Congress has authorized citizenship at birth for children born abroad to unmarried mothers, it cannot impose any post-birth conditions upon the granting of citizenship to the foreign-born children of citizen fathers, that might be characterized as merely a byproduct of the strong presumption that gender-based legal distinctions are suspect. An impartial analysis of the relevant differences between citizen mothers and citizen fathers plainly rebuts that presumption.[26]

The judgment of the Court of Appeals is affirmed.

[26] ...Justice Scalia argues that petitioner's suit must be dismissed because the courts have "no power to provide the relief requested." Because we conclude that there is no constitutional violation to remedy, we express no opinion on this question.

Justice O'Connor, with whom Justice Kennedy joins, concurring in the judgment.

This Court has long applied a presumption against third-party standing as a prudential limitation on the exercise of federal jurisdiction.... The statute ... accords differential treatment to fathers and mothers, not to sons and daughters. Thus, although petitioner is clearly injured by the fact that she has been denied citizenship, the discriminatory impact of the provision falls on petitioner's father, Charlie Miller, who is no longer a party to this suit. Consequently, I do not believe that we should consider petitioner's gender discrimination claim.

. . .

Although petitioner cannot raise her father's rights, she may raise her own.... Her challenge, however, triggers only rational basis scrutiny....

Given that petitioner cannot raise a claim of discrimination triggering heightened scrutiny, she can argue only that § 1409 irrationally discriminates between illegitimate children of citizen fathers and citizen mothers. Although I do not share Justice Stevens' assessment that the provision withstands heightened scrutiny, I believe it passes rational scrutiny for the reasons he gives for sustaining it under the higher standard. It is unlikely, in my opinion, that any gender classifications based on stereotypes can survive heightened scrutiny, but under rational scrutiny, a statute may be defended based on generalized classifications unsupported by empirical evidence.... This is particularly true when the classification is adopted with reference to immigration, an area where Congress frequently must base its decisions on generalizations about groups of people.

. . .

Justice Scalia, with whom Justice Thomas joins, concurring in the judgment.

I agree with the outcome in this case, but for a reason more fundamental than the one relied upon by Justice Stevens. In my view it makes no difference whether or not § 1409(a) passes "heightened scrutiny" or any other test members of the Court might choose to apply. The complaint must be dismissed because the Court has no power to provide the relief requested: conferral of citizenship on a basis other than that prescribed by Congress.

... Petitioner, having been born outside the territory of the United States, is an alien as far as the Constitution is concerned.... If there is no congressional enactment granting petitioner citizenship, she remains an alien.

. . .

By its plain language, § 1409(a) sets forth a precondition to the acquisition of citizenship under § 1401(g) by the illegitimate child of a citizen-father. Petitioner ... acknowledges that she did not meet the last two requirements of that precondition, §§ 1409(a)(3) and (4). She nonetheless asks for a "declaratory judgment that [she] is a citizen of the United States" and an order to the Secretary of State requiring the State Department to grant her application for citizenship, ... because the requirements she did not meet are not also imposed upon illegitimate children of citizen-mothers, and therefore violate the

Equal Protection Clause.[1] Even if we were to agree that the difference in treatment between illegitimate children of citizen-fathers and citizen-mothers is unconstitutional, we could not, consistent with the limited judicial power in this area, remedy that constitutional infirmity by declaring petitioner to be a citizen or ordering the State Department to approve her application for citizenship. "Once it has been determined that a person does not qualify for citizenship, ... the district court has no discretion to ignore the defect and grant citizenship." INS v. Pangilinan, 486 U.S. 875, 884 (1988)....

Judicial power over immigration and naturalization is extremely limited.... Because only Congress has the power to set the requirements for acquisition of citizenship by persons not born within the territory of the United States, federal courts cannot exercise that power under the guise of their remedial authority....

. . .

... I know of no instance ... in which this Court has severed an unconstitutional restriction upon the grant of immigration or citizenship. It is in my view incompatible with the plenary power of Congress over those fields for judges to speculate as to what Congress would have enacted if it had not enacted what it did—whether it would, for example, have preferred to extend the requirements of §§ 1409(a)(3) and (4) to mothers instead of eliminating them for fathers, or even to deny citizenship to illegitimate children entirely....

Justice Ginsburg, with whom Justice Souter and Justice Breyer join, dissenting.

As Justice Breyer convincingly demonstrates, 8 U.S.C. § 1409 classifies unconstitutionally on the basis of gender in determining the capacity of a parent to qualify a child for citizenship. The section rests on familiar generalizations: mothers, as a rule, are responsible for a child born out of wedlock; fathers unmarried to the child's mother, ordinarily, are not. The law at issue might have made custody or support the relevant criterion. Instead, it treats mothers one way, fathers another, shaping government policy to fit and reinforce the stereotype or historic pattern.

Characteristic of sex-based classifications, the stereotypes underlying this legislation may hold true for many, even most, individuals. But in prior decisions the Court has rejected official actions that classify unnecessarily and overbroadly by gender when more accurate and impartial functional lines can be drawn. While the Court is divided on Lorelyn Miller's standing to sue, a solid majority adheres to that vital understanding. As Justice O'Connor's opinion makes plain, distinctions based on gender trigger heightened scrutiny and "[i]t is unlikely ... that any gender classifications based on stereotypes can survive heightened scrutiny."

On the surface, § 1409 treats females favorably. Indeed, it might be seen as a benign preference, an affirmative action of sorts. Compare Mississippi Univ. for Women v. Hogan, 458 U.S. 718, 731, and n. 17 (1982) with id., at 740–744 (Powell, J., dissenting). Two Justices today apparently take this view. Justice Stevens' opinion, in which The Chief Justice joins, portrays § 1409 as

---

[1] ... I accept petitioner's third-party standing....

helpfully recognizing the different situations of unmarried mothers and fathers during the pre-natal period and at birth, and fairly equalizing the "burdens" that each parent bears. But pages of history place the provision in real-world perspective. Section 1409 is one of the few provisions remaining in the United States Code that uses sex as a criterion in delineating citizens' rights. It is an innovation in this respect: During most of our Nation's past, laws on the transmission of citizenship from parent to child discriminated adversely against citizen mothers, not against citizen fathers.

I

[Justice Ginsburg's extensive review of the history of gender distinctions found in federal statutes concerning naturalization and citizenship included the following:]

... [I]n 1855, Congress clarified that citizenship would pass to children born abroad only when the father was a United States citizen....

. . .

Women's inability to transmit their United States citizenship to children born abroad was one among many gender-based distinctions drawn in our immigration and nationality laws. The woman who married a foreign citizen risked losing her United States nationality.... In 1907, Congress ... provided by statute that a female United States citizen automatically lost her citizenship upon marriage to an alien.... This Court upheld the statute, noting that "[t]he identity of husband and wife is an ancient principle of our jurisprudence." Mackenzie v. Hare, 239 U.S. 299, 311 (1915).

. . .

... Congress treated wives and children of male United States citizens or immigrants benevolently. The 1855 legislation automatically granted citizenship to women who married United States citizens.... Under an 1804 statute, if a male alien died after completing the United States residence requirement but before actual naturalization, his widow and children would be "considered as citizens." ... That 1804 measure granted no corresponding dispensation to the husband and children of an alien woman. In addition, Congress provided statutory exemptions to entry requirements for the wives and children of men but not for the husbands and children of women....

In 1934, Congress ... terminated the discrimination against United States citizen mothers in regard to children born abroad....

The 1934 Act's equal respect for the citizenship stature of mothers and fathers of children born abroad did not remain unmodified. [T]he Nationality Act of 1940 ... replaced the ... single provision on citizenship of children born abroad with an array of provisions that turned on whether the child was born in an outlying possession of the United States, whether one or both of the child's parents were United States citizens, and whether the child was born in or out of wedlock. The 1940 Act preserved Congress' earlier recognition of parental equality in regard to children born in wedlock, but established a different regime for children born out of wedlock, one that disadvantaged United States citizen fathers and their children.

Subsequent legislation retained the gender lines drawn in the 1940 Act....
In 1986, ... Congress added further gender-based differentials ... that ...
permitted substitution of a written acknowledgment under oath or adjudication
of paternity prior to age 18 in place of formal legitimation. To that extent,
Congress eased access to citizenship by a child born abroad out of wedlock to a
United States citizen father. At the same time, however, Congress imposed on
such a child two further requirements: production of clear and convincing
evidence of paternity, also a written statement from the father promising
support until the child turned 18. The requirements for a child of a United
States citizen mother remained the same ... No substantive change has been
made since 1986 in the law governing citizenship of children born abroad out of
wedlock.

II

The history of the treatment of children born abroad to United States
citizen parents counsels skeptical examination of the Government's prime
explanation for the gender line drawn by § 1409—the close connection of
mother to child, in contrast to the distant or fleeting father-child link. Or, as
Justice Stevens puts it, a mother's presence at birth, identification on the birth
certificate, and likely "initial custody" of the child give her an "opportunity to
develop a caring relationship with the child," which Congress legitimately could
assume a father lacks. For most of our Nation's past, Congress demonstrated
no high regard or respect for the mother-child affiliation. It bears emphasis,
too, that in 1934, when Congress allowed United States citizen mothers to
transmit their citizenship to their foreign-born children, Congress simulta-
neously and for the first time required that such children (unless both parents
were citizens) fulfill a residence requirement.... Congress largely relied on a
residence requirement, not the sex of the child's citizen parent, to assure an
abiding affiliation with the United States....

Even if one accepts at face value the Government's current rationale, it is
surely based on generalizations (stereotypes) about the way women (or men)
are. These generalizations pervade the opinion of Justice Stevens, which
constantly relates and relies on what "typically," or "normally," or "probably"
happens "often."

We have repeatedly cautioned, however, that when the Government controls "gates to opportunity," it "may not exclude qualified individuals based on
'fixed notions concerning the roles and abilities of males and females.' "United
States v. Virginia, 518 U.S. 515,——(1996) (quoting Mississippi Univ. for
Women v. Hogan, 458 U.S. 718, 725 (1982))....

. . .

**Justice Breyer, with whom Justice Souter and Justice Ginsburg
join, dissenting.**

... The statutes [before us] require (1) that the American parent promise
to provide financial support for the child until the child is 18, and (2) that the
American parent (or a court) legitimate or formally acknowledge the child
before the child turns 18—if and only if the American parent is the father, but
not if the parent is the mother.

What sense does it make to apply these latter two conditions only to fathers and not to mothers in today's world—where paternity can readily be proved and where women and men both are likely to earn a living in the workplace? As Justice O'Connor has observed, and as a majority of the Court agrees, "[i]t is unlikely . . . that any gender classifications based on stereotypes can survive heightened scrutiny." These two gender-based distinctions lack the "exceedingly persuasive" support that the Constitution requires. United States v. Virginia, 518 U.S. 515, 530 (1996). Consequently, the statute that imposes them violates the Fifth Amendment's "equal protection" guarantee. See Bolling v. Sharpe, 347 U.S. 497, 500 (1954).

. . .

II

[Justice Breyer here concluded that petitioner had standing to raise her father's equal protection claims and that there was no impediment to a federal court granting her the relief she sought] for, once the two unconstitutional clauses are excised from the statute, that statute operates automatically to confer citizenship upon Lorelyn "at birth." 8 U.S.C. § 1401. . . .

Nor do I agree with Justice O'Connor's determination that "rational scrutiny" must apply to Lorelyn's assertion of her own rights. Lorelyn belongs to a class made up of children of citizen-fathers, whom the law distinguishes from the class of children of citizen-mothers, solely on grounds of the parent's gender. This Court, I assume, would use heightened scrutiny were it to review discriminatory laws based upon ancestry, say laws that denied voting rights or educational opportunity based upon the religion, or the racial make-up, of a parent or grandparent. And, if that is so, I am not certain that it makes a significant difference whether one calls the rights at issue those of Lorelyn or of her father. . . .

Regardless, like Justice O'Connor, I "do not share," and thus I believe a Court majority does not share, "Justice Stevens' assessment that the provision withstands heightened scrutiny." I also agree with Justice O'Connor that "[i]t is unlikely" that "gender classifications based on stereotypes can survive heightened scrutiny," a view shared by at least five members of this Court. Indeed, for reasons to which I shall now turn, we must subject the provisions here at issue to "heightened scrutiny." And those provisions cannot survive.

III

This case is about American citizenship and its transmission from an American parent to his child. The right of citizenship, as this Court has said, is "a most precious right." Kennedy v. Mendoza–Martinez, 372 U.S. 144, 159 (1963). . . .

Further, the tie of parent to child is a special one, which in other circumstances by itself has warranted special constitutional protection. See, e.g., Wisconsin v. Yoder, 406 U.S. 205 (1972); Pierce v. Society of Sisters, 268 U.S. 510 (1925); Meyer v. Nebraska, 262 U.S. 390 (1923); see also Skinner v. Oklahoma ex rel. Williamson, 316 U.S. 535 (1942).

Moreover, American statutory law has consistently recognized the rights of American parents to transmit their citizenship to their children. . . .

Finally, the classification at issue is gender-based, and we have held that, under the equal protection principle, such classifications may not rest on generalizations about the different capacities of males and females when neutral categories would serve the legislature's end. United States v. Virginia, 518 U.S., at 540–546.

These circumstances mean that courts should not diminish the quality of review—that they should not apply specially lenient standards—when they review these statutes. The statutes focus upon two of the most serious of human relationships, that of parent to child and that of individual to the State. They tie each to the other, transforming both while strengthening the bonds of loyalty that connect family with Nation. Yet because they confer the status of citizenship "at birth," they do not involve the transfer of loyalties that underlies the naturalization of aliens, where precedent sets a more lenient standard of review. See Fiallo v. Bell, 430 U.S. 787 (1977).

To the contrary, the same standard of review must apply when a married American couple travel abroad or temporarily work abroad and have a child as when a single American parent has a child born abroad out of wedlock. If the standard that the law applies is specially lenient, then statutes conferring citizenship upon these children could discriminate virtually free of independent judicial review. And as a result, many such children, lacking citizenship, would be placed outside the domain of basic constitutional protections. Nothing in the Constitution requires so anomalous a result.

I recognize that, ever since the Civil War, the transmission of American citizenship from parent to child, *jus sanguinis*, has played a role secondary to that of the transmission of citizenship by birthplace, *jus soli*.... That lesser role reflects the fact that the Fourteenth Amendment's Citizenship Clause does not mention statutes that might confer citizenship "at birth" to children of Americans born abroad.... But that omission, though it may give Congress the power to decide whether or not to extend citizenship to children born outside the United States, ... does not justify more lenient "equal protection" review of statutes that embody a congressional decision to do so.

Nothing in the language of the Citizenship Clause argues for less close scrutiny of those laws conferring citizenship at birth that Congress decides to enact. Nor have I found any support for a lesser standard in either the history of the Clause or its purpose. To the contrary, those who wrote the Citizenship Clause hoped thereby to assure that courts would not exclude newly freed slaves—born within the United States—from the protections the Fourteenth Amendment provided, including "equal protection of the laws." ... They took special care, lest deprivation of citizenship undermine the Amendment's guarantee of "equal protection of the laws." Care is no less necessary when statutes, transferring citizenship between American parent and child, make the child a citizen "at birth." How then could the Fourteenth Amendment itself provide support for a diminished standard of review?

Nor have I found any such support in the history of the jus sanguinis statutes....

The history of these statutes does reveal considerable discrimination against women, particularly from 1855 to 1934. But that discrimination then cannot justify this discrimination now, when much discrimination that the law once tolerated, including "de jure segregation and the total exclusion of women from juries," is "now unconstitutional even though [it] once coexisted with the

Equal Protection Clause." J.E.B. v. Alabama ex rel. T.B., 511 U.S. 127, 142, n. 15 (1994).

Neither have I found case law that could justify use here of a more lenient standard of review. Justice Stevens points out that this Court has said it will apply a more lenient standard in matters of " 'immigration and naturalization.' " Ante, at 1437, n. 11 (quoting Mathews v. Diaz, 426 U.S. 67, 82, 96 S.Ct. 1883, 1892–1893, 48 L.Ed.2d 478 (1976)). But that language arises in a case involving aliens. The Court did not say it intended that phrase to include statutes that confer citizenship "at birth." And Congress does not believe that this kind of citizenship involves "naturalization." 8 U.S.C. § 1101(a)(23) ("The term 'naturalization' means the conferring of nationality of a state upon a person after birth, by any means whatsoever") (emphasis added). The Court to my knowledge has never said, or held, or reasoned that statutes automatically conferring citizenship "at birth" upon the American child of American parents receive a more lenient standard of review.

The Court has applied a deferential standard of review in cases involving aliens, not in cases in which only citizens' rights were at issue. . . .

In sum, the statutes that automatically transfer American citizenship from parent to child "at birth" differ significantly from those that confer citizenship on those who originally owed loyalty to a different nation. To fail to recognize this difference, and consequently to apply an unusually lenient constitutional standard of review here, could deprive the children of millions of Americans, married and unmarried, working abroad, traveling, say, even temporarily to Canada or Mexico, of the most basic kind of constitutional protection. . . .

IV

If we apply undiluted equal protection standards, we must hold the two statutory provisions at issue unconstitutional. . . .

Distinctions of this kind—based upon gender—are subject to a " 'strong presumption' " of constitutional invalidity. Virginia, 518 U.S., at 532. . . . The Equal Protection Clause permits them only if the Government meets the "demanding" burden of showing an " 'exceedingly persuasive' " justification for the distinction. Virginia, supra, at 533. . . . That distinction must further important governmental objectives, and the discriminatory means employed must be "substantially related" to the achievement of those objectives. Virginia, supra, at 533. . . . This justification "must be genuine, not hypothesized or invented post hoc in response to litigation." Virginia, 518 U.S., at 533. Further, "it must not rely on overbroad generalizations about the different talents, capacities, or preferences of males and females." . . . The fact that the statutes "discriminat[e] against males rather than against females" is beside the point. Mississippi Univ. for Women, 458 U.S., at 723.

The statutory distinctions here violate these standards. They depend for their validity upon the generalization that mothers are significantly more likely than fathers to care for their children, or to develop caring relationships with their children. But consider how the statutes work once one abandons that generalization as the illegitimate basis for legislative line-drawing we have held it to be. . . . First, assume that the American citizen is also the Caretaker Parent. The statute would then require a Male Caretaker Parent to acknowledge his child prior to the child's 18th birthday (or for the parent or child to obtain a court equivalent) and to provide financial support. It would not require a Female Caretaker Parent to do either. The gender-based distinction that would impose added burdens only upon the Male Caretaker Parent would serve no purpose at all. Second, assume that the American citizen is the Non–Caretaker Parent. In that circumstance, the statute would forgive a Female Non–Caretaker Parent from complying with the requirements (for formal acknowledgment and written promises to provide financial support) that it would impose upon a Male Non-Caretaker Parent. Again, the gender based distinction that would impose lesser burdens only upon the Female Non–Caretaker Parent would serve no purpose.

To illustrate the point, compare the family before us—Charlie, Lorelyn, and Luz—with an imagined family—Carlos, a Philippine citizen, Lucy, his daughter, and Lenora, Lucy's mother and an American citizen. Suppose that Lenora, Lucy's unmarried mother, returned to the United States soon after Lucy's birth, leaving Carlos to raise his daughter. Why, under those circumstances, should Lenora not be required to fulfill the same statutory requirements that here apply to Charlie? Alternatively, imagine that Charlie had taken his daughter Lorelyn back to the United States to raise. The statute would not make Lorelyn an American from birth unless Charlie satisfied its two conditions. But had our imaginary family mother, Lenora, taken her child Lucy back to the United States, the statute would have automatically made her an American from birth without anyone having satisfied the two conditions. The example suggests how arbitrary the statute's gender-based distinction is once one abandons the generalization that mothers, not fathers, will act as caretaker parents.

. . . Justice Stevens asserts that subsection (a)(4) serves two interests: first, "ensuring reliable proof of a biological relationship between the potential citizen and its citizen parent," and second, "encouraging" certain relationships or ties. . . . I have no doubt that these interests are important. But the relationship between the statutory requirements and those particular objectives is one of total misfit.

. . . I . . . do not understand the need for the prior-to–18 legitimation-or-acknowledgment requirement. When the statute was written, one might have seen the requirement as offering some protection against false paternity claims. But that added protection is unnecessary in light of inexpensive DNA testing that will prove paternity with certainty. . . .

Moreover, a different provision of the statute, subsection (a)(1), already requires proof of paternity by "clear and convincing evidence." No one contests the validity of that provision, and I believe that biological differences between men and women would justify its imposition where paternity is at issue. In light of that provision, subsection (a)(4)'s protection against false claims is not needed. . . .

. . .

[As for the knowledge-of-birth differential said to serve the purpose of establishing ties to the father and to the United States before the child is 18, t]he distance between this knowledge and the claimed objectives . . . is far too great to satisfy any legal requirement of tailoring or proportionality. And the assumption that this knowledge-of-birth could make a significant gender-related difference rests upon a host of unproved gender-related hypotheses. Simple knowledge of a child's existence may, or may not, be followed by the kinds of relationships for which Justice Stevens hopes. A mother or a father, knowing of a child's birth, may nonetheless fail to care for the child or even to acknowledge the child. A father with strong ties to the child may, simply by lack of knowledge, fail to comply with the statute's formal requirements. A father with weak ties might readily comply. Moreover, the statute does little to assure any tie for, as Justice Stevens acknowledges, a child might obtain an adjudication of paternity "absent any affirmative act by the father, and perhaps even over his express objection."

To make plausible the connection between the statute's requirement and the asserted "relationship" goals, Justice Stevens must find a factual scenario where a father's knowledge—equivalent to the mother's knowledge that she has given birth—could lead to the establishment of a more meaningful parenting relationship or tie to America. It therefore points to what one might term the "war baby" problem—the problem created by American servicemen fathering children overseas and returning to America unaware of the related pregnancy or birth. The statutory remedy before us, however, is disproportionately broad even when considered in relation to that problem. Justice Stevens refers to 683,000 service personnel stationed in the Far East in 1970 when Lorelyn was born. The statute applies, however, to all Americans who live or travel abroad, including the 3.2 million private citizens, and the 925,000 Federal Government employees, who live, or who are stationed, abroad—of whom today only 240,000 are active duty military employees, many of whom are women. U.S. Dept. of State, Private American Citizens Residing Abroad (Nov. 21, 1997).... Nor does the statute seem to have been aimed at the "war baby" problem, for the precursor to the provisions at issue was first proposed in a 1938 report and was first adopted in the Nationality Act of 1940, which was enacted before the United States entered World War II....

Nor is there need for the gender-based discrimination at issue here, for, were Congress truly interested in achieving the goals Justice Stevens posits in the way Justice Stevens suggests, it could simply substitute a requirement of knowledge-of-birth for the present subsection (a)(4); or it could distinguish between caretaker and non-caretaker parents, rather than between men and women. A statute that does not do so, but instead relies upon gender-based distinctions, appears rational only ... if one accepts the legitimacy of gender-based generalizations that, for example, would equate gender and caretaking—generalizations of a kind that this Court has previously found constitutionally impermissible....

For similar reasons, subsection (3) denies Charlie Miller "equal protection" of the laws. That subsection requires an American father to "agre[e] ... to provide financial support" for the child until the child "reaches the age of 18," but does not require the same of an American mother. I agree with the Government that this provision has as one objective helping to assure ties between father and child.... But I do not see why the same need does not exist with respect to a mother. And, where the American parent is the Non-Caretaker Parent, the need for such assurances would seem the same in respect to either sex. Where the American parent is the Caretaker Parent, there would seem no need for the assurance regardless of gender. Since either men or women may be caretakers, and since either men or women may be "breadwinners," one could justify the gender distinction only on the ground that more women are caretakers than men, and more men are "breadwinners" than women. This, again, is the kind of generalization that we have rejected as justifying a gender-based distinction in other cases....

For these reasons, I can find no "exceedingly persuasive" justification for the gender-based distinctions that the statute draws.

. . .

E.   "BENIGN" DISCRIMINATION: AFFIRMATIVE ACTION, QUOTAS, PREFERENCES BASED ON GENDER OR RACE

2.   CLASSIFICATIONS ADVANTAGING RACIAL MINORITIES

Page 887.   Add at end of subsection:

ABRAMS v. JOHNSON, 521 U.S. 74 (1997). The summary report of this case appears, infra on this page.

LAWYER v. DEPARTMENT OF JUSTICE, 521 U.S. 567 (1997). The summary report of this case appears, infra at p. 134.

HUNT v. CROMARTIE, 119 S.Ct. 1545 (1999). The summary report of this case appears, infra at p. 135.

F.   CLASSIFICATIONS DISADVANTAGING ALIENS

Page 896. Add at end of subsection:

Miller v. Albright

523 U.S. 420, 118 S.Ct. 1428, 140 L.Ed.2d 575 (1998).

[The report in this case appears supra, p. 110.]

SECTION 4.   PROTECTION OF PERSONAL LIBERTIES

B.   VOTING AND ELECTIONS

2.   LEGISLATIVE DISTRICTING

Page 983.   Add at end of subsection:

ABRAMS v. JOHNSON, 521 U.S. 74 (1997). On remand from Miller v. Johnson, supra, following a deadlock in the Georgia legislature—the House having adopted a new congressional reapportionment plan providing for two majority-minority districts and the Senate a plan with just one—the district court adopted a plan with one. This time black voters, joined by the United States, challenged the court's remedial plan for "making more changes than necessary to cure constitutional defects in the previous plan [and for] violating §§ 2 and 5 of the Voting Rights Act of 1965 . . . ." By the same 5–4 vote as in *Miller*, the Supreme Court rejected this attack.

Justice Kennedy's majority opinion recounted that the district court had found that another district in the remanded plan was invalid under *Miller*—a conclusion not challenged on this appeal—and had considered several proposed alternatives with two or three majority-minority districts, including a "late submission" from the Justice Department after the evidence closed. After noting "the Justice Department's thorough 'subversion of the redistricting process' since the 1990 census, [however, the district court] based its plan on the *State's 1972 and 1982 plans*"; looked to "Georgia's traditional redistricting principles"; considered "the possibility of creating a second majority-black district but decided doing so would require it to 'subordinate Georgia's traditional districting policies and consider race predominantly, to the exclusion of both constitutional norms and common sense"; and found that "Georgia did not have a black population of sufficient concentration to allow creation of a second majority-black district...." Under these circumstances, and emphasizing particularly that "[i]nterference by the Justice Department, leading the state legislature to act based on an overriding concern with race," rendered deference to post–1990 census state redistricting plans inappropriate, Justice Kennedy concluded that "the trial court acted well within its discretion in deciding it could not draw two majority-black districts without itself engaging in racial gerrymandering." Because "the District Court found, without clear error, that the black population was not sufficiently compact for a second majority-black district" and that there was "insufficient racial polarization in voting to meet the *Gingles* requirements"—a conclusion supported by the fact that "[a]ll three black incumbents won elections under the court plan, two in majority-white districts running against white candidates"—there was no § 2 violation. As for § 5, the "benchmark" for measuring retrogression could not be any of the plans containing two majority-black districts, because "appellants have not demonstrated it was possible to create a second majority-black district within constitutional bounds"; § 5 benchmarks in any event must be based on "plans that have been in effect"; and the 1992 plan, "constitutional defects and all," could not be used. Accordingly, the district court appropriately chose as its benchmark "the 1982 plan, in effect for a decade[,]" and "appellants have not shown that black voters in any particular district suffered a retrogression in their voting strength under the court plan measured against the 1982 plan."

Justice Breyer's dissent argued that the Georgia legislature's post–1990 redistricting plans expressed a preference for at least two majority-black districts and that, because a "two-district plan is not unconstitutional[,]" the majority was wrong not to follow that preference. He thought the district court and the majority improperly had discounted Georgia's plans as tainted by Justice Department interference, whereas the Department's pressure on the Georgia legislature was no more objectionable than other "political pressures" routinely applied in the redistricting process. Moreover, he disagreed with what he understood to be the majority's view "that a two-district plan ... would violate the Constitution as interpreted in *Miller*." He contended that a second compact majority-black district could have been created; noted that the district court had conceded "some degree of vote polarization"; and suggested that the district court had "asked the wrong question":

"... The question is not about whether the evidence proves § 2 *in fact requires* two majority-minority districts. The question is whether the evidence is strong enough to justify a legislature's reasonable belief that that was so. The record rather clearly demonstrates a 'strong basis in the evidence' for *believing* that § 2 or § 5 required two majority-minority districts. The Legislature thus could very reasonably have believed that was so. And, that is what I had believed the law, as set forth in this Court's opinions, required as legal justification for a district that otherwise would violate the basic predominant factor test of *Miller*.

"This legal distinction—between whether a plan really violates § 2 or might well violate § 2—may seem technical. But it is not. A legal rule that permits legislatures to take account of race only when § 2 *really* requires them to do so is a rule that shifts the power to redistrict from legislatures to federal courts (for only the latter can say what § 2 *really* requires). A rule that rests upon a reasonable view of the evidence (i.e., that permits the legislature to use race if it has a *'strong basis' for believing* it necessary to do so) is a rule that leaves at least a modicum of discretionary (race-related) redistricting authority in the hands of legislators. . . ."

Justice Breyer reiterated the dissenters' formerly expressed objections to the *Shaw* line of cases and suggested that "[t]his suit just exacerbates those concerns[,]" because "unlike other cases that use somewhat similar words [to "predominant racial motive"], the Court has not turned to other consider-ations, such as discriminatory intent, or vote dilution, or even a district's bizarre geographical shape, to help explain, or to limit the scope of, the words themselves." That made it "particularly difficult ... [for legislators] to find principled legal answers to what, in the redistricting context, are traditionally political questions [and] increase[d] the risk of significant judicial entanglement in the inherently political redistricting process."

LAWYER v. DEPARTMENT OF JUSTICE, 521 U.S. 567 (1997). Fol-lowing the 1990 census, the Department of Justice refused to preclear a Florida reapportionment plan for state legislative districts because it divided "political-ly cohesive minority populations" in one county area and failed to create a majority-minority district there. The Florida Supreme Court, after concluding that the legislature had reached an impasse in attempting to respond, revised the plan to include "an irregularly shaped Senate District 21, with a voting-age population 45.8% black and 9.4% hispanic and comprising portions of four counties in the Tampa Bay area." After the 1992 and 1994 elections under this Plan 330, Lawyer and others challenged District 21 in federal district court as violating equal protection. Settlement negotiations produced an agreement among the parties, except for Lawyer, to revise District 21 under a new Plan 386 (to "be used in state elections unless Florida adopted a new plan") that reduced its irregular shape "and would include a resident black voting age population reduced from 45.0% to 36.2%." The three-judge court, after seeking and receiving "specific assurances from lawyers for the President of the Senate and the Speaker of the House that they were authorized to represent their respective government bodies in the litigation and enter into the settlement proposed[,]" and after concluding that the plaintiffs had shown "a substantial 'evidentiary and legal' basis" for their challenge, approved the settlement despite Lawyer's objections "that the District Court was required to hold Plan 330 unconstitutional before it could adopt a new districting plan" and "that District 21, as redrawn in Plan 386, would still be unconstitutional because only race could explain its contours[.]" (One judge agreed with the former contention but found Plan 330 unconstitutional and Plan 386 constitutional.)

The Supreme Court affirmed in an opinion by Justice Souter, joined by the other consistent dissenters in this line of cases and by Chief Justice Rehnquist. On the facts of this case, the majority did not think it necessary for the district court to determine that Plan 330's District 21 was unconstitutional before approving the settlement. And the majority found no clear error—the proper standard of review—in the district court's conclusion "that Plan 386 did not subordinate traditional districting principles to race." "The District Court looked to the shape and composition of District 21 as redrawn in Plan 386 and found them 'demonstrably benign and satisfactorily tidy.' " The redrawn district did not stand out in any geographic or jurisdiction-splitting manner from numerous other state legislative districts, and as to composition,

"the District Court found that the residents of District 21 'regard themselves as a community.' Evidence indicated that District 21 comprises a predominantly urban, low-income population, the poorest of the nine districts in the Tampa Bay region and among the poorest districts in the State, whose white and black members alike share a similarly depressed economic condition, ... and interests that reflect it.... The fact that District 21 under Plan 386 is not a majority black district, the black voting-age population being 36.2%, supports the District Court's finding that the district is not a 'safe' one for black-preferred candidates, but one that 'offers to any candidate, without regard to race, the opportunity' to seek and be elected to office."

With respect to Lawyer's objection that it "contains a percentage of black voters significantly higher than the overall percentage of black voters in [the three] counties" from which it draws, the Court said:

"[W]e have never suggested that the percentage of black residents in a district may not exceed the percentage of black residents in any of the counties from which the district is created, and have never recognized similar racial composition of different political districts as being necessary to avoid an inference of racial gerrymandering in any one of them. Since districting can be difficult, after all, just because racial composition varies from place to place, and counties and voting districts do not depend on common principles of size and location, facts about the one do not as such necessarily entail conclusions about the other."

Justice Scalia's dissent, joined by Justices O'Connor, Kennedy and Thomas, did not "consider the constitutionality of the court-drawn district, Plan 386." In their view, the district court had made "an unprecedented intrusion upon state sovereignty" by never having determined that Plan 330's District 21 was in fact unconstitutional and by not having provided "the State an opportunity to do its own redrawing of the district to remedy whatever unconstitutional features it contained."

HUNT v. CROMARTIE, 119 S.Ct. 1545 (1999). After the Supreme Court ruled in *Shaw II* that North Carolina's Twelfth Congressional District constituted an unconstitutional racial gerrymander, the State redrew District 12 in 1997, reducing its black population below a majority, splitting fewer counties, and making it smaller. In a new suit challenging the redrawn district on the same ground, the district court granted the challengers' summary judgment motion, finding as "uncontroverted material facts" that "District 12 was drawn to collect precincts with high racial identification rather than political identification," that "more heavily Democratic precincts ... were bypassed in the drawing of District 12 and included in the surrounding congressional districts," and that "[t]he legislature disregarded traditional districting criteria."

The Supreme Court reversed. Reviewing the record, Justice Thomas, for the majority, noted that "*in toto*, appellees' [circumstantial] evidence tends to support an inference that the State drew its district lines with an impermissible racial motive—even though they presented no direct evidence of intent." Yet

"[t]he District Court nevertheless was only partially correct in stating that the material facts before it were uncontroverted. The legislature's motivation is itself a factual question.... Appellants asserted that the General Assembly drew its district lines with the intent to make District 12 a strong Democratic district. In support, they presented the after-the-fact affidavit testimony of the two members of the General Assembly responsible for developing the State's 1997 plan.... Those legislators further stated that, in crafting their districting law, they attempted to protect incumbents, to adhere to traditional districting criteria, and to preserve the existing partisan balance in the State's congressional delegation ....

"More important, we think, was the affidavit of an expert [who] reviewed racial demographics, party registration, and election result data (the number of people voting for Democratic candidates) .... [T]he data tended to support both a political and racial hypothesis.... He concluded that the State included the more heavily Democratic precinct much more often than the more heavily black precinct, and therefore, that the data as a whole supported a political explanation at least as well as, and somewhat better than, a racial explanation....

"[His] analysis ... support[s] an inference that the General Assembly did no more than create a district of strong partisan Democrats.... [Compared to appellees' evidence, his] more complete analysis [that considered actual voting results] was significant because it showed that in North Carolina, party registration and party preference do not always correspond.

"Accepting appellants' political motivation explanation as true, as the District Court was required to do in ruling on appellees' motion for summary judgment, ... appellees were not entitled to judgment as a matter of law. Our prior decisions have made clear that a jurisdiction may engage in constitutional political gerrymandering, even if it so happens that the most loyal Democrats happen to be black Democrats and even if the State were *conscious* of that fact. See Bush v. Vera, 517 U.S. 952, 968 (Thomas, J., concurring in judgment); *Shaw II*, 517 U.S., at 905; *Miller*, 515 U.S., at 916; *Shaw I*, 509 U.S., at 646. Evidence that blacks constitute even a supermajority in one congressional district while amounting to less than a plurality in a neighboring district will not, by itself, suffice to prove that a jurisdiction was motivated by race in drawing its district lines when the evidence also shows a high correlation between race and party preference.

"... While appellees' evidence might allow the District Court to find that the State acted with an impermissible racial motivation, despite the State's explanation as supported by the Peterson affidavit, it does not require that the court do so. All that can be said on the record before us is that motivation was in dispute...."

The majority would "not ... say that summary judgment in a plaintiff's favor will never be appropriate in a racial gerrymandering case sought to be proved exclusively by circumstantial evidence" and noted that "[p]erhaps, after trial, the evidence will support a finding that race was the State's predominant motive, but" it ruled that this case "was not suited for summary disposition."

In an opinion concurring in the judgment, Justice Stevens, joined by Justices Souter, Ginsburg and Breyer, wrote

"separately to emphasize the importance of two undisputed matters of fact that are firmly established by the historical record and confirmed by the record in this case.

"First, bizarre configuration is the traditional hallmark of the political gerrymander. . . .

"Second, . . . a great many registered Democrats in the South do not always vote for Democratic candidates in federal elections. . . . There was no need for expert testimony to establish the proposition that 'in North Carolina, party registration and party preference do not always correspond.'

. . .

"[A]ppellees' evidence may include nothing more than (i) a bizarre shape, which is equally consistent with either political or racial motivation, (ii) registration data, which are virtually irrelevant when actual voting results were available and which point in a different direction, and (iii) knowledge of the racial composition of the district. Because we do not have before us the question whether the District Court erred in denying the State's motion for summary judgment, I need not decide whether that circumstantial evidence even raises an inference of improper motive."

In a responsive footnote to Justice Stevens, Justice Thomas stated:

". . . We do not necessarily quarrel with the proposition that a district's unusual shape can give rise to an inference of political motivation. But we doubt that a bizarre shape equally supports a political inference and a racial one. . . ."

C. TRAVEL AND INTERSTATE MIGRATION, LENGTH OF STATE RESIDENCE, AND DISADVANTAGING NONRESIDENTS

1. Travel and Interstate Migration

Page 1003. Add at end of subsection:

Saenz v. Roe
___ U.S.___, 119 S.Ct. 1518, ___L.Ed.2d ___ (1999)

[The report in this case appears infra on this page.]

2. Length of State Residence Distinctions

Page 1014. Add before Williams v. Vermont:

Saenz v. Roe
___ U.S. ___, 119 S.Ct. 1518, ___ L.Ed.2d ___ (1999).

Justice Stevens delivered the opinion of the Court.

In 1992, California enacted a statute limiting the maximum welfare benefits available to newly arrived residents. The scheme limits the amount payable to a family that has resided in the State for less than 12 months to the amount payable by the State of the family's prior residence. The questions presented by this case are whether the 1992 statute was constitutional when it was enacted and, if not, whether an amendment to the Social Security Act enacted by Congress in 1996 affects that determination.

I

. . .

... In 1992, in order to make a relatively modest reduction in its vast welfare budget, the California Legislature enacted § 11450.03 of the state Welfare and Institutions Code ... to change the California AFDC program by limiting new residents, for the first year they live in California, to the benefits they would have received in the State of their prior residence. Because in 1992 a state program either had to conform to federal specifications or receive a waiver from the Secretary of Health and Human Services in order to qualify for federal reimbursement, § 11450.03 required approval by the Secretary to take effect. In October 1992, the Secretary issued a waiver purporting to grant such approval.

... [T]hree California residents who were eligible for AFDC benefits challeng[ed] the constitutionality of the durational residency requirement[, each] alleg[ing] that she had recently moved to California to live with relatives in order to escape abusive family circumstances [and] that her monthly AFDC grant for the ensuing 12 months would be substantially lower under § 11450.03 than if the statute were not in effect....

The District Court ... preliminarily enjoined implementation of the statute. The Court of Appeals summarily affirmed....

We granted the State's petition for certiorari [but] were ... unable to reach the merits because the Secretary's approval of § 11450.03 had been invalidated in a separate proceeding, and the State had acknowledged that the Act would not be implemented without further action by the Secretary. We vacated the judgment and directed that the case be dismissed. Anderson v. Green, 513 U.S. 557 (1995) (per curiam). Accordingly, § 11450.03 remained inoperative until after Congress enacted the Personal Responsibility and Work Opportunity Reconciliation Act of 1996 PRWORA, 110 Stat. 2105.

PRWORA replaced the AFDC program with TANF [Temporary Assistance to Needy Families]. The new statute expressly authorizes any State that receives a block grant under TANF to "apply to a family the rules (including benefit amounts) of the [TANF] program ... of another State if the family has moved to the State from the other State and has resided in the State for less than 12 months." 42 U.S.C. § 604(c) (1994 ed., Supp. II). With this federal statutory provision in effect, California no longer needed specific approval from the Secretary to implement § 11450.03....

... [Under the California rules,] the lower level of benefits applies regardless of whether the family was on welfare in the State of prior residence and regardless of the family's motive for moving to California. The instructions also explain that the residency requirement is inapplicable to families that recently arrived from another country.

II

[T]his action ... [presents] essentially the same claims asserted by the plaintiffs in *Anderson v. Green*, but also challeng[es] the constitutionality of PRWORA's approval of the durational residency requirement....

. . .

... [The District Court] again enjoined the implementation of the statute. [T]he Court of Appeals affirmed.... We now affirm.

III

The word "travel" is not found in the text of the Constitution. Yet the "constitutional right to travel from one State to another" is firmly embedded in our jurisprudence. United States v. Guest, 383 U.S. 745, 757 (1966). Indeed, as Justice Stewart reminded us in Shapiro v. Thompson, 394 U.S. 618 (1969), the right is so important that it is "assertable against private interference as well as governmental action ... a virtually unconditional personal right, guaranteed by the Constitution to us all." Id., at 643 (concurring opinion).

. . .

In this case California argues that § 11450.03 was not enacted for the impermissible purpose of inhibiting migration by needy persons and that, unlike the legislation reviewed in *Shapiro*, it does not penalize the right to travel because new arrivals are not ineligible for benefits during their first year of residence. California submits that, instead of being subjected to the strictest scrutiny, the statute should be upheld if it is supported by a rational basis and that the State's legitimate interest in saving over $10 million a year satisfies that test. [T]he United States ... has advanced the novel argument that the enactment of PRWORA allows the States to adopt a "specialized choice-of-law-type provision" that "should be subject to an intermediate level of constitutional review," merely requiring that durational residency requirements be "substantially related to an important governmental objective." The debate about the appropriate standard of review, together with the potential relevance of the federal statute, persuades us that it will be useful to focus on the source of the constitutional right on which respondents rely.

IV

The "right to travel" discussed in our cases embraces at least three different components. It protects the right of a citizen of one State to enter and to leave another State, the right to be treated as a welcome visitor rather than an unfriendly alien when temporarily present in the second State, and, for those travelers who elect to become permanent residents, the right to be treated like other citizens of that State.

... Given that § 11450.03 imposed no obstacle to respondents' entry into California, we think the State is correct when it argues that the statute does not directly impair the exercise of the right to free interstate movement. For the purposes of this case, therefore, we need not identify the source of that particular right in the text of the Constitution. The right of "free ingress and regress to and from" neighboring States, which was expressly mentioned in the text of the Articles of Confederation, may simply have been "conceived from the beginning to be a necessary concomitant of the stronger Union the Constitution created." Id., at 758.

The second component of the right to travel is, however, expressly protected by the text of the Constitution. The first sentence of Article IV, § 2, provides:

> "The Citizens of each State shall be entitled to all Privileges and Immunities of Citizens in the several States."

Thus, by virtue of a person's state citizenship, a citizen of one State who travels in other States, intending to return home at the end of his journey, is entitled to enjoy the "Privileges and Immunities of Citizens in the several States" that he visits. This provision ... provides important protections for nonresidents who enter a State whether to obtain employment, Hicklin v. Orbeck, 437 U.S. 518 (1978), to procure medical services, Doe v. Bolton, 410 U.S. 179, 200 (1973), or even to engage in commercial shrimp fishing, Toomer v. Witsell, 334 U.S. 385 (1948). Those protections are not "absolute," but the Clause "does bar discrimination against citizens of other States where there is no substantial reason for the discrimination beyond the mere fact that they are citizens of other States." Id., at 396. There may be a substantial reason for requiring the nonresident to pay more than the resident for a hunting license, see Baldwin v. Fish and Game Comm'n of Mont., 436 U.S. 371, 390–391 (1978), or to enroll in the state university, see Vlandis v. Kline, 412 U.S. 441, 445 (1973), but our cases have not identified any acceptable reason for qualifying the protection afforded by the Clause for "the 'citizen of State A who ventures into State B' to settle there and establish a home." *Zobel*, 457 U.S., at 74 (O'Connor, J., concurring in judgment). Permissible justifications for discrimination between residents and nonresidents are simply inapplicable to a nonresident's exercise of the right to move into another State and become a resident of that State.

What is at issue in this case, then, is this third aspect of the right to travel—the right of the newly arrived citizen to the same privileges and immunities enjoyed by other citizens of the same State. That right is protected not only by the new arrival's status as a state citizen, but also by her status as a citizen of the United States. That additional source of protection is plainly identified in the opening words of the Fourteenth Amendment:

> "All persons born or naturalized in the United States, and subject to the jurisdiction thereof, are citizens of the United States and of the State wherein they reside. No State shall make or enforce any law which shall abridge the privileges or immunities of citizens of the United States; ...."

Despite fundamentally differing views concerning the coverage of the Privileges or Immunities Clause of the Fourteenth Amendment, most notably expressed in the majority and dissenting opinions in the Slaughter–House Cases, 16 Wall. 36 (1872), it has always been common ground that this Clause protects the third component of the right to travel. Writing for the majority in the *Slaughter-House Cases*, Justice Miller explained that one of the privileges conferred by this Clause "is that a citizen of the United States can, of his own volition, become a citizen of any State of the Union by a *bona fide* residence therein, with the same rights as other citizens of that State." Id., at 80. Justice Bradley, in dissent, used even stronger language to make the same point:

> "The states have not now, if they ever had, any power to restrict their citizenship to any classes or persons. A citizen of the United States has a perfect constitutional right to go to and reside in any State he chooses, and to claim citizenship therein, and an equality of rights with every other citizen; and the whole power of the nation is pledged to sustain him in that right. He is not bound to cringe to any superior, or to pray for any act of grace, as a means of enjoying all the rights and privileges enjoyed by other citizens." Id., at 112–113.

That newly arrived citizens "have two political capacities, one state and one federal," adds special force to their claim that they have the same rights as others who share their citizenship. Neither mere rationality nor some intermediate standard of review should be used to judge the constitutionality of a state rule that discriminates against some of its citizens because they have been domiciled in the State for less than a year. The appropriate standard may be more categorical than that articulated in *Shapiro*, see supra, at ___-___, but it is surely no less strict.

V

Because this case involves discrimination against citizens who have completed their interstate travel, the State's argument that its welfare scheme affects the right to travel only "incidentally" is beside the point. Were we concerned solely with actual deterrence to migration, we might be persuaded that a partial withholding of benefits constitutes a lesser incursion on the right to travel than an outright denial of all benefits. See Dunn v. Blumstein, 405 U.S. 330, 339 (1972). But since the right to travel embraces the citizen's right to be treated equally in her new State of residence, the discriminatory classification is itself a penalty.

It is undisputed that respondents and the members of the class that they represent are citizens of California and that their need for welfare benefits is unrelated to the length of time that they have resided in California. We thus have no occasion to consider what weight might be given to a citizen's length of residence if the bona fides of her claim to state citizenship were questioned. Moreover, because whatever benefits they receive will be consumed while they remain in California, there is no danger that recognition of their claim will encourage citizens of other States to establish residency for just long enough to acquire some readily portable benefit, such as a divorce or a college education, that will be enjoyed after they return to their original domicile. See, e.g., Sosna v. Iowa, 419 U.S. 393 (1975); Vlandis v. Kline, 412 U.S. 441 (1973).

The classifications challenged in this case—and there are many—are defined entirely by (a) the period of residency in California and (b) the location of the prior residences of the disfavored class members. The favored class of beneficiaries includes all eligible California citizens who have resided there for at least one year, plus those new arrivals who last resided in another country or in a State that provides benefits at least as generous as California's. Thus, within the broad category of citizens who resided in California for less than a year, there are many who are treated like lifetime residents. And within the broad sub-category of new arrivals who are treated less favorably, there are many smaller classes whose benefit levels are determined by the law of the States from whence they came. To justify § 11450.03, California must therefore explain not only why it is sound fiscal policy to discriminate against those who have been citizens for less than a year, but also why it is permissible to apply such a variety of rules within that class.

These classifications may not be justified by a purpose to deter welfare applicants from migrating to California for three reasons. First, although it is reasonable to assume that some persons may be motivated to move for the purpose of obtaining higher benefits, the empirical evidence reviewed by the District Judge, which takes into account the high cost of living in California, indicates that the number of such persons is quite small—surely not large enough to justify a burden on those who had no such motive. Second, California has represented to the Court that the legislation was not enacted for any such reason.[19] Third, even if it were, as we squarely held in Shapiro v. Thompson, 394 U.S. 618 (1969), such a purpose would be unequivocally impermissible.

Disavowing any desire to fence out the indigent, California has instead advanced an entirely fiscal justification for its multitiered scheme. The enforcement of § 11450.03 will save the State approximately $10.9 million a year. The question is not whether such saving is a legitimate purpose but whether the State may accomplish that end by the discriminatory means it has chosen. An evenhanded, across-the-board reduction of about 72 cents per month for every beneficiary would produce the same result. But our negative answer to the question does not rest on the weakness of the State's purported fiscal justification. It rests on the fact that the Citizenship Clause of the Fourteenth Amendment expressly equates citizenship with residence: "That Clause does not provide for, and does not allow for, degrees of citizenship based on length of residence." *Zobel*, 457 U.S., at 69. It is equally clear that the Clause does not tolerate a hierarchy of 45 subclasses of similarly situated citizens based on the location of their prior residence.[20] Thus § 11450.03 is doubly vulnerable: Neither the duration of respondents' California residence, nor the identity of their prior States of residence, has any relevance to their need for benefits. Nor do those factors bear any relationship to the State's interest in making an equitable allocation of the funds to be distributed among its needy citizens. . . . In short, the State's legitimate interest in saving money provides no justification for its decision to discriminate among equally eligible citizens.

VI

The question that remains is whether congressional approval of durational residency requirements in the 1996 amendment to the Social Security Act somehow resuscitates the constitutionality of § 11450.03. That question is readily answered, for we have consistently held that Congress may not authorize the States to violate the Fourteenth Amendment. Moreover, the protection

[19] The District Court and the Court of Appeals concluded, however, that the "apparent purpose of § 11450.03 was to deter migration of poor people to California." Roe v. Anderson, 134 F.3d 1400, 1404 (C.A.9 1998).

[20] See Cohen, Discrimination Against New State Citizens: An Update, 11 Const. Comm. 73, 79 (1994) ("[J]ust as it would violate the Constitution to deny these new arrivals state citizenship, it would violate the Constitution to concede their citizenship in name only while treating them as if they were still citizens of other states").

afforded to the citizen by the Citizenship Clause of that Amendment is a limitation on the powers of the National Government as well as the States.

. . . Congress has no affirmative power to authorize the States to violate the Fourteenth Amendment and is implicitly prohibited from passing legislation that purports to validate any such violation. . . .

The Solicitor General does not unequivocally defend the constitutionality of § 11450.03. But he has argued that two features of PRWORA may provide a sufficient justification for state durational requirements to warrant further inquiry before finally passing on the section's validity, or perhaps that it is only invalid insofar as it applies to new arrivals who were not on welfare before they arrived in California.

He first points out that because the TANF program gives the States broader discretion than did AFDC, there will be significant differences among the States which may provide new incentives for welfare recipients to change their residences. He does not, however, persuade us that the disparities under the new program will necessarily be any greater than the differences under AFDC . . . . Moreover, we are not convinced that a policy of eliminating incentives to move to California provides a more permissible justification for classifying California citizens than a policy of imposing special burdens on new arrivals to deter them from moving into the State. Nor is the discriminatory impact of § 11450.03 abated by repeatedly characterizing it as "a sort of specialized choice-of-law rule." California law alone discriminates among its own citizens on the basis of their prior residence.

The Solicitor General also suggests that we should recognize the congressional concern addressed in the legislative history of PRWORA that the "States might engage in a 'race to the bottom' in setting the benefit levels in their TANF programs." Again, it is difficult to see why that concern should be any greater under TANF than under AFDC. The evidence reviewed by the District Court indicates that the savings resulting from the discriminatory policy, if spread equitably throughout the entire program, would have only a miniscule impact on benefit levels. Indeed, as one of the legislators apparently interpreted this concern, it would logically prompt the States to reduce benefit levels sufficiently "to encourage emigration of benefit recipients." But speculation about such an unlikely eventuality provides no basis for upholding § 11450.03.

Finally, the Solicitor General suggests that the State's discrimination might be acceptable if California had limited the disfavored subcategories of new citizens to those who had received aid in their prior State of residence at any time within the year before their arrival in California. The suggestion is ironic for at least three reasons: It would impose the most severe burdens on the neediest members of the disfavored classes; it would significantly reduce the savings that the State would obtain, thus making the State's claimed justification even less tenable; and, it would confine the effect of the statute to what the Solicitor General correctly characterizes as "the invidious purpose of discouraging poor people generally from settling in the State."

* * *

Citizens of the United States, whether rich or poor, have the right to choose to be citizens "of the State wherein they reside." U.S. Const., Amdt. 14, § 1. The States, however, do not have any right to select their citizens. The

Fourteenth Amendment, like the Constitution itself, was, as Justice Cardozo put it, "framed upon the theory that the peoples of the several states must sink or swim together, and that in the long run prosperity and salvation are in union and not division." Baldwin v. G.A.F. Seelig, Inc., 294 U.S. 511, 523 (1935).

. . .

Chief Justice Rehnquist, with whom Justice Thomas joins, dissenting.

The Court today breathes new life into the previously dormant Privileges or Immunities Clause of the Fourteenth Amendment . . . to strike down what I believe is a reasonable measure falling under the head of a "good-faith residency requirement." Because I do not think any provision of the Constitution—and surely not a provision relied upon for only the second time since its enactment 130 years ago—requires this result, I dissent.

I

Much of the Court's opinion is unremarkable and sound. The right to travel clearly embraces the right to go from one place to another, and prohibits States from impeding the free interstate passage of citizens. . . . The Court wisely holds that because Cal. Welf. & Inst.Code Ann. § 11450.03 (West Supp.1999) imposes no obstacle to respondents' entry into California, the statute does not infringe upon the right to travel. Thus, the traditional conception of the right to travel is simply not an issue in this case.

I also have no difficulty with aligning the right to travel with the protections afforded by the Privileges and Immunities Clause of Article IV, § 2, to nonresidents who enter other States "intending to return home at the end of [their] journey." . . . Like the traditional right-to-travel guarantees discussed above, however, this Clause has no application here, because respondents expressed a desire to stay in California and become citizens of that State. Respondents therefore plainly fall outside the protections of Article IV, § 2.

Finally, I agree with the proposition that a "citizen of the United States can, of his own volition, become a citizen of any State of the Union by a *bona fide* residence therein, with the same rights as other citizens of that State." Slaughter–House Cases, 16 Wall. 36, 80, 21 L.Ed. 394 (1872).

But I cannot see how the right to become a citizen of another State is a necessary "component" of the right to travel, or why the Court tries to marry these separate and distinct rights. A person is no longer "traveling" in any sense of the word when he finishes his journey to a State which he plans to make his home. Indeed, under the Court's logic, the protections of the Privileges or Immunities Clause recognized in this case come into play only when an individual stops traveling with the intent to remain and become a citizen of a new State. The right to travel and the right to become a citizen are distinct, their relationship is not reciprocal, and one is not a "component" of the other. Indeed, the same dicta from the *Slaughter-House Cases* quoted by the Court actually treats the right to become a citizen and the right to travel as separate and distinct rights under the Privileges or Immunities Clause of the Fourteenth Amendment. See id., at 79–80. At most, restrictions on an individual's right to become a citizen indirectly affect his calculus in deciding whether to exercise his right to travel in the first place, but such an attenuated and uncertain relationship is no ground for folding one right into the other.

No doubt the Court has, in the past 30 years, essentially conflated the right to travel with the right to equal state citizenship in striking down durational residence requirements similar to the one challenged here. . . .

[T]he Court in these cases held that restricting the provision of welfare benefits, votes, or certain medical benefits to new citizens for a limited time impermissibly "penalized" them under the Equal Protection Clause of the Fourteenth Amendment for having exercised their right to travel. . . . In other cases, the Court recognized that laws dividing new and old residents had little to do with the right to travel and merely triggered an inquiry into whether the resulting classification rationally furthered a legitimate government purpose. See Zobel v. Williams, 457 U.S. 55, 60, n. 6 (1982); Hooper v. Bernalillo County Assessor, 472 U.S. 612, 618 (1985).[22] While *Zobel* and *Hooper* reached the wrong result in my view, they at least put the Court on the proper track in identifying exactly what interests it was protecting; namely, the right of individuals not to be subject to unjustifiable classifications as opposed to infringements on the right to travel.

The Court today tries to clear much of the underbrush created by these prior right-to-travel cases, abandoning its effort to define what residence requirements deprive individuals of "important rights and benefits" or "penalize" the right to travel. Under its new analytical framework, a State, outside certain ill-defined circumstances, cannot classify its citizens by the length of their residence in the State without offending the Privileges or Immunities Clause of the Fourteenth Amendment. The Court thus departs from *Shapiro* and its progeny, and, while paying lipservice to the right to travel, the Court does little to explain how the right to travel is involved at all. Instead, as the Court's analysis clearly demonstrates, this case is only about respondents' right to immediately enjoy all the privileges of being a California citizen in relation to that State's ability to test the good-faith assertion of this right. The Court has thus come full circle by effectively disavowing the analysis of *Shapiro*, segregating the right to travel and the rights secured by Article IV from the right to become a citizen under the Privileges or Immunities Clause, and then testing the residence requirement here against this latter right. For all its misplaced efforts to fold the right to become a citizen into the right to travel, the Court has essentially returned to its original understanding of the right to travel.

II

In unearthing from its tomb the right to become a state citizen and to be treated equally in the new State of residence, however, the Court ignores a State's need to assure that only persons who establish a bona fide residence receive the benefits provided to current residents of the State.

. . .

[22] As Chief Justice Burger aptly stated in *Zobel*: "In reality, right to travel analysis refers to little more than a particular application of equal protection analysis. Right to travel cases have examined, in equal protection terms, state distinctions between newcomers and longer term residents." 457 U.S., at 60, n. 6.

While the physical presence element of a bona fide residence is easy to police, the subjective intent element is not. It is simply unworkable and futile to require States to inquire into each new resident's subjective intent to remain. Hence, States employ objective criteria such as durational residence requirements to test a new resident's resolve to remain before these new citizens can enjoy certain in-state benefits. Recognizing the practical appeal of such criteria, this Court has repeatedly sanctioned the State's use of durational residence requirements before new residents receive in-state tuition rates at state universities. Starns v. Malkerson, 401 U.S. 985 (1971), summarily aff'g 326 F.Supp. 234 (D.Minn.1970) (upholding 1–year residence requirement for in-state tuition) .... The Court has declared: "The State can establish such reasonable criteria for in-state status as to make virtually certain that students who are not, in fact, *bona fide* residents of the State, but have come there solely for educational purposes, cannot take advantage of the in-state rates." See Vlandis v. Kline, 412 U.S. 441, 453–454 (1973). The Court has done the same in upholding a 1–year residence requirement for eligibility to obtain a divorce in state courts, see Sosna v. Iowa, 419 U.S. 393, 406–409 (1975), and in upholding political party registration restrictions that amounted to a durational residency requirement for voting in primary elections, see Rosario v. Rockefeller, 410 U.S. 752, 760–762 (1973).

If States can require individuals to reside in-state for a year before exercising the right to educational benefits, the right to terminate a marriage, or the right to vote in primary elections that all other state citizens enjoy, then States may surely do the same for welfare benefits. Indeed, there is no material difference between a 1–year residence requirement applied to the level of welfare benefits given out by a State, and the same requirement applied to the level of tuition subsidies at a state university. The welfare payment here and in-state tuition rates are cash subsidies provided to a limited class of people, and California's standard of living and higher education system make both subsidies quite attractive. Durational residence requirements were upheld when used to regulate the provision of higher education subsidies, and the same deference should be given in the case of welfare payments....

The Court today recognizes that States retain the ability to determine the bona fides of an individual's claim to residence, but then tries to avoid the issue.... I do not understand how the absence of a link between need and length of residency bears on the State's ability to objectively test respondents' resolve to stay in California. There is no link between the need for an education or for a divorce and the length of residence, and yet States may use length of residence as an objective yardstick to channel their benefits to those whose intent to stay is legitimate.

In one respect, the State has a greater need to require a durational residence for welfare benefits than for college eligibility. The impact of a large number of new residents who immediately seek welfare payments will have a far greater impact on a State's operating budget than the impact of new residents seeking to attend a state university. In the case of the welfare recipients, a modest durational residence requirement to allow for the completion of an annual legislative budget cycle gives the State time to decide how to finance the increased obligations.

The Court tries to distinguish education and divorce benefits by contending that the welfare payment here will be consumed in California, while a college education or a divorce produces benefits that are "portable" and can be enjoyed after individuals return to their original domicile. But this "you can't take it with you" distinction is more apparent than real, and offers little guidance to lower courts who must apply this rationale in the future. Welfare payments are a form of insurance, giving impoverished individuals and their families the means to meet the demands of daily life while they receive the necessary training, education, and time to look for a job. The cash itself will no doubt be spent in California, but the benefits from receiving this income and having the opportunity to become employed or employable will stick with the welfare recipient if they stay in California or go back to their true domicile. Similarly, tuition subsidies are "consumed" in-state but the recipient takes the benefits of a college education with him wherever he goes. A welfare subsidy is thus as much an investment in human capital as is a tuition subsidy, and their attendant benefits are just as "portable." More importantly, this foray into social economics demonstrates that the line drawn by the Court borders on the metaphysical, and requires lower courts to plumb the policies animating certain benefits like welfare to define their "essence" and hence their "portability."
. . .

. . .

Finally, Congress' express approval in 42 U.S.C. § 604(c) of durational residence requirements for welfare recipients like the one established by California only goes to show the reasonableness of a law like § 11450.03. The National Legislature, where people from Mississippi as well as California are represented, has recognized the need to protect state resources in a time of experimentation and welfare reform. As States like California revamp their total welfare packages, . . . they should have the authority and flexibility to ensure that their new programs are not exploited. Congress has decided that it makes good welfare policy to give the States this power. California has reasonably exercised it through an objective, narrowly tailored residence requirement. I see nothing in the Constitution that should prevent the enforcement of that requirement.

Justice Thomas, with whom The Chief Justice joins, dissenting.

. . . In my view, the majority attributes a meaning to the Privileges or Immunities Clause that likely was unintended when the Fourteenth Amendment was enacted and ratified.

. . .

The [American] colonists' repeated assertions that they maintained the rights, privileges and immunities of persons "born within the realm of England" and "natural born" persons suggests that, at the time of the founding, the terms "privileges" and "immunities" (and their counterparts) were understood to refer to those fundamental rights and liberties specifically enjoyed by English citizens, and more broadly, by all persons. Presumably members of the Second Continental Congress so understood these terms when they employed them in the Articles of Confederation .... The Constitution ... similarly guarantees that "[t]he Citizens of each State shall be entitled to all Privileges and Immunities of Citizens in the several States." Art. IV, § 2, cl. 1.

Justice Bushrod Washington's landmark opinion in Corfield v. Coryell, 6 Fed. Cas. 546 (No. 3, 230) (CCED Pa. 1825), reflects this historical understanding. . . .

Washington rejected the proposition that the Privileges and Immunities Clause guaranteed equal access to all public benefits (such as the right to harvest oysters in public waters) that a State chooses to make available. Instead, he endorsed the colonial-era conception of the terms "privileges" and "immunities," concluding that Article IV encompassed only fundamental rights that belong to all citizens of the United States. . . .

Justice Washington's opinion in *Corfield* indisputably influenced the Members of Congress who enacted the Fourteenth Amendment. . . .

That Members of the 39th Congress appear to have endorsed the wisdom of Justice Washington's opinion does not, standing alone, provide dispositive insight into their understanding of the Fourteenth Amendment's Privileges or Immunities Clause. Nevertheless, their repeated references to the *Corfield* decision, combined with what appears to be the historical understanding of the Clause's operative terms, supports the inference that, at the time the Fourteenth Amendment was adopted, people understood that "privileges or immunities of citizens" were fundamental rights, rather than every public benefit established by positive law. Accordingly, the majority's conclusion—that a State violates the Privileges or Immunities Clause when it "discriminates" against citizens who have been domiciled in the State for less than a year in the distribution of welfare benefits appears contrary to the original understanding and is dubious at best.

. . . Because I believe that the demise of the Privileges or Immunities Clause has contributed in no small part to the current disarray of our Fourteenth Amendment jurisprudence, I would be open to reevaluating its meaning in an appropriate case. Before invoking the Clause, however, we should endeavor to understand what the framers of the Fourteenth Amendment thought that it meant. We should also consider whether the Clause should displace, rather than augment, portions of our equal protection and substantive due process jurisprudence. The majority's failure to consider these important questions raises the specter that the Privileges or Immunities Clause will become yet another convenient tool for inventing new rights, limited solely by the "predilections of those who happen at the time to be Members of this Court." Moore v. East Cleveland, 431 U.S. 494, 502 (1977).

I respectfully dissent.

D.   Court Access, Welfare, and the Poor

Page 1029.   Add to end of Note, "Access of the Poor to the Courts in Civil Cases," after Lassiter v. Department of Social Services:

M.L.B. v. S.L.J., 519 U.S. 102 (1996). The Court held that Mississippi could not deny an indigent mother the right to appeal the sufficiency of the evidence supporting a trial court's decision terminating all her parental rights based on her inability to pay substantial costs for preparing the trial record necessary to enable effective appellate review. The majority observed "that the Court's decisions concerning access to judicial processes . . . reflect both equal protection and due process concerns[,]" but that most had relied on equal protection, "as M.L.B.'s plea heavily does, for ... due process does not independently require that the State provide a right to appeal." Though not controlled by precedent because this was a *civil* case involving indigency related to *appellate* review rather than any court access at all, the majority emphasized that a State must have strong justification when a matter of family association so fundamental as that of mother and child is at stake in a way as irrevocable as complete termination of any parental right. It also stressed the "considerable" risk of error evidenced by the frequency of appellate reversal of Mississippi trial court determinations to terminate parental rights, and the relative insignificance of the State's countervailing financial interest "in the tightly circumscribed category of parental status termination cases [where] appeals are few, and not likely to impose an undue burden on the State."

For the majority, Justice Ginsburg distinguished cases holding that the Constitution does not mandate affirmative subsidies to exercise fundamental rights, such as freedom to speak or to choose an abortion procedure, on the basis that those cases involved requests for "state aid to subsidize their privately initiated action or to alleviate the consequences of differences in economic circumstances that existed apart from state action[,]" whereas here the objective was "to defend against the State's destruction of ... family bonds, and to resist the brand associated with a parental unfitness adjudication." She also distinguished Washington v. Davis, 426 U.S. 229 (1976), and like cases holding that otherwise neutral laws do not presumptively violate equal protection simply because they disproportionately have an adverse effect on a racial minority, much less on the poor. Here there was more than just a disproportionate impact, for such rules are "wholly contingent on one's ability to pay, and thus 'visit different consequences on two categories of persons,' ... ; they apply to all indigents and do not reach anyone outside that class." As for concern that extending the State's obligation to pay for transcripts to permit effective appellate review beyond criminal cases to this kind of civil case inevitably would implicate greater financial obligations on the State to pay for transcripts in aid of appellate review in other important civil cases, Justice Ginsburg emphasized that the unique deprivation associated with terminating parental status set this case apart "even from other domestic relations matters such as divorce, paternity, and child custody."

Justice Kennedy concurred in the judgment, asserting that "due process is quite a sufficient basis for our holding." Justice Thomas dissented, joined in full by Justice Scalia and in part by Chief Justice Rehnquist (except for the portion of the opinion declaring Justice Thomas' "inclin[ation] to vote to overrule *Griffin* and its progeny").

CHAPTER 11

DEFINING THE SCOPE OF "LIBERTY" AND "PROPERTY" PROTECTED BY THE DUE PROCESS CLAUSE—THE PROCEDURAL DUE PROCESS CASES

SECTION 1. WHEN DOES DUE PROCESS MANDATE CONSTITUTIONAL PROCEDURES?

A. WHAT "PROPERTY" AND "LIBERTY" IS PROTECTED?

Page 1073. Add after Board of Regents of State Colleges v. Roth:

AMERICAN MANUFACTURERS MUTUAL INSURANCE CO. v. SULLIVAN, 119 S.Ct. 977 (1999). Amendments to Pennsylvania's workers' compensation scheme created a "utilization review" procedure that allows insurers to request review of the "reasonableness and necessity" of medical treatment for injured employees before having to pay their medical bills. Rejecting a claim "that medical benefits are a state-created entitlement, and thus an insurer cannot withhold payment of medical benefits without affording an injured worker due process[,]" the Court reasoned as follows:

"... Under Pennsylvania law, an employee is not entitled to payment for *all* medical treatment once the employer's initial liability is established, as respondents' argument assumes. Instead, the law expressly limits an employee's entitlement to 'reasonable' and 'necessary' medical treatment, and requires that disputes over the reasonableness and necessity of particular treatment must be resolved *before* an employer's obligation to pay— and an employee's entitlement to benefits—arise.... Thus, for an employee's property interest in the payment of medical benefits to attach under state law, the employee must clear two hurdles: First, he must prove that an employer is liable for a work-related injury, and second, he must establish that the particular medical treatment at issue is reasonable and necessary. Only then does the employee's interest parallel that of the beneficiary of welfare assistance in *Goldberg [v. Kelly*, 397 U.S. 254 (1970),] and the recipient of disability benefits in *Mathews [v. Eldridge*, 424 U.S. 319 (1976)].

"... While [respondents] indeed have established their initial *eligibility* for medical treatment, they have yet to make good on their claim that the particular medical treatment they received was reasonable and necessary. Consequently, they do not have a property interest—under the logic of their own argument—in having their providers paid for treatment that has yet to be found reasonable and necessary....

"Having concluded that respondents' due process claim falters for lack of a property interest in the payment of benefits, we need go no further....[13]"

Justice Ginsburg "join[ed] Part III of the Court's opinion on the understanding that the Court rejects specifically, and only, respondents' demands for constant payment of each medical bill, within 30 days of receipt, pending determination of the necessity or reasonableness of the medical treatment. See *ante*, n. 13. I do not doubt, however, that due process requires fair procedures for the adjudication of respondents' claims for workers' compensation benefits, including medical care."

Justice Breyer, joined by Justice Souter, also "agree[d] with Part III insofar as it rejects respondents' facial attack on the statute and also points out that respondents 'do not contend that they have a property interest in their claims for payment, as distinct from the payments themselves.' *Ante*, n. 13. I would add, however, that there may be individual circumstances in which the receipt of earlier payments leads an injured person reasonably to expect their continuation, in which case that person may well possess a constitutionally protected 'property' interest. See, e.g., Board of Regents of State Colleges v. Roth, 408 U.S. 564, 577 (1972)...."

Justice Stevens, concurring in part and dissenting in part, remarked:

"Because the individual respondents suffered work-related injuries, they are entitled to have their employers, or the employers' insurers, pay for whatever 'reasonable' and 'necessary' treatment they may need.... That right—whether described as a 'claim' for payment or a 'cause of action'—is unquestionably a species of property protected by the Due Process Clause of the Fourteenth Amendment. ... Because the resolution of ... disputes [over the reasonableness or necessity of particular treatments] determines the scope of the claimants' property interests, the Constitution requires that the procedure be fair.... It is equally clear that the State's duty to establish and administer a fair procedure for resolving the dispute obtains whether the dispute is initiated by the filing of a claim or by an insurer's decision to withhold payment until the reasonableness issue is resolved."

"... In my opinion the Court of Appeals correctly concluded that the original procedure was deficient because it did not give employees either notice that a request for utilization review would automatically suspend their benefits or an opportunity to provide relevant evidence and argument to the state actor vested with initial decisional authority.... I do not, however, find any constitutional defect in the procedures that are now in place, ... [because i]t is not unfair, in and of itself, for a State to allow either a private or a publicly owned party to withhold payment of a state-created entitlement pending resolution of a dispute over its amount."

---

[13] Respondents do not contend that they have a property interest in their claims for payment, as distinct from the payments themselves, such that the State, the argument goes, could not finally reject their claims without affording them appropriate procedural protections.

CHAPTER 12

Application of the Post Civil War Amendments to Private Conduct: Congressional Power to Enforce the Amendments

SECTION 2. Application of the Constitution to Private Conduct

A. Private performance of "Government" Functions

Page 1116. Add at end of subsection:

AMERICAN MANUFACTURERS MUTUAL INSURANCE CO. v. SULLIVAN, 119 S.Ct. 977 (1999). The Court held that a private insurer could suspend workers' compensation benefits without giving the worker notice or opportunity to be heard. The insurers' decisions to withhold payment for disputed medical treatment were not attributable to the State. The Court rejected an argument that state action was present because the State had delegated to insurers powers traditionally reserved to itself in providing state-mandated "public benefits." The State was not required to provide either medical treatment or workers' compensation benefits to injured workers. Privately owned enterprises providing services that the State would not neces-sarily provide, even though they are extensively regulated, are not state actors.

SECTION 6.   THE SCOPE OF CONGRESSIONAL POWER TO REDEFINE THE AMENDMENTS

B.   "INTERPRETIVE" POWER

Replace pages 1174–1186 with the following:

City of Boerne v. Flores

521 U.S. 507, 117 S.Ct. 2157, 138 L.Ed.2d 624 (1997).

Justice Kennedy delivered the opinion of the Court.*

A decision by local zoning authorities to deny a church a building permit was challenged under the Religious Freedom Restoration Act of 1993 (RFRA), 107 Stat. 1488, 42 U.S.C. § 2000bb et seq. The case calls into question the authority of Congress to enact RFRA. We conclude the statute exceeds Congress' power.

I

Situated on a hill in the city of Boerne, Texas, some 28 miles northwest of San Antonio, is St. Peter Catholic Church. Built in 1923, the church's structure replicates the mission style of the region's earlier history. The church seats about 230 worshippers, a number too small for its growing parish. Some 40 to 60 parishioners cannot be accommodated at some Sunday masses. In order to meet the needs of the congregation the Archbishop of San Antonio gave permission to the parish to plan alterations to enlarge the building.

A few months later, the Boerne City Council passed an ordinance authorizing the city's Historic Landmark Commission to prepare a preservation plan with proposed historic landmarks and districts. Under the ordinance, the Commission must preapprove construction affecting historic landmarks or buildings in a historic district.

---

* Justice Scalia joins all but Part III–A–1 of this opinion.

Soon afterwards, the Archbishop applied for a building permit so construction to enlarge the church could proceed. City authorities, relying on the ordinance and the designation of a historic district (which, they argued, included the church), denied the application. The Archbishop brought this suit challenging the permit denial in the United States District Court for the Western District of Texas.

. . . [T]he litigation has centered on RFRA and the question of its constitutionality. The Archbishop relied upon RFRA as one basis for relief from the refusal to issue the permit. The District Court concluded that by enacting RFRA Congress exceeded the scope of its enforcement power under § 5 of the Fourteenth Amendment. The . . . Fifth Circuit reversed, finding RFRA to be constitutional. We . . . reverse.

II

Congress enacted RFRA in direct response to the Court's decision in Employment Div., Dept. of Human Resources of Ore. v. Smith, 494 U.S. 872 (1990). There we considered a Free Exercise Clause claim brought by members of the Native American Church who were denied unemployment benefits when they lost their jobs because they had used peyote. Their practice was to ingest peyote for sacramental purposes, and they challenged an Oregon statute of general applicability which made use of the drug criminal. In evaluating the claim, we declined to apply the balancing test set forth in Sherbert v. Verner, 374 U.S. 398 (1963), under which we would have asked whether Oregon's prohibition substantially burdened a religious practice and, if it did, whether the burden was justified by a compelling government interest. We stated: "[G]overnment's ability to enforce generally applicable prohibitions of socially harmful conduct . . . cannot depend on measuring the effects of a governmental action on a religious objector's spiritual development. . . ." . . .

The only instances where a neutral, generally applicable law had failed to pass constitutional muster, the Smith Court noted, were cases in which other constitutional protections were at stake. . . . In Wisconsin v. Yoder, 406 U.S. 205 (1972), for example, we invalidated Wisconsin's mandatory school-attendance law as applied to Amish parents who refused on religious grounds to send their children to school. That case implicated not only the right to the free exercise of religion but also the right of parents to control their children's education.

The *Smith* decision acknowledged the Court had employed the *Sherbert* test in considering free exercise challenges to state unemployment compensation rules on three occasions where the balance had tipped in favor of the individual. See *Sherbert*, supra; Thomas v. Review Bd. of Indiana Employment Security Div., 450 U.S. 707 (1981); Hobbie v. Unemployment Appeals Comm'n of Fla., 480 U.S. 136 (1987). Those cases, the Court explained, stand for "the proposition that where the State has in place a system of individual exemptions, it may not refuse to extend that system to cases of religious hardship without compelling reason." . . . By contrast, where a general prohibition, such as Oregon's, is at issue, "the sounder approach, and the approach in accord with the vast majority of our precedents, is to hold the test inapplicable to [free exercise] challenges." . . . . *Smith* held that neutral, generally applicable laws may be applied to religious practices even when not supported by a compelling governmental interest.

Four Members of the Court disagreed. They argued the law placed a substantial burden on the Native American Church members so that it could be upheld only if the law served a compelling state interest and was narrowly tailored to achieve that end....

These points of constitutional interpretation were debated by Members of Congress in hearings and floor debates. Many criticized the Court's reasoning, and this disagreement resulted in the passage of RFRA. Congress announced:

"(1) [T]he framers of the Constitution, recognizing free exercise of religion as an unalienable right, secured its protection in the First Amendment to the Constitution;

"(2) laws 'neutral' toward religion may burden religious exercise as surely as laws intended to interfere with religious exercise;

"(3) governments should not substantially burden religious exercise without compelling justification;

"(4) in Employment Division v. Smith, 494 U.S. 872 (1990), the Supreme Court virtually eliminated the requirement that the government justify burdens on religious exercise imposed by laws neutral toward religion; and

"(5) the compelling interest test as set forth in prior Federal court rulings is a workable test for striking sensible balances between religious liberty and competing prior governmental interests." 42 U.S.C. § 2000bb(a).

The Act's stated purposes are:

"(1) to restore the compelling interest test as set forth in Sherbert v. Verner, 374 U.S. 398 (1963) and Wisconsin v. Yoder, 406 U.S. 205 (1972) and to guarantee its application in all cases where free exercise of religion is substantially burdened; and

"(2) to provide a claim or defense to persons whose religious exercise is substantially burdened by government." § 2000bb(b).

statute

RFRA prohibits "[g]overnment" from "substantially burden[ing]" a person's exercise of religion even if the burden results from a rule of general applicability unless the government can demonstrate the burden "(1) is in furtherance of a compelling governmental interest; and (2) is the least restrictive means of furthering that compelling governmental interest." § 2000bb–1. The Act's mandate applies to any "branch, department, agency, instrumentality, and official (or other person acting under color of law) of the United States," as well as to any "State, or ... subdivision of a State." § 2000bb–2(1). The Act's universal coverage is confirmed in § 2000bb–3(a), under which RFRA "applies to all Federal and State law, and the implementation of that law, whether statutory or otherwise, and whether adopted before or after [RFRA's enactment]." In accordance with RFRA's usage of the term, we shall use "state law" to include local and municipal ordinances.

III

A

Under our Constitution, the Federal Government is one of enumerated powers. McCulloch v. Maryland, 4 Wheat. 316, 405 (1819) ... The judicial authority to determine the constitutionality of laws, in cases and controversies, is based on the premise that the "powers of the legislature are defined and limited; and that those limits may not be mistaken, or forgotten, the constitution is written." Marbury v. Madison, 1 Cranch 137, 176 (1803).

Congress relied on its Fourteenth Amendment enforcement power in enacting the most far reaching and substantial of RFRA's provisions, those which impose its requirements on the States . . . .

D's argument

In defense of the Act respondent contends, with support from the United States as *amicus*, that RFRA is permissible enforcement legislation. Congress, it is said, is only protecting by legislation one of the liberties guaranteed by the Fourteenth Amendment's Due Process Clause, the free exercise of religion, beyond what is necessary under *Smith*. It is said the congressional decision to dispense with proof of deliberate or overt discrimination and instead concentrate on a law's effects accords with the settled understanding that § 5 includes the power to enact legislation designed to prevent as well as remedy constitutional violations. It is further contended that Congress' § 5 power is not limited to remedial or preventive legislation.

ISSUE
Does congress have this power

. . . Legislation which deters or remedies constitutional violations can fall within the sweep of Congress' enforcement power even if in the process it prohibits conduct which is not itself unconstitutional and intrudes into "legislative spheres of autonomy previously reserved to the States." Fitzpatrick v. Bitzer, 427 U.S. 445, 455 (1976). For example, the Court upheld a suspension of literacy tests and similar voting requirements under Congress' parallel power to enforce the provisions of the Fifteenth Amendment . . . as a measure to combat racial discrimination in voting, South Carolina v. Katzenbach, 383 U.S. 301, 308 (1966), despite the facial constitutionality of the tests under Lassiter v. Northampton County Bd. of Elections, 360 U.S. 45 (1959). We have also concluded that other measures protecting voting rights are within Congress' power to enforce the Fourteenth and Fifteenth Amendments, despite the burdens those measures placed on the States. South Carolina v. Katzenbach, . . . (upholding several provisions of the Voting Rights Act of 1965); Katzenbach v. Morgan, [384 U.S. 641 (1966)] (upholding ban on literacy tests that prohibited certain people schooled in Puerto Rico from voting); Oregon v. Mitchell, 400 U.S. 112 (1970) (upholding 5–year nationwide ban on literacy tests and similar voting requirements for registering to vote); City of Rome v. United States, 446 U.S. 156, 161 (1980) (upholding 7–year extension of the Voting Rights Act's requirement that certain jurisdictions preclear any change to a " 'standard, practice, or procedure with respect to voting' ") . . . .

It is also true, however, that "[a]s broad as the congressional enforcement power is, it is not unlimited." Oregon v. Mitchell, supra, at 128 (opinion of Black, J.). In assessing the breadth of § 5's enforcement power, we begin with its text. Congress has been given the power "to enforce" the "provisions of this article." We agree with respondent, of course, that Congress can enact legislation under § 5 enforcing the constitutional right to the free exercise of religion. The "provisions of this article," to which § 5 refers, include the Due Process Clause of the Fourteenth Amendment. Congress' power to enforce the Free Exercise Clause follows from our holding in Cantwell v. Connecticut, 310 U.S. 296, 303 (1940), that the "fundamental concept of liberty embodied in [the

Fourteenth Amendment's Due Process Clause] embraces the liberties guaranteed by the First Amendment." ...

Congress' power under § 5, however, extends only to "enforc[ing]" the provisions of the Fourteenth Amendment. The Court has described this power as "remedial," South Carolina v. Katzenbach, supra, at 326. The design of the Amendment and the text of § 5 are inconsistent with the suggestion that Congress has the power to decree the substance of the Fourteenth Amendment's restrictions on the States. Legislation which alters the meaning of the Free Exercise Clause cannot be said to be enforcing the Clause. Congress does not enforce a constitutional right by changing what the right is. It has been given the power "to enforce," not the power to determine what constitutes a constitutional violation. Were it not so, what Congress would be enforcing would no longer be, in any meaningful sense, the "provisions of [the Fourteenth Amendment]."

Court's argument

While the line between measures that remedy or prevent unconstitutional actions and measures that make a substantive change in the governing law is not easy to discern, and Congress must have wide latitude in determining where it lies, the distinction exists and must be observed. There must be a congruence and proportionality between the injury to be prevented or remedied and the means adopted to that end. Lacking such a connection, legislation may become substantive in operation and effect. History and our case law support drawing the distinction, one apparent from the text of the Amendment.

1

The Fourteenth Amendment's history confirms the remedial, rather than substantive, nature of the Enforcement Clause. The Joint Committee on Reconstruction of the 39th Congress began drafting what would become the Fourteenth Amendment in January 1866. The objections to the Committee's first draft of the Amendment, and the rejection of the draft, have a direct bearing on the central issue of defining Congress' enforcement power. In February, Republican Representative John Bingham of Ohio reported the following draft amendment to the House of Representatives on behalf of the Joint Committee: "The Congress shall have power to make all laws which shall be necessary and proper to secure to the citizens of each State all privileges and immunities of citizens in the several States, and to all persons in the several States equal protection in the rights of life, liberty, and property." ...

history argument

The proposal encountered immediate opposition....

... [T]he Joint Committee began drafting a new article of Amendment, which it reported to Congress on April 30, 1866.

Section 1 of the new draft Amendment imposed self-executing limits on the States. Section 5 prescribed that "[t]he Congress shall have power to enforce, by appropriate legislation, the provisions of this article." ... Under the revised Amendment, Congress' power was no longer plenary but remedial. Congress was granted the power to make the substantive constitutional prohibitions against the States effective....

. . .

The design of the Fourteenth Amendment has proved significant . . . in maintaining the traditional separation of powers between Congress and the Judiciary. . . . As enacted, the Fourteenth Amendment confers substantive rights against the States which, like the provisions of the Bill of Rights, are self-executing. . . . The power to interpret the Constitution in a case or controversy remains in the Judiciary.

2

The remedial and preventive nature of Congress' enforcement power, and the limitation inherent in the power, were confirmed in our earliest cases on the Fourteenth Amendment. In the Civil Rights Cases, 109 U.S. 3 (1883), the Court invalidated sections of the Civil Rights Act of 1875 which prescribed criminal penalties for denying to any person "the full enjoyment of" public accommodations and conveyances, on the grounds that it exceeded Congress' power by seeking to regulate private conduct. The Enforcement Clause, the Court said, did not authorize Congress to pass "general legislation upon the rights of the citizen, but corrective legislation; that is, such as may be necessary and proper for counteracting such laws as the States may adopt or enforce, and which, by the amendment, they are prohibited from making or enforcing. . . ." . . . Although the specific holdings of these early cases might have been superseded or modified, see, e.g., Heart of Atlanta Motel, Inc. v. United States, 379 U.S. 241 (1964); United States v. Guest, 383 U.S. 745 (1966), their treatment of Congress' § 5 power as corrective or preventive, not definitional, has not been questioned.

Recent cases have continued to revolve around the question of whether § 5 legislation can be considered remedial. In South Carolina v. Katzenbach . . . we upheld various provisions of the Voting Rights Act of 1965, finding them to be "remedies aimed at areas where voting discrimination has been most flagrant," . . . and necessary to "banish the blight of racial discrimination in voting, which has infected the electoral process in parts of our country for nearly a century," . . . . We noted evidence in the record reflecting the subsisting and pervasive discriminatory—and therefore unconstitutional—use of literacy tests. . . . The Act's new remedies, which used the administrative resources of the Federal Government, included the suspension of both literacy tests and, pending federal review, all new voting regulations in covered jurisdictions, as well as the assignment of federal examiners to list qualified applicants enabling those listed to vote. The new, unprecedented remedies were deemed necessary given the ineffectiveness of the existing voting rights laws, . . . and the slow costly character of case-by-case litigation. . . .

After South Carolina v. Katzenbach, the Court continued to acknowledge the necessity of using strong remedial and preventive measures to respond to the widespread and persisting deprivation of constitutional rights resulting from this country's history of racial discrimination. . . .

3

Any suggestion that Congress has a substantive, non-remedial power under the Fourteenth Amendment is not supported by our case law. In Oregon v. Mitchell, . . . a majority of the Court concluded Congress had exceeded its enforcement powers by enacting legislation lowering the minimum age of voters from 21 to 18 in state and local elections. The five Members of the Court who reached this conclusion explained that the legislation intruded into an area reserved by the Constitution to the States. . . .

There is language in our opinion in Katzenbach v. Morgan, 384 U.S. 641 (1966), which could be interpreted as acknowledging a power in Congress to enact legislation that expands the rights contained in § 1 of the Fourteenth Amendment. This is not a necessary interpretation, however, or even the best one. In *Morgan*, the Court considered the constitutionality of § 4(e) of the Voting Rights Act of 1965, which provided that no person who had successfully completed the sixth primary grade in a public school in, or a private school accredited by, the Commonwealth of Puerto Rico in which the language of instruction was other than English could be denied the right to vote because of an inability to read or write English. New York's Constitution, on the other hand, required voters to be able to read and write English. The Court provided two related rationales for its conclusion that § 4(e) could "be viewed as a measure to secure for the Puerto Rican community residing in New York nondiscriminatory treatment by government." . . . Under the first rationale, Congress could prohibit New York from denying the right to vote to large segments of its Puerto Rican community, in order to give Puerto Ricans "enhanced political power" that would be "helpful in gaining nondiscriminatory treatment in public services for the entire Puerto Rican community." . . . Section 4(e) thus could be justified as a remedial measure to deal with "discrimination in governmental services." . . . The second rationale, an alternative holding, did not address discrimination in the provision of public services but "discrimination in establishing voter qualifications." . . . The Court perceived a factual basis on which Congress could have concluded that New York's literacy requirement "constituted an invidious discrimination in violation of the Equal Protection Clause." . . . Both rationales for upholding § 4(e) rested on unconstitutional discrimination by New York and Congress' reasonable attempt to combat it. As Justice Stewart explained in Oregon v. Mitchell, . . . interpreting *Morgan* to give Congress the power to interpret the Constitution "would require an enormous extension of that decision's rationale."

If Congress could define its own powers by altering the Fourteenth Amendment's meaning, no longer would the Constitution be "superior paramount law, unchangeable by ordinary means." It would be "on a level with ordinary legislative acts, and, like other acts, . . . alterable when the legislature shall please to alter it." Marbury v. Madison, 1 Cranch, at 177. Under this approach, it is difficult to conceive of a principle that would limit congressional power. . . . Shifting legislative majorities could change the Constitution and effectively circumvent the difficult and detailed amendment process contained in Article V.

We now turn to consider whether RFRA can be considered enforcement legislation under § 5 of the Fourteenth Amendment.

B

Respondent contends that RFRA is a proper exercise of Congress' remedial or preventive power. The Act, it is said, is a reasonable means of protecting the free exercise of religion as defined by *Smith*. It prevents and remedies laws which are enacted with the unconstitutional object of targeting religious beliefs and practices. . . . If Congress can prohibit laws with discriminatory effects in order to prevent racial discrimination in violation of the Equal Protection Clause, . . . then it can do the same, respondent argues, to promote religious liberty.

While preventive rules are sometimes appropriate remedial measures, there must be a congruence between the means used and the ends to be achieved. The appropriateness of remedial measures must be considered in light of the evil presented. . . . Strong measures appropriate to address one harm may be an unwarranted response to another, lesser one. . . .

A comparison between RFRA and the Voting Rights Act is instructive. In contrast to the record which confronted Congress and the judiciary in the voting rights cases, RFRA's legislative record lacks examples of modern instances of generally applicable laws passed because of religious bigotry. The history of persecution in this country detailed in the hearings mentions no episodes occurring in the past 40 years. . . . Rather, the emphasis of the hearings was on laws of general applicability which place incidental burdens on religion. . . . It is difficult to maintain that they are examples of legislation enacted or enforced due to animus or hostility to the burdened religious practices or that they indicate some widespread pattern of religious discrimination in this country. Congress' concern was with the incidental burdens imposed, not the object or purpose of the legislation. . . . This lack of support in the legislative record, however, is not RFRA's most serious shortcoming. Judicial deference, in most cases, is based not on the state of the legislative record Congress compiles but "on due regard for the decision of the body constitutionally appointed to decide." . . . As a general matter, it is for Congress to determine the method by which it will reach a decision.

Regardless of the state of the legislative record, RFRA cannot be considered remedial, preventive legislation, if those terms are to have any meaning. RFRA is so out of proportion to a supposed remedial or preventive object that it cannot be understood as responsive to, or designed to prevent, unconstitutional behavior. It appears, instead, to attempt a substantive change in constitutional protections. Preventive measures prohibiting certain types of laws may be appropriate when there is reason to believe that many of the laws affected by the congressional enactment have a significant likelihood of being unconstitutional. . . .

RFRA is not so confined. Sweeping coverage ensures its intrusion at every level of government, displacing laws and prohibiting official actions of almost every description and regardless of subject matter. RFRA's restrictions apply to every agency and official of the Federal, State, and local Governments. . . . RFRA applies to all federal and state law, statutory or otherwise, whether adopted before or after its enactment. . . . RFRA has no termination date or termination mechanism. Any law is subject to challenge at any time by any individual who alleges a substantial burden on his or her free exercise of religion.

The reach and scope of RFRA distinguish it from other measures passed under Congress' enforcement power, even in the area of voting rights. In South Carolina v. Katzenbach, the challenged provisions were confined to those regions of the country where voting discrimination had been most flagrant, . . . and affected a discrete class of state laws, i.e., state voting laws. Furthermore, to ensure that the reach of the Voting Rights Act was limited to those cases in which constitutional violations were most likely (in order to reduce the possibility of overbreadth), the coverage under the Act would terminate "at the behest of States and political subdivisions in which the danger of substantial voting discrimination has not materialized during the preceding five years." ... The provisions restricting and banning literacy tests, upheld in Katzenbach v. Morgan, ... and Oregon v. Mitchell, ... attacked a particular type of voting qualification, one with a long history as a "notorious means to deny and abridge voting rights on racial grounds." ... In *City of Rome*, ... the Court rejected a challenge to the constitutionality of a Voting Rights Act provision which required certain jurisdictions to submit changes in electoral practices to the Department of Justice for preimplementation review. The requirement was placed only on jurisdictions with a history of intentional racial discrimination in voting.... Like the provisions at issue in South Carolina v. Katzenbach, this provision permitted a covered jurisdiction to avoid preclearance requirements under certain conditions and, moreover, lapsed in seven years. This is not to say, of course, that § 5 legislation requires termination dates, geographic restrictions or egregious predicates. Where, however, a congressional enactment pervasively prohibits constitutional state action in an effort to remedy or to prevent unconstitutional state action, limitations of this kind tend to ensure Congress' means are proportionate to ends legitimate under § 5.

The stringent test RFRA demands of state laws reflects a lack of proportionality or congruence between the means adopted and the legitimate end to be achieved. If an objector can show a substantial burden on his free exercise, the State must demonstrate a compelling governmental interest and show that the law is the least restrictive means of furthering its interest. Claims that a law substantially burdens someone's exercise of religion will often be difficult to contest.... Requiring a State to demonstrate a compelling interest and show that it has adopted the least restrictive means of achieving that interest is the most demanding test known to constitutional law.... Laws valid under *Smith* would fall under RFRA without regard to whether they had the object of stifling or punishing free exercise. We make these observations not to reargue the position of the majority in *Smith* but to illustrate the substantive alteration of its holding attempted by RFRA. Even assuming RFRA would be interpreted in effect to mandate some lesser test, say one equivalent to intermediate scrutiny, the statute nevertheless would require searching judicial scrutiny of state law with the attendant likelihood of invalidation. This is a considerable congressional intrusion into the States' traditional prerogatives and general authority to regulate for the health and welfare of their citizens.

The substantial costs RFRA exacts, both in practical terms of imposing a heavy litigation burden on the States and in terms of curtailing their traditional general regulatory power, far exceed any pattern or practice of unconstitutional conduct under the Free Exercise Clause as interpreted in *Smith*. Simply put, RFRA is not designed to identify and counteract state laws likely to be unconstitutional because of their treatment of religion. In most cases, the state laws to which RFRA applies are not ones which will have been motivated by religious bigotry. If a state law disproportionately burdened a particular class of religious observers, this circumstance might be evidence of an impermissible legislative motive.... RFRA's substantial burden test, however, is not even a discriminatory effects or disparate impact test. It is a reality of the modern regulatory state that numerous state laws, such as the zoning regulations at issue here, impose a substantial burden on a large class of individuals. When the exercise of religion has been burdened in an incidental way by a law of general application, it does not follow that the persons affected have been burdened any more than other citizens, let alone burdened because of their religious beliefs. In addition, the Act imposes in every case a least restrictive means requirement—a requirement that was not used in the pre-*Smith* jurisprudence RFRA purported to codify—which also indicates that the legislation is broader than is appropriate if the goal is to prevent and remedy constitutional violations.

When Congress acts within its sphere of power and responsibilities, it has not just the right but the duty to make its own informed judgment on the meaning and force of the Constitution. This has been clear from the early days of the Republic.... Were it otherwise, we would not afford Congress the presumption of validity its enactments now enjoy.

.   .   .

It is for Congress in the first instance to "determin[e] whether and what legislation is needed to secure the guarantees of the Fourteenth Amendment," and its conclusions are entitled to much deference. Katzenbach v. Morgan, 384 U. S., at 651. Congress' discretion is not unlimited, however, and the courts retain the power, as they have since Marbury v. Madison, to determine if Congress has exceeded its authority under the Constitution. Broad as the power of Congress is under the Enforcement Clause of the Fourteenth Amendment, RFRA contradicts vital principles necessary to maintain separation of powers and the federal balance. The judgment of the Court of Appeals sustaining the Act's constitutionality is reversed.

It is so ordered.

Justice Stevens, concurring.

In my opinion, the Religious Freedom Restoration Act of 1993 (RFRA) is a "law respecting an establishment of religion" that violates the First Amendment to the Constitution.

If the historic landmark on the hill in Boerne happened to be a museum or an art gallery owned by an atheist, it would not be eligible for an exemption from the city ordinances that forbid an enlargement of the structure. Because the landmark is owned by the Catholic Church, it is claimed that RFRA gives its owner a federal statutory entitlement to an exemption from a generally applicable, neutral civil law. Whether the Church would actually prevail under the statute or not, the statute has provided the Church with a legal weapon that no atheist or agnostic can obtain. This governmental preference for religion, as opposed to irreligion, is forbidden by the First Amendment....

Justice Scalia, with whom Justice Stevens joins, concurring in part.

I write to respond briefly to the claim of Justice O'Connor's dissent ...that historical materials support a result contrary to the one reached in Employment Div., Dept. of Human Resources of Ore. v. Smith, 494 U.S. 872 (1990)....

Justice O'Connor, with whom Justice Breyer joins except as to a portion of Part I, dissenting.

I dissent from the Court's disposition of this case. I agree with the Court that the issue before us is whether the Religious Freedom Restoration Act (RFRA) is a proper exercise of Congress' power to enforce § 5 of the Fourteenth Amendment. But as a yardstick for measuring the constitutionality of RFRA, the Court uses its holding in Employment Div., Dept. of Human Resources of Ore. v. Smith, 494 U.S. 872 (1990), the decision that prompted Congress to enact RFRA as a means of more rigorously enforcing the Free Exercise Clause. I remain of the view that *Smith* was wrongly decided, and I would use this case to reexamine the Court's holding there. . . .

I

I agree with much of the reasoning set forth in Part III–A of the Court's opinion. Indeed, if I agreed with the Court's standard in *Smith*, I would join the opinion. . . .

The Court's analysis of whether RFRA is a constitutional exercise of Congress' § 5 power, set forth in Part III–B of its opinion, is premised on the assumption that *Smith* correctly interprets the Free Exercise Clause. This is an assumption that I do not accept. I continue to believe that *Smith* adopted an improper standard for deciding free exercise claims. . . .

. . .

Justice Souter, dissenting.

To decide whether the Fourteenth Amendment gives Congress sufficient power to enact the Religious Freedom Restoration Act, the Court measures the legislation against the free-exercise standard of Employment Div., Dept. of Human Resources of Ore. v. Smith, 494 U.S. 872 (1990). For the reasons stated in my opinion in Church of Lukumi Babalu Aye, Inc. v. Hialeah, 508 U.S. 520, 564–577 (1993) . . . I have serious doubts about the precedential value of the *Smith* rule and its entitlement to adherence. . . . [W]ithout briefing and argument on the merits of that rule . . . , I am not now prepared to join Justice O'Connor in rejecting it or the majority in assuming it to be correct. In order to provide full adversarial consideration, this case should be set down for reargument permitting plenary reexamination of the issue. . . .

Justice Breyer, dissenting.

I agree with Justice O'Connor that the Court should direct the parties to brief the question whether Employment Div., Dept. of Human Resources of Ore. v. Smith, 494 U.S. 872 (1990) was correctly decided, and set this case for reargument. I do not, however, find it necessary to consider the question whether, assuming *Smith* is correct, § 5 of the Fourteenth Amendment would authorize Congress to enact the legislation before us. . . . I therefore join Justice O'Connor's dissent, with the exception of the first paragraph of Part I.

Page 1187. Add at end of chapter:

Saenz v. Roe

___ U.S. ___, 119 S.Ct. 1518, ___ L.Ed.2d ___ (1999).

[The report in this case appears supra, page 137.]

CHAPTER 13

GOVERNMENT CONTROL OF THE CONTENT OF EXPRESSION

SECTION 3. SPEECH CONFLICTING WITH OTHER COMMUNITY VALUES: GOVERNMENT CONTROL OF THE CONTENT OF SPEECH

C. CONTROL OF "FIGHTING WORDS" AND OFFENSIVE SPEECH

Page 1313. **Add after Denver Area Educational Telecommunications Consortium, Inc. v. Federal Communications Commission:**

Reno v. American Civil Liberties Union

521 U.S. 844, 117 S.Ct. 2329, 138 L.Ed.2d 874 (1997).

Justice Stevens delivered the opinion of the Court.

At issue is the constitutionality of two statutory provisions enacted to protect minors from "indecent" and "patently offensive" communications on the Internet. Notwithstanding the legitimacy and importance of the congressional goal of protecting children from harmful materials, we agree with the three-judge District Court that the statute abridges "the freedom of speech" protected by the First Amendment.

I

The District Court made extensive findings of fact, most of which were based on a detailed stipulation prepared by the parties. The findings describe the character and the dimensions of the Internet, the availability of sexually explicit material in that medium, and the problems confronting age verification for recipients of Internet communications. . . .

The Internet

The Internet is an international network of interconnected computers. . . . that, eventually linking with each other, now enable tens of millions of people to communicate with one another and to access vast amounts of information from around the world. The Internet is "a unique and wholly new medium of worldwide human communication."

The Internet has experienced "extraordinary growth." . . . About 40 million people used the Internet at the time of trial, a number that is expected to mushroom to 200 million by 1999.

Individuals can obtain access to the Internet from many different sources, generally hosts themselves or entities with a host affiliation. Most colleges and universities provide access for their students and faculty; many corporations provide their employees with access through an office network; many communities and local libraries provide free access; and an increasing number of storefront "computer coffee shops" provide access for a small hourly fee. Several major national "online services" ... had almost 12 million individual subscribers at the time of trial.

Anyone with access to the Internet may take advantage of a wide variety of communication and information retrieval methods.... [T]hose most relevant to this case are electronic mail ("e-mail"), automatic mailing list services ("mail exploders," sometimes referred to as "listservs"), "newsgroups," "chat rooms," and the "World Wide Web." All of these methods can be used to transmit text; most can transmit sound, pictures, and moving video images. Taken together, these tools constitute a unique medium—known to its users as "cyberspace"—located in no particular geographical location but available to anyone, anywhere in the world, with access to the Internet.

. . .

The best known category of communication over the Internet is the World Wide Web, which allows users to search for and retrieve information stored in remote computers, as well as, in some cases, to communicate back to designated sites. In concrete terms, the Web consists of a vast number of documents stored in different computers all over the world. Some of these documents are simply files containing information. However, more elaborate documents, commonly known as Web "pages," are also prevalent.... Web pages frequently contain information and sometimes allow the viewer to communicate with the page's (or "site's") author. They generally also contain "links" to other documents created by that site's author or to other (generally) related sites....

Navigating the Web is relatively straightforward. A user may either type the address of a known page or enter one or more keywords into a commercial "search engine" in an effort to locate sites on a subject of interest. A particular Web page may contain the information sought by the "surfer," or, through its links, it may be an avenue to other documents located anywhere on the Internet. Users generally explore a given Web page, or move to another, by clicking a computer "mouse" on one of the page's icons or links.... The Web is thus comparable, from the readers' viewpoint, to both a vast library including millions of readily available and indexed publications and a sprawling mall offering goods and services.

From the publishers' point of view, it constitutes a vast platform from which to address and hear from a world-wide audience of millions of readers, viewers, researchers, and buyers. Any person or organization with a computer connected to the Internet can "publish" information.... "No single organization controls any membership in the Web, nor is there any centralized point from which individual Web sites or services can be blocked from the Web." ...

Sexually Explicit Material

Sexually explicit material on the Internet includes text, pictures, and chat and "extends from the modestly titillating to the hardest-core." These files are created, named, and posted in the same manner as material that is not sexually explicit, and may be accessed either deliberately or unintentionally during the course of an imprecise search. "Once a provider posts its content on the Internet, it cannot prevent that content from entering any community." ...

Though such material is widely available, users seldom encounter such content accidentally. "A document's title or a description of the document will usually appear before the document itself ... and in many cases the user will receive detailed information about a site's content before he or she need take the step to access the document. Almost all sexually explicit images are preceded by warnings as to the content." For that reason, the "odds are slim" that a user would enter a sexually explicit site by accident. Unlike communications received by radio or television, "the receipt of information on the Internet requires a series of affirmative steps more deliberate and directed than merely turning a dial. A child requires some sophistication and some ability to read to retrieve material and thereby to use the Internet unattended."

Systems have been developed to help parents control the material that may be available on a home computer with Internet access. A system may either limit a computer's access to an approved list of sources that have been identified as containing no adult material, it may block designated inappropriate sites, or it may attempt to block messages containing identifiable objectionable features. "Although parental control software currently can screen for certain suggestive words or for known sexually explicit sites, it cannot now screen for sexually explicit images." Nevertheless, the evidence indicates that "a reasonably effective method by which parents can prevent their children from accessing sexually explicit and other material which parents may believe is inappropriate for their children will soon be available."

Age Verification

The problem of age verification differs for different uses of the Internet. The District Court categorically determined that there "is no effective way to determine the identity or the age of a user who is accessing material through e-mail, mail exploders, newsgroups or chat rooms." The Government offered no evidence that there was a reliable way to screen recipients and participants in such fora for age. Moreover, even if it were technologically feasible to block minors' access to newsgroups and chat rooms containing discussions of art, politics or other subjects that potentially elicit "indecent" or "patently offensive" contributions, it would not be possible to block their access to that material and "still allow them access to the remaining content, even if the overwhelming majority of that content was not indecent."

Technology exists by which an operator of a Web site may condition access on the verification of requested information such as a credit card number or an adult password. Credit card verification is only feasible, however, either in connection with a commercial transaction in which the card is used, or by payment to a verification agency. Using credit card possession as a surrogate for proof of age would impose costs on non-commercial Web sites that would require many of them to shut down. For that reason, at the time of the trial, credit card verification was "effectively unavailable to a substantial number of Internet content providers." ... Moreover, the imposition of such a requirement "would completely bar adults who do not have a credit card and lack the resources to obtain one from accessing any blocked material."

Commercial pornographic sites that charge their users for access have assigned them passwords as a method of age verification. The record does not contain any evidence concerning the reliability of these technologies. Even if passwords are effective for commercial purveyors of indecent material, the District Court found that an adult password requirement would impose significant burdens on noncommercial sites, both because they would discourage users from accessing their sites and because the cost of creating and maintaining such screening systems would be "beyond their reach."

In sum, the District Court found: "Even if credit card verification or adult password verification were implemented, the Government presented no testimony as to how such systems could ensure that the user of the password or credit card is in fact over 18. The burdens imposed by credit card verification and adult password verification systems make them effectively unavailable to a substantial number of Internet content providers." . . .

II

The Telecommunications Act of 1996 . . . was an unusually important legislative enactment. . . . The major components of the statute have nothing to do with the Internet; they were designed to promote competition in the local telephone service market, the multichannel video market, and the market for over-the-air broadcasting. . . . Title V—known as the "Communications Decency Act of 1996" (CDA)—contains provisions that were either added in executive committee after the hearings were concluded or as amendments offered during floor debate on the legislation. An amendment offered in the Senate was the source of the two statutory provisions challenged in this case. They are informally described as the "indecent transmission" provision and the "patently offensive display" provision.

The first, 47 U.S.C.A. § 223(a) (Supp.1997), prohibits the knowing transmission of obscene or indecent messages to any recipient under 18 years of age. It provides in pertinent part:

"(a) Whoever—

"(1) in interstate or foreign communications—. . .

"(B) by means of a telecommunications device knowingly—

"(i) makes, creates, or solicits, and

"(ii) initiates the transmission of,

"any comment, request, suggestion, proposal, image, or other communication which is obscene or indecent, knowing that the recipient of the communication is under 18 years of age, regardless of whether the maker of such communication placed the call or initiated the communication; . . .

"(2) knowingly permits any telecommunications facility under his control to be used for any activity prohibited by paragraph (1) with the intent that it be used for such activity,

"shall be fined under Title 18, or imprisoned not more than two years, or both. "

The second provision, § 223(d), prohibits the knowing sending or displaying of patently offensive messages in a manner that is available to a person under 18 years of age. It provides:

"(d) Whoever—

"(1) in interstate or foreign communications knowingly—

"(A) uses an interactive computer service to send to a specific person or persons under 18 years of age, or

"(B) uses any interactive computer service to display in a manner available to a person under 18 years of age,

"any comment, request, suggestion, proposal, image, or other communication that, in context, depicts or describes, in terms patently offensive as measured by contemporary community standards, sexual or excretory activities or organs, regardless of whether the user of such service placed the call or initiated the communication; or

"(2) knowingly permits any telecommunications facility under such person's control to be used for an activity prohibited by paragraph (1) with the intent that it be used for such activity,

"shall be fined under Title 18, or imprisoned not more than two years, or both."

The breadth of these prohibitions is qualified by two affirmative defenses.... One covers those who take "good faith, reasonable, effective, and appropriate actions" to restrict access by minors to the prohibited communications. § 223(e)(5)(A). The other covers those who restrict access to covered material by requiring certain designated forms of age proof, such as a verified credit card or an adult identification number or code. § 223(e)(5)(B).

III

On February 8, 1996, immediately after the President signed the statute, 20 plaintiffs filed suit against the Attorney General of the United States and the Department of Justice challenging the constitutionality of §§ 223(a)(1) and 223(d).... [A] three-judge District Court was convened pursuant to § 561 of the Act.... [T]hat Court entered a preliminary injunction against enforcement of both of the challenged provisions....

. . .

The judgment of the District Court enjoins the Government from enforcing the prohibitions in § 223(a)(1)(B) insofar as they relate to "indecent" communications, but expressly preserves the Government's right to investigate and prosecute the obscenity or child pornography activities prohibited therein. The injunction against enforcement of §§ 223(d)(1) and (2) is unqualified because those provisions contain no separate reference to obscenity or child pornography.

The Government appealed under the Act's special review provisions.... In its appeal, the Government argues that the District Court erred in holding that the CDA violated both the First Amendment because it is overbroad and the Fifth Amendment because it is vague. While we discuss the vagueness of the CDA because of its relevance to the First Amendment overbreadth inquiry, we conclude that the judgment should be affirmed without reaching the Fifth Amendment issue. . . .

IV

In arguing for reversal, the Government contends that the CDA is plainly constitutional under three of our prior decisions: (1) Ginsberg v. New York, 390 U.S. 629 (1968); (2) FCC v. Pacifica Foundation, 438 U.S. 726 (1978); and (3) Renton v. Playtime Theatres, Inc., 475 U.S. 41 (1986). A close look at these cases, however, raises—rather than relieves—doubts concerning the constitutionality of the CDA.

In *Ginsberg*, we upheld the constitutionality of a New York statute that prohibited selling to minors under 17 years of age material that was considered obscene as to them even if not obscene as to adults. . . .

In four important respects, the statute upheld in *Ginsberg* was narrower than the CDA. First, we noted in *Ginsberg* that "the prohibition against sales to minors does not bar parents who so desire from purchasing the magazines for their children." . . . Under the CDA, by contrast, neither the parents' consent—nor even their participation—in the communication would avoid the application of the statute. Second, the New York statute applied only to commercial transactions, . . . whereas the CDA contains no such limitation. Third, the New York statute cabined its definition of material that is harmful to minors with the requirement that it be "utterly without redeeming social importance for minors." . . . The CDA fails to provide us with any definition of the term "indecent" as used in § 223(a)(1) and, importantly, omits any requirement that the "patently offensive" material covered by § 223(d) lack serious literary, artistic, political, or scientific value. Fourth, the New York statute defined a minor as a person under the age of 17, whereas the CDA, in applying to all those under 18 years, includes an additional year of those nearest majority.

In *Pacifica*, we upheld a declaratory order of the Federal Communications Commission, holding that the broadcast of a recording of a 12–minute monologue entitled "Filthy Words" that had previously been delivered to a live audience "could have been the subject of administrative sanctions." . . .

. . .

As with the New York statute at issue in *Ginsberg*, there are significant differences between the order upheld in *Pacifica* and the CDA. First, the order in *Pacifica*, issued by an agency that had been regulating radio stations for decades, targeted a specific broadcast that represented a rather dramatic departure from traditional program content in order to designate when—rather than whether—it would be permissible to air such a program in that particular medium. The CDA's broad categorical prohibitions are not limited to particular times and are not dependent on any evaluation by an agency familiar with the unique characteristics of the Internet. Second, unlike the CDA, the Commission's declaratory order was not punitive. . . . Finally, the Commission's order applied to a medium which as a matter of history had "received the most limited First Amendment protection," . . . , in large part because warnings could not adequately protect the listener from unexpected program content. The Internet, however, has no comparable history. Moreover, the District Court found that the risk of encountering indecent material by accident is remote because a series of affirmative steps is required to access specific material.

In *Renton*, we upheld a zoning ordinance that kept adult movie theatres out of residential neighborhoods. The ordinance was aimed, not at the content of the films shown in the theaters, but rather at the "secondary effects"—such as crime and deteriorating property values—that these theaters fostered. . . . [T]he purpose of the CDA is to protect children from the primary effects of "indecent" and "patently offensive" speech, rather than any "secondary" effect of such speech. . . .

These precedents, then, surely do not require us to uphold the CDA and are fully consistent with the application of the most stringent review of its provisions.

V

. . . [S]ome of our cases have recognized special justifications for regulation of the broadcast media that are not applicable to other speakers. . . . In these cases, the Court relied on the history of extensive government regulation of the broadcast medium, . . . the scarcity of available frequencies at its inception, . . . and its "invasive" nature. . . .

Those factors are not present in cyberspace. Neither before nor after the enactment of the CDA have the vast democratic fora of the Internet been subject to the type of government supervision and regulation that has attended the broadcast industry. Moreover, the Internet is not as "invasive" as radio or television. The District Court specifically found that "[c]ommunications over the Internet do not 'invade' an individual's home or appear on one's computer screen unbidden. Users seldom encounter content 'by accident.' " It also found that "[a]lmost all sexually explicit images are preceded by warnings as to the content," and cited testimony that " 'odds are slim' that a user would come across a sexually explicit sight by accident."

. . .

Finally, unlike the conditions that prevailed when Congress first authorized regulation of the broadcast spectrum, the Internet can hardly be considered a "scarce" expressive commodity. It provides relatively unlimited, low-cost capacity for communication of all kinds. The Government estimates that "[a]s many as 40 million people use the Internet today, and that figure is expected to grow to 200 million by 1999." This dynamic, multifaceted category of communication includes not only traditional print and news services, but also audio, video, and still images, as well as interactive, real-time dialogue. Through the use of chat rooms, any person with a phone line can become a town crier with a voice that resonates farther than it could from any soapbox. Through the use of Web pages, mail exploders, and newsgroups, the same individual can become a pamphleteer. As the District Court found, "the content on the Internet is as diverse as human thought." . . .

VI

Regardless of whether the CDA is so vague that it violates the Fifth Amendment, the many ambiguities concerning the scope of its coverage render it problematic for purposes of the First Amendment. For instance, each of the two parts of the CDA uses a different linguistic form. The first uses the word "indecent," ... while the second speaks of material that "in context, depicts or describes, in terms patently offensive as measured by contemporary community standards, sexual or excretory activities or organs," .... Given the absence of a definition of either term, this difference in language will provoke uncertainty among speakers about how the two standards relate to each other and just what they mean. Could a speaker confidently assume that a serious discussion about birth control practices, homosexuality, the First Amendment issues raised by the Appendix to our *Pacifica* opinion, or the consequences of prison rape would not violate the CDA? This uncertainty undermines the likelihood that the CDA has been carefully tailored to the congressional goal of protecting minors from potentially harmful materials.

The vagueness of the CDA is a matter of special concern for two reasons. First, the CDA is a content-based regulation of speech. The vagueness of such a regulation raises special First Amendment concerns because of its obvious chilling effect on free speech.... Second, the CDA is a criminal statute.... The severity of criminal sanctions may well cause speakers to remain silent rather than communicate even arguably unlawful words, ideas, and images....

The Government argues that the statute is no more vague than the obscenity standard this Court established in Miller v. California, 413 U.S. 15 (1973).... Because the CDA's "patently offensive" standard (and, we assume *arguendo*, its synonymous "indecent" standard) is one part of the three-prong *Miller* test, the Government reasons, it cannot be unconstitutionally vague.

The Government's assertion is incorrect as a matter of fact. The second prong of the *Miller* test—the purportedly analogous standard—contains a critical requirement that is omitted from the CDA: that the proscribed material be "specifically defined by the applicable state law." This requirement reduces the vagueness inherent in the open-ended term "patently offensive" as used in the CDA. Moreover, the *Miller* definition is limited to "sexual conduct," whereas the CDA extends also to include (1) "excretory activities" as well as (2) "organs" of both a sexual and excretory nature.

The Government's reasoning is also flawed. Just because a definition including three limitations is not vague, it does not follow that one of those limitations, standing by itself, is not vague. Each of *Miller*'s additional two prongs ... critically limits the uncertain sweep of the obscenity definition. The second requirement is particularly important because, unlike the "patently offensive" and "prurient interest" criteria, it is not judged by contemporary community standards.... This "societal value" requirement, absent in the CDA, allows appellate courts to impose some limitations and regularity on the definition by setting, as a matter of law, a national floor for socially redeeming value. The Government's contention that courts will be able to give such legal limitations to the CDA's standards is belied by *Miller*'s own rationale for having juries determine whether material is "patently offensive" according to community standards: that such questions are essentially ones of *fact*.

In contrast to *Miller* and our other previous cases, the CDA thus presents a greater threat of censoring speech that, in fact, falls outside the statute's scope. Given the vague contours of the coverage of the statute, it unquestionably silences some speakers whose messages would be entitled to constitutional protection. That danger provides further reason for insisting that the statute not be overly broad. The CDA's burden on protected speech cannot be justified if it could be avoided by a more carefully drafted statute.

VII

We are persuaded that the CDA lacks the precision that the First Amendment requires when a statute regulates the content of speech. In order to deny minors access to potentially harmful speech, the CDA effectively suppresses a large amount of speech that adults have a constitutional right to receive and to address to one another. That burden on adult speech is unacceptable if less restrictive alternatives would be at least as effective in achieving the legitimate purpose that the statute was enacted to serve.

. . .

It is true that we have repeatedly recognized the governmental interest in protecting children from harmful materials. . . . But that interest does not justify an unnecessarily broad suppression of speech addressed to adults. . . .

. . .

In arguing that the CDA does not so diminish adult communication, the Government relies on the incorrect factual premise that prohibiting a transmission whenever it is known that one of its recipients is a minor would not interfere with adult-to-adult communication. The findings of the District Court make clear that this premise is untenable. Given the size of the potential audience for most messages, in the absence of a viable age verification process, the sender must be charged with knowing that one or more minors will likely view it. Knowledge that, for instance, one or more members of a 100–person chat group will be minor—and therefore that it would be a crime to send the group an indecent message—would surely burden communication among adults.

The District Court found that at the time of trial existing technology did not include any effective method for a sender to prevent minors from obtaining access to its communications on the Internet without also denying access to adults. . . . By contrast, the District Court found that "[d]espite its limitations, currently available *user-based* software suggests that a reasonably effective method by which *parents* can prevent their children from accessing sexually explicit and other material which *parents* may believe is inappropriate for their children will soon be widely available." . . .

The breadth of the CDA's coverage is wholly unprecedented. Unlike the regulations upheld in *Ginsberg* and *Pacifica*, the scope of the CDA is not limited to commercial speech or commercial entities. Its open-ended prohibitions embrace all nonprofit entities and individuals posting indecent messages or displaying them on their own computers in the presence of minors. The general, undefined terms "indecent" and "patently offensive" cover large amounts of nonpornographic material with serious educational or other value. Moreover, the "community standards" criterion as applied to the Internet means that any communication available to a nation-wide audience will be judged by the standards of the community most likely to be offended by the message. The regulated subject matter includes any of the seven "dirty words" used in the *Pacifica* monologue, the use of which the Government's expert acknowledged could constitute a felony. . . . It may also extend to discussions about prison rape or safe sexual practices, artistic images that include nude subjects, and arguably the card catalogue of the Carnegie Library.

For the purposes of our decision, we need neither accept nor reject the Government's submission that the First Amendment does not forbid a blanket prohibition on all "indecent" and "patently offensive" messages communicated to a 17–year old—no matter how much value the message may contain and regardless of parental approval. It is at least clear that the strength of the Government's interest in protecting minors is not equally strong throughout the coverage of this broad statute. Under the CDA, a parent allowing her 17–year-old to use the family computer to obtain information on the Internet that she, in her parental judgment, deems appropriate could face a lengthy prison term. . . . Similarly, a parent who sent his 17–year-old college freshman information on birth control via e-mail could be incarcerated even though neither he, his child, nor anyone in their home community, found the material "indecent" or "patently offensive," if the college town's community thought otherwise.

The breadth of this content-based restriction of speech imposes an especially heavy burden on the Government to explain why a less restrictive provision would not be as effective as the CDA. It has not done so. The arguments in this Court have referred to possible alternatives such as requiring that indecent material be "tagged" in a way that facilitates parental control of material coming into their homes, making exceptions for messages with artistic or educational value, providing some tolerance for parental choice, and regulating some portions of the Internet—such as commercial web sites—differently than others, such as chat rooms. Particularly in the light of the absence of any detailed findings by the Congress, or even hearings addressing the special problems of the CDA, we are persuaded that the CDA is not narrowly tailored if that requirement has any meaning at all.

VIII

In an attempt to curtail the CDA's facial overbreadth, the Government advances three additional arguments for sustaining the Act's affirmative prohibitions: (1) that the CDA is constitutional because it leaves open ample "alternative channels" of communication; (2) that the plain meaning of the Act's "knowledge" and "specific person" requirement significantly restricts its permissible applications; and (3) that the Act's prohibitions are "almost always" limited to material lacking redeeming social value.

The Government first contends that, even though the CDA effectively censors discourse on many of the Internet's modalities—such as chat groups, newsgroups, and mail exploders—it is nonetheless constitutional because it provides a "reasonable opportunity" for speakers to engage in the restricted speech on the World Wide Web. This argument is unpersuasive because the CDA regulates speech on the basis of its content. A "time, place, and manner" analysis is therefore inapplicable. . . . It is thus immaterial whether such speech would be feasible on the Web. . . . The Government's position is equivalent to arguing that a statute could ban leaflets on certain subjects as long as individuals are free to publish books. . . .

The Government also asserts that the "knowledge" requirement of both §§ 223(a) and (d), especially when coupled with the "specific child" element found in § 223(d), saves the CDA from overbreadth. Because both sections prohibit the dissemination of indecent messages only to persons known to be under 18, the Government argues, it does not require transmitters to "refrain from communicating indecent material to adults; they need only refrain from disseminating such materials to persons they know to be under 18."

This argument ignores the fact that most Internet fora—including chat rooms, newsgroups, mail exploders, and the Web—are open to all comers. . . . Even the strongest reading of the "specific person" requirement of § 223(d) . . . would confer broad powers of censorship, in the form of a "heckler's veto," upon any opponent of indecent speech who might simply log on and inform the would-be discoursers that his 17–year-old child—a "specific person . . . under 18 years of age," . . .—would be present.

Finally, we find no textual support for the Government's submission that material having scientific, educational, or other redeeming social value will necessarily fall outside the CDA's "patently offensive" and "indecent" prohibitions. . . .

IX

The Government's three remaining arguments focus on the defenses provided in § 223(e)(5). First, relying on the "good faith, reasonable, effective, and appropriate actions" provision, the Government suggests that "tagging" provides a defense that saves the constitutionality of the Act. The suggestion assumes that transmitters may encode their indecent communications in a way that would indicate their contents, thus permitting recipients to block their reception with appropriate software. It is the requirement that the good faith action must be "effective" that makes this defense illusory. The Government recognizes that its proposed screening software does not currently exist. Even if it did, there is no way to know whether a potential recipient will actually block the encoded material. Without the impossible knowledge that every guardian in America is screening for the "tag," the transmitter could not reasonably rely on its action to be "effective."

For its second and third arguments concerning defenses—which we can consider together—the Government relies on the latter half of § 223(e)(5), which applies when the transmitter has restricted access by requiring use of a verified credit card or adult identification. Such verification is not only technologically available but actually is used by commercial providers of sexually explicit material. These providers, therefore, would be protected by the defense. Under the findings of the District Court, however, it is not economically feasible for most noncommercial speakers to employ such verification. Accordingly, this defense would not significantly narrow the statute's burden on noncommercial speech. Even with respect to the commercial pornographers that would be protected by the defense, the Government failed to adduce any evidence that these verification techniques actually preclude minors from posing as adults. . . . The Government thus failed to prove that the proffered defense would significantly reduce the heavy burden on adult speech produced by the prohibition on offensive displays.

... [T]he CDA places an unacceptably heavy burden on protected speech, and ... the defenses do not constitute the sort of "narrow tailoring" that will save an otherwise patently invalid unconstitutional provision. ...

X

At oral argument, the Government relied heavily on its ultimate fall-back position: If this Court should conclude that the CDA is insufficiently tailored, it urged, we should save the statute's constitutionality by honoring the severability clause, ... and construing nonseverable terms narrowly. In only one respect is this argument acceptable.

A severability clause requires textual provisions that can be severed. We will follow § 608's guidance by leaving constitutional textual elements of the statute intact in the one place where they are, in fact, severable.... Appellees do not challenge the application of the statute to obscene speech, which, they acknowledge, can be banned totally because it enjoys no First Amendment protection.... As set forth by the statute, the restriction of "obscene" material enjoys a textual manifestation separate from that for "indecent" material, which we have held unconstitutional. Therefore, we will sever the term "or indecent" from the statute, leaving the rest of § 223(a) standing. In no other respect, however, can § 223(a) or § 223(d) be saved by such a textual surgery.

The Government also draws on an additional, less traditional aspect of the CDA's severability clause, 47 U.S. C., § 608, which asks any reviewing court that holds the statute facially unconstitutional not to invalidate the CDA in application to "other persons or circumstances" that might be constitutionally permissible....

. . .

... In considering a facial challenge, this Court may impose a limiting construction on a statute only if it is "readily susceptible" to such a construction.... The open-ended character of the CDA provides no guidance whatever for limiting its coverage.

This case is therefore unlike those in which we have construed a statute narrowly because the text or other source of congressional intent identified a clear line that this Court could draw.... [O]ur decision in United States v. Treasury Employees, 513 U.S. 454, 479, n. 26 (1995), is applicable. In that case, we declined to "dra[w] one or more lines between categories of speech covered by an overly broad statute, when Congress has sent inconsistent signals as to where the new line or lines should be drawn" because doing so "involves a far more serious invasion of the legislative domain." This Court "will not rewrite a ... law to conform it to constitutional requirements." ...

XI

In this Court, though not in the District Court, the Government asserts that—in addition to its interest in protecting children—its "[e]qually significant" interest in fostering the growth of the Internet provides an independent basis for upholding the constitutionality of the CDA. The Government apparently assumes that the unregulated availability of "indecent" and "patently offensive" material on the Internet is driving countless citizens away from the medium because of the risk of exposing themselves or their children to harmful material.

We find this argument singularly unpersuasive. The dramatic expansion of this new marketplace of ideas contradicts the factual basis of this contention. The record demonstrates that the growth of the Internet has been and continues to be phenomenal. As a matter of constitutional tradition, in the absence of evidence to the contrary, we presume that governmental regulation of the content of speech is more likely to interfere with the free exchange of ideas than to encourage it. The interest in encouraging freedom of expression in a democratic society outweighs any theoretical but unproven benefit of censorship.

For the foregoing reasons, the judgment of the district court is affirmed.

It is so ordered.

Justice O'Connor with whom The Chief Justice joins, concurring in the judgment in part and dissenting in part.

I write separately to explain why I view the Communications Decency Act of 1996(CDA) as little more than an attempt by Congress to create "adult zones" on the Internet. Our precedent indicates that the creation of such zones can be constitutionally sound. Despite the soundness of its purpose, however, portions of the CDA are unconstitutional because they stray from the blueprint our prior cases have developed for constructing a "zoning law" that passes constitutional muster.

. . .

I

Our cases make clear that a "zoning" law is valid only if adults are still able to obtain the regulated speech. . . . If the law does not unduly restrict adults' access to constitutionally protected speech, however, it may be valid. . . .

The Court in *Ginsberg* concluded that the New York law created a constitutionally adequate adult zone simply because, on its face, it denied access only to minors. The Court did not question—and therefore necessarily assumed—that an adult zone, once created, would succeed in preserving adults' access while denying minors' access to the regulated speech. Before today, there was no reason to question this assumption, for the Court has previously only considered laws that operated in the physical world, a world that with two characteristics that make it possible to create "adult zones": geography and identity. . . . A minor can see an adult dance show only if he enters an establishment that provides such entertainment. And should he attempt to do so, the minor will not be able to conceal completely his identity (or, consequently, his age). Thus, the twin characteristics of geography and identity enable the establishment's proprietor to prevent children from entering the establishment, but to let adults inside.

The electronic world is fundamentally different. . . . [I]t is not currently possible to exclude persons from accessing certain messages on the basis of their identity.

Cyberspace differs from the physical world in another basic way: Cyberspace is malleable. Thus, it is possible to construct barriers in cyberspace and use them to screen for identity, making cyberspace more like the physical world and, consequently, more amenable to zoning laws. This transformation of cyberspace is already underway.... Internet speakers (users who post material on the Internet) have begun to zone cyberspace itself through the use of "gateway" technology. Such technology requires Internet users to enter information about themselves—perhaps an adult identification number or a credit card number—before they can access certain areas of cyberspace, much like a bouncer checks a person's driver's license before admitting him to a nightclub. Internet users who access information have not attempted to zone cyberspace itself, but have tried to limit their own power to access information in cyberspace, much as a parent controls what her children watch on television by installing a lock box. This user-based zoning is accomplished through the use of screening software (such as Cyber Patrol or SurfWatch) or browsers with screening capabilities, both of which search addresses and text for keywords that are associated with "adult" sites and, if the user wishes, blocks access to such sites....

Despite this progress, the transformation of cyberspace is not complete. Although gateway technology has been available on the World Wide Web for some time now, ... it is not available to all Web speakers, and is just now becoming technologically feasible for chat rooms and USENET newsgroups. Gateway technology is not ubiquitous in cyberspace, and because without it "there is no means of age verification," cyberspace still remains largely unzoned—and unzoneable.... User-based zoning is also in its infancy....

Although the prospects for the eventual zoning of the Internet appear promising, I agree with the Court that we must evaluate the constitutionality of the CDA as it applies to the Internet as it exists today. Given the present state of cyberspace, I agree with the Court that the "display" provision cannot pass muster....

The "indecency transmission" and "specific person" provisions present a closer issue, for they are not unconstitutional in all of their applications.... [T]he "indecency transmission" provision makes it a crime to transmit knowingly an indecent message to a person the sender knows is under 18 years of age.... The "specific person" provision proscribes the same conduct, although it does not as explicitly require the sender to know that the intended recipient of his indecent message is a minor.... Appellant urges the Court to construe the provision to impose such a knowledge requirement, and I would do so....

So construed, both provisions are constitutional as applied to a conversation involving only an adult and one or more minors—e.g., when an adult speaker sends an e-mail knowing the addressee is a minor, or when an adult and minor converse by themselves or with other minors in a chat room. In this context, these provisions are no different from the law we sustained in *Ginsberg*....

The analogy to *Ginsberg* breaks down, however, when more than one adult is a party to the conversation. If a minor enters a chat room otherwise occupied by adults, the CDA effectively requires the adults in the room to stop using indecent speech.... The CDA is therefore akin to a law that makes it a crime for a bookstore owner to sell pornographic magazines to anyone once a minor enters his store.... [T]he absence of any means of excluding minors from chat rooms in cyberspace restricts the rights of adults to engage in indecent speech in those rooms. The "indecency transmission" and "specific person" provisions share this defect.

. . . I agree with the Court that the provisions are overbroad in that they cover any and all communications between adults and minors, regardless of how many adults might be part of the audience to the communication.

This conclusion does not end the matter, however. . . . I would . . . sustain the "indecency transmission" and "specific person" provisions to the extent they apply to the transmission of Internet communications where the party initiating the communication knows that all of the recipients are minors.

II

Whether the CDA substantially interferes with the First Amendment rights of minors, and thereby runs afoul of the second characteristic of valid zoning laws, presents a closer question. . . .

The Court neither "accept[s] nor reject[s]" the argument that the CDA is facially overbroad because it substantially interferes with the First Amendment rights of minors. I would reject it. . . . Because the CDA denies minors the right to obtain material that is "patently offensive"—even if it has some redeeming value for minors and even if it does not appeal to their prurient interests— Congress' rejection of the *Ginsberg* "harmful to minors" standard means that the CDA could ban some speech that is "indecent" (i.e., "patently offensive") but that is not obscene as to minors.

I do not deny this possibility, but to prevail in a facial challenge, it is not enough for a plaintiff to show "some" overbreadth. Our cases require a proof of "real" and "substantial" overbreadth. . . . In my view, the universe of speech constitutionally protected as to minors but banned by the CDA—i.e., the universe of material that is "patently offensive," but which nonetheless has some redeeming value for minors or does not appeal to their prurient interest— is a very small one. . . . Accordingly, in my view, the CDA does not burden a substantial amount of minors' constitutionally protected speech.

Thus, the constitutionality of the CDA as a zoning law hinges on the extent to which it substantially interferes with the First Amendment rights of adults. . . . I would invalidate the CDA only to that extent. Insofar as the "indecency transmission" and "specific person" provisions prohibit the use of indecent speech in communications between an adult and one or more minors, however, they can and should be sustained. The Court reaches a contrary conclusion, and from that holding that I respectfully dissent.

D.   REGULATION OF COMMERCIAL SPEECH

Page 1359.   Add at end of chapter:

Glickman v. Wileman Brothers & Elliott, Inc.

521 U.S. 457, 117 S.Ct. 2130, 138 L.Ed.2d 585 (1997).

[The report in this case appears infra, page 209.]

Greater New Orleans Broadcasting Association, Inc. v. United States

___ U.S. ___, 119 S.Ct. 1923, ___ L.Ed.2d ___ (1999).

Justice Stevens delivered the opinion of the Court.

Federal law prohibits some, but by no means all, broadcast advertising of lotteries and casino gambling. In United States v. Edge Broadcasting Co., 509 U. S. 418 (1993), we upheld the constitutionality of 18 U. S. C. § 1304 as applied to broadcast advertising of Virginia's lottery by a radio station located in North Carolina, where no such lottery was authorized. Today we hold that § 1304 may not be applied to advertisements of private casino gambling that are broadcast by radio or television stations located in Louisiana, where such gambling is legal.

I

Through most of the 19th and the first half of the 20th centuries, Congress adhered to a policy that not only discouraged the operation of lotteries and similar schemes, but forbade the dissemination of information concerning such enterprises by use of the mails, even when the lottery in question was chartered by a state legislature. . . .[W]e found that the notion that "lotteries . . . are supposed to have a demoralizing influence upon the people" provided sufficient justification for excluding circulars concerning such enterprises from the federal postal system. Ex parte Jackson, 96 U. S. 727, 736–737 (1878). We likewise deferred to congressional judgment in upholding the similar exclusion for newspapers that contained either lottery advertisements or prize lists. In re Rapier, 143 U. S. 110, 134–135 (1892) . . . The current versions of these early antilottery statutes are now codified at 18 U. S. C. §§ 1301–1303.

Congress extended its restrictions on lottery-related information to broadcasting as communications technology made that practice both possible and profitable. It enacted the statute at issue in this case as § 316 of the Communications Act of 1934, 48 Stat. 1088. Now codified at 18 U. S. C. § 1304 ("Broadcasting lottery information"), the statute prohibits radio and television broadcasting, by any station for which a license is required, of

> "any advertisement of or information concerning any lottery, gift enterprise, or similar scheme, offering prizes dependent in whole or in part upon lot or chance, or any list of the prizes drawn or awarded by means of any such lottery, gift enterprise, or scheme, whether said list contains any part or all of such prizes."

. . . Although § 1304 is a criminal statute, . . . in practice, the provision traditionally has been enforced by the Federal Communications Commission (FCC), which imposes administrative sanctions on radio and television licensees for violations of the agency's implementing regulation. . . .Petitioners now concede that the broadcast ban in § 1304 and the FCC's regulation encompasses advertising for privately owned casinos . . .

During the second half of this century, Congress dramatically narrowed the scope of the broadcast prohibition in § 1304. The first inroad was minor: In 1950, certain not-for-profit fishing contests were exempted as "innocent pastimes ... far removed from the reprehensible type of gambling activity which it was paramount in the congressional mind to forbid." ...

Subsequent exemptions were more substantial. Responding to the growing popularity of State-run lotteries, in 1975 Congress enacted the provision that gave rise to our decision in *Edge.* ... With subsequent modifications, that amendment now exempts advertisements of State-conducted lotteries from the nationwide postal restrictions in §§ 1301 and 1302, and from the broadcast restriction in § 1304, when "broadcast by a radio or television station licensed to a location in ... a State which conducts such a lottery." ... The § 1304 broadcast restriction remained in place, however, for stations licensed in States that do not conduct lotteries. In *Edge,* we held that this remaining restriction on broadcasts from nonlottery States, such as North Carolina, supported the "laws against gambling" in those jurisdictions and properly advanced the "congressional policy of balancing the interests of lottery and nonlottery States."

In 1988, Congress enacted two additional statutes that significantly curtailed the coverage of § 1304. First, the Indian Gaming Regulatory Act (IGRA) ... exempted "any gaming conducted by an Indian tribe pursuant to" the Act from both the postal and transportation restrictions in 18 U. S. C. §§ 1301–1302, and the broadcast restriction in § 1304. ... Second, the Charity Games Advertising Clarification Act of 1988 ... extended the exemption from §§ 1301–1304 for state-run lotteries to include any other lottery, gift enterprise, or similar scheme—not prohibited by the law of the State in which it operates—when conducted by: (i) any governmental organization; (ii) any not-for-profit organization; or (iii) a commercial organization as a promotional activity "clearly occasional and ancillary to the primary business of that organization." [U]nlike the 1975 broadcast exemption for advertisements of and information concerning State-conducted lotteries, the exemptions in both of these 1988 statutes are not geographically limited; they shield messages from § 1304's reach in States that do not authorize such gambling as well as those that do.

A separate statute, the 1992 Professional and Amateur Sports Protection Act, ... proscribes most sports betting and advertising thereof. ... However, the Act also includes a variety of exemptions, some with obscured congressional purposes: (i) gambling schemes conducted by States or other governmental entities at any time between January 1, 1976, and August 31, 1990; (ii) gambling schemes authorized by statutes in effect on October 2, 1991; (iii) gambling "conducted exclusively in casinos" located in certain municipalities if the schemes were authorized within one year of the effective date of the Act and, for "commercial casino gaming scheme[s]," that had been in operation for the preceding ten years pursuant to a State constitutional provision and comprehensive State regulation applicable to that municipality; and (iv) gambling on parimutuel animal racing or jai-alai games. ... These exemptions make the scope of § 3702's advertising prohibition somewhat unclear, but the prohibition is not limited to broadcast media and does not depend on the location of a broadcast station or other disseminator of promotional materials.

Thus, unlike the uniform federal antigambling policy that prevailed in 1934 when 18 U. S. C. § 1304 was enacted, federal statutes now accommodate both pro-gambling and antigambling segments of the national polity.

II

Petitioners are an association of Louisiana broadcasters and its members who operate FCC-licensed radio and television stations in the New Orleans metropolitan area. But for the threat of sanctions ..., petitioners would broadcast promotional advertisements for gaming available at private, for-profit casinos that are lawful and regulated in both Louisiana and neighboring Mississippi. According to an FCC official, however, "[u]nder appropriate conditions, some broadcast signals from Louisiana broadcasting stations may be heard in neighboring states including Texas and Arkansas," where private casino gambling is unlawful.

Petitioners brought this action against the United States and the FCC in the District Court for the Eastern District of Louisiana, praying for a declaration that § 1304 and the FCC's regulation violate the First Amendment as applied to them, and for an injunction preventing enforcement of the statute and the rule against them. [T]he District Court ruled in favor of the Government. . . .

A divided panel of the Court of Appeals for the Fifth Circuit ... affirmed the grant of summary judgment to the Government. . . .

. . .

While the broadcasters' petition for certiorari was pending in this Court, we decided 44 Liquormart, Inc. v. Rhode Island, ... [W]e ... remanded the case for further consideration. . . .

On remand, the Fifth Circuit majority adhered to its prior conclusion. . . . We now reverse.

III

In a number of cases involving restrictions on speech that is "commercial"in nature, we have employed *Central Hudson's* four-part test to resolve First Amendment challenges ...

... [P]etitioners as well as certain judges, scholars, and amici curiae have advocated repudiation of the *Central Hudson* standard and implementation of a more straightforward and stringent test for assessing the validity of governmental restrictions on commercial speech. As the opinions in *44 Liquormart* demonstrate, reasonable judges may disagree about the merits of such proposals. It is, however, an established part of our constitutional jurisprudence that we do not ordinarily reach out to make novel or unnecessarily broad pronouncements on constitutional issues when a case can be fully resolved on a narrower ground. . . . In this case, there is no need to break new ground. *Central Hudson*, as applied in our more recent commercial speech cases, provides an adequate basis for decision.

IV

All parties to this case agree that the messages petitioners wish to broadcast constitute commercial speech, and that these broadcasts would satisfy the first part of the *Central Hudson* test: Their content is not misleading and concerns lawful activities ...

The second part of the *Central Hudson* test asks whether the asserted governmental interest served by the speech restriction is substantial. The Solicitor General identifies two such interests: (1) reducing the social costs associated with "gambling" or " 'casino gambling,' " and (2) assisting States that "restrict gambling" or "prohibit casino gambling" within their own borders. . . .

We can accept the characterization of these two interests as "substantial," but that conclusion is by no means self-evident. . . . Despite its awareness of the potential social costs, Congress has not only sanctioned casino gambling for Indian tribes through tribal-state compacts, but has enacted other statutes that reflect approval of state legislation that authorizes a host of public and private gambling activities. . . . That Congress has generally exempted state-run lotteries and casinos from federal gambling legislation reflects a decision to defer to, and even promote, differing gambling policies in different States. . . . Whatever its character in 1934 when § 1304 was adopted, the federal policy of discouraging gambling in general, and casino gambling in particular, is now decidedly equivocal.

. . . Even though the Government has identified substantial interests, when we consider both their quality and the information sought to be suppressed, the crosscurrents in the scope and application of § 1304 become more difficult for the Government to defend.

V

The third part of the *Central Hudson* test asks whether the speech restriction directly and materially advances the asserted governmental interest. . . .

The fourth part of the test complements the direct-advancement inquiry of the third, asking whether the speech restriction is not more extensive than necessary to serve the interests that support it. . . . .

. . . § 1304 cannot satisfy these standards. With regard to the first asserted interest—alleviating the social costs of casino gambling by limiting demand—the Government contends that its broadcasting restrictions directly advance that interest because "promotional" broadcast advertising concerning casino gambling increases demand for such gambling, which in turn increases the amount of casino gambling that produces those social costs. . . . [I]t does not necessarily follow that the Government's speech ban has directly and materially furthered the asserted interest. . . . [A]ny measure of the effectiveness of the Government's attempt to minimize the social costs of gambling cannot ignore Congress' simultaneous encouragement of tribal casino gambling, which may well be growing at a rate exceeding any increase in gambling or compulsive gambling that private casino advertising could produce. And, . . . the Government fails to "connect casino gambling and compulsive gambling with broadcast advertising for casino' "—let alone broadcast advertising for non-Indian commercial casinos. . . .

We need not resolve the question whether any lack of evidence in the record fails to satisfy the standard of proof under *Central Hudson*, however, because the flaw in the Government's case is more fundamental: The operation of § 1304 and its attendant regulatory regime is so pierced by exemptions and inconsistencies that the Government cannot hope to exonerate it. . . . Under current law, a broadcaster may not carry advertising about privately operated commercial casino gambling, regardless of the location of the station or the casino. . . . On the other hand, advertisements for tribal casino gambling authorized by state compacts—whether operated by the tribe or by a private party pursuant to a management contract—are subject to no such broadcast ban, even if the broadcaster is located in or broadcasts to a jurisdiction with the strictest of antigambling policies. . . . Government-operated, nonprofit, and "occasional and ancillary" commercial casinos are likewise exempt. . . .

The FCC's interpretation and application of §§ 1304 and 1307 underscore the statute's infirmity. Attempting to enforce the underlying purposes and policy of the statute, the FCC has permitted broadcasters to tempt viewers with claims of "Vegas-style excitement" at a commercial "casino'" if "casino" is part of the establishment's proper name and the advertisement can be taken to refer to the casino's amenities, rather than directly promote its gaming aspects. While we can hardly fault the FCC in view of the statute's focus on the suppression of certain types of information, the agency's practice is squarely at odds with the governmental interests asserted in this case.

From what we can gather, the Government is committed to prohibiting accurate product information, not commercial enticements of all kinds, and then only when conveyed over certain forms of media and for certain types of gambling—indeed, for only certain brands of casino gambling—and despite the fact that messages about the availability of such gambling are being conveyed over the airwaves by other speakers.

Even putting aside the broadcast exemptions for arguably distinguishable sorts of gambling that might also give rise to social costs about which the Federal Government is concerned—such as state lotteries and parimutuel betting on horse and dog races, . . . —the Government presents no convincing reason for pegging its speech ban to the identity of the owners or operators of the advertised casinos. The Government cites revenue needs of States and tribes that conduct casino gambling, and notes that net revenues generated by the tribal casinos are dedicated to the welfare of the tribes and their members. . . . Yet the Government admits that tribal casinos offer precisely the same types of gambling as private casinos. . . . The Government's suggestion that Indian casinos are too isolated to warrant attention is belied by a quick review of tribal geography and the Government's own evidence regarding the financial success of tribal gaming. If distance were determinative, Las Vegas might have remained a relatively small community, or simply disappeared like a desert mirage.

Ironically, the most significant difference identified by the Government between tribal and other classes of casino gambling is that the former are "heavily regulated." . . . If such direct regulation provides a basis for believing that the social costs of gambling in tribal casinos are sufficiently mitigated to make their advertising tolerable, one would have thought that Congress might have at least experimented with comparable regulation before abridging the speech rights of federally unregulated casinos. . . . There surely are practical and nonspeech-related forms of regulation—including a prohibition or supervision of gambling on credit; limitations on the use of cash machines on casino premises; controls on admissions; pot or betting limits; location restrictions;

and licensing requirements—that could more directly and effectively alleviate some of the social costs of casino gambling.

. . .

Given the special federal interest in protecting the welfare of Native Americans, . . . we recognize that there may be valid reasons for imposing commercial regulations on non-Indian businesses that differ from those imposed on tribal enterprises. It does not follow, however, that those differences also justify abridging non-Indians' freedom of speech more severely than the freedom of their tribal competitors. For the power to prohibit or to regulate particular conduct does not necessarily include the power to prohibit or regulate speech about that conduct. . . . And to the extent that the purpose and operation of federal law distinguishes among information about tribal, governmental, and private casinos based on the identity of their owners or operators, the Government presents no sound reason why such lines bear any meaningful relationship to the particular interest asserted: minimizing casino gambling and its social costs by way of a (partial) broadcast ban. . . .

The second interest asserted by the Government—the derivative goal of "assisting" States with policies that disfavor private casinos—adds little to its case. We cannot see how this broadcast restraint, ambivalent as it is, might directly and adequately further any state interest in dampening consumer demand for casino gambling if it cannot achieve the same goal with respect to the similar federal interest.

Furthermore, even assuming that the state policies on which the Federal Government seeks to embellish are more coherent and pressing than their federal counterpart, § 1304 sacrifices an intolerable amount of truthful speech about lawful conduct . . . .

VI

. . . Had the Federal Government adopted a more coherent policy, or accommodated the rights of speakers in States that have legalized the underlying conduct, . . . this might be a different case. But under current federal law, as applied to petitioners and the messages that they wish to convey, the broadcast prohibition in 18 U. S. C. § 1304 . . . (1998) violates the First Amendment. The judgment of the Court of Appeals is therefore

Reversed.

Chief Justice Rehnquist, concurring.

. . .

Were Congress to undertake substantive regulation of the gambling industry, rather than simply the manner in which it may broadcast advertisements, "exemptions and inconsistencies' "such as those in § 1304 might well prove constitutionally tolerable. . . . Williamson v. Lee Optical . . .

But when Congress regulates commercial speech, the *Central Hudson* test imposes a more demanding standard of review. I agree with the Court that that standard has not been met here and I join its opinion.

Justice Thomas, concurring in the judgment.

I continue to adhere to my view that . . . the *Central Hudson* test should not be applied because [it] can no more justify regulation of "commercial speech" than it can justify regulation of "noncommercial speech."

CHAPTER 14

RESTRICTIONS ON TIME, PLACE OR MANNER OF EXPRESSION

SECTION 1. THE TRADITIONAL PUBLIC FORUM: SPEECH ACTIVITIES IN STREETS AND PARKS

Page 1377. Add after Madsen v. Women's Health Center, Inc.:

SCHENCK v. PRO–CHOICE NETWORK OF WESTERN NEW YORK, 519 U.S. 357 (1997). The Court held that an injunction requiring a "floating buffer zone"—requiring protesters to stay 15 feet from those entering or leaving an abortion clinic—burdened more speech than necessary, and violated the First Amendment. On the other hand, an injunction imposing a "fixed buffer zone"—requiring protesters to remain 15 feet from clinic doorways, driveways, and driveway entrances—was necessary to insure access to the clinic.

SECTION 2. THE NON-TRADITIONAL FORUM–SPEECH ACTIVITIES IN PUBLIC PROPERTY OTHER THAN PARKS AND STREETS

Page 1393. Add at end of section:

Arkansas Educational Television Commission v. Forbes

523 U.S. 666, 118 S.Ct. 1633, 140 L.Ed.2d 875 (1998).

Justice Kennedy delivered the opinion of the Court.

A state-owned public television broadcaster sponsored a candidate debate from which it excluded an independent candidate with little popular support. The issue before us is whether, by reason of its state ownership, the station had a constitutional obligation to allow every candidate access to the debate. We conclude that, unlike most other public television programs, the candidate debate was subject to constitutional constraints applicable to nonpublic fora under our forum precedents. Even so, the broadcaster's decision to exclude the candidate was a reasonable, viewpoint-neutral exercise of journalistic discretion.

I

Petitioner, the Arkansas Educational Television Commission (AETC), is an Arkansas state agency owning and operating a network of five noncommercial television stations (Arkansas Educational Television Network or AETN). The eight members of AETC are appointed by the Governor for 8–year terms and are removable only for good cause. ...To insulate its programming decisions from political pressure, AETC employs an Executive Director and professional staff who exercise broad editorial discretion in planning the network's programming. AETC has also adopted the Statement of Principles of Editorial Integrity in Public Broadcasting, which counsel adherence to "generally accepted broadcasting industry standards, so that the programming service is free from pressure from political or financial supporters."

In the spring of 1992, AETC staff began planning a series of debates between candidates for federal office in the November 1992 elections. AETC decided to televise a total of five debates, scheduling one for the Senate election and one for each of the four congressional elections in Arkansas. ...AETC staff developed a debate format allowing about 53 minutes during each 1–hour debate for questions to and answers by the candidates. Given the time constraint, the staff and Simmons "decided to limit participation in the debates to the major party candidates or any other candidate who had strong popular support."

On June 17, 1992, AETC invited the Republican and Democratic candidates for Arkansas' Third Congressional District to participate in the AETC debate for that seat. Two months later, after obtaining the 2,000 signatures required by Arkansas law, ... respondent Ralph Forbes was certified as an independent candidate qualified to appear on the ballot for the seat. Forbes was a perennial candidate who had sought, without success, a number of elected offices in Arkansas. On August 24, 1992, he wrote to AETC requesting permission to participate in the debate for his district, scheduled for October 22, 1992. On September 4, AETC Executive Director Susan Howarth denied Forbes' request, explaining that AETC had "made a bona fide journalistic judgement that our viewers would be best served by limiting the debate" to the candidates already invited.

On October 19, 1992, Forbes filed suit against AETC, seeking injunctive and declaratory relief as well as damages. Forbes claimed he was entitled to participate in the debate under both the First Amendment and 47 U. S. C. § 315, which affords political candidates a limited right of access to television air time. ...The District Court ... dismissed Forbes' action for failure to state a claim.

Sitting en banc, the Court of Appeals affirmed the dismissal of Forbes' statutory claim, holding that he had failed to exhaust his administrative remedies. The court reversed, however, the dismissal of Forbes' First Amendment claim ... , and ... remanded the action for further proceedings.

On remand, the District Court found as a matter of law that the debate was a nonpublic forum, and the issue became whether Forbes' views were the reason for his exclusion. At trial, ... [t]he jury made express findings that AETC's decision to exclude Forbes had not been influenced by political pressure or disagreement with his views. The District Court entered judgment for AETC.

The Court of Appeals again reversed. ...AETC had "opened its facilities to a particular group—candidates running for the Third District Congressional seat." AETC's action ... made the debate a public forum, to which all candidates "legally qualified to appear on the ballot" had a presumptive right of access. Applying strict scrutiny, the court determined that AETC's assessment of Forbes' "political viability" was neither a "compelling nor [a] narrowly tailored" reason for excluding him from the debate.

... We now reverse.

II

Forbes has long since abandoned his statutory claims under 47 U. S. C. § 315, and so the issue is whether his exclusion from the debate was consistent with the First Amendment. ...At the outset ... it is instructive to ask whether public forum principles apply to the case at all.

Having first arisen in the context of streets and parks, the public forum doctrine should not be extended in a mechanical way to the very different context of public television broadcasting. ...[B]road rights of access for outside speakers would be antithetical, as a general rule, to the discretion that stations and their editorial staff must exercise to fulfill their journalistic purpose and statutory obligations.

Congress has rejected the argument that "broadcast facilities should be open on a nonselective basis to all persons wishing to talk about public issues." Columbia Broadcasting System, Inc. v. Democratic National Committee, 412 U. S. 94, 105 (1973). Instead, television broadcasters enjoy the "widest journalistic freedom" consistent with their public responsibilities. ...Among the broadcaster's responsibilities is the duty to schedule programming that serves the "public interest, convenience, and necessity." 47 U. S. C. § 309(a). Public and private broadcasters alike are not only permitted, but indeed required, to exercise substantial editorial discretion in the selection and presentation of their programming.

As a general rule, the nature of editorial discretion counsels against subjecting broadcasters to claims of viewpoint discrimination. Programming decisions would be particularly vulnerable to claims of this type because even principled exclusions rooted in sound journalistic judgment can often be characterized as viewpoint-based. To comply with their obligation to air programming that serves the public interest, broadcasters must often choose among speakers expressing different viewpoints. ...Much like a university selecting a commencement speaker, a public institution selecting speakers for a lecture series, or a public school prescribing its curriculum, a broadcaster by its nature will facilitate the expression of some viewpoints instead of others. Were the judiciary to require, and so to define and approve, pre-established criteria for access, it would risk implicating the courts in judgments that should be left to the exercise of journalistic discretion.

When a public broadcaster exercises editorial discretion in the selection and presentation of its programming, it engages in speech activity. ....Although programming decisions often involve the compilation of the speech of third parties, the decisions nonetheless constitute communicative acts. ...

Claims of access under our public forum precedents could obstruct the legitimate purposes of television broadcasters. ..."The result would be a further erosion of the journalistic discretion of broadcasters," transferring "control over the treatment of public issues from the licensees who are accountable for broadcast performance to private individuals" who bring suit under our forum precedents. 412 U. S., at 124. In effect, we would "exchange 'public trustee' broadcasting, with all its limitations, for a system of self-appointed editorial commentators." Id., at 125.

In the absence of any congressional command to "[r]egimen[t] broadcasters" in this manner, id., at 127, we are disinclined to do so through doctrines of our own design. This is not to say the First Amendment would bar the legislative imposition of neutral rules for access to public broadcasting. Instead, we say that, in most cases, the First Amendment of its own force does not compel public broadcasters to allow third parties access to their programming.

Although public broadcasting as a general matter does not lend itself to scrutiny under the forum doctrine, candidate debates present the narrow exception to the rule. For two reasons, a candidate debate like the one at issue here is different from other programming. First, unlike AETC's other broadcasts, the debate was by design a forum for political speech by the candidates. Consistent with the long tradition of candidate debates, the implicit representation of the broadcaster was that the views expressed were those of the candidates, not its own. The very purpose of the debate was to allow the candidates to express their views with minimal intrusion by the broadcaster. In this respect the debate differed even from a political talk show, whose host can express partisan views and then limit the discussion to those ideas.

Second, in our tradition, candidate debates are of exceptional significance in the electoral process. ...Deliberation on the positions and qualifications of candidates is integral to our system of government, and electoral speech may have its most profound and widespread impact when it is disseminated through televised debates. A majority of the population cites television as its primary source of election information, and debates are regarded as the "only occasion during a campaign when the attention of a large portion of the American public is focused on the election, as well as the only campaign information format which potentially offers sufficient time to explore issues and policies in depth in a neutral forum." Congressional Research Service, Campaign Debates in Presidential General Elections, summ. (June 15, 1993).

As we later discuss, in many cases it is not feasible for the broadcaster to allow unlimited access to a candidate debate. Yet the requirement of neutrality remains; a broadcaster cannot grant or deny access to a candidate debate on the basis of whether it agrees with a candidate's views. ...

The special characteristics of candidate debates support the conclusion that the AETC debate was a forum of some type. The question of what type must be answered by reference to our public forum precedents, to which we now turn.

III

Forbes argues, and the Court of Appeals held, that the debate was a public forum to which he had a First Amendment right of access. Under our precedents, however, the debate was a nonpublic forum, from which AETC could exclude Forbes in the reasonable, viewpoint-neutral exercise of its journalistic discretion.

A

For our purposes, it will suffice to employ the categories of speech fora already established and discussed in our cases. "[T]he Court [has] identified three types of fora: the traditional public forum, the public forum created by government designation, and the nonpublic forum." Cornelius v. NAACP Legal Defense & Ed. Fund, Inc., 473 U. S. 788, 802 (1985). Traditional public fora are defined by the objective characteristics of the property, such as whether, "by long tradition or by government fiat," the property has been "devoted to assembly and debate." Perry Ed. Assn. v. Perry Local Educators' Assn., 460 U. S., 37, 45 (1983). The government can exclude a speaker from a traditional public forum "only when the exclusion is necessary to serve a compelling state interest and the exclusion is narrowly drawn to achieve that interest." . . .

Designated public fora, in contrast, are created by purposeful governmental action. "The government does not create a [designated] public forum by inaction or by permitting limited discourse, but only by intentionally opening a nontraditional public forum for public discourse." 473 U. S., at 802; accord, International Soc. for Krishna Consciousness, Inc. v. Lee, 505 U. S. 672, 678 (1992) (*ISKCON*) (designated public forum is "property that the State has opened for expressive activity by all or part of the public"). Hence "the Court has looked to the policy and practice of the government to ascertain whether it intended to designate a place not traditionally open to assembly and debate as a public forum." *Cornelius*, 473 U. S., at 802. If the government excludes a speaker who falls within the class to which a designated public forum is made generally available, its action is subject to strict scrutiny. Ibid.; United States v. Kokinda, 497 U. S. 720, 726–727 (1990) (plurality opinion of O'Connor, J.).

Other government properties are either nonpublic fora or not fora at all. . . . The government can restrict access to a nonpublic forum "as long as the restrictions are reasonable and [are] not an effort to suppress expression merely because public officials oppose the speaker's view." . . .

In summary, traditional public fora are open for expressive activity regardless of the government's intent. The objective characteristics of these properties require the government to accommodate private speakers. The government is free to open additional properties for expressive use by the general public or by a particular class of speakers, thereby creating designated public fora. Where the property is not a traditional public forum and the government has not chosen to create a designated public forum, the property is either a nonpublic forum or not a forum at all.

B

The parties agree the AETC debate was not a traditional public forum. The Court has rejected the view that traditional public forum status extends beyond its historic confines . . . and even had a more expansive conception of traditional public fora been adopted, . . ., the almost unfettered access of a traditional public forum would be incompatible with the programming dictates a television broadcaster must follow. The issue, then, is whether the debate was a designated public forum or a nonpublic forum.

Under our precedents, the AETC debate was not a designated public forum. To create a forum of this type, the government must intend to make the property "generally available," Widmar v. Vincent, 454 U. S. 263, 264 (1981), to a class of speakers. In *Widmar*, for example, a state university created a public forum for registered student groups by implementing a policy that expressly made its meeting facilities "generally open" to such groups. . . .

A designated public forum is not created when the government allows selective access for individual speakers rather than general access for a class of speakers. In *Perry*, for example, the Court held a school district's internal mail system was not a designated public forum even though selected speakers were able to gain access to it. The basis for the holding in *Perry* was explained by the Court in *Cornelius*:

> "In contrast to the general access policy in Widmar, school board policy did not grant general access to the school mail system. The practice was to require permission from the individual school principal before access to the system to communicate with teachers was granted."

And in *Cornelius* itself, the Court held the Combined Federal Campaign (CFC) charity drive was not a designated public forum because "[t]he Government's consistent policy ha[d] been to limit participation in the CFC to 'appropriate' [i.e., charitable rather than political] voluntary agencies and to require agencies seeking admission to obtain permission from federal and local Campaign officials."

These cases illustrate the distinction between "general access," . . . which indicates the property is a designated public forum, and "selective access," . . . which indicates the property is a nonpublic forum. On one hand, the government creates a designated public forum when it makes its property generally available to a certain class of speakers, as the university made its facilities generally available to student groups in *Widmar*. On the other hand, the government does not create a designated public forum when it does no more than reserve eligibility for access to the forum to a particular class of speakers, whose members must then, as individuals, "obtain permission," . . . to use it. For instance, the Federal Government did not create a designated public forum in *Cornelius* when it reserved eligibility for participation in the CFC drive to charitable agencies, and then made individual, non-ministerial judgments as to which of the eligible agencies would participate. . . .

The *Cornelius* distinction between general and selective access furthers First Amendment interests. By recognizing the distinction, we encourage the government to open its property to some expressive activity in cases where, if faced with an all-or-nothing choice, it might not open the property at all. That this distinction turns on governmental intent does not render it unprotective of speech. Rather, it reflects the reality that, with the exception of traditional public fora, the government retains the choice of whether to designate its property as a forum for specified classes of speakers.

Here, the debate did not have an open-microphone format. Contrary to the assertion of the Court of Appeals, AETC did not make its debate generally available to candidates for Arkansas' Third Congressional District seat. Instead, just as the Federal Government in *Cornelius* reserved eligibility for participation in the CFC program to certain classes of voluntary agencies, AETC reserved eligibility for participation in the debate to candidates for the Third Congressional District seat (as opposed to some other seat). At that point, just as the Government in Cornelius made agency-by-agency determinations as to which of the eligible agencies would participate in the CFC, AETC made candidate-by-candidate determinations as to which of the eligible candidates would participate in the debate. "Such selective access, unsupported by evidence of a purposeful designation for public use, does not create a public forum." ... Thus the debate was a nonpublic forum.

In addition to being a misapplication of our precedents, the Court of Appeals' holding would result in less speech, not more. In ruling that the debate was a public forum open to all ballot-qualified candidates, the Court of Appeals would place a severe burden upon public broadcasters who air candidates' views. In each of the 1988, 1992, and 1996 Presidential elections, for example, no fewer than 22 candidates appeared on the ballot in at least one State. ....In the 1996 congressional elections, it was common for 6 to 11 candidates to qualify for the ballot for a particular seat.... In the 1993 New Jersey gubernatorial election, to illustrate further, sample ballot mailings included the written statements of 19 candidates. ...On logistical grounds alone, a public television editor might, with reason, decide that the inclusion of all ballot-qualified candidates would "actually undermine the educational value and quality of debates."

Were it faced with the prospect of cacophony, on the one hand, and First Amendment liability, on the other, a public television broadcaster might choose not to air candidates' views at all. A broadcaster might decide "'the safe course is to avoid controversy,' ... and by so doing diminish the free flow of information and ideas." Turner Broadcasting System, Inc., 512 U. S., at 656 (quoting Miami Herald Publishing Co. v. Tornillo, 418 U. S. 241, 257 (1974)). In this circumstance, a "[g]overnment-enforced right of access inescapably 'dampens the vigor and limits the variety of public debate.' "

These concerns are more than speculative. As a direct result of the Court of Appeals' decision in this case, the Nebraska Educational Television Network canceled a scheduled debate between candidates in Nebraska's 1996 United States Senate race. ... A First Amendment jurisprudence yielding these results does not promote speech but represses it.

C

The debate's status as a nonpublic forum, however, did not give AETC unfettered power to exclude any candidate it wished. ...To be consistent with the First Amendment, the exclusion of a speaker from a nonpublic forum must not be based on the speaker's viewpoint and must otherwise be reasonable in light of the purpose of the property. ...

In this case, the jury found Forbes' exclusion was not based on "objections or opposition to his views." The record provides ample support for this finding, demonstrating as well that AETC's decision to exclude him was reasonable. AETC Executive Director Susan Howarth testified Forbes' views had 'absolutely' no role in the decision to exclude him from the debate. She further testified Forbes was excluded because (1) "the Arkansas voters did not consider him a serious candidate"; (2) "the news organizations also did not consider him a serious candidate"; (3) "the Associated Press and a national election result reporting service did not plan to run his name in results on election night"; (4) Forbes "apparently had little, if any, financial support, failing to report campaign finances to the Secretary of State's office or to the Federal Election Commission"; and (5) "there [was] no 'Forbes for Congress' campaign headquarters other than his house." Forbes himself described his campaign organization as "bedlam" and the media coverage of his campaign as "zilch." It is, in short, beyond dispute that Forbes was excluded not because of his viewpoint but because he had generated no appreciable public interest. . . .

There is no substance to Forbes' suggestion that he was excluded because his views were unpopular or out of the mainstream. His own objective lack of support, not his platform, was the criterion. Indeed, the very premise of Forbes' contention is mistaken. A candidate with unconventional views might well enjoy broad support by virtue of a compelling personality or an exemplary campaign organization. By the same token, a candidate with a traditional platform might enjoy little support due to an inept campaign or any number of other reasons.

Nor did AETC exclude Forbes in an attempted manipulation of the political process. The evidence provided powerful support for the jury's express finding that AETC's exclusion of Forbes was not the result of "political pressure from anyone inside or outside [AETC]." There is no serious argument that AETC did not act in good faith in this case. AETC excluded Forbes because the voters lacked interest in his candidacy, not because AETC itself did.

The broadcaster's decision to exclude Forbes was a reasonable, viewpoint-neutral exercise of journalistic discretion consistent with the First Amendment. The judgment of the Court of Appeals is

Reversed.

Justice Stevens, with whom Justice Souter and Justice Ginsburg join, dissenting.

The Court has decided that a state-owned television network has no "constitutional obligation to allow every candidate access to" political debates that it sponsors. I do not challenge that decision. The judgment of the Court of Appeals should nevertheless be affirmed. The official action that led to the exclusion of respondent Forbes from a debate with the two major-party candidates for election to one of Arkansas' four seats in Congress does not adhere to well-settled constitutional principles. The ad hoc decision of the staff of the Arkansas Educational Television Commission (AETC) raises precisely the concerns . . . "that a law subjecting the exercise of First Amendment freedoms to the prior restraint of a license, without narrow, objective, and definite standards to guide the licensing authority, is unconstitutional."

In its discussion of the facts, the Court barely mentions the standardless character of the decision to exclude Forbes from the debate. In its discussion of the law, the Court understates the constitutional importance of the distinction between state ownership and private. . . .

I

Two months before Forbes was officially certified as an independent candidate qualified to appear on the ballot under Arkansas law, the AETC staff had already concluded that he "should not be invited" to participate in the televised debates because he was "not a serious candidate as determined by the voters of Arkansas." He had, however, been a serious contender for the

Republican nomination for Lieutenant Governor in 1986 and again in 1990. Although he was defeated in a run-off election, in the three-way primary race conducted in 1990—just two years before the AETC staff decision—he had received 46.88% of the statewide vote and had carried 15 of the 16 counties within the Third Congressional District by absolute majorities. Nevertheless, the staff concluded that Forbes did not have "strong popular support."

Given the fact that the Republican winner in the Third Congressional District race in 1992 received only 50.22% of the vote and the Democrat received 47.20%, it would have been necessary for Forbes, who had made a strong showing in recent Republican primaries, to divert only a handful of votes from the Republican candidate to cause his defeat. Thus, even though the AETC staff may have correctly concluded that Forbes was "not a serious candidate," their decision to exclude him from the debate may have determined the outcome of the election in the Third District.

If a comparable decision were made today by a privately owned network, it would be subject to scrutiny under the Federal Election Campaign Act unless the network used "pre-established objective criteria to determine which candidates may participate in [the] debate." ... No such criteria governed AETC's refusal to permit Forbes to participate in the debate. Indeed, whether that refusal was based on a judgment about "newsworthiness"—as AETC has argued in this Court—or a judgment about "political viability"—as it argued in the Court of Appeals—the facts in the record presumably would have provided an adequate basis either for a decision to include Forbes in the Third District debate or a decision to exclude him, and might even have required a cancellation of two of the other debates.

The apparent flexibility of AETC's purported standard suggests the extent to which the staff had nearly limitless discretion to exclude Forbes from the debate based on ad hoc justifications. ...

II

... [T]he Court seriously underestimates the importance of the difference between private and public ownership of broadcast facilities, despite the fact that Congress and this Court have repeatedly recognized that difference.

In Columbia Broadcasting System, Inc. v. Democratic National Committee, 412 U. S. 94 (1973), the Court held that a licensee is neither a common carrier, ... nor a public forum that must accommodate " 'the right of every individual to speak, write, or publish,' " ...

While noncommercial, educational stations generally have exercised the same journalistic independence as commercial networks, in 1981 Congress enacted a statute forbidding stations that received a federal subsidy from engaging in "editorializing." Relying primarily on cases involving the rights of commercial entities, a bare majority of this Court held the restriction invalid. ... Responding to the dissenting view that "the interest in keeping the Federal Government out of the propaganda arena" justified the restriction, ... the majority emphasized the broad coverage of the statute and concluded that it "impermissibly sweeps within its prohibition a wide range of speech by wholly private stations on topics that ... have nothing whatever to do with federal, state, or local government." ... The Court noted that Congress had considered and rejected a ban that would have applied only to stations operated by state or local governmental entities, and reserved decision on the constitutionality of such a limited ban.

The *League of Women Voters* case implicated the right of "wholly private stations" to express their own views on a wide range of topics that "have nothing whatever to do with ... government." ... The case before us today involves only the right of a state-owned network to regulate speech that plays a central role in democratic government. Because AETC is owned by the State, deference to its interest in making ad hoc decisions about the political content of its programs necessarily increases the risk of government censorship and propaganda in a way that protection of privately owned broadcasters does not.

III

The ... First Amendment will not tolerate a state agency's arbitrary exclusion from a debate forum based, for example, on an expectation that the speaker might be critical of the Governor, or might hold unpopular views about abortion or the death penalty. Indeed, the Court so holds today.

It seems equally clear, however, that the First Amendment will not tolerate arbitrary definitions of the scope of the forum. We have recognized that "[o]nce it has opened a limited forum, ... the State must respect the lawful boundaries it has itself set." Rosenberger v. Rector and Visitors of Univ. of Va., 515 U. S. 819, 829 (1995). It follows, of course, that a State's failure to set any meaningful boundaries at all cannot insulate the State's action from First Amendment challenge. The dispositive issue in this case, then, is not whether AETC created a designated public forum or a nonpublic forum, as the Court concludes, but whether AETC defined the contours of the debate forum with sufficient specificity to justify the exclusion of a ballot-qualified candidate.

AETC asks that we reject Forbes' constitutional claim on the basis of entirely subjective, ad hoc judgments about the dimensions of its forum. The First Amendment demands more ...

AETC's control was comparable to that of a local government official authorized to issue permits to use public facilities for expressive activities. In cases concerning access to a traditional public forum, we have found an analogy between the power to issue permits and the censorial power to impose a prior restraint on speech. ...

We recently reaffirmed this approach when considering the constitutionality of an assembly and parade ordinance that authorized a county official to exercise discretion in setting the amount of the permit fee. ... Forsyth County v. Nationalist Movement, 505 U. S. 123 (1992). ... Perhaps the discretion of the AETC staff in controlling access to the 1992 candidate debates was not quite as unbridled as that of the Forsyth County administrator. Nevertheless, it was surely broad enough to raise the concerns that controlled our decision in that case. No written criteria cabined the discretion of the AETC staff. Their subjective judgment about a candidate's "viability" or "newsworthiness" allowed them wide latitude either to permit or to exclude a third participant in any debate. ...

The televised debate forum at issue in this case may not squarely fit within our public forum analysis, but its importance cannot be denied. Given the special character of political speech, particularly during campaigns for elected office, the debate forum implicates constitutional concerns of the highest order, as the majority acknowledges. . . .

. . . The importance of avoiding arbitrary or viewpoint-based exclusions from political debates militates strongly in favor of requiring the controlling state agency to use (and adhere to) pre-established, objective criteria to determine who among qualified candidates may participate. . . . A constitutional duty to use objective standards—i.e., "neutral principles"—for determining whether and when to adjust a debate format would impose only a modest requirement that would fall far short of a duty to grant every multiple-party request. Such standards would also have the benefit of providing the public with some assurance that state-owned broadcasters cannot select debate participants on arbitrary grounds.

Like the Court, I do not endorse the view of the Court of Appeals that all candidates who qualify for a position on the ballot are necessarily entitled to access to any state-sponsored debate. . . . Requiring government employees to set out objective criteria by which they choose which candidates will benefit from the significant media exposure that results from state-sponsored political debates would alleviate some of the risk inherent in allowing government agencies—rather than private entities—to stage candidate debates.

Accordingly, I would affirm the judgment of the Court of Appeals.

SECTION 5.   GOVERNMENT SUBSIDIES TO SPEECH

Page 1438. Add at end of Chapter:

National Endowment for the Arts v. Finley

524 U.S. 569, 118 S.Ct. 2168, 141 L.Ed.2d 500 (1998).

Justice O'Connor delivered the opinion of the Court.

The National Foundation on the Arts and Humanities Act, as amended in 1990, requires the Chairperson of the National Endowment for the Arts (NEA) to ensure that "artistic excellence and artistic merit are the criteria by which [grant] applications are judged, taking into consideration general standards of decency and respect for the diverse beliefs and values of the American public." 20 U. S. C. § 954(d)(1). In this case, we review the Court of Appeals' determination that § 954(d)(1), on its face, impermissibly discriminates on the basis of viewpoint and is void for vagueness under the First and Fifth Amendments. We conclude that § 954(d)(1) is facially valid, as it neither inherently interferes with First Amendment rights nor violates constitutional vagueness principles.

I

A

With the establishment of the NEA in 1965, Congress embarked on a "broadly conceived national policy of support for the . . . arts in the United States," see § 953(b), pledging federal funds to "help create and sustain not only a climate encouraging freedom of thought, imagination, and inquiry but also the material conditions facilitating the release of ... creative talent." § 951(7). The enabling statute vests the NEA with substantial discretion to award grants; it identifies only the broadest funding priorities, including "artistic and cultural significance, giving emphasis to American creativity and cultural diversity," "professional excellence," and the encouragement of "'public knowledge, education, understanding, and appreciation of the arts." See §§ 954(c)(1)-(10).

Applications for NEA funding are initially reviewed by advisory panels composed of experts in the relevant field of the arts. Under the 1990 Amendments to the enabling statute, those panels must reflect "diverse artistic and cultural points of view" and include "wide geographic, ethnic, and minority representation," as well as "lay individuals who are knowledgeable about the arts." §§ 959(c)(1)-(2). The panels report to the 26–member National Council on the Arts (Council), which, in turn, advises the NEA Chairperson. The Chairperson has the ultimate authority to award grants but may not approve an application as to which the Council has made a negative recommendation. § 955(f).

Since 1965, the NEA has distributed over three billion dollars in grants to individuals and organizations, funding that has served as a catalyst for increased state, corporate, and foundation support for the arts. Congress has recently restricted the availability of federal funding for individual artists, confining grants primarily to qualifying organizations and state arts agencies, and constraining sub-granting. ...

Throughout the NEA's history, only a handful of the agency's roughly 100,000 awards have generated formal complaints about misapplied funds or abuse of the public's trust. Two provocative works, however, prompted public controversy in 1989 and led to congressional revaluation of the NEA's funding priorities and efforts to increase oversight of its grant-making procedures. The Institute of Contemporary Art at the University of Pennsylvania had used $30,000 of a visual arts grant it received from the NEA to fund a 1989 retrospective of photographer Robert Mapplethorpe's work. The exhibit, entitled The Perfect Moment, included homoerotic photographs that several Members of Congress condemned as pornographic. ... Members also denounced artist Andres Serrano's work Piss Christ, a photograph of a crucifix immersed in urine. ... Serrano had been awarded a $15,000 grant from the Southeast Center for Contemporary Art, an organization that received NEA support.

When considering the NEA's appropriations for fiscal year 1990, Congress reacted to the controversy surrounding the Mapplethorpe and Serrano photographs by eliminating $45,000 from the agency's budget, the precise amount contributed to the two exhibits by NEA grant recipients. Congress also enacted an amendment providing that no NEA funds "may be used to promote, disseminate, or produce materials which in the judgment of [the NEA] may be considered obscene, including but not limited to, depictions of sadomasochism, homoeroticism, the sexual exploitation of children, or individuals engaged in sex acts and which, when taken as a whole, do not have serious literary, artistic, political, or scientific value." ... The NEA implemented Congress' mandate by instituting a requirement that all grantees certify in writing that they would not utilize federal funding to engage in projects inconsistent with the criteria in the 1990 appropriations bill. That certification requirement was subsequently invalidated as unconstitutionally vague by a Federal District Court, see Bella Lewitzky Dance Foundation v. Frohnmayer, 754 F. Supp. 774 (CD Cal. 1991), and the NEA did not appeal the decision.

In the 1990 appropriations bill, Congress also agreed to create an Independent Commission of constitutional law scholars to review the NEA's grant-making procedures and assess the possibility of more focused standards for public arts funding. The Commission's report, issued in September 1990, concluded that there is no constitutional obligation to provide arts funding, but also recommended that the NEA rescind the certification requirement and cautioned against legislation setting forth any content restrictions. Instead, the Commission suggested procedural changes to enhance the role of advisory panels and a statutory reaffirmation of "the high place the nation accords to the fostering of mutual respect for the disparate beliefs and values among us."
. . .

Informed by the Commission's recommendations, and cognizant of pending judicial challenges to the funding limitations in the 1990 appropriations bill, Congress debated several proposals to reform the NEA's grant-making process when it considered the agency's reauthorization in the fall of 1990. The House rejected the Crane Amendment, which would have virtually eliminated the NEA, . . . and the Rohrabacher Amendment, which would have introduced a prohibition on awarding any grants that could be used to "promote, distribute, disseminate, or produce matter that has the purpose or effect of denigrating the beliefs, tenets, or objects of a particular religion" or "of denigrating an individual, or group of individuals, on the basis of race, sex, handicap, or national origin,". . . . Ultimately, Congress adopted the Williams/Coleman Amendment, a bipartisan compromise between Members opposing any funding restrictions and those favoring some guidance to the agency. In relevant part, the Amendment became § 954(d)(1), which directs the Chairperson, in establishing procedures to judge the artistic merit of grant applications, to "tak[e] into consideration general standards of decency and respect for the diverse beliefs and values of the American public."

The NEA has not promulgated any official interpretation of the provision, but in December 1990, the Council unanimously adopted a resolution to implement § 954(d)(1) merely by ensuring that the members of the advisory panels that conduct the initial review of grant applications represent geographic, ethnic, and aesthetic diversity. . . .John Frohnmayer, then Chairperson of the NEA, also declared that he would "count on [the] procedures" ensuring diverse membership on the peer review panels to fulfill Congress' mandate.

B

The four individual respondents in this case . . . are performance artists who applied for NEA grants before § 954(d)(1) was enacted. An advisory panel recommended approval of respondents' projects,. . . . A majority of the Council subsequently recommended disapproval, and in June 1990, the NEA informed respondents that they had been denied funding. Respondents filed suit, alleging that the NEA had violated their First Amendment rights by rejecting the applications on political grounds,. . . . When Congress enacted § 954(d)(1), respondents, now joined by the National Association of Artists' Organizations

(NAAO), amended their complaint to challenge the provision as void for vagueness and impermissibly viewpoint based.

. . .

The District Court ... granted summary judgment in favor of respondents on their facial constitutional challenge to § 954(d)(1) and enjoined enforcement of the provision. ...

A divided panel of the Court of Appeals affirmed the District Court's ruling. ...

. . .

We ... reverse the judgment of the Court of Appeals.

II

A

Respondents raise a facial constitutional challenge to § 954(d)(1), and consequently they confront "a heavy burden" in advancing their claim. ...

Respondents argue that the provision is a paradigmatic example of viewpoint discrimination because it rejects any artistic speech that either fails to respect mainstream values or offends standards of decency. The premise of respondents' claim is that § 954(d)(1) constrains the agency's ability to fund certain categories of artistic expression. The NEA, however, reads the provision as merely hortatory, and contends that it stops well short of an absolute restriction. Section 954(d)(1) adds "considerations" to the grant-making process; it does not preclude awards to projects that might be deemed "indecent" or "disrespectful," nor place conditions on grants, or even specify that those factors must be given any particular weight in reviewing an application. Indeed, the agency asserts that it has adequately implemented § 954(d)(1) merely by ensuring the representation of various backgrounds and points of view on the advisory panels that analyze grant applications. ...We do not decide whether the NEA's view—that the formulation of diverse advisory panels is sufficient to comply with Congress' command—is in fact a reasonable reading of the statute. It is clear, however, that the text of § 954(d)(1) imposes no categorical requirement. The advisory language stands in sharp contrast to congressional efforts to prohibit the funding of certain classes of speech. When Congress has in fact intended to affirmatively constrain the NEA's grant-making authority, it has done so in no uncertain terms. See § 954(d)(2) ("[O]bscenity is without artistic merit, is not protected speech, and shall not be funded").

Furthermore, like the plain language of § 954(d), the political context surrounding the adoption of the "decency and respect" clause is inconsistent with respondents' assertion that the provision compels the NEA to deny funding on the basis of viewpoint discriminatory criteria. The legislation was a bipartisan proposal introduced as a counterweight to amendments aimed at eliminating the NEA's funding or substantially constraining its grant-making authority. ...[T]he criteria in § 954(d)(1) inform the assessment of artistic merit, but Congress declined to disallow any particular viewpoints. ...

That § 954(d)(1) admonishes the NEA merely to take "decency and respect" into consideration, and that the legislation was aimed at reforming procedures rather than precluding speech, undercut respondents' argument that the provision inevitably will be utilized as a tool for invidious viewpoint discrimination. . . .

. . . As respondents' own arguments demonstrate, the considerations that the provision introduces, by their nature, do not engender the kind of directed viewpoint discrimination that would prompt this Court to invalidate a statute on its face. Respondents assert, for example, that "[o]ne would be hard-pressed to find two people in the United States who could agree on what the 'iverse beliefs and values of the American public' are, much less on whether a particular work of art 'respects' them"; and they claim that " '[d]ecency' is likely to mean something very different to a septegenarian in Tuscaloosa and a teenager in Las Vegas.". . . . Accordingly, the provision does not introduce considerations that, in practice, would effectively preclude or punish the expression of particular views. Indeed, one could hardly anticipate how "decency" or "respect" would bear on grant applications in categories such as funding for symphony orchestras.

Respondents' claim that the provision is facially unconstitutional may be reduced to the argument that the criteria in § 954(d)(1) are sufficiently subjective that the agency could utilize them to engage in viewpoint discrimination. Given the varied interpretations of the criteria and the vague exhortation to "take them into consideration," it seems unlikely that this provision will introduce any greater element of selectivity than the determination of "artistic excellence" itself. And we are reluctant, in any event, to invalidate legislation "on the basis of its hypothetical application to situations not before the Court." . . .

The NEA's enabling statute contemplates a number of indisputably constitutional applications for both the "decency" prong of § 954(d)(1) and its reference to "respect for the diverse beliefs and values of the American public." Educational programs are central to the NEA's mission. . . . And it is well established that 'decency' is a permissible factor where "educational suitability" motivates its consideration. . . .

Permissible applications of the mandate to consider "respect for the diverse beliefs and values of the American public" are also apparent. In setting forth the purposes of the NEA, Congress explained that "[i]t is vital to democracy to honor and preserve its multicultural artistic heritage." § 951(10). The agency expressly takes diversity into account, giving special consideration to "projects and productions . . . that reach, or reflect the culture of, a minority, inner city, rural, or tribal community," § 954(c)(4), as well as projects that generally emphasize "cultural diversity," § 954(c)(1). Respondents do not contend that the criteria in § 954(d)(1) are impermissibly applied when they may be justified, as the statute contemplates, with respect to a project's intended audience.

We recognize, of course, that reference to these permissible applications would not alone be sufficient to sustain the statute against respondents' First Amendment challenge. But neither are we persuaded that, in other applications, the language of § 954(d)(1) itself will give rise to the suppression of protected expression. Any content-based considerations that may be taken into account in the grant-making process are a consequence of the nature of arts funding. The NEA has limited resources and it must deny the majority of the grant applications that it receives, including many that propose "artistically excellent" projects. The agency may decide to fund particular projects for a wide variety of reasons, "such as the technical proficiency of the artist, the creativity of the work, the anticipated public interest in or appreciation of the work, the work's contemporary relevance, its educational value, its suitability for or appeal to special audiences (such as children or the disabled), its service to a rural or isolated community, or even simply that the work could increase public knowledge of an art form." . . . .

Respondent's reliance on our decision in Rosenberger v. Rector and Visitors of Univ. of Va., 515 U. S. 819 (1995), is therefore misplaced. In *Rosenberger*, a public university declined to authorize disbursements from its Student Activities Fund to finance the printing of a Christian student newspaper. We held that by subsidizing the Student Activities Fund, the University had created a limited public forum, from which it impermissibly excluded all publications with religious editorial viewpoints. . . . .Although the scarcity of NEA funding does not distinguish this case from *Rosenberger*, . . . the competitive process according to which the grants are allocated does. In the context of arts funding, in contrast to many other subsidies, the Government does not indiscriminately "encourage a diversity of views from private speakers," . . . The NEA's mandate is to make aesthetic judgments, and the inherently content-based "excellence" threshold for NEA support sets it apart from the subsidy at issue in *Rosenberger*—which was available to all student organizations that were " 'related to the educational purpose of the University,' " . . .— and from comparably objective decisions on allocating public benefits, such as access to a school auditorium or a municipal theater, see Lamb's Chapel v. Center Moriches Union Free School Dist., 508 U. S. 384, 386 (1993); Southeastern Promotions, Ltd. v. Conrad, 420 U. S. 546, 555 (1975), or the second class mailing privileges available to " 'all newspapers and other periodical publications,' " see Hannegan v. Esquire, Inc., 327 U. S. 146, 148, n. 1 (1946).

Respondents do not allege discrimination in any particular funding decision. (In fact, after filing suit to challenge § 954(d)(1), two of the individual respondents received NEA grants. . . .) Thus, we have no occasion here to address an as-applied challenge in a situation where the denial of a grant may be shown to be the product of invidious viewpoint discrimination. If the NEA were to leverage its power to award subsidies on the basis of subjective criteria into a penalty on disfavored viewpoints, then we would confront a different case. . . .Unless and until § 954(d)(1) is applied in a manner that raises concern about the suppression of disfavored viewpoints, however, we uphold the constitutionality of the provision. . . .

B

Finally, although the First Amendment certainly has application in the subsidy context, we note that the Government may allocate competitive funding according to criteria that would be impermissible were direct regulation of speech or a criminal penalty at stake. So long as legislation does not infringe on other constitutionally protected rights, Congress has wide latitude to set spending priorities. . . .In the 1990 Amendments that incorporated § 954(d)(1), Congress modified the declaration of purpose in the NEA's enabling act to provide that arts funding should ' "contribute to public support and confidence in the use of taxpayer funds," and that "[p]ublic funds ... must ultimately serve public purposes the Congress defines." ' § 951(5). ...Congress may "selectively fund a program to encourage certain activities it believes to be in the public interest, without at the same time funding an alternative program which seeks to deal with the problem in another way."....

III

The lower courts also erred in invalidating § 954(d)(1) as unconstitutionally vague. ....The terms of the provision are undeniably opaque, and if they appeared in a criminal statute or regulatory scheme, they could raise substantial vagueness concerns. It is unlikely, however, that speakers will be compelled to steer too far clear of any "forbidden area" in the context of grants of this nature. ...We recognize, as a practical matter, that artists may conform their speech to what they believe to be the decision-making criteria in order to acquire funding. ...But when the Government is acting as patron rather than as sovereign, the consequences of imprecision are not constitutionally severe.

In the context of selective subsidies, it is not always feasible for Congress to legislate with clarity. Indeed, if this statute is unconstitutionally vague, then so too are all government programs awarding scholarships and grants on the basis of subjective criteria such as "excellence." ... To accept respondents' vagueness argument would be to call into question the constitutionality of these valuable government programs and countless others like them.

Section 954(d)(1) merely adds some imprecise considerations to an already subjective selection process. It does not, on its face, impermissibly infringe on First or Fifth Amendment rights. Accordingly, the judgment of the Court of Appeals is reversed and the case is remanded for further proceedings consistent with this opinion.

It is so ordered.

Justice Scalia with whom Justice Thomas joins, concurring in the judgment.

"The operation was a success, but the patient died." What such a procedure is to medicine, the Court's opinion in this case is to law. It sustains the constitutionality of 20 U. S. C. § 954(d)(1) by gutting it. The most avid congressional opponents of the provision could not have asked for more. I write separately because, unlike the Court, I think that § 954(d)(1) must be evaluated as written, rather than as distorted by the agency it was meant to control. By its terms, it establishes content-and-viewpoint-based criteria upon which grant applications are to be evaluated. And that is perfectly constitutional.

I

THE STATUTE MEANS WHAT IT SAYS

. . .

... I am at a loss to understand what the Court has in mind (other than the gutting of the statute) when it speculates that the statute is merely "advisory." ... This does not mean that those factors must always be dispositive, but it does mean that they must always be considered. The method of compliance proposed by the National Endowment for the Arts (NEA)—selecting diverse review panels of artists and nonartists that reflect a wide range of geographic and cultural perspectives—is so obviously inadequate that it insults the intelligence. A diverse panel membership increases the odds that, if and when the panel takes the factors into account, it will reach an accurate assessment of what they demand. But it in no way increases the odds that the panel will take the factors into consideration—much less ensures that the panel will do so, which is the Chairperson's duty under the statute. Moreover, the NEA's fanciful reading of § 954(d)(1) would make it wholly superfluous. Section 959(c) already requires the Chairperson to "issue regulations and establish procedures . . . to ensure that all panels are composed, to the extent practicable, of individuals reflecting . . . diverse artistic and cultural points of view."

. . .

I agree with the Court that § 954(d)(1) "imposes no categorical requirement," in the sense that it does not require the denial of all applications that violate general standards of decency or exhibit disrespect for the diverse beliefs and values of Americans. But the factors need not be conclusive to be discriminatory. To the extent a particular applicant exhibits disrespect for the diverse beliefs and values of the American public or fails to comport with general standards of decency, the likelihood that he will receive a grant diminishes. In other words, the presence of the "tak[e] into consideration" clause "cannot be regarded as mere surplusage; it means something," . . . And the "something" is that the decisionmaker, all else being equal, will favor applications that display decency and respect, and disfavor applications that do not.

This unquestionably constitutes viewpoint discrimination. That conclusion is not altered by the fact that the statute does not "compe[l]" the denial of funding, any more than a provision imposing a five-point handicap on all black applicants for civil service jobs is saved from being race discrimination by the fact that it does not compel the rejection of black applicants. If viewpoint discrimination in this context is unconstitutional (a point I shall address anon), the law is invalid unless there are some situations in which the decency and respect factors do not constitute viewpoint discrimination. And there is none. . . .

. . .

II

WHAT THE STATUTE SAYS IS CONSTITUTIONAL

. . . With the enactment of § 954(d)(1), Congress did not abridge the speech of those who disdain the beliefs and values of the American public, nor did it abridge indecent speech. Those who wish to create indecent and disrespectful art are as unconstrained now as they were before the enactment of this statute. Avant-garde artistes such as respondents remain entirely free to epater les bourgeois; they are merely deprived of the additional satisfaction of having the bourgeoisie taxed to pay for it. . . .

One might contend, I suppose, that a threat of rejection by the only available source of free money would constitute coercion and hence "abridgment" within the meaning of the First Amendment. . . . I would not agree with such a contention, which would make the NEA the mandatory patron of all art too indecent, too disrespectful, or even too kitsch to attract private support. But even if one accepts the contention, it would have no application here. The NEA is far from the sole source of funding for art—even indecent, disrespectful, or just plain bad art. Accordingly, the Government may earmark NEA funds for projects it deems to be in the public interest without thereby abridging speech. . . .

Section 954(d)(1) is no more discriminatory, and no less constitutional, than virtually every other piece of funding legislation enacted by Congress. . . . [T]he agency itself discriminates—and is required by law to discriminate—in favor of artistic (as opposed to scientific, or political, or theological) expression. . . .

Respondents, relying on Rosenberger v. Rector and Visitors of Univ. of Va., 515 U. S. 819, 833 (1995), argue that viewpoint-based discrimination is impermissible unless the government is the speaker or the government is "disbursing public funds to private entities to convey a governmental message." . It is impossible to imagine why that should be so; one would think that directly involving the government itself in the viewpoint discrimination (if it is unconstitutional) would make the situation even worse. Respondents are mistaken. It is the very business of government to favor and disfavor points of view on (in modern times, at least) innumerable subjects—which is the main reason we have decided to elect those who run the government, rather than save money by making their posts hereditary. And it makes not a bit of difference, insofar as either common sense or the Constitution is concerned, whether these officials further their (and, in a democracy, our) favored point of view by achieving it directly (having government-employed artists paint pictures, for example, or government-employed doctors perform abortions); or by advocating it officially (establishing an Office of Art Appreciation, for example, or an Office of Voluntary Population Control); or by giving money to others who achieve or advocate it (funding private art classes, for example, or Planned Parenthood). [None of this has anything to do with abridging anyone's speech. *Rosenberger* . . . found the viewpoint discrimination unconstitutional, not because funding of "private" speech was involved, but because the government had established a limited public forum—to which the NEA's granting of highly selective (if not highly discriminating) awards bears no resemblance.

The nub of the difference between me and the Court is that I regard the distinction between 'abridging' speech and funding it as a fundamental divide, on this side of which the First Amendment is inapplicable. The Court, by contrast, seems to believe that the First Amendment, despite its words, has some ineffable effect upon funding, imposing constraints of an indeterminate nature which it announces (without troubling to enunciate any particular test) are not violated by the statute here—or, more accurately, are not violated by the quite different, emasculated statute that it imagines. . . .

. . .

. . . The Congress that felt it necessary to enact § 954(d)(1) evidently thought it much more noteworthy that any money exacted from American taxpayers had been used to produce a crucifix immersed in urine, or a display of homoerotic photographs. It is no secret that the provision was prompted by, and directed at, the funding of such offensive productions. Instead of banning the funding of such productions absolutely, which I think would have been entirely constitutional, Congress took the lesser step of requiring them to be disfavored in the evaluation of grant applications. The Court's opinion today renders even that lesser step a nullity. For that reason, I concur only in the judgment.

Justice Souter, dissenting.

. . . .

The decency and respect proviso mandates viewpoint-based decisions in the disbursement of government subsidies, and the Government has wholly failed to explain why the statute should be afforded an exemption from the fundamental rule of the First Amendment that viewpoint discrimination in the exercise of public authority over expressive activity is unconstitutional. The Court's conclusions that the proviso is not viewpoint based, that it is not a regulation, and that the NEA may permissibly engage in viewpoint-based discrimination, are all patently mistaken. Nor may the question raised be answered in the Government's favor on the assumption that some constitutional applications of the statute are enough to satisfy the demand of facial constitutionality, leaving claims of the proviso's obvious invalidity to be dealt with later in response to challenges of specific applications of the discriminatory standards. This assumption is irreconcilable with our long standing and sensible doctrine of facial overbreadth, applicable to claims brought under the First Amendment's speech clause. I respectfully dissent.

I

It goes without saying that artistic expression lies within this First Amendment protection. . . . The constitutional protection of artistic works turns not on the political significance that may be attributable to such productions, though they may indeed comment on the political, but simply on their expressive character, which falls within a spectrum of protected "speech" extending outward from the core of overtly political declarations. . . .

When called upon to vindicate this ideal, we characteristically begin by asking "whether the government has adopted a regulation of speech because of disagreement with the message it conveys. . . ." . . . The answer in this case is damning. One need do nothing more than read the text of the statute to conclude that Congress's purpose in imposing the decency and respect criteria was to prevent the funding of art that conveys an offensive message; the decency and respect provision on its face is quintessentially viewpoint based, and quotations from the Congressional Record merely confirm the obvious legislative purpose. . . . Indeed, if there were any question at all about what Congress had in mind, a definitive answer comes in the succinctly accurate remark of the proviso's author, that the bill "add[s] to the criteria of artistic excellence and artistic merit, a shell, a screen, a viewpoint that must be constantly taken into account." . . .

II

In the face of such clear legislative purpose, so plainly expressed, the Court has its work cut out for it in seeking a constitutional reading of the statute. . . .

A

The Court says, first, that because the phrase "general standards of decency and respect for the diverse beliefs and values of the American public" is imprecise and capable of multiple interpretations, "the considerations that the provision introduces, by their nature, do not engender the kind of directed viewpoint discrimination that would prompt this Court to invalidate a statute on its face." . . .

. . . "[T]he inextricability of indecency from expression," . . . is beyond dispute in a certain amount of entirely lawful artistic enterprise. Starve the mode, starve the message.

Just as self-evidently, a statute disfavoring speech that fails to respect America's "diverse beliefs and values" is the very model of viewpoint discrimination; it penalizes any view disrespectful to any belief or value espoused by someone in the American populace. Boiled down to its practical essence, the limitation obviously means that art that disrespects the ideology, opinions, or convictions of a significant segment of the American public is to be disfavored, whereas art that reinforces those values is not. After all, the whole point of the proviso was to make sure that works like Serrano's ostensibly blasphemous portrayal of Jesus would not be funded, while a reverent treatment, conventionally respectful of Christian sensibilities, would not run afoul of the law. Nothing could be more viewpoint based than that. . . . The fact that the statute disfavors art insufficiently respectful of America's "diverse" beliefs and values alters this conclusion not one whit: the First Amendment does not validate the ambition to disqualify many disrespectful viewpoints instead of merely one. . . .

B

Another alternative for avoiding unconstitutionality that the Court appears to regard with some favor is the Government's argument that the NEA may comply with § 954(d) merely by populating the advisory panels that analyze grant applications with members of diverse backgrounds. Would that it were so easy . . .

. . . .

C

A third try at avoiding constitutional problems is the Court's disclaimer of any constitutional issue here because "[s]ection 954(d)(1) adds 'considerations' to the grant-making process; it does not preclude awards to projects that might be deemed 'indecent' or 'disrespectful,' . . ." . . .

That is not a fair reading. Just as the statute cannot be read as anything but viewpoint based, or as requiring nothing more than diverse review panels, it cannot be read as tolerating awards to spread indecency or disrespect, so long as the review panel, the National Counsel on the Arts, and the Chairperson have given some thought to the offending qualities and decided to underwrite them anyway. That, after all, is presumably just what prompted the congressional outrage in the first place . . .

But even if I found the Court's view of "consideration" plausible, that would make no difference at all on the question of constitutionality. . . . [T]he First Amendment bars the government from considering viewpoint when it decides whether to subsidize private speech, and a statute that mandates the consideration of viewpoint is quite obviously unconstitutional. . . .

III

A second basic strand in the Court's treatment of today's question, and the heart of Justice Scalia's, in effect assumes that whether or not the statute mandates viewpoint discrimination, there is no constitutional issue here because government art subsidies fall within a zone of activity free from First Amendment restraints. The Government calls attention to the roles of government-as-speaker and government-as-buyer, in which the government is of course entitled to engage in viewpoint discrimination: if the Food and Drug Administration launches an advertising campaign on the subject of smoking, it may condemn the habit without also having to show a cowboy taking a puff on the opposite page; and if the Secretary of Defense wishes to buy a portrait to decorate the Pentagon, he is free to prefer George Washington over George the Third.

The Government freely admits, however, that it neither speaks through the expression subsidized by the NEA, nor buys anything for itself with its NEA grants. On the contrary, . . . the Government acts as a patron, financially underwriting the production of art by private artists and impresarios for independent consumption. Accordingly, the Government would have us liberate government-as-patron from First Amendment strictures not by placing it squarely within the categories of government-as-buyer or government-as-speaker, but by recognizing a new category by analogy to those accepted ones. The analogy is, however, a very poor fit, and this patronage falls embarrassingly on the wrong side of the line between government-as-buyer or-speaker and government-as-regulator-of-private-speech.

. . .

Rosenberger controls here. The NEA, like the student activities fund in *Rosenberger*, is a subsidy scheme created to encourage expression of a diversity of views from private speakers. Congress brought the NEA into being to help all Americans "achieve a better understanding of the past, a better analysis of the present, and a better view of the future.' § 951(3). The NEA's purpose is to 'support new ideas' and 'to help create and sustain . . . a climate encouraging freedom of thought, imagination, and inquiry." §§ 951(10),(7) . . . Given this congressional choice to sustain freedom of expression, *Rosenberger* teaches that the First Amendment forbids decisions based on viewpoint popularity. So long as Congress chooses to subsidize expressive endeavors at large, it has no business requiring the NEA to turn down funding applications of artists and exhibitors who devote their "freedom of thought, imagination, and inquiry" to defying our tastes, our beliefs, or our values. . . .

The Court says otherwise, claiming to distinguish *Rosenberger* on the ground that the student activities funds in that case were generally available to most applicants, whereas NEA funds are disbursed selectively and competitively to a choice few. But the Court in *Rosenberger* anticipated and specifically rejected just this distinction when it held in no uncertain terms that "[t]he government cannot justify viewpoint discrimination among private speakers on the economic fact of scarcity." . . . Scarce money demands choices, of course, but choices "on some acceptable [viewpoint] neutral principle," like artistic excellence and artistic merit;.... If the student activities fund at issue in *Rosenberger* had awarded competitive, merit-based grants to only 50%, or even 5%, of the applicants, on the basis of "journalistic merit taking into consideration the message of the newspaper," it is obvious beyond peradventure that the Court would not have come out differently, leaving the University free to refuse funding after considering a publication's Christian perspective.

A word should be said, finally, about a proposed alternative to this failed analogy. As the Solicitor General put it at oral argument, "there is something unique ... about the Government funding of the arts for First Amendment purposes." However different the governmental patron may be from the governmental speaker or buyer, the argument goes, patronage is also singularly different from traditional regulation of speech, and the limitations placed on the latter would be out of place when applied to viewpoint discrimination in distributing patronage. To this, there are two answers. The first, again, is *Rosenberger*, which forecloses any claim that the NEA and the First Amendment issues that arise under it are somehow unique. But even if we had no *Rosenberger*, and even if I thought the NEA's program of patronage was truly singular, I would not hesitate to reject the Government's plea to recognize a new, categorical patronage exemption from the requirement of viewpoint neutrality. . . . .

. . .

IV

Although I, like the Court, recognize that "facial challenges to legislation are generally disfavored," ... the proviso is the type of statute that most obviously lends itself to such an attack. The NEA does not offer a list of reasons when it denies a grant application, and an artist or exhibitor whose subject raises a hint of controversy can never know for sure whether the decency and respect criteria played a part in any decision by the NEA to deny funding. ...

. . .

There is an "exception to th[e] [capable-of-constitutional-application] rule recognized in our jurisprudence [for] facial challenge[s] based upon First Amendment free-speech grounds. ..." ... [W]e have routinely understood the overbreadth doctrine to apply where the plaintiff mounts a facial challenge to a law investing the government with discretion to discriminate on viewpoint when it parcels out benefits in support of speech. ...

To be sure, such a "facial challenge will not succeed unless the statute is 'substantially' overbroad,' ..." ... But that is no impediment to invalidation here. ...[T]his is certainly a case in which the challenged statute "reaches a substantial number of impermissible applications," not one in which the statute's "legitimate reach dwarfs its arguably impermissible applications." ...

The Government takes a different tack, arguing that overbreadth analysis is out of place in this case because the 'prospect for 'chilling' expressive conduct, ... "is not present here." But that is simply wrong. We have explained before that the prospect of a denial of government funding necessarily carries with it the potential to "chil[l] ... individual thought and expression." ... In the world of NEA funding, this is so because the makers or exhibitors of potentially controversial art will either trim their work to avoid anything likely to offend, or refrain from seeking NEA funding altogether. Either way, to whatever extent NEA eligibility defines a national mainstream, the proviso will tend to create a timid esthetic. . . .

Since the decency and respect proviso of § 954(d)(1) is substantially overbroad and carries with it a significant power to chill artistic production and display, it should be struck down on its face.

V

The Court does not strike down the proviso, however. Instead, it preserves the irony of a statutory mandate to deny recognition to virtually any expression capable of causing offense in any quarter as the most recent manifestation of a scheme enacted to "create and sustain . . . a climate encouraging freedom of thought, imagination, and inquiry." § 951(7).

CHAPTER 15

PROTECTION OF PENUMBRAL FIRST AMENDMENT RIGHTS

SECTION 3. FREEDOM OF ASSOCIATION

D. COMPULSORY ASSOCIATION MEMBERSHIP

Page 1474. Add at end of subsection:

Glickman v. Wileman Brothers & Elliott, Inc.

521 U.S. 457, 117 S.Ct. 2130, 138 L.Ed.2d 585 (1997).

Justice Stevens delivered the opinion of the Court.

A number of growers, handlers, and processors of California tree fruits (respondents) brought this proceeding to challenge the validity of various regulations contained in marketing orders promulgated by the Secretary of Agriculture. The orders impose assessments on respondents that cover the expenses of administering the orders, including the cost of generic advertising of California nectarines, plums, and peaches. The question presented to us is whether the requirement that respondents finance such generic advertising is a law "abridging the freedom of speech" within the meaning of the First Amendment.

I

Congress enacted the Agricultural Marketing Agreement Act of 1937 (AMAA) ... in order to establish and maintain orderly marketing conditions and fair prices for agricultural commodities.... Marketing orders promulgated pursuant to the AMAA are a species of economic regulation that has displaced competition in a number of discrete markets; they are expressly exempted from the antitrust laws.... Collective action, rather than the aggregate consequences of independent competitive choices, characterizes these regulated markets.... Pursuant to the policy of collective, rather than competitive marketing, the orders also authorize joint research and development projects, inspection procedures that ensure uniform quality, and even certain standardized packaging requirements. ...

Marketing orders must be approved by either two-thirds of the affected producers or by producers who market at least two-thirds of the volume of the commodity.... The orders are implemented by committees composed of producers and handlers of the regulated commodity, appointed by the Secretary, who recommend rules to the Secretary governing marketing matters such as

209

fruit size and maturity levels. . . . The committee also determines the annual rate of assessments to cover the expenses of administration, inspection services, research, and advertising and promotion. . . .

Among the collective activities that Congress authorized for certain specific commodities is "any form of marketing promotion including paid advertising." . . . The central message of the generic advertising at issue in this case is that "California Summer Fruits" are wholesome, delicious, and attractive to discerning shoppers. . . .

II

The regulations at issue in this litigation . . . authorized . . . generic advertising of California nectarines, plums, and peaches.

Respondent Wileman Bros. & Elliott, Inc., is a large producer of these fruits. . . . In 1988 it filed a . . . petition [with the Secretary of Agriculture] challenging . . . the generic advertising regulations. . . . [T]he Judicial Officer of the Department of Agriculture [rejected the challenge]. Wileman, along with 15 other handlers, then sought review of the Judicial Officer's decision by filing this action in the District Court, [which upheld the Department] and entered judgment of $3.1 million in past due assessments against the handlers.

In the Court of Appeals the handlers challenged the generic advertising provisions of the orders as violative of . . . the First Amendment. . . .

. . .

The Court of Appeals concluded . . . that government enforced contributions to pay for generic advertising violated the First Amendment rights of the handlers. . . .

. . .

We . . . reverse.

III

. . . [T]he Court of Appeals invalidated the entire program on the theory that the program could not survive Central Hudson [Gas & Electric Corp. v. Public Serv. Comm'n of N.Y., 447 U.S. 557 (1980)] because the Government had failed to prove that generic advertising was more effective than individual advertising in increasing consumer demand for California nectarines, plums, and peaches. That holding did not depend at all on either the content of the advertising, or on the respondents' claimed disagreement with any particular message. Although respondents have continued in this Court to argue about their disagreement with particular messages, those arguments, while perhaps calling into question the administration of portions of the program, have no bearing on the validity of the entire program.

For purposes of our analysis, we neither accept nor reject the factual assumption underlying the Court of Appeals' invalidation of the program—namely that generic advertising may not be the most effective method of promoting the sale of these commodities. The legal question that we address is whether being compelled to fund this advertising raises a First Amendment issue for us to resolve, or rather is simply a question of economic policy for Congress and the Executive to resolve.

In answering that question we stress the importance of the statutory context in which it arises. California nectarines and peaches are marketed pursuant to detailed marketing orders that have displaced many aspects of independent business activity that characterize other portions of the economy in which competition is fully protected by the antitrust laws. The business entities that are compelled to fund the generic advertising at issue in this litigation do so as a part of a broader collective enterprise in which their freedom to act independently is already constrained by the regulatory scheme. It is in this context that we consider whether we should review the assessments used to fund collective advertising, together with other collective activities, under the standard appropriate for the review of economic regulation or under a heightened standard appropriate for the review of First Amendment issues.

IV

Three characteristics of the regulatory scheme at issue distinguish it from laws that we have found to abridge the freedom of speech protected by the First Amendment. First, the marketing orders impose no restraint on the freedom of any producer to communicate any message to any audience. Second, they do not compel any person to engage in any actual or symbolic speech. Third, they do not compel the producers to endorse or to finance any political or ideological views. Indeed, since all of the respondents are engaged in the business of marketing California nectarines, plums, and peaches, it is fair to presume that they agree with the central message of the speech that is generated by the generic program. Thus, none of our First Amendment jurisprudence provides any support for the suggestion that the promotional regulations should be scrutinized under a different standard than that applicable to the other anticompetitive features of the marketing orders.

. . . Respondents argue that the assessments for generic advertising impinge on their First Amendment rights because they reduce the amount of money that producers have available to conduct their own advertising. This is equally true, however, of assessments to cover employee benefits, inspection fees, or any other activity that is authorized by a marketing order. . . .

The Court of Appeals, perhaps recognizing the expansive nature of respondents' argument, did not rely on the claim that the assessments for generic advertising indirectly limit the extent of the handlers' own advertising. Rather, the Court of Appeals apparently accepted respondents' argument that the assessments infringe First Amendment rights because they constitute compelled speech. Our compelled speech case law, however, is clearly inapplicable to the regulatory scheme at issue here. The use of assessments to pay for advertising does not require respondents to repeat an objectional message out of their own mouths, cf. West Virginia Bd. of Ed. v. Barnette, 319 U.S. 624, 632 (1943), require them to use their own property to convey an antagonistic ideological message, cf. Wooley v. Maynard, 430 U.S. 705 (1977), Pacific Gas & Elec. Co. v. Public Util. Comm'n of Cal., 475 U.S. 1, 18 (1986) (plurality opinion), force them to respond to a hostile message when they "would prefer to remain silent," see ibid., or require them to be publicly identified or associated with another's message, cf. PruneYard Shopping Center v. Robins,

447 U.S. 74, 88 (1980). Respondents are not required themselves to speak, but are merely required to make contributions for advertising. With trivial exceptions on which the court did not rely, none of the generic advertising conveys any message with which respondents disagree. Furthermore, the advertising is attributed not to them, but to the California Tree Fruit Agreement or "California Summer Fruits."

Although this regulatory scheme may not compel speech as recognized by our case law, it does compel financial contributions that are used to fund advertising. As the Court of Appeals read our decision in *Abood*, just as the First Amendment prohibits compelled speech, it prohibits—at least without sufficient justification by the government—compelling an individual to "render financial support for others' speech." However, *Abood*, and the cases that follow it, did not announce a broad First Amendment right not to be compelled to provide financial support for any organization that conducts expressive activities. Rather, *Abood* merely recognized a First Amendment interest in not being compelled to contribute to an organization whose expressive activities conflict with one's "freedom of belief." . . . We held that compelled contributions to support activities related to collective bargaining were "constitutionally justified by the legislative assessment of the important contribution of the union shop" to labor relations. . . . Relying on our compelled-speech cases, however, the Court found that compelled contributions for political purposes unrelated to collective bargaining implicated First Amendment interests because they interfere with the values lying at the "heart of the First Amendment[-]the notion that an individual should be free to believe as he will, and that in a free society one's beliefs should be shaped by his mind and his conscience rather than coerced by the State." . . .

Here, however, requiring respondents to pay the assessments cannot be said to engender any crisis of conscience. None of the advertising in this record promotes any particular message other than encouraging consumers to buy California tree fruit. Neither the fact that respondents may prefer to foster that message independently in order to promote and distinguish their own products, nor the fact that they think more or less money should be spent fostering it, makes this case comparable to those in which an objection rested on political or ideological disagreement with the content of the message. . . .

. . .

We are not persuaded that any greater weight should be given to the fact that some producers do not wish to foster generic advertising than to the fact that many of them may well object to the marketing orders themselves because they might earn more money in an unregulated market. Respondents' criticisms of generic advertising provide no basis for concluding that factually accurate advertising constitutes an abridgment of anybody's right to speak freely. Similar criticisms might be directed at other features of the regulatory orders that impose restraints on competition that arguably disadvantage particular producers for the benefit of the entire market. Although one may indeed question the wisdom of such a program, its debatable features are insufficient to warrant special First Amendment scrutiny. It was therefore error for the Court of Appeals to rely on *Central Hudson* for the purpose of testing the constitutionality of market order assessments for promotional advertising.

V

The Court of Appeals' decision to apply the *Central Hudson* test is inconsistent with the very nature and purpose of the collective action program at issue here. The Court of Appeals concluded that the advertising program does not "directly advance" the purposes of the marketing orders because the Secretary had failed to prove that generic advertising is any more effective in stimulating consumer demand for the commodities than the advertising that might otherwise be undertaken by producers acting independently. We find this an odd burden of proof to assign to the administrator of marketing orders that reflect a policy of displacing unrestrained competition with government supervised cooperative marketing programs. . . . The basic policy decision that underlies the entire statute rests on an assumption that in the volatile markets for agricultural commodities the public will be best served by compelling cooperation among producers in making economic decisions that would be made independently in a free market. It is illogical, therefore, to criticize any cooperative program authorized by this statute on the ground that competition would provide greater benefits than joint action.

On occasion it is appropriate to emphasize the difference between policy judgments and constitutional adjudication. Judges who have endorsed the view that the Sherman Act is a charter of economic liberty, naturally approach laws that command competitors to participate in joint ventures with a jaundiced eye. Doubts concerning the policy judgments that underlie many features of this legislation do not, however, justify reliance on the First Amendment as a basis for reviewing economic regulations. Appropriate respect for the power of Congress to regulate commerce among the States provides abundant support for the constitutionality of these marketing orders. . . .

. . .

. . . In sum, what we are reviewing is a species of economic regulation that should enjoy the same strong presumption of validity that we accord to other policy judgments made by Congress. The mere fact that one or more producers "do not wish to foster" generic advertising of their product is not a sufficient reason for overriding the judgment of the majority of market participants, bureaucrats, and legislators who have concluded that such programs are beneficial.

The judgment of the Court of Appeals is reversed.

It is so ordered.

Justice Souter, with whom The Chief Justice and Justice Scalia join, and with whom Justice Thomas joins except as to Part II, dissenting.

. . . [T]he very reasons for recognizing that commercial speech falls within the scope of First Amendment protection likewise justifies the protection of those who object to subsidizing it against their will. I therefore conclude that forced payment for commercial speech should be subject to the same level of judicial scrutiny as any restriction on communications in that category. Because I believe that the advertising scheme here fails that test, I respectfully dissent.

I

The nub of the Court's opinion is its reading of the line of cases following Abood v. Detroit Bd. of Ed., 431 U.S. 209 (1977) ... *Abood* appears more readily in its proper size if we begin our analysis with two more basic principles of First Amendment law: that speech as such is subject to some level of protection unless it falls within a category, such as obscenity, placing it beyond the Amendment's scope, and that protected speech may not be made the subject of coercion to speak or coercion to subsidize speech.

. . . .

B

Since commercial speech is not subject to any categorical exclusion from First Amendment protection, and indeed is protectible as a speaker's chosen medium of commercial enterprise, it becomes subject to a second First Amendment principle: that compelling cognizable speech officially is just as suspect as suppressing it, and is typically subject to the same level of scrutiny....

As a familiar corollary to the principle that what may not be suppressed may not be coerced, we have recognized (thus far, outside the context of commercial speech) that individuals have a First Amendment interest in freedom from compulsion to subsidize speech and other expressive activities undertaken by private and quasi-private organizations.... *Abood* ... relied on compelled-speech cases such as *Barnette* ... in concluding that just as the government may not (without a compelling reason) prohibit a person from contributing money to propagate ideas, neither may it force an individual to contribute money to support some group's distinctly expressive activities....

C

... Since *Abood* struck down the mandatory "service fee" only insofar as it funded the union's expression of support for "ideological causes not germane to its duties as collective-bargaining representative," ... the Court reads *Abood* for the proposition that the First Amendment places no limits on government's power to force one individual to pay for another's speech, except when the speech in question both is ideological or political in character and is not germane to an otherwise lawful regulatory program.

1

The Court's first mistaken conclusion lies in treating *Abood* as permitting any enforced subsidy for speech that is germane to permissible economic regulation.... But *Abood* ... is not nearly so permissive.... In *Abood*, we recognized that even in matters directly related to collective bargaining, compulsory funding of union activities has an impact on employees' First Amendment interests, since the employees might disagree with positions taken by the union on issues such as the inclusion of abortion in a medical benefit plan, or negotiating no-strike agreements, or even the desirability of unionism in general.... Collective bargaining, and related activities such as grievance arbitration and contract administration, are part and parcel of the very economic transactions between employees and employer that Congress can regulate, and which it could not regulate without these potential impingements on the employees' First Amendment interests. *Abood* is thus a specific instance of the general principle that government retains its full power to regulate commercial transactions directly, despite elements of speech and association inherent in such transactions. . . .

[*Abood*'s] limited sanction for laws affecting First Amendment interests may not be expanded to cover every imposition that is in some way "germane" to a regulatory program in the sense of relating sympathetically to it. Rather, to survive scrutiny under *Abood*, a mandatory fee must not only be germane to some otherwise legitimate regulatory scheme; it must also be justified by vital policy interests of the government and not add significantly to the burdening of free speech inherent in achieving those interests. . . .

. . .

2

The Court's second misemployment of *Abood* . . . is its reliance on [it] for the proposition that when government neither forbids speech nor attributes it to an objector, it may compel subsidization for any objectionable message that is not political or ideological. But this, of course, is entirely at odds with the principle that speech significant enough to be protected at some level is outside the government's power to coerce or to support by mandatory subsidy without further justification. Since a commercial speaker (who does not mislead) may generally promote commerce as he sees fit, the government requires some justification (such as its necessity for otherwise valid regulation) before it may force him to subsidize commercial speech to which he objects. While it is perfectly true that . . . *Abood* . . . did involve political or ideological speech, . . . nothing . . . suggests that government has free rein to compel funding of nonpolitical speech (which might include art, for example, as well as commercial advertising). While an individual's First Amendment interest in commercial speech, and thus the government's burden in justifying a regulation of it, may well be less weighty than the interest in ideological speech, *Abood* continues to stand for the proposition that being compelled to make expenditures for protected speech "works no less an infringement of . . . constitutional rights" than being prohibited from making such expenditures. . . . The fact that no prior case of this Court has applied this principle to commercial and nonideological speech simply reflects the fortuity that this is the first commercial-speech subsidy case to come before us.

. . .

II

. . . I would . . . adhere to the principle laid down in our compelled-speech cases: laws requiring an individual to engage in or pay for expressive activities are reviewed under the same standard that applies to laws prohibiting one from engaging in or paying for such activities. . . . In this case, the Secretary has failed to establish that the challenged advertising programs satisfy any of these three prongs of the *Central Hudson* test.

A

. . .

Here, the AMAA's authorization of compelled advertising programs is so random and so randomly implemented, in light of the Act's stated purposes, as to unsettle any inference that the Government's asserted interest is either substantial or even real. First, the Act authorizes paid advertising programs in marketing orders for 25 listed fruits, nuts, vegetables, and eggs, but not for any other agricultural commodity. . . . The only thing the limited list unambiguously shows is that a need for promotional control does not go hand-in-hand with a need for market and economic stability, since the authorization for marketing orders bears no such narrow restriction to specific types of produce. But no general criterion for selection is stated in the text, and neither Congress nor the Secretary has so much as suggested that such a criterion exists. Instead, the legislative history shows that from time to time Congress has simply amended the Act to add particular commodities to the list at the request of interested producers or handlers, without ever explaining why compelled advertising programs were necessary for the specific produce chosen and not others. . . .

. . .

A second element of the arbitrary in this statutory and regulatory scheme inheres in the geographical limitations on the marketing orders that include the advertising programs challenged in this case, which apply only to peaches, plums, and nectarines grown in California, unaccompanied by counterparts for advertising the same commodities grown elsewhere. Some geographical restriction, it must be said, follows from the general provision of the AMAA limiting marketing orders to the smallest production or marketing area practicable and consistent with the policy of the Act. . . . But this provision merely explains why a substantial governmental interest in advertising a type of produce would have to be manifested in as many orders under the AMAA as there are defined production or marketing areas; it does nothing to explain the oddity that a government interest worth vindicating should occur within such geographically select boundaries and nowhere else, or to negate the suggestion of the evidence already mentioned, that the government's asserted interest is nothing more than the preference of a local interest group.

. . .

B

Even if the Secretary could establish a sufficiently substantial interest, he would need also to show how the compelled advertising programs directly advance that interest, that is, how the schemes actually contribute to stabilizing agricultural markets and maintaining farm income by stimulating consumer demand. . . .

. . . [T]he Government has to show that its mandatory scheme appreciably increases the total amount of advertising for a commodity or somehow does a better job of sparking the right level of consumer demand than a wholly voluntary system would. There is no evidence of this in the record here.

C

Finally, a regulation of commercial speech must be narrowly tailored to achieving the government's interests. . . . Respondents argue that the mandatory advertising schemes for California peaches, plums, and nectarines fail this narrow tailoring requirement, because they deny handlers any credit toward their assessments for some or all of their individual advertising expenditures. The point is well-taken.... [T]he remarkable thing is that the AMAA itself provides for exactly such credits for individual advertising expenditures under marketing orders for almonds, filberts, raisins, walnuts, olives, and Florida Indian River grapefruit, but not for other commodities....

. . .

Although the government's obligation is not a heavy one in *Central Hudson* ..., we have understood it to call for some showing beyond plausibility, and there has been none here. I would accordingly affirm the judgment of the Ninth Circuit.

Justice Thomas, with whom Justice Scalia joins as to Part II, dissenting.

I

I join Justice Souter's dissent, with the exception of Part II. My join is thus limited because I continue to disagree with the use of the *Central Hudson* balancing test and the discounted weight given to commercial speech generally....

II

I write separately to note my disagreement with the majority's conclusion that coerced funding of advertising by others does not involve "speech" at all and does not even raise a First Amendment "issue." ...

. . .

What we are now left with, if we are to take the majority opinion at face value, is one of two disturbing consequences: Either (1) paying for advertising is not speech at all, while such activities as draft card burning, flag burning, armband wearing, public sleeping, and nude dancing are, or (2) compelling payment for third party communication does not implicate speech, and thus the Government would be free to force payment for a whole variety of expressive conduct that it could not restrict. In either case, surely we have lost our way.

SECTION 4. APPLICATION OF THE FIRST AMENDMENT TO GOVERNMENT REGULATION OF ELECTIONS

A.   CHOOSING AND ELECTING CANDIDATES FOR PUBLIC OFFICE

Page 1491. Add at end of subsection:

Timmons v. Twin Cities Area New Party

520 U.S. 351, 117 S.Ct. 1364, 137 L.Ed.2d 589 (1997).

Chief Justice Rehnquist delivered the opinion of the Court.

Most States prohibit multiple-party, or "fusion," candidacies for elected office. The Minnesota laws challenged in this case prohibit a candidate from appearing on the ballot as the candidate of more than one party. We hold that such a prohibition does not violate the First and Fourteenth Amendments to the United States Constitution.

Respondent is a chartered chapter of the national New Party. Petitioners are Minnesota election officials....

The New Party filed suit in United States District Court, contending that Minnesota's antifusion laws violated the Party's associational rights under the First and Fourteenth Amendments. The District Court granted summary judgment for the state defendants ...

The Court of Appeals reversed.... We ... reverse.

Fusion was a regular feature of Gilded Age American politics. Particularly in the West and Midwest, candidates of issue-oriented parties like the Grangers, Independents, Greenbackers, and Populists often succeeded through fusion with the Democrats, and vice versa. Republicans, for their part, sometimes arranged fusion candidacies in the South, as part of a general strategy of encouraging and exploiting divisions within the dominant Democratic Party. See generally Argersinger, "A Place at the Table": Fusion Politics and Antifusion Laws, 85 Amer. Hist. Rev. 287, 288–290 (1980).

Fusion was common in part because political parties, rather than local or state governments, printed and distributed their own ballots. ...[A]fter the 1888 presidential election, which was widely regarded as having been plagued by fraud, many States moved to the "Australian ballot system." Under that system, an official ballot, containing the names of all the candidates legally nominated by all the parties, was printed at public expense and distributed by public officials at polling places.... [M]any States enacted other election-related reforms, including bans on fusion candidacies.... Minnesota banned fusion in 1901. Today, multiple-party candidacies are permitted in just a few States, and fusion plays a significant role only in New York.

. . .

When deciding whether a state election law violates First and Fourteenth Amendment associational rights, we weigh the " 'character and magnitude' "of the burden the State's rule imposes on those rights against the interests the State contends justify that burden, and consider the extent to which the State's concerns make the burden necessary.... Regulations imposing severe burdens on plaintiffs' rights must be narrowly tailored and advance a compelling state interest. Lesser burdens, however, trigger less exacting review, and a State's " 'important regulatory interests,' " will usually be enough to justify " 'reasonable, nondiscriminatory restrictions.' " No bright line separates permissible election-related regulation from unconstitutional infringements on First Amendment freedoms....

The New Party's claim that it has a right to select its own candidate is uncontroversial, so far as it goes.... It does not follow, though, that a party is absolutely entitled to have its nominee appear on the ballot as that party's candidate. A particular candidate might be ineligible for office, unwilling to serve, or, as here, another party's candidate. That a particular individual may not appear on the ballot as a particular party's candidate does not severely burden that party's association rights. . . .

The New Party relies on Eu v. San Francisco County Democratic Central Comm., [489 U.S. 214 (1989)] and Tashjian v. Republican Party of Conn. . . . In *Eu*, we struck down California election provisions that prohibited political parties from endorsing candidates in party primaries and regulated parties' internal affairs and structure. . . . But while *Tashjian* and *Eu* involved regulation of political parties' internal affairs and core associational activities, Minnesota's fusion ban does not. The ban, which applies to major and minor parties alike, simply precludes one party's candidate from appearing on the ballot, as that party's candidate, if already nominated by another party. . . . Whether the Party still wants to endorse a candidate who, because of the fusion ban, will not appear on the ballot as the Party's candidate, is up to the Party.

The Court of Appeals also held that Minnesota's laws "keep the New Party from developing consensual political alliances and thus broadening the base of public participation in and support for its activities." . . .

But Minnesota has not directly precluded minor political parties from developing and organizing. . . . Nor has Minnesota excluded a particular group of citizens, or a political party, from participation in the election process. . . . The New Party remains free to endorse whom it likes, to ally itself with others, to nominate candidates for office, and to spread its message to all who will listen. . . .

The Court of Appeals emphasized its belief that, without fusion-based alliances, minor parties cannot thrive. This is a predictive judgment which is by no means self-evident. But, more importantly, the supposed benefits of fusion to minor parties does not require that Minnesota permit it. Many features of our political system—e.g., single-member districts, "first past the post" elections, and the high costs of campaigning—make it difficult for third parties to succeed in American politics. . . .

. . .

It is true that Minnesota's fusion ban prevents the New Party from using the ballot to communicate to the public that it supports a particular candidate who is already another party's candidate. . . . We are unpersuaded, however, by the Party's contention that it has a right to use the ballot itself to send a particularized message, to its candidate and to the voters, about the nature of its support for the candidate. Ballots serve primarily to elect candidates, not as fora for political expression. . . . Like all parties in Minnesota, the New Party is able to use the ballot to communicate information about itself and its candidate to the voters, so long as that candidate is not already someone else's candidate. The Party retains great latitude in its ability to communicate ideas to voters and candidates through its participation in the campaign, and Party members may campaign for, endorse, and vote for their preferred candidate even if he is listed on the ballot as another party's candidate. . . .

In sum, Minnesota's laws do not restrict the ability of the New Party and its members to endorse, support, or vote for anyone they like. The laws do not directly limit the Party's access to the ballot. They are silent on parties' internal structure, governance, and policy-making. Instead, these provisions reduce the universe of potential candidates who may appear on the ballot as the

Party's nominee only by ruling out those few individuals who both have already agreed to be another party's candidate and also, if forced to choose, themselves prefer that other party. They also limit, slightly, the Party's ability to send a message to the voters and to its preferred candidates. We conclude that the burdens Minnesota imposes on the Party's First and Fourteenth Amendment associational rights—though not trivial—are not severe.

. . .

. . . Minnesota argues here that its fusion ban is justified by its interests in avoiding voter confusion, promoting candidate competition (by reserving limited ballot space for opposing candidates), preventing electoral distortions and ballot manipulations, and discouraging party splintering and "unrestrained factionalism."

. . . Petitioners contend that a candidate or party could easily exploit fusion as a way of associating his or its name with popular slogans and catchphrases. For example, members of a major party could decide that a powerful way of "sending a message" via the ballot would be for various factions of that party to nominate the major party's candidate as the candidate for the newly-formed "No New Taxes," "Conserve Our Environment," and "Stop Crime Now" parties. In response, an opposing major party would likely instruct its factions to nominate that party's candidate as the "Fiscal Responsibility," "Healthy Planet," and "Safe Streets" parties' candidate.

. . . [B]ecause the burdens the fusion ban imposes on the Party's associational rights are not severe, the State need not narrowly tailor the means it chooses to promote ballot integrity. The Constitution does not require that Minnesota compromise the policy choices embodied in its ballot-access requirements to accommodate the New Party's fusion strategy. . . .

. . . Minnesota fears that fusion would enable minor parties, by nominating a major party's candidate, to bootstrap their way to major-party status in the next election and circumvent the State's nominating-petition requirement for minor parties. . . . The State surely has a valid interest in making sure that minor and third parties who are granted access to the ballot are bona fide and actually supported, on their own merits, by those who have provided the statutorily required petition or ballot support. . . .

States also have a strong interest in the stability of their political systems. . . . This interest does not permit a State to completely insulate the two-party system from minor parties' or independent candidates' competition and influence, . . . nor is it a paternalistic license for States to protect political parties from the consequences of their own internal disagreements. . . . That said, the States' interest permits them to enact reasonable election regulations that may, in practice, favor the traditional two-party system, . . . and that temper the destabilizing effects of party-splintering and excessive factionalism. The Constitution permits the Minnesota Legislature to decide that political stability is best served through a healthy two-party system. . . . And while an interest in securing the perceived benefits of a stable two-party system will not justify unreasonably exclusionary restrictions, . . . States need not remove all of the many hurdles third parties face in the American political arena today.

. . .

We conclude that the burdens Minnesota's fusion ban imposes on the New Party's associational rights are justified by "correspondingly weighty" valid state interests in ballot integrity and political stability. In deciding that Minnesota's fusion ban does not unconstitutionally burden the New Party's First and Fourteenth Amendment rights, we express no views on the New Party's policy-based arguments concerning the wisdom of fusion. It may well be that, as support for new political parties increases, these arguments will carry the day in some States' legislatures. But the Constitution does not require Minnesota, and the approximately 40 other States that do not permit fusion, to allow it. The judgment of the Court of Appeals is reversed.

It is so ordered.

Justice Stevens with whom Justice Ginsburg joins, and with whom Justice Souter joins as to Parts I and II, dissenting.

. . .

The Court's conclusion that the Minnesota statute prohibiting multiple-party candidacies is constitutional rests on three dubious premises: (1) that the statute imposes only a minor burden on the Party's right to choose and to support the candidate of its choice; (2) that the statute significantly serves the State's asserted interests in avoiding ballot manipulation and factionalism; and (3) that, in any event, the interest in preserving the two-party system justifies the imposition of the burden at issue in this case. I disagree with each of these premises.

I

. . .

. . . The fact that the Party may nominate its second choice surely does not diminish the significance of a restriction that denies it the right to have the name of its first choice appear on the ballot. Nor does the point that it may use some of its limited resources to publicize the fact that its first choice is the nominee of some other party provide an adequate substitute for the message that is conveyed to every person who actually votes when a party's nominees appear on the ballot.

. . .

II

Minnesota argues that the statutory restriction on the New Party's right to nominate the candidate of its choice is justified by the State's interests in avoiding voter confusion, preventing ballot clutter and manipulation, encouraging candidate competition, and minimizing intraparty factionalism. None of these rationales can support the fusion ban because the State has failed to explain how the ban actually serves the asserted interests.

. . .

The State's concern about ballot manipulation, readily accepted by the majority, is . . . farfetched. The possibility that members of the major parties will begin to create dozens of minor parties with detailed, issue-oriented titles for the sole purpose of nominating candidates under those titles is entirely hypothetical....

. . .

... I turn ... to what appears to be the true basis for the Court's holding—the interest in preserving the two-party system.

III

. . .

... [The State's interest in preserving the two-party system is not] sufficient to justify the fusion ban. In most States, perhaps in all, there are two and only two major political parties.... The fact that the law was both intended to disadvantage minor parties and has had that effect is a matter that should weigh against, rather than in favor of, its constitutionality.

Our jurisprudence in this area reflects a certain tension: on the one hand, we have been clear that political stability is an important state interest and that incidental burdens on the formation of minor parties are reasonable to protect that interest ...; on the other, we have struck down state elections laws specifically because they give "the two old, established parties a decided advantage over any new parties struggling for existence," .... Between these boundaries, we have acknowledged that there is "no litmus-paper test for separating those restrictions that are valid from those that are invidious ..."....

Nothing in the Constitution prohibits the States from maintaining single-member districts with winner-take-all voting arrangements. And these elements of an election system do make it significantly more difficult for third parties to thrive. But these laws are different in two respects from the fusion bans at issue here. First, the method by which they hamper third-party development is not one that impinges on the associational rights of those third parties; minor parties remain free to nominate candidates of their choice, and to rally support for those candidates. The small parties' relatively limited likelihood of ultimate success on election day does not deprive them of the right to try. Second, the establishment of single-member districts correlates directly with the States' interests in political stability. Systems of proportional representation, for example, may tend toward factionalism and fragile coalitions that diminish legislative effectiveness. In the context of fusion candidacies, the risks to political stability are extremely attenuated. Of course, the reason minor parties so ardently support fusion politics is because it allows the parties to build up a greater base of support, as potential minor party members realize that a vote for the smaller party candidate is not necessarily a "wasted" vote. Eventually, a minor party might gather sufficient strength that—were its members so inclined—it could successfully run a candidate not endorsed by any major party, and legislative coalition-building will be made more difficult by the presence of third party legislators. But the risks to political stability in that scenario are speculative at best.

In some respects, the fusion candidacy is the best marriage of the virtues of the minor party challenge to entrenched viewpoints and the political stability that the two-party system provides....

. . . It demeans the strength of the two-party system to assume that the major parties need to rely on laws that discriminate against independent voters and minor parties in order to preserve their positions of power. . . .

In my opinion legislation that would otherwise be unconstitutional because it burdens First Amendment interests and discriminates against minor political parties cannot survive simply because it benefits the two major parties. Accordingly, I respectfully dissent.

Justice Souter, dissenting.

I join parts I and II of Justice Stevens's dissent. . . .

. . . I would judge the challenged statutes only on the interests the State has raised in their defense and would hold them unconstitutional.

I am, however, unwilling to go the further distance of considering and rejecting the majority's "preservation of the two-party system" rationale. For while Minnesota has made no such argument before us, I cannot discount the possibility of a forceful one. . . .

Surely the majority is right that States "have a strong interest in the stability of their political systems," that is, in preserving a political system capable of governing effectively. If it could be shown that the disappearance of the two-party system would undermine that interest, and that permitting fusion candidacies poses a substantial threat to the two-party scheme, there might well be a sufficient predicate for recognizing the constitutionality of the state action presented by this case. Right now, however, no State has attempted even to make this argument, and I would therefore leave its consideration for another day.

C. DISCLOSURE REQUIREMENTS

Page 1525. Add at end of subsection:

BUCKLEY v. AMERICAN CONSTITUTIONAL LAW FOUNDATION, 119 S.Ct. 636 (1999). The Court held invalid a number of Colorado's controls on the process of soliciting signatures to qualify initiatives for the ballot: a requirement that petition circulators be registered voters; a requirement that petition circulators wear identification badges; requirements to report the circulators' names and addresses, and the amount paid to each circulator. The Court concluded that the restrictions significantly inhibited communication with voters, and were not warranted by state interests in administrative efficiency, fraud detection, and informing voters. Justice O'Connor, joined by Justice Breyer in dissent, argued that the requirement that petition circulators be registered voters was a neutral qualification that only "indirectly and incidentally" burdened the communicative aspects of petition circulation. They also dissented from invalidation of the disclosure requirements whose burdens were "incremental and insubstantial." Chief Justice Rehnquist's dissent argued that the Court's rationale for invalidating the requirement that petition circulators be registered voters threatened a "whole host of historically established" regulations of the electoral process.

CHAPTER 16

FREEDOM OF THE PRESS

SECTION 6. SPECIAL PROBLEMS OF THE ELECTRONIC MEDIA

Page 1601. Add at end of chapter:

Turner Broadcasting System v. Federal Communications Commission

520 U.S. 180, 117 S.Ct. 1174, 137 L.Ed.2d 369 (1997).

Justice Kennedy delivered the opinion of the Court, except as to a portion of Part II–A–1.

Sections 4 and 5 of the Cable Television Consumer Protection and Competition Act of 1992 require cable television systems to dedicate some of their channels to local broadcast television stations. Earlier in this case, we held the so-called "must-carry" provisions to be content-neutral restrictions on speech, subject to intermediate First Amendment scrutiny under United States v. O'Brien, 391 U.S. 367, 377 (1968). [Turner Broadcasting System, Inc. v. FCC, 512 U.S. 622 (1994) (*Turner*).] A plurality of the Court considered the record as then developed insufficient to determine whether the provisions were narrowly tailored to further important governmental interests, and we remanded the case to the District Court for the District of Columbia for additional factfinding.

On appeal from the District Court's grant of summary judgment for appellees, the case now presents the two questions left open during the first appeal: First, whether the record as it now stands supports Congress' predictive judgment that the must-carry provisions further important governmental interests; and second, whether the provisions do not burden substantially more speech than necessary to further those interests. We answer both questions in the affirmative, and conclude the must-carry provisions are consistent with the First Amendment.

I

. . . Soon after Congress enacted the Cable Television Consumer Protection and Competition Act of 1992, Pub. L. 102–385, 106 Stat. 1460 (Cable Act), appellants brought suit . . . in the United States District Court for the District of Columbia, challenging the constitutionality of the must-carry provisions under the First Amendment. The three-judge District Court, in a divided opinion, granted summary judgment for the Government and intervenor-defendants. . . .

On appeal, we agreed with the District Court that must-carry does not "distinguish favored speech from disfavored speech on the basis of the ideas or views expressed," ... but is a content-neutral regulation designed "to prevent cable operators from exploiting their economic power to the detriment of broadcasters," and "to ensure that all Americans, especially those unable to subscribe to cable, have access to free television programming—whatever its content." ... We held that, under the intermediate level of scrutiny applicable to content-neutral regulations, must-carry would be sustained if it were shown to further an important or substantial governmental interest unrelated to the suppression of free speech, provided the incidental restrictions did not "burden substantially more speech than is necessary to further" those interests.... [A] four-Justice plurality concluded genuine issues of material fact remained regarding whether "the economic health of local broadcasting is in genuine jeopardy and need of the protections afforded by must-carry," and whether must-carry " 'burden[s] substantially more speech than is necessary to further the government's legitimate interests.' " ...

The District Court oversaw another 18 months of factual development on remand "yielding a record of tens of thousands of pages" of evidence.... Upon consideration of the expanded record, a divided panel of the District Court again granted summary judgment to appellees....

. . .

... [W]e now affirm.

II

We begin where the plurality ended in *Turner*, applying the standards for intermediate scrutiny enunciated in *O'Brien*.... As noted in *Turner*, must-carry was designed to serve "three interrelated interests: (1) preserving the benefits of free, over-the-air local broadcast television, (2) promoting the widespread dissemination of information from a multiplicity of sources, and (3) promoting fair competition in the market for television programming." ... We decided then, and now reaffirm, that each of those is an important governmental interest....

On remand, and again before this Court, both sides have advanced new interpretations of these interests in an attempt to recast them in forms "more readily proven." ... The Government downplays the importance of showing a risk to the broadcast industry as a whole and suggests the loss of even a few broadcast stations "is a matter of critical importance." Taking the opposite approach, appellants argue Congress' interest in preserving broadcasting is not implicated unless it is shown the industry as a whole would fail without must-carry, and suggest Congress' legitimate interest in "assuring that the public has access to a multiplicity of information sources" extends only as far as preserving "a minimum amount of television broadcast service."

These alternative formulations are inconsistent with Congress' stated interests in enacting must-carry. The congressional findings do not reflect concern that, absent must-carry, "a few voices, would be lost from the television marketplace." In explicit factual findings, Congress expressed clear concern that the "marked shift in market share from broadcast television to cable television services" ... resulting from increasing market penetration by cable services, as well as the expanding horizontal concentration and vertical integration of cable operators, combined to give cable systems the incentive and ability to delete, reposition, or decline carriage to local broadcasters in an attempt to favor affiliated cable programmers.... Congress predicted that "absent the reimposition of [must-carry], additional local broadcast signals will be deleted, repositioned, or not carried," ... with the end result that "the economic viability of free local broadcast television and its ability to originate quality local programming will be seriously jeopardized." ...

At the same time, Congress was under no illusion that there would be a complete disappearance of broadcast television nationwide in the absence of must-carry. Congress recognized broadcast programming (and network programming in particular) "remains the most popular programming on cable systems," .... Indeed, reflecting the popularity and strength of some broadcasters, Congress included in the Cable Act a provision permitting broadcasters to charge cable systems for carriage of the broadcasters' signals.... Congress was concerned not that broadcast television would disappear in its entirety without must-carry, but that without it, "significant numbers of broadcast stations will be refused carriage on cable systems," and those "broadcast stations denied carriage will either deteriorate to a substantial degree or fail altogether." ...

Nor do the congressional findings support appellants' suggestion that legitimate legislative goals would be satisfied by the preservation of a rump broadcasting industry providing a minimum of broadcast service to Americans without cable.... Congress enacted must-carry to "preserve the existing structure of the Nation's broadcast television medium while permitting the concomitant expansion and development of cable television." ...

Although Congress set no definite number of broadcast stations sufficient for these purposes, the Cable Act's requirement that all cable operators with more than 12 channels set aside one-third of their channel capacity for local broadcasters ... refutes the notion that Congress contemplated preserving only a bare minimum of stations. Congress' evident interest in "preserv[ing] the existing structure," ... of the broadcast industry discloses a purpose to prevent any significant reduction in the multiplicity of broadcast programming sources available to noncable households. To the extent the appellants question the substantiality of the Government's interest in preserving something more than a minimum number of stations in each community, their position is meritless. It is for Congress to decide how much local broadcast television should be preserved for noncable households, and the validity of its determination " 'does not turn on a judge's agreement with the responsible decisionmaker concerning' ... the degree to which [the Government's] interests should be promoted." ...

The dissent proceeds on the assumption that must-carry is designed solely to be (and can only be justified as) a measure to protect broadcasters from cable operators' anticompetitive behavior. Federal policy, however, has long favored preserving a multiplicity of broadcast outlets regardless of whether the conduct that threatens it is motivated by anticompetitive animus or rises to the level of an antitrust violation.... Congress has an independent interest in preserving a multiplicity of broadcasters to ensure that all households have access to information and entertainment on an equal footing with those who subscribe to cable.

A

... The expanded record now permits us to consider whether the must-carry provisions were designed to address a real harm, and whether those provisions will alleviate it in a material way.... We turn first to the harm or risk which prompted Congress to act. The Government's assertion that "the economic health of local broadcasting is in genuine jeopardy and in need of the protections afforded by must-carry," rests on two component propositions: First, "significant numbers of broadcast stations will be refused carriage on cable systems" absent must-carry. Second, "the broadcast stations denied carriage will either deteriorate to a substantial degree or fail altogether."

In reviewing the constitutionality of a statute, "courts must accord substantial deference to the predictive judgments of Congress." Our sole obligation is "to assure that, in formulating its judgments, Congress has drawn reasonable inferences based on substantial evidence." As noted in the first appeal, substantiality is to be measured in this context by a standard more deferential than we accord to judgments of an administrative agency. We owe Congress' findings deference in part because the institution "is far better equipped than the judiciary to 'amass and evaluate the vast amounts of data' bearing upon" legislative questions. ... This principle has special significance in cases, like this one, involving congressional judgments concerning regulatory schemes of inherent complexity and assessments about the likely interaction of industries undergoing rapid economic and technological change. Though different in degree, the deference to Congress is in one respect akin to deference owed to administrative agencies because of their expertise.... This is not the sum of the matter, however. We owe Congress' findings an additional measure of deference out of respect for its authority to exercise the legislative power. Even in the realm of First Amendment questions where Congress must base its conclusions upon substantial evidence, deference must be accorded to its findings as to the harm to be avoided and to the remedial measures adopted for that end, lest we infringe on traditional legislative authority to make predictive judgments when enacting nationwide regulatory policy.

1

We have no difficulty in finding a substantial basis to support Congress' conclusion that a real threat justified enactment of the must-carry provisions. We examine first the evidence before Congress and then the further evidence presented to the District Court on remand to supplement the congressional determination.

As to the evidence before Congress, there was specific support for its conclusion that cable operators had considerable and growing market power over local video programming markets. Cable served at least 60 percent of American households in 1992.... Only one percent of communities are served by more than one cable system....

Evidence indicated the structure of the cable industry would give cable operators increasing ability and incentive to drop local broadcast stations from their systems, or reposition them to a less-viewed channel. Horizontal concentration was increasing as a small number of multiple system operators (MSO's) acquired large numbers of cable systems nationwide. . . .

Vertical integration in the industry also was increasing. . . . Extensive testimony indicated that cable operators would have an incentive to drop local broadcasters and to favor affiliated programmers. . . .

. . .

The reasonableness of Congress' conclusion was borne out by the evidence on remand, which also reflected cable industry favoritism for integrated programmers. . . .

In addition, evidence before Congress, supplemented on remand, indicated that cable systems would have incentives to drop local broadcasters in favor of other programmers less likely to compete with them for audience and advertisers. Independent local broadcasters tend to be the closest substitutes for cable programs, because their programming tends to be similar, . . . and because both primarily target the same type of advertiser: those interested in cheaper (and more frequent) ad spots than are typically available on network affiliates. . . . The ability of broadcast stations to compete for advertising is greatly increased by cable carriage, which increases viewership substantially. . . . With expanded viewership, broadcast presents a more competitive medium for television advertising. Empirical studies indicate that cable-carried broadcasters so enhance competition for advertising that even modest increases in the numbers of broadcast stations carried on cable are correlated with significant decreases in advertising revenue to cable systems. . . . Empirical evidence also indicates that demand for premium cable services (such as pay-per-view) is reduced when a cable system carries more independent broadcasters. . . . Thus, operators stand to benefit by dropping broadcast stations.

Cable systems also have more systemic reasons for seeking to disadvantage broadcast stations: Simply stated, cable has little interest in assisting, through carriage, a competing medium of communication. . . . Congress could therefore reasonably conclude that cable systems would drop broadcasters in favor of programmers—even unaffiliated ones—less likely to compete with them for audience and advertisers. . . .

The dissent contends Congress could not reasonably conclude cable systems would engage in such predation because cable operators, whose primary source of revenue is subscriptions, would not risk dropping a widely viewed broadcast station in order to capture advertising revenues. However, if viewers are faced with the choice of sacrificing a handful of broadcast stations to gain access to dozens of cable channels (plus network affiliates), it is likely they would still subscribe to cable even if they would prefer the dropped television stations to the cable programming that replaced them. Substantial evidence introduced on remand bears this out. . . .

It was more than a theoretical possibility in 1992 that cable operators would take actions adverse to local broadcasters; indeed, significant numbers of broadcasters had already been dropped. . . .

Substantial evidence demonstrated that absent must-carry the already "serious" . . . problem of noncarriage would grow worse because "additional local broadcast signals will be deleted, repositioned, or not carried," . . . .

Additional evidence developed on remand supports the reasonableness of Congress' predictive judgment. Approximately 11 percent of local broadcasters were not carried on the typical cable system in 1989. . . . The figure had grown to even more significant proportions by 1992. According to one of appellants' own experts, between 19 and 31 percent of all local broadcast stations, including network affiliates, were not carried by the typical cable system. . . .

The dissent cites evidence indicating that many dropped broadcasters were stations few viewers watch, and it suggests that must-carry thwarts noncable viewers' preferences. Undoubtedly, viewers without cable . . . would have a strong preference for carriage of any broadcast program over any cable program, for the simple reason that it helps to preserve a medium to which they have access. . . . [T]he broadcasters added by must-carry had ratings greater than or equal to the cable programs they replaced. . . . On average, even the lowest-rated station added pursuant to must-carry had ratings better than or equal to at least nine basic cable program services carried on the system. . . . If cable systems refused to carry certain local broadcast stations because of their subscribers' preferences for the cable services carried in their place, one would expect that all cable programming services would have ratings exceeding those of broadcasters not carried. That is simply not the case.

The evidence on remand also indicated that the growth of cable systems' market power proceeded apace. The trend towards greater horizontal concentration continued . . .

This is not a case in which we are called upon to give our best judgment as to the likely economic consequences of certain financial arrangements or business structures, or to assess competing economic theories and predictive judgments, as we would in a case arising, say, under the antitrust laws. . . . The issue before us is whether, given conflicting views of the probable development of the television industry, Congress had substantial evidence for making the judgment that it did. We need not put our imprimatur on Congress' economic theory in order to validate the reasonableness of its judgment.

2

The harm Congress feared was that stations dropped or denied carriage would be at a "serious risk of financial difficulty," and would "deteriorate to a substantial degree or fail altogether." Congress had before it substantial evidence to support its conclusion. . . .

. . . We hold Congress could conclude from the substantial body of evidence before it that "absent legislative action, the free local off-air broadcast system is endangered." . . .

The evidence assembled on remand confirms the reasonableness of the congressional judgment. . . .

To be sure, the record also contains evidence to support a contrary conclusion. Appellants . . . make much of the fact that the number of broadcast stations and their advertising revenue continued to grow during the period without must-carry, albeit at a diminished rate. . . . Appellants . . . contend that in light of such evidence, it is clear "the must-carry law is not necessary to assure the economic viability of the broadcast system as a whole."

This assertion misapprehends the relevant inquiry. The question is not whether Congress, as an objective matter, was correct to determine must-carry is necessary to prevent a substantial number of broadcast stations from losing cable carriage and suffering significant financial hardship. Rather, the question is whether the legislative conclusion was reasonable and supported by substantial evidence in the record before Congress.... In making that determination, we are not to "re-weigh the evidence *de novo*, or to replace Congress' factual predictions with our own." Rather, we are simply to determine if the standard is satisfied. If it is, summary judgment for defendants-appellees is appropriate regardless of whether the evidence is in conflict. We have noted in another context, involving less deferential review than is at issue here, that " 'the possibility of drawing two inconsistent conclusions from the evidence does not prevent ... [a] finding from being supported by substantial evidence.' " American Textile Mfrs. Institute, Inc. v. Donovan, 452 U.S. 490, 523 (1981) ...

Although evidence of continuing growth in broadcast could have supported the opposite conclusion, a reasonable interpretation is that expansion in the cable industry was causing harm to broadcasting. Growth continued, but the rate of growth fell to a considerable extent during the period without must-carry.... At the same time, ... stations began to fail in increasing numbers.... While these phenomena could be thought to stem from factors quite separate from the increasing market power of cable (for example, a recession in 1990–1992), it was for Congress to determine the better explanation....

Despite the considerable evidence before Congress and adduced on remand indicating that the significant numbers of broadcast stations are at risk, the dissent believes yet more is required before Congress could act. It demands more information.... The level of detail in factfinding required by the dissent would be an improper burden for courts to impose on the Legislative Branch. That amount of detail is as unreasonable in the legislative context as it is constitutionally unwarranted....

We think it apparent must-carry serves the Government's interests "in a direct and effective way." ... Must-carry ensures that a number of local broadcasters retain cable carriage, with the concomitant audience access and advertising revenues needed to support a multiplicity of stations. Appellants contend that even were this so, must-carry is broader than necessary to accomplish its goals. We turn to this question.

B

The second portion of the *O'Brien* inquiry concerns the fit between the asserted interests and the means chosen to advance them. Content-neutral regulations do not pose the same "inherent dangers to free expression" that content-based regulations do, and thus are subject to a less rigorous analysis, which affords the Government latitude in designing a regulatory solution.... Under intermediate scrutiny, the Government may employ the means of its choosing " 'so long as the ... regulation promotes a substantial governmental interest that would be achieved less effectively absent the regulation,' " and does not " 'burden substantially more speech than is necessary to further' " that interest....

The must-carry provisions have the potential to interfere with protected speech in two ways. First, the provisions restrain cable operators' editorial discretion in creating programming packages by "reduc[ing] the number of channels over which [they] exercise unfettered control." Second, the rules "render it more difficult for cable programmers to compete for carriage on the limited channels remaining."

Appellants say the burden of must-carry is great, but the evidence adduced on remand indicates the actual effects are modest. Significant evidence indicates the vast majority of cable operators have not been affected in a significant manner by must-carry. Cable operators have been able to satisfy their must-carry obligations 87 percent of the time using previously unused channel capacity ...; 94.5 percent of the 11,628 cable systems nationwide have not had to drop any programming in order to fulfill their must-carry obligations; the remaining 5.5 percent have had to drop an average of only 1.22 services from their programming ...; and cable operators nationwide carry 99.8 percent of the programming they carried before enactment of must-carry.... Appellees note that only 1.18 percent of the approximately 500,000 cable channels nationwide is devoted to channels added because of must-carry.... Appellees contend the burdens of must-carry will soon diminish as cable channel capacity increases, as is occurring nationwide....

We do not understand appellants to dispute in any fundamental way the accuracy of those figures, only their significance. They note national averages fail to account for greater crowding on certain (especially urban) cable systems, and contend that half of all cable systems, serving two-thirds of all cable subscribers, have no available capacity. Appellants argue that the rate of growth in cable programming outstrips cable operators' creation of new channel space, that the rate of cable growth is lower than claimed, and that must-carry infringes First Amendment rights now irrespective of future growth. Finally, they say that regardless of the percentage of channels occupied, must-carry still represents "thousands of real and individual infringements of speech." ...

While the parties' evidence is susceptible of varying interpretations, a few definite conclusions can be drawn about the burdens of must-carry. It is undisputed that broadcast stations gained carriage on 5,880 channels as a result of must-carry.... Appellants concede most of those stations would be dropped in the absence of must-carry, so the figure approximates the benefits of must-carry as well.

Because the burden imposed by must-carry is congruent to the benefits it affords, we conclude must-carry is narrowly tailored to preserve a multiplicity of broadcast stations for the 40 percent of American households without cable.... Congress took steps to confine the breadth and burden of the regulatory scheme. For example, the more popular stations (which appellants concede would be carried anyway) will likely opt to be paid for cable carriage under the "retransmission consent" provision of the Cable Act; those stations will nonetheless be counted towards systems' must-carry obligations. Congress exempted systems of 12 or fewer channels, and limited the must-carry obligation of larger systems to one-third of capacity ...; allowed cable operators discretion in choosing which competing and qualified signals would be carried ...; and permitted operators to carry public stations on unused public, educational, and governmental channels in some circumstances....

Appellants say the must-carry provisions are overbroad because they require carriage in some instances when the Government's interests are not implicated: the must-carry rules prohibit a cable system operator from dropping a broadcaster "even if the operator has no anticompetitive motives, and even if the broadcaster that would have to be dropped . . . would survive without cable access." . . . We are not persuaded that either possibility is so prevalent that must-carry is substantially overbroad. . . . Even on the doubtful assumption that a narrower but still practicable must-carry rule could be drafted to exclude all instances in which the Government's interests are not implicated, our cases establish that content-neutral regulations are not "invalid simply because there is some imaginable alternative that might be less burdensome on speech." . . .

Appellants posit a number of alternatives in an effort to demonstrate a less-restrictive means to achieve the Government's aims. . . . Our precedents establish that when evaluating a content-neutral regulation which incidentally burdens speech, we will not invalidate the preferred remedial scheme because some alternative solution is marginally less intrusive on a speaker's First Amendment interests. "So long as the means chosen are not substantially broader than necessary to achieve the government's interest, . . . the regulation will not be invalid simply because a court concludes that the government's interest could be adequately served by some less-speech-restrictive alternative." . . .

In any event, after careful examination of each of the alternatives suggested by appellants, we cannot conclude that any of them is an adequate alternative to must-carry for promoting the Government's legitimate interests. . . .

. . .

There is a final argument made by appellants that we do not reach. Appellant Time Warner Entertainment raises in its brief a separate First Amendment challenge to a subsection of the Cable Act . . . that requires carriage on unfilled must-carry channels of low power broadcast stations if the FCC determines that the station's programming "would address local news and informational needs which are not being adequately served by full power television broadcast stations because of the geographic distance of such full power stations from the low power station's community of license." . . . Because this question has received "only the most glancing" attention from the District Court and the parties, we have no more information about "the operation of, and justifications for, the low-power broadcast provisions" on which to base an informed determination than we did on the earlier appeal. . . . Even if the issue is "fairly included" in the broadly worded question presented, it is tangential to the main issue, and prudence dictates that we not decide this question based on such scant argumentation. . . .

III

Judgments about how competing economic interests are to be reconciled in the complex and fast-changing field of television are for Congress to make. Those judgments "cannot be ignored or undervalued simply because [appellants] cas[t] [their] claims under the umbrella of the First Amendment." . . . Appellants' challenges to must-carry reflect little more than disagreement over the level of protection broadcast stations are to be afforded and how protection is to be attained. We cannot displace Congress' judgment respecting content-neutral regulations with our own, so long as its policy is grounded on reasonable factual findings supported by evidence that is substantial for a legislative determination. Those requirements were met in this case, and in these circumstances the First Amendment requires nothing more. The judgment of the District Court is affirmed.

It is so ordered.

Justice Stevens concurring.

. . . If this statute regulated the content of speech rather than the structure of the market, our task would be quite different. . . . Though I write to emphasize this important point, I fully concur in the Court's thorough opinion.

Justice Breyer concurring in part.

I join the opinion of the Court except insofar as Part II–A–1 relies on an anticompetitive rationale. . . . My conclusion rests, however, not upon the principal opinion's analysis of the statute's efforts to "promot[e] fair competition," but rather upon its discussion of the statute's other objectives. . . .

. . .

In particular, I note (and agree) that a cable system, physically dependent upon the availability of space along city streets, at present (perhaps less in the future) typically faces little competition, that it therefore constitutes a kind of bottleneck that controls the range of viewer choice (whether or not it uses any consequent economic power for economically predatory purposes), and that some degree—at least a limited degree—of governmental intervention and control through regulation can prove appropriate when justified under *O'Brien* (at least when not "content based"). . . .

. . .

Justice O'Connor with whom Justice Scalia, Justice Thomas and Justice Ginsburg join, dissenting.

. . . [T]he Court errs in two crucial respects. First, the Court disregards one of the principal defenses of the statute urged by appellees on remand: that it serves a substantial interest in preserving "diverse," "quality" programming that is "responsive" to the needs of the local community. The course of this litigation on remand and the proffered defense strongly reinforce my view that the Court adopted the wrong analytic framework in the prior phase of this case. . . . Second, the Court misapplies the "intermediate scrutiny" framework it adopts. Although we owe deference to Congress' predictive judgments and its evaluation of complex economic questions, we have an independent duty to identify with care the Government interests supporting the scheme, to inquire into the reasonableness of congressional findings regarding its necessity, and to examine the fit between its goals and its consequences. . . . The Court fails to discharge its duty here.

I

I did not join those portions of the principal opinion in *Turner* holding that the must-carry provisions of the Cable Act are content neutral and therefore subject to intermediate First Amendment scrutiny. The Court there referred to the "unusually detailed statutory findings" accompanying the Act, in which Congress recognized the importance of preserving sources of local news, public affairs, and educational programming. Nevertheless, the Court minimized the significance of these findings, suggesting that they merely reflected Congress' view of the "intrinsic value" of broadcast programming generally, rather than a congressional preference for programming with local, educational, or informational content.

In *Turner*, the Court drew upon Senate and House reports to identify three "interests" that the must-carry provisions were designed to serve: "(1) preserving the benefits of free, over-the-air local broadcast television, (2) promoting the widespread dissemination of information from a multiplicity of sources, and (3) promoting fair competition in the market for television programming." ... The Court reiterates these interests here, but neither the principal opinion nor the partial concurrence ever explains the relationship between them with any clarity.

Much of the principal opinion treats the must-carry provisions as a species of antitrust regulation enacted by Congress in response to a perceived threat that cable system operators would otherwise engage in various forms of anticompetitive conduct resulting in harm to broadcasters.... [T]he Court now asks whether Congress could reasonably have thought the must-carry regime necessary to prevent a *"significant* reduction in the multiplicity of broadcast programming sources available to noncable households."

I fully agree that promoting fair competition is a legitimate and substantial Government goal. But the Court nowhere examines whether the breadth of the must-carry provisions comports with a goal of preventing anticompetitive harms. Instead, in the course of its inquiry into whether the must-carry provisions are "narrowly tailored," the principal opinion simply assumes that most adverse carriage decisions are anticompetitively motivated, and that must-carry is therefore a measured response to a problem of anticompetitive behavior....

Perhaps because of the difficulty of defending the must-carry provisions as a measured response to anticompetitive behavior, the Court asserts an "independent" interest in preserving a "multiplicity" of broadcast programming sources. In doing so, the Court posits existence of "conduct that threatens" the availability of broadcast television outlets, quite apart from anticompetitive conduct.... [W]hen separated from anticompetitive conduct, this interest in preserving a "multiplicity of broadcast programming sources" becomes poorly defined.... The proper analysis, in my view, necessarily turns on the present *distribution* of broadcast stations among the local broadcast markets that make up the national broadcast "system." Whether cable poses a "significant" threat to a local broadcast market depends first on how many broadcast stations in that market will, in the absence of must-carry, remain available to viewers in noncable households. It also depends on whether viewers actually watch the stations that are dropped or denied carriage.... [T]he Court proceeds from the assumptions that adverse carriage decisions nationwide will affect broadcast markets in proportion to their size; and that all broadcast programming is watched by viewers. Neither assumption is logical or has any factual basis in the record.

. . .

II

The principal opinion goes to great lengths to avoid acknowledging that preferences for "quality," "diverse," and "responsive" local programming underlie the must-carry scheme, although the partial concurrence's reliance on such preferences is explicit.... I take the principal opinion at its word and evaluate the claim that the threat of anticompetitive behavior by cable operators supplies a content-neutral basis for sustaining the statute. It does not.

. . .

A

. . .

What was not resolved in *Turner* was whether "reasonable inferences based on substantial evidence" supported Congress' judgment that the must-carry provisions were necessary "to prevent cable operators from exploiting their economic power to the detriment of broadcasters." Because I remain convinced that the statute is not a measured response to congressional concerns about monopoly power, in my view the principal opinion's discussion on this point is irrelevant. But even if it were relevant, it is incorrect.

1

The *Turner* plurality recognized that Congress' interest in curtailing anticompetitive behavior is substantial "in the abstract." The principal opinion now concludes that substantial evidence supports the congressional judgment that cable operators have incentives to engage in significant anticompetitive behavior. It appears to accept two related arguments on this point: first, that vertically integrated cable operators prefer programming produced by their affiliated cable programming networks to broadcast programming, and second, that potential advertising revenues supply cable system operators, whether affiliated with programmers or not, with incentives to prefer cable programming to broadcast programming.

... [E]ven accepting as reasonable Congress' conclusion that cable operators have incentives to favor affiliated programmers, Congress has already limited the number of channels on a cable system that can be occupied by affiliated programmers.... Once a cable system operator reaches that cap, it can no longer bump a broadcaster in favor of an affiliated programmer. If Congress were concerned that broadcasters favored too many affiliated programmers, it could simply adjust the cap. Must-carry simply cannot be justified as a response to the allegedly "substantial" problem of vertical integration.

The second argument, that the quest for advertising revenue will supply cable operators with incentives to drop local broadcasters, takes two forms. First, some cable programmers offer blank slots within a program into which a cable operator can insert advertisements; appellees argue that "[t]he opportunity to sell such advertising gives cable programmers an additional value to operators above broadcast stations...." But that "additional value" arises only because the must-carry provisions *require* cable operators to carry broadcast signals without alteration.... Second, appellees claim that since cable operators compete directly with broadcasters for some advertising revenue, operators will profit if they can drive broadcasters out of the market and capture their advertising revenue. Even if the record before Congress included substantial evidence ..., it does not necessarily follow that Congress could reasonably find that the quest for advertising revenues supplies cable operators with incentives to engage in predatory behavior, or that must-carry is a reasonable response to such incentives. There is no dispute that a cable system depends primarily upon its subscriber base for revenue. A cable operator is therefore unlikely to drop a widely viewed station in order to capture advertising revenues.... In doing so, it would risk losing subscribers. Nevertheless, appellees contend that cable operators will drop some broadcast stations in spite of, and not because of, viewer preferences. The principal opinion suggests that viewers are likely subscribe to cable even though they prefer certain over-the-air programming to cable programming, because they would be willing to trade access to their preferred channel for access to dozens of cable channels. Even assuming that, at the margin, advertising revenues would drive cable systems to drop some stations ... the strategy's success would depend upon the additional untested premise that the advertising revenues freed by dropping a broadcast station will flow to cable operators rather than to *other* broadcasters.

2

. . .

... When appellees are pressed to explain the Government's "substantial interest" in preserving noncable viewers' access to "vulnerable" or "marginal" stations with "relatively small" audiences, it becomes evident that the interest has nothing to do with anticompetitive behavior, but has everything to do with content-preserving "quality" local programming that is "responsive" to community needs. Indeed, Justice Breyer expressly declines to accept the anticompetitive rationale for the must-carry rules embraced by the principal opinion, and instead explicitly relies on a need to preserve a "rich mix" of "quality" programming.

3

I turn now to the evidence of harm to broadcasters denied carriage or repositioned.... The record on remand does not permit the conclusion, at the summary judgment stage, that Congress could reasonably have predicted serious harm to a significant number of stations in the absence of must-carry.

The purported link between an adverse carriage decision and severe harm to a station depends on yet another untested premise. Even accepting the conclusion that a cable system operator has a monopoly over cable services to the home, it does not necessarily follow that the operator also has a monopoly over all video services to cabled households. Cable subscribers using an input selector switch and an antenna can receive broadcast signals.... Growing use of direct-broadcast satellite television also tends to undercut the notion that cable operators have an inevitable monopoly over video services entering cable households....

. . .

In sum, appellees are not entitled to summary judgment on whether Congress could conclude, based on reasonable inferences drawn from substantial evidence, that " 'absent legislative action, the free local off-air broadcast system is endangered.' " ... The principal opinion disavows a need to closely scrutinize the logic of the regulatory scheme at issue on the ground that it "need not put [its] imprimatur on Congress' economic theory in order to validate the reasonableness of its judgment." That approach trivializes the First Amendment issue at stake in this case. A highly dubious economic theory has been advanced as the "substantial interest" supporting a First Amendment burden on cable operators and cable programmers. In finding that must-carry serves a substantial interest, the principal opinion necessarily accepts that theory. The partial concurrence does not, but neither does it articulate what threat to the availability of a "multiplicity" of broadcast stations would exist in a perfectly competitive market.

B

I turn now to the second portion of the *O'Brien* inquiry, which concerns the fit between the Government's asserted interests and the means chosen to advance them. The Court observes that "broadcast stations gained carriage on 5,880 channels as a result of must-carry," and recognizes that this forced carriage imposes a burden on cable system operators and cable programmers. . . .

Even assuming that the Court is correct that the 5,880 channels occupied by added broadcasters "represent the actual burden of the regulatory scheme," the Court's leap to the conclusion that must-carry "is narrowly tailored to preserve a multiplicity of broadcast stations" is nothing short of astounding. The Court's logic is circular. Surmising that most of the 5,880 channels added by the regulatory scheme would be dropped in its absence, the Court concludes that the figure also approximates the "benefit" of must-carry. . . . The "evi[l] the Government seeks to eliminate," is not the failure of cable operators to carry *these 5,880 stations*. Rather, to read the first half of the principal opinion, the "evil" is *anticompetitive behavior* by cable operators. . . . Without a sense whether *most* adverse carriage decisions are anticompetitively motivated, it is improper to conclude that the statute is narrowly tailored simply because it prevents *some* adverse carriage decisions. . . .

In my view, the statute is not narrowly tailored to serve a substantial interest in preventing anticompetitive conduct. . . . Congress has commandeered up to one third of each cable system's channel capacity for the benefit of local broadcasters, without any regard for whether doing so advances the statute's alleged goals. . . .

Finally, I note my disagreement with the Court's suggestion that the availability of less-speech-restrictive alternatives is never relevant to *O'Brien*'s narrow tailoring inquiry. . . .

Our cases suggest only that we have not interpreted the narrow tailoring inquiry to "require elimination of *all* less restrictive alternatives." . . . It is one thing to say that a regulation need not be the *least*-speech-restrictive means of serving an important governmental objective. It is quite another to suggest, as I read the majority to do here, that the availability of less-speech-restrictive alternatives cannot establish or confirm that a regulation is substantially broader than necessary to achieve the Government's goals. . . . [T]he availability of less intrusive approaches to a problem serves as a benchmark for assessing the reasonableness of the fit between Congress' articulated goals and the means chosen to pursue them. . . .

. . . If Congress truly sought to address anticompetitive behavior by cable system operators, it passed the wrong law. . . . The availability of less restrictive alternatives—a leased-access regime and subsidies—reinforces my conclusion that the must-carry provisions are overbroad.

. . .

III

Finally, I note my disagreement with the Court's decision to sidestep a question reserved in *Turner* . . .: whether the must-carry rules requiring carriage of low power stations . . . survive constitutional scrutiny. A low power station qualifies for carriage only if the Federal Communications Commission determines that the station's programming "would address local news and informational needs which are not being adequately served by full power television broadcast stations because of the geographic distance of such full power stations from the low power station's community of license." . . . As the *Turner* Court noted, "this aspect of § 4 appears to single out certain low-power broadcasters for special benefits on the basis of content." Because I believe that the must-carry provisions fail even intermediate scrutiny, it is clear that they would fail scrutiny under a stricter content-based standard.

. . .

In any event, the Court lets stand the District Court's seriously flawed legal reasoning on the point. The District Court concluded that the provisions "are very close to content-based legislation triggering strict scrutiny," but held that they do not "cross the line." That conclusion appears to have been based on the fact that the low power provisions are *viewpoint*-neutral. Whether a provision is viewpoint-neutral is irrelevant to the question whether it is also *content*-neutral. . . .

IV

In sustaining the must-carry provisions of the Cable Act, the Court ignores the main justification of the statute urged by appellees and subjects restrictions on expressive activity to an inappropriately lenient level of scrutiny. The principal opinion then misapplies the analytic framework it chooses, exhibiting an extraordinary and unwarranted deference for congressional judgments, a profound fear of delving into complex economic matters, and a willingness to substitute untested assumptions for evidence. . . .

Justice Breyer disavows the principal opinion's position on anticompetitive behavior, and instead treats the must-carry rules as a "speech-enhancing" measure designed to ensure access to "quality" programming for noncable households. Neither the principal opinion nor the partial concurrence explains the nature of the alleged threat to the availability of a "multiplicity of broadcast programming sources," if that threat does not arise from cable operators' anticompetitive conduct. . . .

I therefore respectfully dissent, and would reverse the judgment below.

Reno v. American Civil Liberties Union

521 U.S. 844, 117 S.Ct. 2329, 138 L.Ed.2d 874 (1997).

[The report in this case appears supra, p. 164.]

Arkansas Educational Television Commission v. Forbes

523 U.S. 666, 118 S.Ct. 1633, 140 L.Ed.2d 875 (1998).

[The report in this case appears supra, page 185.]

Greater New Orleans Broadcasting Association, Inc. v. United States

__ U.S. __, 119 S.Ct. 1923, __ L.Ed.2d __ (1999).

[The report in this case appears supra, page 179.]

CHAPTER 17

RELIGION AND THE CONSTITUTION

SECTION 1. THE ESTABLISHMENT CLAUSE

B. GOVERNMENT RELIGIOUS EXERCISES, CEREMONIES, DISPLAYS, AND PRACTICES

2. RELIGIOUS SPEECH AND DISPLAYS ON PUBLIC PROPERTY

Page 1638. Add after County of Allegheny v. American Civil Liberties Union:

EQUAL ACCESS FOR RELIGIOUS SPEECH ON PUBLIC PROPERTY*

Religious speakers denied access to public property have sought to compel access on free speech grounds, while the government-owner of the property has sought to justify denial of access on establishment grounds. In Widmar v. Vincent, 454 U.S. 263 (1981), a student group was denied permission to conduct meetings on state university facilities because of a policy denying use of university facilities "for purposes of religious worship or religious teaching." (The group was an organization of evangelical Christian students whose on-campus meetings, open to the public, included prayer, hymns, Bible commentary, and religious discussion.) The exclusion was held to violate the First Amendment's Free Speech Clause. The "discriminatory exclusion" was "content-based," and could only be justified if "necessary to serve a compelling state interest and ... narrowly drawn to achieve that end." The exclusion was not necessary to serve the University's interest in maintaining separation of church and State because the religious group's benefit from access to the University's public forum was "incidental."

In Board of Education v. Mergens, 496 U.S. 226 (1990), students at a public secondary school were denied permission to form a Christian club "to read and discuss the Bible, to have fellowship, and to pray together" because school officials decided that a religious club at school would violate the Establishment Clause. The Court held that the school had violated a federal statute, the Equal Access Act, 20 U.S.C. §§ 4071–4074. The Act prohibits public secondary schools receiving federal funds, and maintaining a "limited public forum," from denying "equal access" to students on the basis of the content of their speech. By a vote of eight to one, but without a majority opinion, the Court held that the Equal Access Act did not violate the Establishment Clause. Justice O'Connor, joined by Chief Justice Rehnquist and Justices White and Blackmun, applied the three-part *Lemon* test. Granting equal access to secular

* The editors thank Professor Richard F. Duncan of the University of Nebraska for suggestions that inspired this note. Professor Duncan has no responsibility for its content.

and religious speech: was a secular purpose; did not have the primary effect of advancing religion because high school students will understand that the school does not endorse speech it merely permits; did not involve excessive entanglement because the Act prohibits faculty from regularly attending, directing or controlling activities of religious student groups. Justice Kennedy, joined by Justice Scalia, said there was no Establishment Clause violation because religious groups were not given benefits to a degree that established a state religion, and students were not coerced to participate in religious activity.

In Lamb's Chapel v. Center Moriches Union Free School District, 508 U.S. 384 (1993), exclusion of a non-student's religious speech from a public secondary school was held to violate the Free Speech Clause. An evangelical church and its pastor were denied permission to use school facilities to show a six-part film series containing lectures concerning "Christian family values." The Court relied on *Widmar* for its conclusion that the school district's "posited fears of an Establishment Clause violation are unfounded."

C.   FINANCIAL AID TO CHURCH-RELATED SCHOOLS

1.   ELEMENTARY AND SECONDARY SCHOOLS

Page 1647. Replace Grand Rapid School District v. Ball, Aguilar v. Felton, and Board of Education of Kiryas Joel Village School District v. Grumet (pages 1647–1669) with the following:

Agostini v. Felton

521 U.S. 203, 117 S.Ct. 1997, 138 L.Ed.2d 391 (1997).

Justice O'Connor delivered the opinion of the Court.

In Aguilar v. Felton, 473 U.S. 402 (1985), this Court held that the Establishment Clause of the First Amendment barred the city of New York from sending public school teachers into parochial schools to provide remedial education to disadvantaged children pursuant to a congressionally mandated program. On remand, the District Court for the Eastern District of New York entered a permanent injunction reflecting our ruling. Twelve years later, petitioners—the parties bound by that injunction—seek relief from its operation. Petitioners maintain that *Aguilar* cannot be squared with our intervening Establishment Clause jurisprudence and ask that we explicitly recognize what our more recent cases already dictate: *Aguilar* is no longer good law. We agree with petitioners that *Aguilar* is not consistent with our subsequent Establishment Clause decisions and further conclude that, on the facts presented here, petitioners are entitled under Federal Rule of Civil Procedure 60(b)(5) to relief from the operation of the District Court's prospective injunction.

I

In 1965, Congress enacted Title I of the Elementary and Secondary Education Act of 1965, 79 Stat. 27, as modified, 20 U.S.C. § 6301 et seq., to "provid[e] full educational opportunity to every child regardless of economic background." ... Toward that end, Title I channels federal funds, through the States, to "local educational agencies" (LEA's).... The LEA's spend these funds to provide remedial education, guidance, and job counseling to eligible students.... An eligible student is one (i) who resides within the attendance boundaries of a public school located in a low-income area ... ; and (ii) who is failing, or is at risk of failing, the State's student performance standards.... Title I funds must be made available to *all* eligible children, regardless of whether they attend public schools, ... and the services provided to children attending private schools must be "equitable in comparison to services and other benefits for public school children." ...

An LEA providing services to children enrolled in private schools is subject to a number of constraints that are not imposed when it provides aid to public schools. Title I services may be provided only to those private school students eligible for aid, and cannot be used to provide services on a "school-wide" basis.... In addition, the LEA must retain complete control over Title I funds; retain title to all materials used to provide Title I services; and provide those services through public employees or other persons independent of the private school and any religious institution.... The Title I services themselves must be "secular, neutral, and nonideological," ... and must "supplement, and in no case supplant, the level of services" already provided by the private school ....

Petitioner Board of Education of the City of New York (Board), an LEA, first applied for Title I funds in 1966 and has grappled ever since with how to provide Title I services to the private school students within its jurisdiction. Approximately 10% of the total number of students eligible for Title I services are private school students. Recognizing that more than 90% of the private schools within the Board's jurisdiction are sectarian, ... the Board initially arranged to transport children to public schools for after-school Title I instruction. But this enterprise was largely unsuccessful. Attendance was poor, teachers and children were tired, and parents were concerned for the safety of their children.... The Board then moved the after-school instruction onto private school campuses, as Congress had contemplated when it enacted Title I. ...After this program also yielded mixed results, the Board implemented the plan we evaluated in Aguilar v. Felton....

That plan called for the provision of Title I services on private school premises during school hours. Under the plan, only public employees could serve as Title I instructors and counselors.... Assignments to private schools were made on a voluntary basis and without regard to the religious affiliation of the employee or the wishes of the private school.... As the Court of Appeals in *Aguilar* observed, a large majority of Title I teachers worked in nonpublic schools with religious affiliations different from their own.... The vast majority of Title I teachers also moved among the private schools, spending fewer than five days a week at the same school....

Before any public employee could provide Title I instruction at a private school, she would be given a detailed set of written and oral instructions emphasizing the secular purpose of Title I and setting out the rules to be followed to ensure that this purpose was not compromised. Specifically, employees would be told that (i) they were employees of the Board and accountable only to their public school supervisors; (ii) they had exclusive responsibility for selecting students for the Title I program and could teach only those children who met the eligibility criteria for Title I; (iii) their materials and equipment would be used only in the Title I program; (iv) they could not engage in team-teaching or other cooperative instructional activities with private school teachers; and (v) they could not introduce any religious matter into their teaching or become involved in any way with the religious activities of the private schools.... All religious symbols were to be removed from classrooms used for Title I services.... The rules acknowledged that it might be necessary for Title I teachers to consult with a student's regular classroom teacher to assess the student's particular needs and progress, but admonished instructors to limit those consultations to mutual professional concerns regarding the student's education.... To ensure compliance with these rules, a publicly employed field supervisor was to attempt to make at least one unannounced visit to each teacher's classroom every month....

In 1978, six federal taxpayers—respondents here—sued the Board in the District Court for the Eastern District of New York. Respondents sought declaratory and injunctive relief, claiming that the Board's Title I program violated the Establishment Clause.... The District Court granted summary judgment for the Board, but the Court of Appeals for the Second Circuit reversed.... [T]his Court affirmed on the ground that the Board's Title I program necessitated an "excessive entanglement of church and state in the administration of [Title I] benefits." ... On remand, the District Court permanently enjoined the Board "from using public funds for any plan or program under [Title I] to the extent that it requires, authorizes or permits public school teachers and guidance counselors to provide teaching and counseling services on the premises of sectarian schools within New York City."

The Board, like other LEA's across the United States, modified its Title I program so it could continue serving those students who attended private religious schools. Rather than offer Title I instruction to parochial school students at their schools, the Board reverted to its prior practice of providing instruction at public school sites, at leased sites, and in mobile instructional units (essentially vans converted into classrooms) parked near the sectarian school. The Board also offered computer-aided instruction, which could be provided "on premises" because it did not require public employees to be physically present on the premises of a religious school.

It is not disputed that the additional costs of complying with *Aguilar*'s mandate are significant. Since the 1986–1987 school year, the Board has spent over $100 million providing computer-aided instruction, leasing sites and mobile instructional units, and transporting students to those sites.... These "*Aguilar* costs" ... reduce the amount of Title I money an LEA has available for remedial education, and LEA's have had to cut back on the number of students who receive Title I benefits....

In October and December of 1995, petitioners—the Board and a new group of parents of parochial school students entitled to Title I services—filed motions in the District Court seeking relief under Federal Rule of Civil Procedure 60(b) from the permanent injunction entered by the District Court on remand from our decision in Aguilar.... Specifically, petitioners pointed to the statements of five Justices in Board of Ed. of Kiryas Joel Village School Dist. v. Grumet, 512 U.S. 687 (1994), calling for the overruling of *Aguilar*. The District Court denied the motion.... The Court of Appeals for the Second Circuit [affirmed.] We ... reverse.

II

The question we must answer is a simple one: Are petitioners entitled to relief from the District Court's permanent injunction under Rule 60(b)? Rule 60(b)(5), the subsection under which petitioners proceeded below, states: "On motion and upon such terms as are just, the court may relieve a party . . . from a final judgment [or] order . . . [when] it is no longer equitable that the judgment should have prospective application." . . . [I]t is appropriate to grant a Rule 60(b)(5) motion when the party seeking relief from an injunction or consent decree can show "a significant change either in factual conditions or in law." A court may recognize subsequent changes in either statutory or decisional law. . . .

Petitioners point to three changes in the factual and legal landscape that they believe justify their claim for relief under Rule 60(b)(5). They first contend that the exorbitant costs of complying with the District Court's injunction constitute a significant factual development warranting modification of the injunction. Petitioners also argue that there have been two significant legal developments since *Aguilar* was decided: a majority of Justices have expressed their views that *Aguilar* should be reconsidered or overruled; and *Aguilar* has in any event been undermined by subsequent Establishment Clause decisions, including Witters v. Washington Dept. of Servs. for Blind, 474 U.S. 481 (1986), Zobrest v. Catalina Foothills School Dist., 509 U.S. 1 (1993), and Rosenberger v. Rector and Visitors of Univ. of Va., 515 U.S. 819 (1995).

. . .

. . . [P]etitioners have failed to establish . . . significant change in factual conditions. . . . Both petitioners and this Court were, at the time *Aguilar* was decided, aware that additional costs would be incurred if Title I services could not be provided in parochial school classrooms. . . .

. . . [T]he statements made by five Justices in *Kiryas Joel* do not, in themselves, furnish a basis for concluding that our Establishment Clause jurisprudence has changed. In *Kiryas Joel*, we considered the constitutionality of a New York law that carved out a public school district to coincide with the boundaries of the village of Kiryas Joel, which was an enclave of the Satmar Hasidic sect. Before the new district was created, Satmar children wishing to receive special educational services under the Individuals with Disabilities Education Act (IDEA), 20 U.S.C. § 1400 et seq., could receive those services at public schools located outside the village. Because Satmar parents rarely permitted their children to attend those schools, New York created a new public school district within the boundaries of the village so that Satmar children could stay within the village but receive IDEA services on public school premises from publicly employed instructors. In the course of our opinion, we observed that New York had created the special school district in response to our decision in *Aguilar*, which had required New York to cease providing IDEA services to Satmar children on the premises of their private religious schools. . . . Five Justices joined opinions calling for reconsideration of *Aguilar*. [O'Connor, Kennedy, Scalia, Rehnquist and Thomas.] But the question of *Aguilar*'s propriety was not before us. The views of five Justices that the case should be reconsidered or overruled cannot be said to have effected a change in Establishment Clause law.

In light of these conclusions, petitioners' ability to satisfy the prerequisites of Rule 60(b)(5) hinges on whether our later Establishment Clause cases have so undermined *Aguilar* that it is no longer good law. We now turn to that inquiry.

III

A

In order to evaluate whether *Aguilar* has been eroded by our subsequent Establishment Clause cases, it is necessary to understand the rationale upon which *Aguilar*, as well as its companion case, School Dist. of Grand Rapids v. Ball, 473 U.S. 373 (1985), rested.

In *Ball*, the Court evaluated two programs implemented by the School District of Grand Rapids, Michigan. The district's Shared Time program, the one most analogous to Title I, provided remedial and "enrichment" classes, at public expense, to students attending nonpublic schools. The classes were taught during regular school hours by publicly employed teachers, using materials purchased with public funds, on the premises of nonpublic schools. The Shared Time courses were in subjects designed to supplement the "core curriculum" of the nonpublic schools.... Of the 41 nonpublic schools eligible for the program, 40 were " 'pervasively sectarian' " in character—that is, "the purpos[e] of [those] schools [was] to advance their particular religions." ...

The Court conducted its analysis by applying the three-part test set forth in Lemon v. Kurtzman, 403 U.S. 602 (1971):.... [I]t ultimately concluded that the program had the impermissible effect of advancing religion....

The Court found that the program violated the Establishment Clause's prohibition against "government-financed or government-sponsored indoctrination into the beliefs of a particular religious faith" in at least three ways.... First, drawing upon the analysis in Meek v. Pittenger, 421 U.S. 349 (1975), the Court observed that "the teachers participating in the programs may become involved in intentionally or inadvertently inculcating particular religious tenets or beliefs".... *Meek* invalidated a Pennsylvania program in which full-time public employees provided supplemental "auxiliary services"—remedial and accelerated instruction, guidance counseling and testing, and speech and hearing services—to nonpublic school children at their schools.... Although the auxiliary services themselves were secular, they were mostly dispensed on the premises of parochial schools, where "an atmosphere dedicated to the advancement of religious belief [was] constantly maintained." ... Instruction in that atmosphere was sufficient to create "[t]he potential for impermissible fostering of religion." ... Cf. Wolman v. Walter, 433 U.S., at 248 (upholding programs employing public employees to provide remedial instruction and guidance counseling to nonpublic school children at sites away from the nonpublic school).

... [A] majority found a " 'substantial risk' " that teachers—even those who were not employed by the private schools—might "subtly (or overtly) conform their instruction to the [pervasively sectarian] environment in which they [taught]." ...

The presence of public teachers on parochial school grounds had a second, related impermissible effect: It created a "graphic symbol of the 'concert or union or dependency' of church and state," . . . .

Third, the Court found that the Shared Time program impermissibly financed religious indoctrination by subsidizing "the primary religious mission of the institutions affected." . . . The Court separated its prior decisions evaluating programs that aided the secular activities of religious institutions into two categories: those in which it concluded that the aid resulted in an effect that was "indirect, remote, or incidental" (and upheld the aid); and those in which it concluded that the aid resulted in "a direct and substantial advancement of the sectarian enterprise" (and invalidated the aid). . . . . In light of *Meek* and *Wolman*, Grand Rapids' program fell into the latter category. In those cases, the Court ruled that a state loan of instructional equipment and materials to parochial schools was an impermissible form of "direct aid" because it "advanced the primary, religion-oriented educational function of the sectarian school," . . . by providing "in-kind" aid (e.g., instructional materials) that could be used to teach religion and by freeing up money for religious indoctrination that the school would otherwise have devoted to secular education. Given the holdings in *Meek* and *Wolman*, the Shared Time program— which provided teachers as well as instructional equipment and materials—was surely invalid. Id., at 395. The *Ball* Court likewise placed no weight on the fact that the program was provided to the student rather than to the school. Nor was the impermissible effect mitigated by the fact that the program only supplemented the courses offered by the parochial schools. . . .

The New York City Title I program challenged in *Aguilar* closely resembled the Shared Time program struck down in *Ball*, but the Court found fault with an aspect of the Title I program not present in *Ball*: The Board had "adopted a system for monitoring the religious content of publicly funded Title I classes in the religious schools." . . . Even though this monitoring system might prevent the Title I program from being used to inculcate religion, the Court concluded, as it had in *Lemon* and *Meek*, that the level of monitoring necessary to be "certain" that the program had an exclusively secular effect would "inevitably resul[t] in the excessive entanglement of church and state," thereby running afoul of *Lemon*'s third prong. . . .

Distilled to essentials, the Court's conclusion that the Shared Time program in *Ball* had the impermissible effect of advancing religion rested on three assumptions: (i) any public employee who works on the premises of a religious school is presumed to inculcate religion in her work; (ii) the presence of public employees on private school premises creates a symbolic union between church and state; and (iii) any and all public aid that directly aids the educational function of religious schools impermissibly finances religious indoctrination, even if the aid reaches such schools as a consequence of private decisionmaking. Additionally, in *Aguilar* there was a fourth assumption: that New York City's Title I program necessitated an excessive government entanglement with religion because public employees who teach on the premises of religious schools must be closely monitored to ensure that they do not inculcate religion.

B

Our more recent cases have undermined the assumptions upon which *Ball* and *Aguilar* relied. To be sure, the general principles we use to evaluate whether government aid violates the Establishment Clause have not changed since *Aguilar* was decided. For example, we continue to ask whether the government acted with the purpose of advancing or inhibiting religion, and the nature of that inquiry has remained largely unchanged.... Likewise, we continue to explore whether the aid has the "effect" of advancing or inhibiting religion. What has changed since we decided *Ball* and *Aguilar* is our understanding of the criteria used to assess whether aid to religion has an impermissible effect.

1

As we have repeatedly recognized, government inculcation of religious beliefs has the impermissible effect of advancing religion. Our cases subsequent to *Aguilar* have, however, modified in two significant respects the approach we use to assess indoctrination. First, we have abandoned the presumption erected in *Meek* and *Ball* that the placement of public employees on parochial school grounds inevitably results in the impermissible effect of state-sponsored indoctrination or constitutes a symbolic union between government and religion. In Zobrest v. Catalina Foothills School Dist., 509 U.S. 1 (1993), we examined whether the IDEA, 20 U.S.C. § 1400 et seq., was constitutional as applied to a deaf student who sought to bring his state-employed sign-language interpreter with him to his Roman Catholic high school. We held that this was permissible, expressly disavowing the notion that "the Establishment Clause [laid] down [an] absolute bar to the placing of a public employee in a sectarian school." ... Because the only *government* aid in *Zobrest* was the interpreter, who was herself not inculcating any religious messages, no *government* indoctrination took place and we were able to conclude that "the provision of such assistance [was] not barred by the Establishment Clause." ... *Zobrest* therefore expressly rejected the notion—relied on in *Ball* and *Aguilar*—that, solely because of her presence on private school property, a public employee will be presumed to inculcate religion in the students. *Zobrest* also implicitly repudiated another assumption on which *Ball* and *Aguilar* turned: that the presence of a public employee on private school property creates an impermissible "symbolic link" between government and religion.

Justice Souter contends that *Zobrest* ... held that the Establishment Clause tolerates the presence of public employees in sectarian schools "only in ... limited circumstances"—i.e., when the employee "simply translates for one student the material presented to the class for the benefit of all students." The sign-language interpreter in Zobrest is unlike the remedial instructors in *Ball* and *Aguilar*....

In *Zobrest*, however, we did not expressly or implicitly rely upon the basis Justice Souter now advances for distinguishing *Ball* and *Aguilar*.... The signer in *Zobrest* had the same opportunity to inculcate religion in the performance of her duties as do Title I employees, and there is no genuine basis upon which to confine *Zobrest*'s underlying rationale....

Second, we have departed from the rule relied on in *Ball* that all government aid that directly aids the educational function of religious schools is invalid. In Witters v. Washington Dept. of Servs. for Blind, 474 U.S. 481 (1986), we held that the Establishment Clause did not bar a State from issuing a vocational tuition grant to a blind person who wished to use the grant to attend a Christian college and become a pastor, missionary, or youth director. Even though the grant recipient clearly would use the money to obtain religious education, we observed that the tuition grants were " 'made available generally without regard to the sectarian-nonsectarian, or public-nonpublic nature of the institution benefited.' " . . . The grants were disbursed directly to students, who then used the money to pay for tuition at the educational institution of their choice. In our view, this transaction was no different from a State's issuing a paycheck to one of its employees, knowing that the employee would donate part or all of the check to a religious institution. In both situations, any money that ultimately went to religious institutions did so "only as a result of the genuinely independent and private choices of" individuals. . . . The same logic applied in *Zobrest*. . . . Because the private school would not have provided an interpreter on its own, we also concluded that the aid in *Zobrest* did not indirectly finance religious education by "reliev[ing] the sectarian schoo[l] of costs [it] otherwise would have borne in educating [its] students."

Zobrest and *Witters* make clear that, under current law, the Shared Time program in *Ball* and New York City's Title I program in *Aguilar* will not, as a matter of law, be deemed to have the effect of advancing religion through indoctrination. Indeed, each of the premises upon which we relied in *Ball* to reach a contrary conclusion is no longer valid. First, there is no reason to presume that, simply because she enters a parochial school classroom, a full-time public employee such as a Title I teacher will depart from her assigned duties and instructions and embark on religious indoctrination, any more than there was a reason in *Zobrest* to think an interpreter would inculcate religion by altering her translation of classroom lectures. . . .

As discussed above, *Zobrest* also repudiates *Ball*'s assumption that the presence of Title I teachers in parochial school classrooms will, without more, create the impression of a "symbolic union" between church and state. Justice Souter maintains that . . . Title I continues to foster a "symbolic union" between the Board and sectarian schools because it mandates "the involvement of public teachers in the instruction provided within sectarian schools," and "fus[es] public and private faculties." Justice Souter does not disavow the notion, uniformly adopted by lower courts, that Title I services may be provided to sectarian school students in off-campus locations. . . . Taking this view, the only difference between a constitutional program and an unconstitutional one is the location of the classroom. . . . We do not see any perceptible (let alone dispositive) difference in the degree of symbolic union between a student receiving remedial instruction in a classroom on his sectarian school's campus and one receiving instruction in a van parked just at the school's curbside. . . .

   . . .

Justice Souter . . . points to three differences he perceives between the programs: (i) Title I services are distributed by LEA's "directly to the religious schools" instead of to individual students pursuant to a formal application process; (ii) Title I services "necessarily reliev[e] a religious school of 'an expense that it otherwise would have assumed' "; and (iii) Title I provides services to more students than did the programs in *Witters* and *Zobrest*. None of these distinctions is meaningful. While it is true that individual students may not directly apply for Title I services, it does not follow from this premise that those services are distributed "directly to the religious schools". . . . Title I funds are instead distributed to a public agency (an LEA) that dispenses services directly to the eligible students within its boundaries, no matter where they choose to attend school. . . .

We are also not persuaded that Title I services supplant the remedial instruction and guidance counseling already provided in New York City's sectarian schools. Although Justice Souter maintains that the sectarian schools provide such services and that those schools reduce those services once their students begin to receive Title I instruction, his claims rest on speculation about the impossibility of drawing any line between supplemental and general education, and not on any evidence in the record that the Board is in fact violating Title I regulations by providing services that supplant those offered in the sectarian schools. . . .

What is most fatal to the argument that New York City's Title I program directly subsidizes religion is that it applies with equal force when those services are provided off-campus, and *Aguilar* implied that providing the services off-campus is entirely consistent with the Establishment Clause. . . .

2

Although we examined in *Witters* and *Zobrest* the criteria by which an aid program identifies its beneficiaries, we did so solely to assess whether any use of that aid to indoctrinate religion could be attributed to the State. A number of our Establishment Clause cases have found that the criteria used for identifying beneficiaries are relevant in a second respect, apart from enabling a court to evaluate whether the program subsidizes religion. Specifically, the criteria might themselves have the effect of advancing religion by creating a financial incentive to undertake religious indoctrination. . . . This incentive is not present, however, where the aid is allocated on the basis of neutral, secular criteria that neither favor nor disfavor religion, and is made available to both religious and secular beneficiaries on a nondiscriminatory basis. . . .

In *Ball* and *Aguilar*, the Court gave this consideration no weight. Before and since those decisions, we have sustained programs that provided aid to all eligible children regardless of where they attended school. . . .

    . . .

3

We turn now to *Aguilar*'s conclusion that New York City's Title I program resulted in an excessive entanglement between church and state. . . . [T]he factors we use to assess whether an entanglement is "excessive" are similar to the factors we use to examine "effect." . . . Indeed, in *Lemon* itself, the entanglement that the Court found "independently" to necessitate the program's invalidation also was found to have the effect of inhibiting religion. . . . Thus, it is simplest to recognize why entanglement is significant and treat it . . . as an aspect of the inquiry into a statute's effect.

Not all entanglements, of course, have the effect of advancing or inhibiting religion. . . . Entanglement must be "excessive" before it runs afoul of the Establishment Clause. . . .

The pre-*Aguilar* Title I program does not result in an "excessive" entanglement that advances or inhibits religion. As discussed previously, the Court's finding of "excessive" entanglement in *Aguilar* rested on three grounds: (i) the program would require "pervasive monitoring by public authorities" to ensure that Title I employees did not inculcate religion; (ii) the program required "administrative cooperation" between the Board and parochial schools; and (iii) the program might increase the dangers of "political divisiveness." . . . Under our current understanding of the Establishment Clause, the last two considerations are insufficient by themselves to create an "excessive" entanglement. They are present no matter where Title I services are offered, and no court has held that Title I services cannot be offered off-campus. . . . Further, the assumption underlying the first consideration has been undermined. . . . [A]fter *Zobrest* we no longer presume that public employees will inculcate religion simply because they happen to be in a sectarian environment. Since we have abandoned the assumption that properly instructed public employees will fail to discharge their duties faithfully, we must also discard the assumption that *pervasive* monitoring of Title I teachers is required. There is no suggestion in the record before us that unannounced monthly visits of public supervisors are insufficient to prevent or to detect inculcation of religion by public employees. Moreover, we have not found excessive entanglement in cases in which States imposed far more onerous burdens on religious institutions than the monitoring system at issue here. . . .

. . . We . . . hold that a federally funded program providing supplemental, remedial instruction to disadvantaged children on a neutral basis is not invalid under the Establishment Clause when such instruction is given on the premises of sectarian schools by government employees pursuant to a program containing safeguards such as those present here. . . . Accordingly, we must acknowledge that *Aguilar*, as well as the portion of *Ball* addressing Grand Rapids' Shared Time program, are no longer good law.

C

The doctrine of *stare decisis* does not preclude us from recognizing the change in our law and overruling *Aguilar* and those portions of *Ball* inconsistent with our more recent decisions. . . . [It] is at its weakest when we interpret the Constitution because our interpretation can be altered only by constitutional amendment or by overruling our prior decisions. . . . As discussed above, our Establishment Clause jurisprudence has changed significantly since we decided *Ball* and *Aguilar*, so our decision to overturn those cases rests on far more than "a present doctrinal disposition to come out differently . . ." . . .

Nor does the "law of the case" doctrine place any additional constraints on our ability to overturn *Aguilar*. Under this doctrine, a court should not reopen issues decided in earlier stages of the same litigation. . . . The doctrine does not apply if the court is "convinced that [its prior decision] is clearly erroneous and would work a manifest injustice." . . .

IV

. . . We are only left to decide whether this change in law entitles petitioners to relief under Rule 60(b)(5). We conclude that it does. Our general practice is to apply the rule of law we announce in a case to the parties before us. . . .

We do not acknowledge, and we do not hold, that other courts should conclude our more recent cases have, by implication, overruled an earlier precedent. We reaffirm that "if a precedent of this Court has direct application in a case, yet appears to rest on reasons rejected in some other line of decisions, the Court of Appeals should follow the case which directly controls, leaving to this Court the prerogative of overruling its own decisions." ... Adherence to this teaching by the District Court and Court of Appeals in this case does not insulate a legal principle on which they relied from our review to determine its continued vitality. The trial court acted within its discretion in entertaining the motion with supporting allegations, but it was also correct to recognize that the motion had to be denied unless and until this Court reinterpreted the binding precedent.

. . .

Respondents nevertheless contend that we should not grant Rule 60(b)(5) relief here, in spite of its propriety in other contexts. They contend that petitioners have used Rule 60(b)(5) in an unprecedented way—not as a means of recognizing changes in the law, but as a vehicle for effecting them. If we were to sanction this use of Rule 60(b)(5), respondents argue, we would encourage litigants to burden the federal courts with a deluge of Rule 60(b)(5) motions premised on nothing more than the claim that various judges or Justices have stated that the law has changed.... We think their fears are overstated. As we noted above, a judge's stated belief that a case should be overruled does not make it so.

... The clause of Rule 60(b)(5) that petitioners invoke applies by its terms only to "judgment[s] hav[ing] prospective application." Intervening developments in the law by themselves rarely constitute the extraordinary circumstances required for relief under Rule 60(b)(6), the only remaining avenue for relief on this basis from judgments lacking any prospective component.... Our decision will have no effect outside the context of ordinary civil litigation where the propriety of continuing prospective relief is at issue....

. . .

As a final matter, we see no reason to wait for a "better vehicle" in which to evaluate the impact of subsequent cases on *Aguilar*'s continued vitality.... [I]t would be particularly inequitable for us to bide our time waiting for another case to arise while the city of New York labors under a continuing injunction forcing it to spend millions of dollars on mobile instructional units and leased sites when it could instead be spending that money to give economically disadvantaged children a better chance at success in life by means of a program that is perfectly consistent with the Establishment Clause.

For these reasons, we reverse the judgment of the Court of Appeals and remand to the District Court with instructions to vacate its September 26, 1985, order.

It is so ordered.

Justice Souter with whom Justice Stevens and Justice Ginsburg join, and with whom Justice Breyer joins as to Part II, dissenting.

In this novel proceeding, petitioners seek relief from an injunction the District Court entered 12 years ago to implement our decision in Aguilar v. Felton.... The result is to repudiate the very reasonable line drawn in *Aguilar* and *Ball*, and to authorize direct state aid to religious institutions on an unparalleled scale, in violation of the Establishment Clause's central prohibition against religious subsidies by the government.

I respectfully dissent.

I

. . .

. . . I believe *Aguilar* was a correct and sensible decision, and my only reservation about its opinion is that the emphasis on the excessive entanglement produced by monitoring religious instructional content obscured those facts that independently called for the application of two central tenets of Establishment Clause jurisprudence. The State is forbidden to subsidize religion directly and is just as surely forbidden to act in any way that could reasonably be viewed as religious endorsement. . . .

. . . [T]he flat ban on subsidization . . . expresses the hard lesson . . . that religions supported by governments are compromised just as surely as the religious freedom of dissenters is burdened when the government supports religion. . . . The human tendency, of course, is to forget the hard lessons, and to overlook the history of governmental partnership with religion when a cause is worthy, and bureaucrats have programs. That tendency to forget is the reason for having the Establishment Clause (along with the Constitution's other structural and libertarian guarantees), in the hope of stopping the corrosion before it starts.

These principles were violated by the programs at issue in *Aguilar* and *Ball*, as a consequence of several significant features common to both Title I, as implemented in New York City before Aguilar, and the Grand Rapids Shared Time program: each provided classes on the premises of the religious schools, covering a wide range of subjects including some at the core of primary and secondary education, like reading and mathematics; while their services were termed "supplemental," the programs and their instructors necessarily assumed responsibility for teaching subjects that the religious schools would otherwise have been obligated to provide . . .; while the programs offered aid to nonpublic school students generally (and Title I went to public school students as well), participation by religious school students in each program was extensive . . .; and, finally, aid under Title I and Shared Time flowed directly to the schools in the form of classes and programs, as distinct from indirect aid that reaches schools only as a result of independent private choice. . . .

What, therefore, was significant in *Aguilar* and *Ball* about the placement of state-paid teachers into the physical and social settings of the religious schools was not only the consequent temptation of some of those teachers to reflect the schools' religious missions in the rhetoric of their instruction, with a resulting need for monitoring and the certainty of entanglement. . . . What was so remarkable was that the schemes in issue assumed a teaching responsibility indistinguishable from the responsibility of the schools themselves. The obligation of primary and secondary schools to teach reading necessarily extends to teaching those who are having a hard time at it, and the same is true of math. Calling some classes remedial does not distinguish their subjects from the schools' basic subjects, however inadequately the schools may have been addressing them.

What was true of the Title I scheme as struck down in *Aguilar* will be just as true when New York reverts to the old practices with the Court's approval after today. There is simply no line that can be drawn between the instruction paid for at taxpayers' expense and the instruction in any subject that is not identified as formally religious. While it would be an obvious sham, say, to channel cash to religious schools to be credited only against the expense of "secular" instruction, the line between "supplemental" and general education is likewise impossible to draw. If a State may constitutionally enter the schools to teach in the manner in question, it must in constitutional principle be free to assume, or assume payment for, the entire cost of instruction provided in any ostensibly secular subject in any religious school. This Court explicitly recognized this in *Ball*. . . .

It may be objected that there is some subsidy in remedial education even when it takes place off the religious premises, some subsidy, that is, even in the way New York City has administered the Title I program after *Aguilar*. In these circumstances, too, what the State does, the religious school need not do; the schools save money and the program makes it easier for them to survive and concentrate their resources on their religious objectives. This argument may, of course, prove too much, but if it is not thought strong enough to bar even off-premises aid in teaching the basics to religious school pupils (an issue not before the Court in *Aguilar* or today), it does nothing to undermine the sense of drawing a line between remedial teaching on and off-premises. The off-premises teaching is arguably less likely to open the door to relieving religious schools of their responsibilities for secular subjects simply because these schools are less likely (and presumably legally unable) to dispense with those subjects from their curriculums or to make patently significant cut-backs in basic teaching within the schools to offset the outside instruction; if the aid is delivered outside of the schools, it is less likely to supplant some of what would otherwise go on inside them and to subsidize what remains. On top of that, the difference in the degree of reasonably perceptible endorsement is substantial. Sharing the teaching responsibilities within a school having religious objectives is far more likely to telegraph approval of the school's mission than keeping the State's distance would do. . . . When, moreover, the aid goes overwhelmingly to one religious denomination, minimal contact between state and church is the less likely to feed the resentment of other religions that would like access to public money for their own worthy projects.

In sum, if a line is to be drawn short of barring all state aid to religious schools for teaching standard subjects, the *Aguilar-Ball* line was a sensible one capable of principled adherence. It is no less sound, and no less necessary, today.

II

The Court today ignores this doctrine and claims that recent cases rejected the elemental assumptions underlying *Aguilar* and much of *Ball*. But the Court errs. . . .

A

. . .

In *Zobrest* the Court did indeed recognize that the Establishment Clause lays down no absolute bar to placing public employees in a sectarian school, . . . but the rejection of such a *per se* rule was hinged expressly on the nature of the employee's job. . . . The signer could . . . be seen as more like a hearing aid than a teacher, and the signing could not be understood as an opportunity to inject religious content in what was supposed to be secular instruction. *Zobrest* accordingly holds only that in these limited circumstances where a public employee simply translates for one student the material presented to the class for the benefit of all students, the employee's presence in the sectarian school does not violate the Establishment Clause. . . .

. . .

B

The Court next claims that *Ball* rested on the assumption that "any and all public aid that directly aids the educational function of religious schools impermissibly finances religious indoctrination, even if the aid reaches such schools as a consequence of private decision-making." After *Ball*, the opinion continues, the Court departed from the rule that "all government aid that directly aids the educational function of religious schools is invalid." But this mischaracterizes *Ball*'s discussion on the point, and misreads *Witters* and *Zobrest* as repudiating the more modest proposition on which *Ball* in fact rested.

Ball did not establish that "any and all" such aid to religious schools necessarily violates the Establishment Clause. It held that the Shared Time program subsidized the religious functions of the parochial schools by taking over a significant portion of their responsibility for teaching secular subjects. . . . In *Witters*, the Court noted that the State would issue the disputed vocational aid directly to one student who would then transmit it to the school of his choice, and that there was no record evidence that "any significant portion of the aid expended under the Washington program as a whole will end up flowing to religious education." . . . *Zobrest* also presented an instance of a single beneficiary, . . . and emphasized that the student (who had previously received the interpretive services in a public school) determined where the aid would be used, that the aid at issue was limited, and that the religious school was "not relieved of an expense that it otherwise would have assumed in educating its students." . . .

. . .

. . . In *Zobrest* and *Witters*, . . . individual students were themselves applicants for individual benefits on a scale that could not amount to a systemic supplement. But under Title I, a local educational agency (which in New York City is the Board of Education) may receive federal funding by proposing programs approved to serve individual students who meet the criteria of need, which it then uses to provide such programs at the religious schools; students eligible for such programs may not apply directly for Title I funds. The aid, accordingly, is not even formally aid to the individual students (and even formally individual aid must be seen as aid to a school system when so many individuals receive it that it becomes a significant feature of the system) ...

In sum, nothing since *Ball* and *Aguilar* and before this case has eroded the distinction between "direct and substantial" and "indirect and incidental." That principled line is being breached only here and now.

C

The Court notes that aid programs providing benefits solely to religious groups may be constitutionally suspect, while aid allocated under neutral, secular criteria is less likely to have the effect of advancing religion.... If a scheme of government aid results in support for religion in some substantial degree, or in endorsement of its value, the formal neutrality of the scheme does not render the Establishment Clause helpless or the holdings in *Aguilar* and *Ball* inapposite.

III

Finally, there is the issue of precedent. *Stare decisis* is no barrier in the Court's eyes because it reads *Aguilar* and *Ball* for exaggerated propositions that *Witters* and *Zobrest* are supposed to have limited to the point of abandoned doctrine.... The Court's dispensation from *stare decisis* is, accordingly, no more convincing than its reading of those cases. Since *Aguilar* came down, no case has held that there need be no concern about a risk that publicly paid school teachers may further religious doctrine; no case has repudiated the distinction between direct and substantial aid and aid that is indirect and incidental; no case has held that fusing public and private faculties in one religious school does not create an impermissible union or carry an impermissible endorsement; and no case has held that direct subsidization of religious education is constitutional or that the assumption of a portion of a religious school's teaching responsibility is not direct subsidization.

The continuity of the law, indeed, is matched by the persistence of the facts. When *Aguilar* was decided everyone knew that providing Title I services off the premises of the religious schools would come at substantial cost in efficiency, convenience, and money.... No predictions have gone so awry as to excuse the case from the claim of precedent....

That is not to deny that the facts just recited are regrettable; the object of Title I is worthy without doubt, and the cost of compliance is high. In the short run there is much that is genuinely unfortunate about the administration of the scheme under *Aguilar*'s rule. But constitutional lines have to be drawn, and on one side of every one of them is an otherwise sympathetic case that provokes impatience with the Constitution and with the line. But constitutional lines are the price of constitutional government.

Justice Ginsburg, with whom Justice Stevens, Justice Souter, and Justice Breyer join, dissenting.

The Court today finds a way to rehear a legal question decided in respondents' favor in this very case some 12 years ago.... This Court's Rules do not countenance the rehearing here granted. For good reason, a proper application of those rules and the Federal Rules of Civil Procedure would lead us to defer reconsideration of *Aguilar* until we are presented with the issue in another case.

We have a rule on rehearing, Rule 44, but it provides only for petitions filed within 25 days of the entry of the judgment in question.... Moreover, nothing in our procedures allows us to grant rehearing, timely or not, "except ... at the instance of a Justice who concurred in the judgment or decision." This Court's Rule 44.1. Petitioners have not been so bold (or so candid) as to style their plea as one for rehearing in this Court, and the Court has not taken up the petition at the instance of Justice Stevens, the only still-sitting member of the *Aguilar* majority.

Lacking any rule or practice allowing us to reconsider the *Aguilar* judgment directly, the majority accepts as a substitute a rule governing relief from judgments or orders of the federal trial courts. See Fed. Rule Civ. Proc. 60(b)(5). The service to which Rule 60(b) has been impressed is unprecedented, and neither the Court nor those urging reconsideration of *Aguilar* contend otherwise. The Court makes clear, fortunately, that any future efforts to expand today's ruling will not be favored. I therefore anticipate that the extraordinary action taken in this case will remain aberrational.

. . .

Unlike the majority, I find just cause to await the arrival of ... another case in which our review appropriately may be sought, before deciding whether *Aguilar* should remain the law of the land. That cause lies in the maintenance of integrity in the interpretation of procedural rules, preservation of the responsive, non-agenda-setting character of this Court, and avoidance of invitations to reconsider old cases based on "speculat[ions] on chances from changes in [the Court's membership]." ...

SECTION 2. THE FREE EXERCISE OF RELIGION

Page 1707. Add at end of chapter:

City of Boerne v. Flores

521 U.S. 507, 117 S.Ct. 2157, 138 L.Ed.2d 624 (1997).

[The report in this case appears supra, page 153.]